Anson Yeager's
In Two Volumes
STORIES
Volume I: Northern Plains Adventures

THE CENTER FOR WESTERN STUDIES
Augustana College
2001

Anson Yeager's
≡ In Two Volumes ≡
STORIES
Volume I: Northern Plains Adventures

© 2000 by The Center for Western Studies

ALL RIGHTS RESERVED

The Center for Western Studies
Box 727, Augustana College
Sioux Falls, South Dakota 57197

Copies of our book catalog may be obtained by calling 605-274-4007 or by visiting our home page at http://inst.augie.edu/CWS/

The Center for Western Studies is an archives, library, museum, publishing house, and educational agency concerned principally with collecting, preserving and interpreting prehistoric, historic, and contemporary materials that document native and immigrant cultures of the northern prairie/plains. The Center promotes understanding of the region through exhibits, publications, art shows, conferences, and academic programs. It is committed, ultimately, to defining the contribution of the region to American civilization.

Library of Congress Cataloging-in-Publication Data:

Yeager, Anson, 1919-
    Anson Yeager's stories / by Anson Yeager.
      p. cm.
    Includes index.
    Contents: v. 1. Northern Plains adventures — v. 2. Famous faces and places.
    ISBN 0-931170-76-1—ISBN 0-931170-77-x (pbk.)
    1. South Dakota—Social life and customs—20th century—Anecdotes. 2. South Dakota—Description and travel—Anecdotes. 3. South Dakota—Biography—Anecdotes. 4. Politicians—United States—Biography—Anecdotes. 5. United States—Description and travel—Anecdotes. I. Argus-leader (Sioux Falls, S.D.: 1891) II. Title.

F651.6.Y4 2000
978.3'03'0922—dc21

00-047428

Cover Photo by Harold's Photo

Foreword

South Dakota's people have a great passion: a love for their state, their neighbors, and their High Plains position on the North American continent. It has been the author's privilege to meet many South Dakotans, their elected officials, and especially voters who approve or reject them. It was a joy to cover the South Dakota Legislature for the Argus Leader over a ten-year period, 1949-1959. I have known many governors and lieutenant governors, other constitutional officers, judges, prosecutors, Sioux Falls and Minnehaha County officials, and school teachers and officials, from the past through present day. Republican, Democrat, or undesignated political persuasion, they have served their state well. The South Dakota citizen's legislature has produced a host of men and women who have served their state through countless hours at Pierre and at home and answered for their actions at the polls. I have also known the state's congressional delegations since 1948 through the present. These people, Democrat or Republican, have been my friends, and I appreciate their friendship. This book is a collection of writings that hopefully give a glimpse of South Dakotans and their passion for this state. My wife, Ada May Yeager, and my son, Harry Yeager, and Mat Nelson, computer consultant and University of Sioux Falls senior, collaborated in collecting and preparing this material for publication.

Jack Marsh, former executive editor, and David Ledford, executive editor of the Argus Leader, were helpful and cooperative in extending permission for publication of Argus Leader articles and pictures. Sharon Rehfeldt, the newspaper's librarian, extended invaluable assistance.

I also want to thank my friend and former Argus Leader publisher Larry Fuller for his confidence in me and his nomination of me for the Minnesota Award in journalism. He encouraged me to start a personal column in 1978 and arranged for me to continue my writings in retirement.

During my years at the Argus Leader, I worked for two private ownerships, and two newspaper chains. Each experience helped provide a unique insight into the workings of the Fourth Estate in South Dakota. This former editor appreciated opportunities provided by former publishers: John A. Kennedy and his associate, Howard L. Chernoff; William H. Leopard and Dean Smith. Editor Fred C. Christopherson who hired me as a reporter, was a longtime friend. My newspaper career spanned the days of linotypes and computers, letterpress and offset printing. It has been a great thrill to see it all and to have known many editors, publishers, staff members, and printers of other South Dakota daily and weekly papers.

Anson Yeager
Sioux Falls, June 1, 2000

Life is a journey for my wife, Ada May, and me. It has been a great ride. This volume offers facets of our trip from family roots to enjoying Sioux Falls, my work at the Argus Leader, and a glimpse of some of the people and events that make up this chronicle: *Anson Yeager's Stories*.

Table of Contents

Opening Chapter
    Retirement can mean new adventures 1
    With gadgets and comforts, the best is always yet to come 2
    Happy retirees keep busy doing what they enjoy 3
    S.D. travel offers beauty without crowds 4
    Get the deal you really want for tour trips 5
    Mountains stand tall among best travel sights in U.S., the world 7
    Retirement a good time to check your roots 8
    This traveler biased to homespun beauty of S.D. 9
    Rural numbering travels across S.D., other states 10
    S.D. towns should trumpet their heroes and attractions 11

Perspective
    South Dakota in the 30's; gains despite misfortune 14

Roots
    Oslo—7 hours from New York:
        Norwegians hate the Germans, but drive their Volkswagens 20
    Time stands still in Norway; Stavanger mixes Presley, Grieg 21
    Visitor from U.S.A. surprises kin in mountains of Norway 23
    To get away from it all: try a motor tour of Norway 26
    Touring Norway by auto should be done at a leisurely pace 28
    A larger 747? Not for this traveler 32
    U.S.A. conjures that old feeling 33
    Father, son seek German family roots 34
    Americans meet their English cousins 36
    Iowa woman investigates her family tree, writes book 37

The Yeager Family 39
    The ending of a successful life 48
    Ride in 18-wheeler offers a different perspective 50
    A letter to a daughter from a proud dad 52
    Coming to the end of life's road 54
    A son's mortality comes into focus following the death of his mother 56
    Precautions, nice people help in on-the-road emergencies 57
    Lessons on hearts, housekeeping 58
    Traveling progression lands in Texas 60

Columns About Yeager
    Making of an editor 63
    Behind the bylines 63
    Years as a newsman fail to spoil Anson's optimism 65
    Anson Yeager, Argus Leader editorial page editor, to retire June 1 67

Anson Yeager, A class newspaperman: 1947-1987 68
There's another side to this story, and Yeagers all over the country 72
Anson Yeager, a city journalist who still loves to come home to Faith 74
50 years of newspapering was his window to the world 75

The Argus Leader
    The Way it was in 1947 77
    Argus Leader editorial wins first place award 83
    Prize-winning editorial one of 101 Inland contest entries 84
    A helping hand for our Indians 85
    Argus wins awards; group honors Yeager 87
    Anson Yeager's deserved honor 87
    Congratulations, Anson 89
    Argus Leader's Yeager wins Casey Award 89
    It's time to do something different 90
    Anson Yeager citation for the honorary degree doctor of public service 93
    Herb Bechtold, Argus Leader city editor, stricken at age 51 94
    A nostalgic return to 1927 96
    The Leprechaun of Laguna Beach 98
    How a day in Sioux Falls changed industry's course 100
    A bad day in Sioux Falls 103
    SDSU misses getting No. 1 103
    "Extra"—an uncommon occurrence 105
    "Chris" watched, guided city through 93 years of change 108
    Photo keeps winning honors 110

Christmas Nostalgia
    Reflection on a bygone Christmas era 112
    Christmas and other mail 113
    It's time for family, home and church 114
    Christmas season takes us back to one-room schools 115
    Christmas present more enjoyable than Christmases past 116
    Christmas traditions live on today despite subtle changes 118
    Christmas memories among older set are fond 118
    It's time to sort memories of Christmases in S.D. past 120
    Christmas cards, photos denote special times, places 121

Columns on S.D. Life
    Dakotas' low murder rate 123
    Best days of the year 123
    The mourning ties that bind 125
    Beating the heat 126
    Quartzite posts lasting markers of state boundary 127
    Life off state's main highways worth preserving 129

S.D. Life—People
    Four Balcers schooled under their dad 131
    History students show that they know their stuff 132
    Historic bridge comes home to Centerville...................................133
    Reunion brings victims, rescuers back together 135

CONTENTS

Widows find thrill with B&B on Strawberry Hill 136
Snowbirds help keep Parker vans on move 137

S.D. Life—Towns
The Prairie Oasis Mall, built by the Faith-ful 141
America's small rural towns will have to fight to survive 144
Faith small but big in celebrating 146
Future will bring better times 149

S.D. Life—Cities
Why city has "good thing going" 152
City has much to offer passing motorists 153
Pierre attractions include capitol, heritage center 154

S.D. Life—Sights
A glimpse into the military past 156
DeSmet preserves frontier history of Laura Ingalls Wilder 157
Faulkton's on the map 158
Don't skip the DakotaDome when you visit Vermillion 159
Museum offers fascinating look at Old West 161
Exhibitions are spectacular at Shrine to Music Museum 162
Wall Drug opens its photo-filled backyard to tourists 163
Visit Murdo for great show of cars 165
Indian-Pioneer Museum is spirited 167

S.D. Life—Variety
North Dakota follows lead in tourist stops 169
Legends enhance S.D. image 170
Winter travel opportunity great close to home 171
Cyclists have room to roam in S.D. 172
Let South Dakota lure family for more visits 173

South Dakota Centennial
Dakotas boast strong treasury of history 175
Famous South Dakotans coming to city for homecoming 176
A special welcome for some special people 178
Historian gets centennial show on the road 181
State's pride surfaced this summer 182
South Dakota celebrated its centennial with style 183

Books
Book describes poor family's life in S.D. dust bowl days 187
Story constructs state capitol history 188
Brookings author describes Civilian Conservation Corps 190
Stuntman's story fascinates 191
This Custer bio also love story 192
Riggs story is treasure of early S.D. 193

South Dakota Trails and Tracks
Tracing the wagon trail 195

Custer an ardent Black Hills booster 196
Army avenged Custer's defeat with attack in northwest S.D. 198
Imagination takes a journey to ghost towns 200
Ash blazed trail into South Dakota history 202
Paper points out attractiveness of Highway 212 203

Scenic South Dakota
S.D. travel offers beauty without crowds 205
South Dakota's infinite mix of sights leaves a lasting impression 206
Pierre, Buffalo, Sturgis, Faith are a joy to visit 207
Cattle country offers color treat. 208
Stopovers across state provide good places to visit 209
S.D. beckons for travelers 210
Nicollet's towering S.D. feats honored 211

South Dakota Spectacle
Sioux ties to land enduring, reverent 214
Pope pleased by Crazy Horse scale model, invited to visit 217
State honors the living. 219
Center for Western Studies preserves, interprets heartland. 220
Ex-Washington High coach settles in the Hills 221
New lodge has rustic appeal in Hills 224
Blizzard baffles today's travel advantages 226

State-City-Government; S.D. Politics
S.D. public figures as close to constituents as nearest phone 228
Solons' ordeal 228
Veep's trip a groundbreaker 230
Milwaukee's history won't die 231
Saving state track a wise move 233
Only five of 23 S.D. senators from West River, Pressler book reveals 235
Panda diplomacy reflects changing world times 237
Voters' watchful eyes have always focused on city hall 238
Janklow offers sound ideas for helping with local governments 240
Put some warmth in your winter: take a trip to the legislature 241
Two of state's old political names face new and exciting challenges 243
Gambling would help Deadwood 244
Mundt archives offer nostalgic view of state's longest-serving lawmaker 246
"Fair Chance" offers insight to famous politician 247
About mayoral longevity 248

Profiles
"Tired American" area prize 250
Carnegie's zest born in S.D. 251
A tale of two area contributors 253
Balcer's roles 255
California wine producer makes a nostalgic return to S.D. 257
Fuller, a lawyer's lawyer, devoted to church 258
40 years' worth of changes 261
Koplow never first in line—salute to remarkable vet 262

CONTENTS

Kroeger helped build boys and structures 263
Death ends brilliant career of Canton native who helped U.S. win WWII 264
Floyd LeBlanc didn't take pharmacy for granted 265
A free spirit who lived for each day 267
Madison woman chronicles prairie memories 269
This fellow rents most everything, and has boxes of ideas 270
Mr. Bookstore 273
Retiring REA head's happiest job moment: when rates cut 25% 275
Gordon Olson views retirement like life's work: positively 277
Lawyer has record of accomplishments 279
Minister's friends, collegues pay their last, loving respects 281
Anderson knew state inside out 282
History buff pushes idea of living-history farm for S.D. 284
Enoch L. Schetnan 285

National Guard, Military

"Justy" starts new chapter after 37 years in cockpit 287
Foss happy spreading "The Word" 290
S.F. native governor of Wake Island 292
Mann leaves Guard after long, distinguished career 294
Eulogy—Citizen-Soldier Scurr gave much to state and country 296
S.D. loses another good one 298
Iverson was always on guard to protect state, country 299

Commentary

Book chronicles diversified role of "Peace Keeper Frontier Post" 301
The national anthem and S.D. 303
Anniversary of V-E Day stirs memories for American veterans 303
Memorial is a touching tribute to victims of an unpopular war 305
45 years ago—U.S. goes to war 306
Tour of East offers look at old battlefields 309
Park memorializes monumental battle 310
Don't pass up miliary museums 311
A military on the march 312
Veterans constitute 11 percent of state 313
WWII brought many major challenges to S.D. 314
Observance, like Pearl Harbor, can't be forgotten 315
History on display at Fort Sill, Okla. 316

Key Hints on Motorhome Travel

Travel veterans offer hints on living in motorhome 319
Motorhome travel needs compromise 320
Good trip starts before leaving 321
Make traveling easier with planning tips 322
South Dakotans join thousands at toyland for motorhomes 323
Tips can help plan for great trip in RV 324
Vagabonds learn about life on road at rally 326
Don't let thieves ruin good trip 327

OPENING CHAPTER

RETIREMENT CAN MEAN NEW ADVENTURES

Argus Leader, Sunday, Nov. 11, 1990

Retirement brings many joys, the principal one being the realization that you can control your own time.

If you're fortunate enough to have good health and an adequate retirement, you can do what you've always wanted to do.

This in turn brings many decisions, ranging from what to do with your home, whether to move, buy a vacation home or hit the road and see America.

My wife and I early on decided we wanted to retain our home of many years. We also decided to travel part of the year and not to buy a vacation home in the Sunbelt. After more than six years of retirement, we still like it this way.

What were the right decisions for us aren't necessarily the right ones for others. The great thing about this country is that you have a choice.

Couples who spend winter or summer months elsewhere have innumerable choices to make. Questions include whether to live in a motorhome, rent a trailer or stationary mobile home on the site, buy a vacation home, etc.

The choices can become very involved. Some couples like small motorhomes, some like 'em big. Some tow a car. Others think trailers are the way to go. Couples who've had motorhomes or trailers before retirement know what suits them.

First-timers should realize that a motorhome or travel trailer is a small home. Its electric, plumbing and heating systems usually work well, but they do require attention. Keeping your motorhome, car or pickup in excellent mechanical condition is a must. Do it and travel days are happy days. Neglect it, and you have problems.

Networking with friends is a good way to get a line on apartments or vacation homes to rent, whether your destination is Hawaii, the Southwest or Florida.

New retirees probably will be happier if they reconnoiter on their first trip. They can see their friends in a retirement park setting and get their advice before deciding on their own dream location.

You can do what you please and live where you want—within some limits, of course. You can see the national parks, or stay in a trailer park and golf by day and play cards at night. Or travel abroad.

If organizations and activities are your bowl of cherries, you can help yourself. You can pursue your hobbies fulltime. See your kids, or visit other relatives. It's your call.

But please don't brag about being busier than ever. It just seems that way because it takes longer to do things. That's a result of being lucky enough to enjoy the privilege of growing old.

There are also many things that make retirement easier these days than might have been the case in the past.

We can thank our friendly bankers for part of this. Direct deposit has made life much simpler. All our Social Security and retirement checks are deposited directly. Banks will also pay utility bills.

While traveling, we carry a minimum of cash. We start out with travelers checks and rely on automatic teller machines for cash. Thanks to the electronic age, the ATM produces cash and usually our Sioux Falls balance in minutes although we may be 1,800 miles away in California.

Once in a while we get fooled. We were in a state recently that didn't have service for our bank card. The solution was to use credit cards at ATMs. Almost any bank teller will help you with a cash advance on a Mastercard or Visa.

The Post Office will hold your mail for 30 days, forward all of it or forward only first class.

A travel club is a good thing to join. You get maps, travel information and brochures that take much of the guesswork out of your trips. Travel agencies can save you money, time and effort in arranging airline, hotel and other reservations.

WITH GADGETS AND COMFORTS, THE BEST IS ALWAYS YET TO COME

Argus Leader, Saturday, Feb. 15, 1986

Imagine the surprise and future shock that a youngster of the 1920s or early 1930s would have in stepping off a time machine into 1986.

The biggest change would probably be today's small world and the immediacy of the news as brought by television.

When Charles A. Lindbergh flew nonstop from New York to Paris in 33 1/2 hours in 1927, his exploit was reported in the newspapers and by radio.

If you didn't live in a city and had no radio, you had to wait for the newspaper to come in the mail.

A youth vaulting from 1930 to January 1986 would find people watching the fiery loss of Challenger and its crew as it happened, in color, on television in their homes.

Sixty years ago it took about a week to cross the Atlantic by ocean liner. Few persons could afford to make the trip.

Today, airline travelers cross the Atlantic, and half of the North American continent, in seven or eight hours. World travel is commonplace and comparatively inexpensive.

Yesteryear's pictures in the newspapers were all black and white. Today, newspapers are using more and better color pictures than ever.

The picture comparison—from black and white to today's color photography—symbolizes one way things have changed.

One of the chores for farm boys in South Dakota 50 years ago was filling the water reservoir on the kitchen stove. The reservoir was next to the firebox. Hot water heaters have long since taken over this function in farm homes.

There would be other surprises in today's home: dishwashers, microwave ovens, video recorders, power lawnmowers, snowblowers and the like.

Today's comfortable, stylish and smaller automobiles would be eyestoppers for a youth transported from the mid-1930s to 1986. The prevalence of four cylinder engines would bring questions about whatever happened to Henry Ford's promising V-8.

Fifty years ago a farm kid was lucky if he had a horse to ride to school. He would envy today's teens on wheels financed out of part-time earnings.

Interstate highways and much wider, better built all-weather primary roads would be another revelation. South Dakotans were lucky before World War II if they lived on a graveled street or highway.

OPENING CHAPTER

Business courses in a small town high school in the 1930s included typing, bookkeeping and shorthand. About the only resemblance between yesterday's manual typewriters and today's sleek electronic models is the layout of the keyboard.

Computers, copying machines, credit cards and other appurtenances of today's times would all be new to the time traveler who was a child when Herbert Hoover and Franklin D. Roosevelt were presidents.

He would be intrigued by such things as automatic and flash cameras (indirect descendants of box-like Kodaks), touch button telephones, pocket radios and headsets and the great sound of FM radio.

Fifty years ago when you went to the store, the clerk tallied grocery items by hand on a sales slip with carbon. Today's clerks whisk an item's bar code past a scanner and the cash register prints each specific item and price on the slip.

Cashing a check was sometimes difficult 50 years ago. Today, you can punch in a request for cash in a machine in Rapid City and get currency plus a ticket that gives your balance in your Sioux Falls bank.

Another surprise would be the amount of pocket change necessary to get through a week. The day of nickel candy bars, ice cream cones and inexpensive clothing is long gone.

The dollar, of course, was stronger then than now—but today's distribution is much better. Say what you will, there is a lot more fun today than there was long ago. Parents have more leisure time. There are more things to do in South Dakota now than there were during the Depression.

Today's youngsters are taller and healthier in most respects than their parents.

It would be nice to know what the year 2040 will be like. However, President Dwight D. Eisenhower had it right when he said that, fortunately, man cannot read tomorrow's newspapers. If we could, some of us would see our own obituary before we really wanted to know about it.

It's better to enjoy hindsight which shows that today beats the so-called good old days. It will be that way, too, in the next century for today's youngsters when they're senior citizens.

Their best is yet to come—in shapes and forms that will outdo today's gadgets and comforts.

HAPPY RETIREES KEEP BUSY DOING WHAT THEY ENJOY

Argus Leader, Saturday, Sept. 27, 1980

"Poor Joe. Last time I saw him he asked me, 'What in the world do you do to pass the time?'"

"I've got so many things I'm interested in that I don't have enough time. Joe's problem was that he didn't have any hobbies or interests."

This anecdote related by a friend points up a problem that many retirees face for the rest of their lives.

My friend's solution is a happy one. He has kept his old hobbies, like photography, and is working on some new ones. He has a computer and enjoys using it as a word processor.

A retired businessman, he retains his interest in today's highly competitive scene. He reads and marks business news stories for the attention of family members who are still active in the firm. Otherwise, he keeps out of their way.

In addition, my friend has continued his lifelong habit of reading material relating to technical and scientific achievements. He's thrilled by space age advances.

All these things occupy his time whether he's at home in South Dakota or pursuing warmer climes in the winter.

He has not immersed himself in numerous civic or volunteer causes, nor has he participated in various senior citizen activities.

My friend's solutions about what to do with his time deserve consideration by today's prospective retirees.

They offer something different from 1) watching the daytime soaps, 2) full-time square-dancing, basket weaving or rock carving in an Arizona trailer camp or 3) endless pursuit of golf, bingo or cards.

Not all retirees, of course, are as fortunate in their income and other circumstances as my friend. But, most retirees can find a way to keep their lifetime hobbies and interests in retirement.

The big gift of retirement days, of course, is time to use as you please. The change is marked when you take your first trip away from home. You're no longer compelled to cut short a pleasant vacation and return to work. You can stay away longer. When you return home, you can spend your time on hobbies or other retirement pursuits.

If you want to do woodworking in your own shop, restore an old car or keep up with numerous magazines and newspapers at the library, there's time to do it. There's also more time for hunting, fishing and enjoying South Dakota's outdoors. There's time for a walk. South Dakotans are fortunate in their longevity. Retirement brings more time for grandparents to enjoy the company of their children's children. Retirement can strengthen family ties that bind senior citizens to offspring and siblings.

Golden years of old age can be especially enjoyable for homemakers. Mothers and grandmothers, like their husbands cut adrift by retirement from lifetime occupations, find new fulfillment in watching younger generations grow and develop.

Another friend and I were discussing the advantages of keeping a home base once retirement comes. This friend and spouse returned to his home state to retire. They were back in Sioux Falls in two months. "We discovered this is our home," he said.

During my retirement, my Mrs. and I met some brave couples who cut all ties and spend all their time on the American road. One couple's home base is a mail drop in Nevada; their home is a recreational vehicle. My guess is that eventually they, too, will want a home or apartment where they can rest a few months out of the year.

The best retirement is what suits the individual. If it's keeping up with daytime television or a retirement center's busy activity schedule or whatever pleases you, fine.

There are many opportunities for fun and friendship in senior citizens' groups in most South Dakota cities and towns. There also are many civic and fraternal organizations that welcome senior volunteers.

The important thing to remember is that in retirement you and your wife decide how to use your newly found 24 hours a day.

S.D. TRAVEL OFFERS BEAUTY WITHOUT CROWDS

Argus Leader, Sunday, Dec. 8, 1991

When the weather outside is frightful, it's a good time to think about next year's travels.
For some of the nation's most spectacular scenery, explore western South Dakota.

Kevin Costner's *Dances With Wolves* has won rave reviews for the remarkable outdoor scenes filmed northwest of Pierre on former Lt. Gov. Roy Houck's buffalo ranch.

The movie cameras didn't lie. They captured the appeal of the "big sky," the open range and what life on the frontier must have been like in territorial days.

That scenery can be duplicated many times in western South Dakota as you drive great distances: from Pierre to Sturgis via Highway 34, from Gettysburg to Belle Fourche via Faith and Newell, from Mobridge to Buffalo and on Highway 85 from the North Dakota line through Buffalo to Sturgis. There are also South Dakota big sky vistas from Platte through Winner to Martin, Pine Ridge and Hot Springs and from Pickstown through Gregory, Winner, White River, Cedar Pass and Scenic to Rapid City.

The variety of scenery is compelling: hills, buttes, long low-lying ridges, river and creek bottoms, grasslands that meet the sky and hilltops that reveal another valley and another range of hills to climb.

Costner saw South Dakota's big sky from afoot and horseback. You can see it from your favorite vehicle.

Part of the appeal of western South Dakota is the scarcity of people. It's easy to commune with nature when you and your companion are driving roads with few other vehicles. That's a plus of living in a state with a large area (South Dakota ranks 15th) and a small population (No. 45).

South Dakota has about 700,000 people who live within 77,116 square miles. That figures out to a population density of about 9.1 persons per square mile. Of course, there are many square miles in the countryside that have no residents.

South Dakota tourism not many years ago used the slogan "Roam free," a message that has not been lost. It is one reason the Black Hills Motor Classic at Sturgis is so popular. Motorcyclists come to South Dakota because they can enjoy their bikes on our uncrowded highways. It's no fun riding busy interstates and other highways in urban areas.

South Dakota has many other outdoor attractions that can enhance your life during the four seasons. The Great Lakes of the Missouri, the northeast lake region and the vast expanse of prairie from Minnesota and Iowa to the Missouri River all have appeal. The state's parks, hunting and fishing are among the least crowded in the nation.

The Black Hills offer great mountain scenery with variety. Mount Rushmore National Memorial, born-again Deadwood and lowstakes gambling, Crazy Horse Memorial, Custer State Park, Wind and Jewell Caves and skiing and snowmobile trails are among top attractions.

If your family is planning a reunion next summer, now or January is the time to make arrangements. Choice campgrounds, motels or other accommodations require reservations many months in advance.

GET THE DEAL YOU REALLY WANT FOR TOUR TRIPS

Argus Leader, Sunday, Dec. 12, 1993

Tour participants invariably compare notes on the deals they got from their travel agent and what they should do next time.

Our trip to Australia a year ago is a case in point. We were able to stop over in Honolulu because we had made arrangements beforehand. We didn't like the prospect of flying 14 hours nonstop from Los Angeles to Sydney.

The tour operator initially tried to discourage us from the Honolulu stopovers, saying they would cost extra. That is to be expected. We suggested that we would buy somebody else's tour if the operator would not make the arrangements we wanted.

Friends we had made on the Australian tour were disgusted that they couldn't stop over in Honolulu on the way back to the United States. They said that the tour operator told them it couldn't be done. This was after they were already committed to the tour and the air arrangements were final.

It's really up to the individual to decide what he or she wants on a tour—and then go for it.

As senior citizens, we like tours in foreign countries in which transportation, motels and some meals are packaged. It's easier to let an energetic, pleasant American or foreign tour guide check on plane departures, baggage, hotel reservations, etc., than to do it yourself.

If we were younger, we'd probably attempt some foreign countries on our own. Even so, it's easier and usually cheaper to have your travel agent make key hotel and rental car reservations abroad for you.

Traffic is difficult in many countries. Left-hand drive in Britain, Australia and New Zealand can be a vexing problem for Americans, whether you drive or walk. City streets and country byways can be hazardous to a pedestrian's health.

We're fortunate to be able to leave Sioux Falls in the morning for flights to Hawaii, the Caribbean or the Gulf of Mexico for fun in the sun. Thanks to jets, snorkeling, sailing and the beach are just a day away.

There are so many travel opportunities available that today's customers can pick and choose what they want. Your travel agent will help you piggy-back an extra tour on another one if you ask.

One way to make your overseas arrival easier is to buy foreign exchange from your own bank before you leave. Allow the bank a week or two to obtain the currency. Then you can go directly to the taxi stand or bus and pay in the local currency without stopping at an airport bank.

You'll probably get a better rate from your own bank than paying foreign hotels or shops the sometimes inflated commissions they charge for exchange. Be sure to save some U.S. bills and quarters for your arrival back in the States. You'll need U.S. money for luggage carts, telephones and taxi.

Don't worry about running out of cash overseas. You can use your credit cards to obtain local currency or pay for goods. Many foreign banks and stores are hooked up electronically to the U.S. credit card network.

In years of travel, we have never lost a bag, although a couple of times our baggage arrived late. Check your baggage stubs. The new scanner tags are great. They help your airline keep track of your baggage while you're enroute.

During 1993, we changed planes three times on a trip to Alaska via United. Some connections were close—but our baggage arrived with us in Fairbanks and in Sioux Falls on our return.

Northwest Airlines, which we've used several times this year for trips within the United States and to Europe, does a fantastic job of dispensing gate information while you're in the air.

Be sure to check your airline tickets carefully against your itinerary as soon as you receive your tickets. Follow your airline's instructions on reconfirming your return trip.

OPENING CHAPTER

MOUNTAINS STAND TALL AMONG BEST TRAVEL SIGHTS IN U.S., THE WORLD

Argus Leader, Sunday, Feb. 20, 1994

Here are my nominations for the top 10 sights I've been privileged to see.
- 1. Alaska, the United States' crown jewel. Its mountain ranges, wildlife, fjords and glaciers are majestic and massive. What a thrill it is to spot bears, caribou, eagles and other wild creatures in Denali National Park and to see Mount McKinley on a clear day. Or to travel the Inland Passage through Alaska's fjords and see green forests and towering peaks hugging the coastline. And to ride the state-owned Alaska Railroad between Anchorage and Fairbanks. Try Alaska—you'll like it!
- 2. Rocky Mountains of the United States and the Canadian Rockies. Their size and grandeur make man seem small. There is so much to see that you'll never see it all.
- 3. Hawaii, America's playground. The Hawaiian Islands are hassle-free and weather (except rainy days) is always OK for sportswear. Hawaii's scenic attractions—mountains, sandy and rock-lined beaches, lava beds and active volcanoes—are among the world's most dramatic and awesome. Stay a short time and you'll want to extend your visit. You'll also plan a return visit.
- 4. Mount Rushmore National Memorial in the Black Hills of South Dakota. The shrine to four great American presidents is one of the world's most photographed objects. Its setting amidst Black Hills evergreens and mountain peaks is inspiring. The story of Gutzon Borglum, sculptor, is equally inspiring.
- 5. Norway, its mountains, green forests and fjords appear to be packaged as one huge national park on the rooftop of Europe. There's no sight to compare to what you see from a ferry in a fjord in Norway on a bright July day. From the ship's railing you have a 360-degree arc of mountain peaks, white clouds, clear water and trees that cling precariously to hillsides. Time stands still between ports.
- 6. Mount Fuji, Japan's highest mountain. During U.S. Army occupation in 1945 and 1946, you could clearly see its snow-covered peak from Yokohama, port city on the coast. In today's times, vehicular smog more often than not obscures the view. Japanese consider the mountain sacred. Its setting amidst a resort area in mountains near Tokyo makes it appealing to tourists.
- 7. The Great Barrier Reef of Australia. The reef—a giant living coral formation—arches in broken chains for some 1,250 miles along the northeast coast of Australia. Coastal waters are clear and inviting to swimmers. But beware of sharks! Traveling from shore to the reef in excursion boats will give you a day you'll long remember.
- 8. The Matterhorn, famous peak in the Swiss Alps. Its pyramidal shape rises like a sentinel over the border with Italy. Taking an electric train from the village of Zermatt to a viewing spot several miles from the mountain makes a memorable half-day trip. Younger tourists ascend walking trails to the base of the Matterhorn.
- 9. The Panama Canal, built by the United States early in this century, spared ships and sailors a circuitous journey around Cape Horn at the tip of South America. The canal cut the 13,000-mile trip from New York to San Francisco to approximately 5,200 miles. The canal was an engineering triumph in the use of locks and artificial lakes to link the Atlantic and Pacific Oceans. Its completion marked medical advances as well; the U.S. Army under Col. William Gorgas, a physician, wiped out yellow fever and malaria by destroying mos-

quitoes that carried the diseases. Today's travelers can see the canal from the decks and comfort of cruise ships.
- 10 Mexico's Copper Canyon in western Chihuahua is large enough to hold several U.S. Grand Canyons. Today's tourists can view the Copper Canyon from a Mexican railroad which crosses the Continental Divide at nearly 9,000 feet and descends to the Gulf of California via hairpin curves and many tunnels.

RETIREMENT A GOOD TIME TO CHECK YOUR ROOTS

Argus Leader, Sunday, Oct. 2, 1994

Why do so many expectant retirees and their friends talk about traveling in their golden years and then never follow through?

More often than not, such individuals lose their resolve upon retirement and simply don't get around to carrying out their dreams of visiting faraway places.

If you can keep your focus while all around you your friends are losing theirs, you'll wind up seeing William Shakespeare's England and also searching out your roots.

Some Americans retiring these days may expect 10, 15 or even 20 years of good health in which to pursue their dreams.

It's important during your early months of retirement to act on your yen to do things differently.

For instance, most Americans can't take the time while they're working to set aside two weeks or more to attend some outstanding national or world event.

That situation changes when you join retirement ranks.

My Mrs. and I attended the 1984 Summer Olympics in Los Angeles the first year I was retired. We repeated Olympic attendance at the winter games in Calgary in 1988.

If your retirement comes up soon and you've always wanted to attend the Olympics, you can go to the summer games in Atlanta in 1996. You'll have plenty of time to arrange your trip, buy your tickets and invite sons or daughters or friends to accompany you.

Individuals searching their roots either in this country or abroad can make their journey more pleasant by compiling information ahead of time.

This information may be in a family Bible, someone's diary or newspaper clippings that your parents passed on to you. It may be something you've gained yourself in a pathfinding trip to the land your ancestors left generations ago.

Church records in Europe often contain complete birth to death records of family members. When relatives or contacts show you something with a family connection on your first trip overseas, write it down. Better yet, transfer your notes to a large-scale topographical map of the European area from whence your ancestors came.

When you return on a second trip, or when other relatives make the trip, your numbered notes on a map can be invaluable in helping them.

Most Americans prefer to travel with someone instead of going solo. If you can't line up a companion, don't chuck your own plans. Make your first trip on your own.

What to take? Travel light. If you're going to ride trains, don't take anything you can't carry for several blocks. A sweater or jacket may be better for you than a dress coat.

Study overseas temperatures before you leave and plan your wardrobe accordingly. If you're going to spend the winter in the U.S. Sunbelt, take what's comfortable. Travel by motorhome will permit you to take more and still not crowd your portable quarters.

Washing machines in motels or campgrounds are a boon to travelers. You can take fewer changes of clothing.

Start a wish book for retirement travels. Clip news stories about interesting places you want to see for yourself. Use your auto or other travel club to obtain maps, tour books and routings.

Ask travel agents to help you. Tell them what you want to do and ask them to obtain brochures for you.

There are good reasons for postponing travel because of illness of yourself or a family member. But you'll never realize your dreams if you let less serious excuses keep you home.

Take a look at your family tree and make a guess on your own mortality. Make every year count. Don't let a year slide by without checking off a coveted destination on your wish list.

THIS TRAVELER BIASED TO HOMESPUN BEAUTY OF S.D.

Argus Leader, Sunday, Oct. 23, 1994

Here are some of my obviously prejudiced selections of favorite South Dakota places and sights.

• Favorite city: Sioux Falls, where my wife and I have lived for more than 47 years with one two-year absence.

We have seen the city grow from almost 50,000 population to today's estimated 110,000.

It's easy and truthful to say that nearly everything about Sioux Falls has come up roses since World War II ended.

Large national firms looking for a headquarters city found many advantages in Sioux Falls in serving South Dakota and corners of Minnesota, Iowa and Nebraska.

Expansion of wholesale distribution, retailing, medical, banking and other services continued apace. Being at the intersection of east-west and north-south interstate highways helped. So did development of Joe Foss Field into a regional airport.

My wife and I enjoyed the benefits of a 4 percent GI loan on our first and only home in Sioux Falls. We have lived at our present address for 42 years and grown accustomed to the place. We considered moving but instead remodeled several times.

Sioux Falls' excellent school system, colleges, vocational schools, churches, and forward-looking civic leadership enhanced our regard for our city of choice. This is a caring community.

Sioux Falls' baseball and soccer fields, playgrounds, parks, bike trails and other attractions are part of the mix that makes the city so appealing.

Sioux Falls' No. 1 rating by Money magazine in 1992 is positive proof that we're living in an outstanding city.

• My favorite city attractions: Great Plains Zoo and Museum, Battleship South Dakota Memorial and Sherman Park hill. There you can imagine what the locale was like when Indians were here and the settlers came. You can hear the lions roar at night. The Old Courthouse and Pettigrew Museums are also neat.

• Favorite smaller South Dakota city: Brookings, home of my alma mater, South Dakota State University.

• Favorite small town: Faith, population 548, where I graduated from high school. Faith's block-long mall was completed by local people in 1976. The town's strong livestock market serves a wide area.

- Favorite state capital city among the dozen or so I've seen: Pierre. The Capitol, restored to its original splendor, is beautiful. The Cultural Heritage Center nearby is world class. Pierre's historic beginnings as a cowtown, its river location and the Oahe Dam are part of its ambiance. Similarly, Fort Pierre's background is intriguing: it's where the Verendrye brothers buried a lead plate in 1743 to claim the region for France. Fort Pierre was the locale of 19th century fur traders and gateway to the open range.
- Favorite mountains: Black Hills. Favorite scenic drive: the Needles highway. Favorite observation point: top of Bear Butte where you can see the state's "big sky" country to the north and east.
- Favorite country place: Maurine, in northwestern South Dakota where I grew up. The post office has been discontinued. A two-room grade school at Maurine has replaced the one-room Red Top school I once attended two miles west along Highway 212.
- Favorite backyard scenes: from our kitchen window where we can see the trees, flower gardens, etc., in our neighbors' yards. Also, the view from Maurine: looking northwest to the ramparts of the Slim Buttes.
- Favorite sports facility: the University of South Dakota's DakotaDome at Vermillion. The Dome made fall football enjoyable in bad weather—and made high school football playoffs possible.
- Favorite day trip: to the northeast lake region, Sisseton, Nicollet Tower, Fort Sisseton State Park, Whetstone Valley, Milbank and Webster.
- Favorite season: fall.

RURAL NUMBERING TRAVELS ACROSS S.D., OTHER STATES

Argus Leader, Sunday, Feb. 11, 1996

Have you ever wondered about street signs sprouting in rural South Dakota, like "475th Avenue" and "250th Street" marking the Baltic corner?

It's not a fanciful extension of the city limits of Sioux Falls, Dell Rapids or whatever town you may be near.

The "475th" designation marks the north-south section line in South Dakota that is 375 miles east of the Wyoming-Montana border.

The "250th" marks the east-west section line that is 150 miles south of the border between North and South Dakota.

It's part of the rural addressing system that was developed several years ago to make response to a 911 call more efficient. It does it by numbering every section line in South Dakota.

Two base lines were chosen: the Wyoming-Montana and North Dakota borders. Each base line is No. 100. The first north-south section line east of the Wyoming-Montana border is 101. The first east-west section line south of North Dakota is 101. To figure miles east or south of the baselines, subtract 100 from the section line figure.

Fifteen of South Dakota's 66 counties (including Minnehaha and Pennington) have completed rural addressing, Thomas Kurtenbach, 911 state coordinator, said. His Pierre office is part of Emergency Management in the State Department of Military and Veterans Affairs.

Twenty-two counties are in the process of adopting the system and four other counties are just getting started.

Rural addressing was fostered by the South Dakota County Commissioners Association and South Dakota Municipal League. A state 911 Task Force carried it out.

OPENING CHAPTER

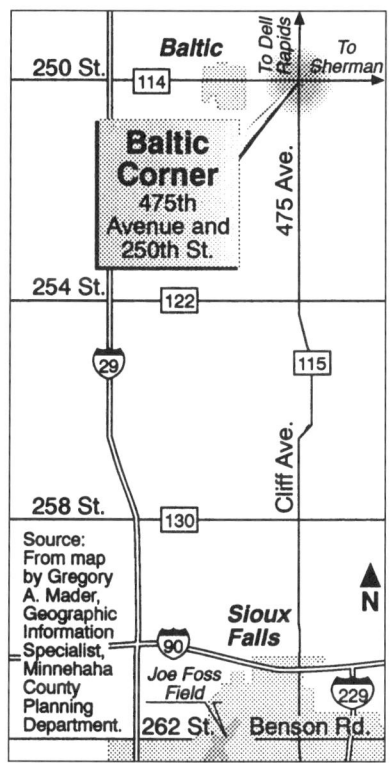

Rural Addressing System.
—Argus Leader drawing by Linda Smith

Other benefits include understandable rural addresses that people can find and to which private parcel carriers can deliver. Firms couldn't deliver to a post office box number.

Sponsors sought a voluntary rather than mandated approach. Erection of signs along rural section lines, for instance, is voluntary. But most counties have put up the signs. They are popping up all over South Dakota rural areas.

Lincoln County rural addressing is virtually complete, Chad Skiles, 911 coordinator, said. Erecting the last few remaining house signs was the last task to be done. Lincoln County addresses have been changed to the new system. All section line signs have been erected.

Dave Queal, Minnehaha County planning director, said that Sioux Falls city addresses were extended into the countryside. Rural addressing street and avenue numbers were used beyond areas adjacent to Sioux Falls.

Dean Westfall, 911 director for Minnehaha County and Sioux Falls, said the system helps local government cope with population changes in rural areas. Twenty years ago, volunteers in a local fire department knew where everybody lived. That is no longer true, Westfall said. The grid system makes it possible to pinpoint locations.

Enhanced 911 in the Safety Building shows the name of the phone subscriber, mail address, phone number and the suggested emergency response—which police or sheriff and fire departments are responsible for serving the caller.

A "South Dakota Rural Addressing Procedural Handbook" published by the 911 Task Force tells county government how to do it. Questions should be directed to 911 Coordinator, Division of Emergency Management, 500 E. Capitol, Pierre, SD 57501; phone (605) 773-3231.

Large-scale county maps may be purchased from the S.D. Department of Transportation, Reproduction Section, 500 E. Capitol, Pierre SD 57501; phone (605) 773-3277. Cost is $1 per map plus tax and handling. Some counties have two maps. Ask for your county's rural addressing grid map.

You may purchase an 11x17-inch Minnehaha County Geographic Information Systems map in color showing rural streets and highways for $3 from the Planning Department in the Courthouse.

S.D. TOWNS SHOULD TRUMPET THEIR HEROES AND ATTRACTIONS

Argus Leader, Sunday, Jan. 12, 1997

WALKING-DRIVING BROCHURES HELP

What can a small South Dakota town or village do to enhance its attractiveness to tourist who may stop to smell the roses on the rural scene next summer?

Do some of the things that towns or cities—like Faulkton or Sioux Falls—have done.

Compile literature that details a walking tour of your town and that gives essential historical information on important buildings or streets.

Pierre and Brookings have emphasized historical material in their walking tours. Watertown lists 40 attractions, including historic homes, in its new walking-driving brochure. Besides writing a walking or driving tour pamphlet, list essential general information about your town on a separate sheet.

Give population figures, form of government, names of key officers and major businesses or industry. List parks and points of interest. These may be described in detail in the walking tour guide.

List the town's motels and restaurants. Include directions or a sketch map showing locations.

Talk your club or group into spending a few dollars to have the material printed or copied. You'll find some bargain rates at instant print shops which have sprung up in the larger cities.

This is a suitable project for a commercial club, a church or study group or simply a coffee shop gathering.

None of these ideas is new.

Many of them helped make the U.S. Bicentennial and South Dakota Centennial celebrations more successful. They brought increased community participation.

• What are some of the attractions you might list?

If you live in Hurley, its marvelous Civil War statue in the City Park would be a sure thing for the walking tour guide.

Hurley veterans of the Civil War and their Grand Army of the Republic (GAR) veterans' organization erected the statue. The GAR thrived in every Northern community until "Taps" was bugled for the last survivors.

Major old buildings, particularly City Hall or post office structures or former large retail buildings, often have a fascinating story to tell of the days when your town was younger.

Someone in the community—a relative or an acquaintance of the building owner—can provide essential information about it.

Nearly every town has a hero or heroine who went on to win fame or fortune or both away from home. Alpena, Eureka and several other towns including Sioux Falls remember Al Neuharth, who founded USA Today. Yankton can't forget Tom Brokaw, NBC evening news anchor.

Both Madison and Sioux Falls remember Mary Hart of "Entertainment Tonight."

Doland remembers famous high school graduates Vice President Hubert Humphrey and Olympic wrestlers Dennis and Duane Koslowski on its Heritage Wall. The South Dakota Department of Transportation marks hometowns and residences of Gov. William Janklow, U.S. Sens. Tom Daschle and Tim Johnson and U.S. Rep. John Thune with highway signs.

The South Dakota State Historical Society with DOT assistance erects historical markers that include information on founders and pioneers.

Many small South Dakota towns trumpet their championship football, basketball or rodeo teams with billboard or smaller signs along the highway.

Why not include sports heroes and highlights in your town's folders?

If there's a historical marker in town or countryside, describe it.

Review travel literature from several of South Dakota's larger cities and smaller longtime tourist destinations. Their brochures and folders will give you some ideas.

OPENING CHAPTER

Tourism is South Dakota's second largest industry. Every town could give local tourism a boost by bragging a bit about local attractions.

Repeat customers at a gas station wouldn't pick up a fact sheet or walking guide every time they stopped for gas. But many tourists would appreciate getting a nugget of information about the locale they're driving through. Some of the state's daily papers and several weeklies publish tabloid visitors guides for their areas.

The Mobridge Tribune and the Redfield Press are among the larger weeklies doing this every year. Editors and publishers of smaller weekly papers could do the same thing for their region.

Commercial clubs or other tourist boosters in smaller towns could enlist sponsors for local advertising extolling hometown tourist attractions. One good example is the Roberts County National Bank ad in the Sisseton Courier.

Banker Harold L. Torness often boosts a local or area tourist attraction in his weekly ad. He also often includes local history vignettes and anecdotes about regional personalities.

Small-town tourist boosters should seek help from their local editor and radio station manager and their advertising people.

Ask them to devise catchy ads to encourage tourists to linger a while in their corner of the Mount Rushmore State.

PERSPECTIVE

SOUTH DAKOTA IN THE 30'S; GAINS DESPITE MISFORTUNE

Argus Leader, Saturday, April 25, 1981

Editor's Note: Thanks to Chris Fees for sending this very interesting article!

Sure the 1930s in South Dakota were tough.

I wouldn't call them "good, old days." But they were mighty interesting. And I'm glad I witnessed them.

However the comparison with today's South Dakota shows the Sunshine Coyote State and its people are much better off in practically every way than they were then.

What South Dakota was like during the 1930s is difficult to explain to teenagers. It's part of the generation gap.

There was no television

There was a a lot of hard scrabble for most of the population.

U.S. money was hard and a dollar bought a lot. But there were very few dollars.

I was 11 years old in 1930 when my family moved from Denver to western South Dakota. That was where my mother had grown up and where my grandfather and great uncle had homesteaded

There was adventure in the new life, going to a one-room country school—Red Top, west of Maurine, which is between Faith and Newell on Highway 212.

A younger brother and I often got a ride with our teacher Anna Still. She sometimes drove the 13 miles from her home at Bixby (a one time Moreau River post office and stage stop) to school and back. Much of the time, however my brother and I and other pupils walked to school. It was about two miles away.

Like other youngsters then and now, we were highly aware of automobile identification. Mrs. Hilt had a green Chevrolet.

Automobiles were much simpler than they are today. They included dependable Chevy sixes, Ford Model A's and later Henry Ford's first V-8. Bob Price, a friendly and well-liked individual, who had a general store, post office and garage at Maurine, owned a Buick.

In 1930, the state was only 41 years old and the last homestead rush in northwestern South Dakota had been only 20 years before.

Faith, 30 miles to the east, was starting its third decade. The Milwaukee Road operated a daily train each way to Mobridge. The tracks, so carefully laid in 1910, were ripped up about a year ago.

Highway 212—a federal highway—was meandering dirt grade for more than half the 85 miles between Faith and Newell. There were many tales—all true—about the perils of becoming stuck in the gumbo east of Newell when it rained. Reaching gravel 25 miles east of Newell determined whether you could make it the rest of the way to the Black Hills.

It wasn't until after World War II that the state constructed a new road—blacktop for all its length—between Faith and Newell. The Highway Department cut a new grade through hills and ravines instead of going around them.

The countryside over most of South Dakota during the 1930s was much darker at night than it is today. A few farm and ranch homes had their own light plants with generator and batteries. Most rural homes had Coleman gasoline table lamps (with the same type of mantle used in camping lanterns today) or kerosene lamps.

PERSPECTIVE

Clay-Union at Vermillion was South Dakota's first rural electric association; it hooked up farm homes in 1937. Sioux Valley Electric at Colman was second—in 1940. REAs lit up the rest of the state after World War II. Rural electrification and getting the remaining major state and local roads out of the mud were two of the biggest boons of the last 40 years.

In the 1930s, as today, drought hit western South Dakota the hardest. Most of the state from Huron and Mitchell west, was in the Dust Bowl. Dust storms that sent topsoil flying high and drifting along fence lines and roads were common. Parts of the state are seeing that on a smaller scale this year.

Many ranchers and farmers who had survived the first thinning out of homesteaders and the farm slump in the 1920s packed their belongings in the family car and headed west in the early 1930s—to Washington, Oregon and California.

Those who stayed in South Dakota encountered about five years of drought. Some ranchers fed Russian thistles to livestock during several of those years. They saw cattle slaughtered in Faith as part of a livestock reduction plan that also included hogs and sheep in South Dakota.

Government farm programs and scores of Federal agencies—a duke's mixture of alphabetical shorthand, like PWA, WPA, etc.—sprang from President Franklin D. Roosevelt's administration to combat drought and depression.

The relief rolls in December 1934 comprised 39 percent of the state's population. This was the highest relief load for any state. North Dakota was next in rank. More than half the farmers in South Dakota in December 1934 were receiving emergency relief.

Farmers using teams of horses built new grades for country roads in one of the programs designed to provide assistance. There were many others, including public works projects, the Civilian Conservation Corps for young men and the National Youth Administration for students.

Roosevelt initiated the public works program which would tame the Mighty Missouri and spare downstream states the ravages of its floods. The Fort Peck Dam in Montana was the first of six mainstem dams. The others—one in North Dakota and four in South Dakota—would follow after World War II.

Today, South Dakota is still trying to exploit the benefit of water resources in return for the half million acres of choice Missouri River bottomland given up for the dams.

When rains come in time, western South Dakota rangeland is among the country's and the world's best.

I spent an enjoyable month herding cows for an uncle in the summer of 1933. I got $15, plus room and board. The cash bought a sweater, corduroy slacks and other clothes with which to start high school.

The grass was good that summer along Sulphur Creek in Meade County. It wasn't very good for several years after that.

Pop and candy bars were a nickel in those days—compared with two bits or 30 cents today.

Sunday afternoons in the summer usually included a baseball game. Storekeeper Price loaded team gear, some players and fans in his truck—and headed for Imogene (former Perkins county post office and store), Faith or wherever Maurine was playing on a Sunday. Home games were on a diamond just south of the Maurine store and across the road.

It was fun to cheer the Maurine team and see them win the area tournament in Faith one summer.

Dedication in 1930 of Prairie Home Church (Presbyterian) three miles west of Maurine, S.D., provided new meeting facilities for the community. The Rev. Robert McElwee of Bison was the pastor. —Faith Photo Finishers photo

Despite drought and economic adversity which afflicted the entire nation, growing up in western South Dakota was pleasant.

Townspeople and country residents coped. They made their own entertainment, had lots of card games in the winter (whist was a favorite) and coffee and desserts to please everyone. The Wapuzo Theatre at Faith had all the current movies—and soon after their release. There were town and country dances, too.

Lawrence Welk was playing on WNAX; KFYR came booming in from Bismarck. There was no FM. Today's multiplicity of radio stations in towns large and small was still in the future.

Small town newspapers took in grain or farm produce for subscriptions. Arthur Nisselius, Spearfish publisher who owned the Sturgis Tribune during the 1930s, offered a year's subscription to the Tribune for two bushels of wheat. That was when wheat was bringing much less than a dollar.

I sometimes rode horseback to our country high school at Fox Ridge, three miles east of Maurine. I liked that pony—a red and white pinto that was half Shetland. He survived—well fed and cared for on my folk's ranch—until the early 1960s.

Another sign of the affluent times is shown in one of today's SDSU students telling a reporter that he lost $500 worth of stereo equipment in an electrical fire in his dormitory room.

College students in the 1930s did a lot of hitchhiking. They also shared rides at Christmas time to travel home from Brookings. If you had the bucks, you could take the Chicago & Northwestern's passenger train from Brookings to Black Hills or Minnesota destinations.

I hitchhiked many times and spent an occasional overnight in a Gettysburg or other midway hotel on my way home to Maurine.

Once, several of us ran out of rides near Onida. This was probably circumstance—there wasn't much traffic. However, the Onida area had been the scene of a brutal slaying of a schoolteacher by hitchhikers a year or so earlier. A telephone call by a companion brought his father from Dupree to pick us up.

A couple of years ago while visiting Faith, I walked over much of the town—and found it difficult to compare with that of the 1930s.

PERSPECTIVE

The biggest difference—and one that accounted for a major change in appearance—came from today's trees. There are lots of them and they give Faith a nice appearance in the summer. During the 1930s, there were very few trees.

Faith today never looked better. Main Street is black-topped. The Prairie Oasis Mall occupies one block on Main Street. There are other excellent business buildings. Today's homes in Faith also reflect prosperity that is typical of much of South Dakota.

Many small towns, of course, have faded away since the 1930s.

But Faith, which has a large trading area, has been fortunate in its civic leadership and also its adaptability. This was shown several years ago when Faith won renown for turning down a federal grant to build a new grandstand. The residents and ranchers who call Faith their hometown built their own. The town has thrived, and its residents along with it.

Faith's population in 1980 was the same as 1970, 576. In 1930 the population was 607; in 1940, 522.

Faith businessmen and western South Dakota ranchers alike are watching the sky this spring, waiting and hoping for rain. It will make all the difference—like it did in the late 1930s.

Another favorite city off mine—Brookings—also reflects changes for the better that are typical in South Dakota. During the 1930s, Brookings and the college were attempting to cope with drastic cuts that the state's dire financial condition imposed on SDSU and other state campuses.

The state appropriation for SDSU was $185,000 in 1937-38, when there were about 1,000 students on campus. In Fiscal 1980, the comparable state appropriation was $10 million, with about 6,200 students.

High school in Faith was an interesting experience, highlighted by working as a printer's devil and linotype operator for the Democratic Faith Independent during my junior year, and its Republican opposition, the Faith Gazette, the next. Pay was room, board and $2 a week during school; this was raised to $5 in summer.

The Independent absorbed the Gazette during World War II and is the surviving paper today. Competition between the two was tough. The scramble for a limited amount of revenue was characteristic of the times.

Attending the South Dakota State (College then, University now) in Brookings during the late 1930s was easily done on $400 a year or less if you had the $400. Today, tuition, board and room are approximately $2,200 a year on the Brookings campus. Tuition in 1937 was $70 a year; today, $718.

There were about 1,200 students on campus during the late 1930s, compared with about 6,500 today. There were possibly a dozen cars on campus then; today there are 3,999 registered at State. There were few parking problems in the 1930s.

Brookings has expanded from a pleasant little college town of 5,346 in 1940 to one of South Dakota's larger cities, 14,951 in 1980. The latter figure, however, counts approximately 6,000 students. The 1940 figure didn't count 1,150 students.

The expansion of the campus and improvements in Brookings homes and businesses over the last 40 years are definitely upbeat.

That resurgence started in the late 1930s, coinciding with the economic upturn throughout the country.

It was a desirable time from a student's standpoint: Nick's hamburgers in downtown Brookings were still a nickel. You could eat for a week on a $5 meal ticket. A nice room in a private home off campus was only $2 a week.

Construction of a dormitory, the Pugsley Student Union and some classrooms—all federal projects—commenced near the end of the decade. This was cheered by students and faculty alike. The buildings marked the end of an era in which all state campuses had done without.

I had a pleasant summer in 1939 when I worked several weeks putting out the West River Progress in Dupree for E.L. Schetnan, a friend from my days in Faith.

Schetnan was a remarkable South Dakota character, who had homesteaded near Dupree. He had lost his hearing on his way to this country, via Canada, from Norway. Despite this handicap, he persevered in publishing a weekly paper, first at Red Elm and then at Dupree. He did everything: set the type on a linotype, fed the press, made up the forms.

He wrote notes to anyone he would meet on the street to get his news.

He also owned the Eagle Butte News. At week's end, after printing the Progress, we'd take the Milwaukee Road train at Dupree in the morning to Eagle Butte 20 miles away. We were loaded down with several galleys of type for the News' front page. We printed the News on a small Diamond Press in Eagle Butte, mailed it at the post office and took the train back to Dupree in the afternoon.

The daily train to and from Mobridge had a legend all its own. According to some stories, engineers and conductors had favorite sloughs enroute where they stopped during season to hunt waterfowl. And according to a box the Faith Gazette used to carry on its front page, Faith was the largest initial shipper of grain in the Milwaukee's entire system.

The railroad engineer had an elite status—somewhat like airplane pilots today. The train crews, like the star mail route drivers to Sturgis, Newell and other towns, were a link with the outside world.

As the decade drew to a close, events in Europe, which had cast their shadow before Munich, Czechoslovakia and "peace in our time," came into sharper focus for collegians and their acquaintants.

PERSPECTIVE

It was dramatized on Sept. 1, 1939. The Daily Argus-Leader delivered in Brookings that Friday afternoon carried three headlines across the top of page one: NAZIS INVADE POLAND, BOMB WARSAW; POLES ASK AID FROM ENGLAND, FRANCE; President Says America Can Keep Out of War.

Adolf Hitler changed the world that day. This was despite the fact that the war in Europe after his conquest of Poland seemed to become a "phony" one. There was inactivity between opposing forces on France's Maginot Line and Germany's Siegfried Line.

College students repeated ditties like, "We're going to hang our washing on the Siegfried Line."

In April 1940, Hitler invaded Denmark and Norway. In May, he sent his army and air force against The Netherlands, Belgium and Luxembourg. Hitler's tanks went around the Maginot Line and drove the combined British and French forces off the continent at Dunkirk.

Nineteen forty would bring the draft to the United States and a further build up of this country's armed forces.

College students had already witnessed increased interest in ROTC (Reserve Officers Training Corps) and the forerunners of courses geared to help the nation in its defense build up. These programs were speeded up. They included pilot training, aviation mechanics, machine shop and other trade courses.

Despite Roosevelt's stated position that the country could stay out of the war in Europe, it was evident that conflict was on its way.

The people who lived in South Dakota in the 1930s had a unique experience: they survived the state's economic downturn, a national depression and a drought over two-thirds of the state.

They saw the state, like the nation, approach recovery just before the war crisis heightened. And fortunately, the weather cycle changed for the better.

The people who moved from South Dakota during the decade because of economic circumstances or for other reasons never forgot their home state, either.

Many of them—second and third generations of South Dakotans who moved West in the 1930s—still come back to see family homesteads or find their roots in the Sunshine State.

Thanks to government writing projects, the 1930s were well chronicled in South Dakota. The decade reflects some remarkable achievements by South Dakotans despite adversity. The decade also set the stage for what was to come.

I well recall shooting the bull with a college friend just after the 1930s had run their course. We were talking about the lights going out in Western Europe—and the historic nature of the times.

The consensus was that we didn't want to miss that part of history, although there were drawbacks ahead compared with the 1930s.

My friend concluded our high-level talk with: "I wish the times weren't quite so historic. "

ROOTS

OSLO—7 HOURS FROM NEW YORK: NORWEGIANS HATE THE GERMANS, BUT DRIVE THEIR VOLKSWAGENS

Argus Leader, Sunday, April 30, 1961

OSLO, Norway—Norway, which has close ties with South Dakota because thousands of its citizens are of Scandinavian descent, is closer than ever now.

This is because of new jet airliner service started to Scandinavia April 21 by Pan American Airways. The jets put Oslo only seven hours non-stop from New York on the eastbound flight. It takes an hour longer west from Oslo to New York because of prevailing headwinds.

The jets make it possible for an individual like this writer to leave Sioux Falls on a Thursday, spend a day in Washington, four days in Norway and be home a week later.

Pan American asked me to participate in their inaugural flight. Other American editors, writers, travel representatives, businessmen and government officials were on the eastbound flight. Coming home on the westbound inaugural flight with the Americans were Norwegian, Swedish and Finnish citizens in the same line of work.

The Americans were given a choice of Oslo, Stockholm or Helsinki. I chose Oslo because Norway is the birthplace of my mother, Mrs. Nels Afdahl of Maurine, S.D., and also of my stepfather.

Oslo, a city of half a million, is 1,000 years old. It has much to offer the tourist in the way of scenic attractions. When I arrived on that overcast Saturday, it seemed somber, grey and moody.

When I left it last Tuesday evening, it was gay in the spring sunshine which lasts until 10:30 at night. Trees were budding and the grass was green. Beautiful women, dressed like the women of New York, Washington and Sioux Falls, give the capital a glamorous look.

Oslo has a parking problem, a telephone problem and a housing problem. Like American cities, it is widening its streets and putting in double lanes on some thoroughfares.

Twenty-seven thousand persons are on the waiting list for a telephone in Oslo. The situation is so bad that the applicants have even formed an association of applicants for telephones. The association hasn't had much luck getting telephones out of the government-run system.

Rents are reasonable—once you get an apartment. They vary from $20 to $40 a month for family-size apartments. But getting one is another matter. You have to plunk down the equivalent of from $1,400 to $3,500 as a deposit. This money buys a share—your share—in the building. You get it back if you move out.

The housing shortage has been the order of things in Norway since the end of World War II. It is most acute in the capital and other cities, and is also found in rural districts.

Food and other expenses in this socialistic state are fairly reasonable. Average family income is said to be something over $2,000 a year. But the tax bite, by which Norway finances its socialistic setup, is a stiff one.

Import taxes virtually double the prices on automobiles. That is one reason why you see so many Volkswagens in Norway. The Volkswagen, which sells for about $1,000 in Germany, sells for $2,000 in Norway. The smallest American cars bring about $4,000 in Norway, or double their price in the U.S.A.

There are some American cars on the road. But they're out-numbered heavily by English, German and Swedish cars, nearly all of which are of compact or small size. The mileage per gallon takes on extra importance in Norway because of the high price of gasoline. Gasoline costs nearly 70 cents a gallon. The difference between the American price and the Norwegian price represents the government's "take." Liquors cost double or more than they do elsewhere in the world. One Norwegian said to me: "If I profiteered like that the government would put me in jail."

Sales tax runs about 10 per cent on many domestic items. Income taxes—20 per cent. Sedans are considered a luxury and pay a heavier tax than panel delivery trucks, for instance, which produce income because of their commercial use.

The tax situation is something that makes capitalists wary—and that makes it hard for the individual Norwegian to become a capitalist. Most Norwegians are in very modest circumstances. There seems to be a wide gulf between the common people and the very rich.

Norwegians generally seem to be happy. They like their country and their king. Their lot is tied with that of the West. NATO headquarters for Northern Europe is on the outskirts of Oslo.

Gallant sentries walk stiffly and pompously in front of the royal palace in Oslo. They take measured steps, wheel and turn in the bright sunshine. There is plumage on their uniform hats and a bright red stripe on their trousers. They seem part of a very old, old system. The bayonets on their rifles gleam sharply. But their rifles are American M1s.

Norwegians are realists. They don't get nervous about the Mr. K. in Moscow—or about Mr. K. in Washington, for that matter. They seem to take life as it comes.

They drive Volkswagens—but will never forgive or forget the Germans for their cruel occupation of Norway in World War II. It is said that they don't like the Swedes. As one Norwegian put it, "The Swedes are still trying to be neutral."

TIME STANDS STILL IN NORWAY; STAVANGER MIXES PRESLEY, GRIEG

Argus Leader, Monday, May 1, 1961

OSLO, Norway—My trip inside Norway was almost as fast as my trip to Norway.

I learned Monday afternoon, April 17th, that I was going to Norway four days later. There was a passport to get. Smallpox vaccination. Things to tell Mama and the kids.

I called my brother, George Afdahl, in Faith. Would he please drive to Maurine and ask our mother to send me a letter with the birthplaces of herself and my stepfather in Norway? He would. The letter got to me before I left Sioux Falls Thursday for Washington to pick up my passport.

Pan American's Jet Clipper Gauntlet took off from Idlewild airport at New York Friday evening. Seven hours and 4,000 miles later it touched down at an airport north of Oslo, to inaugurate Pan American's new jet service to Scandinavia. It was Saturday morning in Norway.

The Lord Mayor of Oslo, the United States Ambassador—Clifton Wharon—and others met the plane. There was an honor guard of Norwegian airmen drawn up at the plane. A children's band struck up a march.

A short time later the Gauntlet left for Stockholm and Helsinki. The Americans who got off in Norway were headed for Oslo in a Swedish made bus.

The bus driver was a throttle jockey who wheeled the large vehicle with ease over a bumpy, narrow road. He slowed down for oncoming cars and for pedestrians, who never looked back.

If Americans tried walking on roads in the U.S.A. like the Norwegians do, there wouldn't be any pedestrians left. But there's more time for everything in Norway.

There are fewer automobiles, more bicycles and motorcycles and more people walking the sidewalks and streets. Youngsters and oldsters think nothing of walking several miles. Many of them had packs on their backs. Some were headed for a weekend in the mountains. Everyone walking seemed to have rosy cheeks.

Saturday afternoon I was in the front seat of an Opel Capital—a German four-door sedan. A young blond Norwegian in a chauffeur's uniform was driving me toward Roikenvik, north of Oslo, where my mother was born. His English wasn't the best—but he knew my purpose in going to Roikenvik.

I think it's hardest for an American to comprehend the age and tradition of a European country like Norway. The last parts of western South Dakota were settled in 1910 by homesteaders. One thousand years ago Norman invaders were building cathedrals in Norway.

In a pine-dotted setting by a lake I found the village of Roikenvik. High on a hill within a few miles of the village I found an old red brick church called Thingelstad, which was my mother's family name.

My mother had left Norway as a child in 1905, with her parents, brothers and sister and an uncle. In 1961 there were no relatives left in Norway. Fifty-six years is almost a lifetime—but in the history of Norway it is only a short time. The beautiful mountains and the tiny farms seemed timeless, indeed.

Sunday morning I was flying to Stavanger, on the west coast of Norway. Stavanger is opposite the northern part of Scotland. It is called "The Golden Key" to the fjord country.

My brief experiences in Stavanger convinced me that the world is pretty much the same all over. South Dakota, with its tourist business as the No. 2 industry, would like to increase that crop. So would Stavanger.

"Ten years ago there was not a tourist in Stavenger," a personable young Norwegian, Petter Schultz-Persen, told me. He is manager of the Stavanger Travel Association.

Stavanger leaders decided to do something about it. Sigvald Bergesen, a big shipowner, got behind a move to build the Atlantic Hotel, perhaps the finest hostelry in Norway. It was opened in 1952.

The night before I arrived Stavanger opened its new concert hall, built next to the hotel. They asked Elvis Presley to come. When he couldn't make it, they played his records alternately with those of Edvard Grieg, the immortal Norwegian composer. "Something for the young, something for the old" is the way they passed off that combination.

Hotel managers from western Norway came to Stavanger for the dedication ceremonies. All of them talked of ways to bring more tourists, particularly Americans, to Norway.

The tourist is king. In Oslo, for instance, the hotels tell Norwegian trade groups when they may hold conventions. It is not in the summer when tourist pinch the already short supply of hotel rooms.

Stavanger intends to preserve its medieval-like business section behind a facade of modernistic buildings in the heart of the city. Traffic will be sealed off from the narrow streets in the area of old shops. They will call it a "living museum" in which the shops will be kept open and do business at the same stands of the last several hundred years—but with modern interiors, of course.

A fishing festival in August is another tourist lure.

Speed has come to the fjords in the form of Italian-made hydro-foil boats. The Vingstor sped me from Stavanger to Bergen in 3 1/2 hours. The trip used to take 10 hours by overnight steamer. The Vingstor does about 40 miles per hour.

I found myself in Bergen for my second night in Norway—Sunday night.

VISITOR FROM U.S.A.
SURPRISES KIN IN MOUNTAINS OF NORWAY

Argus Leader, Tuesday, May 2, 1961

Bergen, Norway—Johan Christian Moe, fortyish and the director of the most modern hotel in Bergen—the Orion—personifies the successful Norwegian career businessman of the post-war era.

He told me something about his life and about life in Norway as we sped from Stavanger to Bergen aboard the Vingstor, a fast Italian-made boat.

Before World War II he spent several months in Switzerland in hotel training. He spent the last six months of the war in a German prison camp. He was soon back in hotel work—and married a girl from his hometown of Kristiansand in the south of Norway.

His blonde wife and their teen-age son met us at the dock, which is half a block from their hotel. Previously, he had managed tourist hotels in the mountains. Now he was in this exciting new job in the second largest city of Norway.

"Dinner at nine?" they invited me pleasantly. And so Sunday evening, April 23rd, I had dinner with Mr. and Mrs. Moe and Olav Sandven, who owns two hotels near Bergen.

That Sunday had been a glorious spring day in Bergen. The temperature was 63. The trees and grass were green. Mrs. Moe had spent the afternoon walking in the mountains.

Talk over the fillet of sole included some needling and joking about the dedication ceremonies for the concert hall in Stavanger the night before. The party at the concert hall broke up about 5 in the morning. It sounded like an American convention.

Sandven told us that he planned to hire a cook the next day. He had a line on a young man at cook's school, whom he would sign up for work at his mountain hotel.

I told them about my jet trip to Norway aboard Pan American Airway's inaugural flight. And about visiting my mother's birthplace near Oslo and that my stepfather, Nels Afdahl of Maurine, S.D., had been born near Voss, 2 1/2 hours from Bergen by train.

I showed them the letter from my mother, which gave a line on my stepfather's relatives. He had had no contact with them for 40 years.

Moe went to the telephone book and found an Olav Afdal at the head of the list for Voss. He offered to call him up. He left the dinner table and placed the call.

A few minutes later, he returned and told me that Olav Afdal was my stepfather's brother—and they would meet me at the railroad station in Voss the next afternoon.

At three o'clock Monday afternoon I stepped from the train at Voss, in the mountains of Norway and on the main railroad line between Bergen and Oslo.

A grey-haired man with a younger man approached me. "Mr. Afdal?" I asked. He nodded. He was Anders, 55. The young man was J. Vangen Lirus, a grocer in Voss who speaks English. I met Olav, 62, a minute later.

My stepfather is 76. He left Norway when he was about 21, or in 1906. Surprise was written on the faces of his brothers. I was to see more surprised faces when I met two other brothers. They hadn't heard from America for so long that they thought Nels was dead. The phone call from Mr. Moe to Olav had changed their world, and mine, somehow.

At Anders' home in the village of Voss we lunched and visited. Later, we headed for Olav's farm home where we had more lunch and more visiting.

"Do you want to go the the Afdal farm?" they asked me.

NORTHERN PLAINS ADVENTURES

Mr. and Mrs. Anders Afdahl and
J. Liaton Virhus, interpreter.

Nels Afdahl 1960.
—Anson Yeager photo

Four of Nels Afdahl's younger brothers; Knud, Olav, Anders, George in Voss, 1961.

24

Left: Afdahl farm, April 24, 1961. Right: Waterfall near Afdahl farm.

"Of course." I replied. So we got in Anders' Opel station wagon and headed out of Voss for the mountain farm where my stepfather was born.

A few miles from Voss we stopped to look up at a waterfall which sent water thundering down the mountainside. "The farm is above the falls," they said.

We drove to the top of the mountain "This is a new road," they told me. "It wasn't here when Nels was a boy. The German POWs built it after the surrender in 1945."

The Germans did it by hand. Like other Norwegians, the Afdals preferred to say nothing about the occupation days in World War II. Resentment against the Germans is deep and bitter.

Voss was one of the big battles of the brief Norwegian campaign in 1940. The Germans told the Norwegians if they didn't surrender Voss, its rail terminal and its airport, they would burn the town. The Norwegians gave them their version of Gen. McAuliffe's "nuts" at Bastogne. The town was burned.

"That's why all the buildings in town are new," they explained. The church, almost a thousand years old, escaped the bombing, however.

Atop the mountain I met two more brothers, George, 73, and Knud, 52, and Knud's family. His son Knud Jr. will take over the farm someday. If my stepfather had stayed in Norway, the farm would have been his. But he saw his opportunity in America.

Below was the valley and across it another mountain range. The small field was ready for planting. There was timber in the process of finishing. Snow lingered at this elevation. The stream that was to become a torrent for the falls below was running fast at the farm.

Here, in the mountains of Norway, I thought to myself, are a very rugged people. We visited—and marveled that of the 10 brothers and sisters of whom Nels is the oldest, all are alive and well.

Eight hours after I arrived at Voss' railroad station I was saying goodbye to Anders and the English-speaking grocer who had interpreted for us.

I got on the night train for Oslo. It was 11 o'clock Monday night. My three days in Norway seemed like a lifetime. Tuesday night I'd be back in New York. And Wednesday night in Sioux Falls. I couldn't believe it.

Left: A rental car is an ideal way to see Norway. Evergreens and grass are lush in these hills north of Oslo. Right: A Norwegian trucker heads up a mountain grade west of Gjovik. Lumber is an important cash product of Norwegian farms.

TO GET AWAY FROM IT ALL: TRY A MOTOR TOUR OF NORWAY

Argus Leader, Sunday, Aug. 1, 1971

Oslo, Norway—uncrowded . . . unspoiled . . . and a new scenery spectacular around every curve in the road and turn in the fjord.

The American who wants to get away from it all will find a motor tour of Norway to his liking if he digs mountain scenery, more green foliage than you can imagine and a yen to see what's beyond the horizon.

Here in Norway, at the top of Europe, the American motorist can take his own time going from one scenic spectacular to another.

It's relatively easy to make arrangements for a rental car through your travel agent in Sioux Falls, pick up a car in Oslo and drop it in Bergen, or vice versa, when your tour is finished.

Prior Planning Helpful

A trip of this kind ideally should be planned several months in advance, to allow time to make car and hotel reservations. Hotel reservations are essential in Oslo and Bergen. They are not so necessary for the casual traveler motoring in Norway along the main tourist routes.

Perhaps the quickest way to get the feel of Norway is to stay in Oslo for about a week. This will permit you to view some of the major attractions of Norway's capital city and also take some drives into the nearby countryside.

Oslo's traffic is heavy. The stateside driver will find the traffic circles confusing. Woe to the driver who gets in the wrong lane! Your problems are comparable to being in the same situation on the Los Angeles freeway at 5 p.m.

Journeys outside the capital will quickly solve your traffic problem New highways provide easy access to nearby districts. Roads are not crowded in rural areas.

A Beautiful Lake

An interesting side trip from Oslo is a tour along the Randsfjord, an inland lake 45 miles long. It lies north and slightly west of Oslo. It is Norway's fourth largest lake.

There are water and wood scenes here to delight the most avid amateur photographer. At Tingelstad there's a beautiful red brick church, built in the Middle Ages. Nearby is the Hadeland Folk Museum.

Brandbu Mountain, a prominent landmark, overlooks the Randsfjord, a lake north of Oslo. Road sign marks the junction at Bleiken Station, a rail stop on the Oslo-Gjovik line.

At Roykenvik, a white frame church built in 1736 nestles among trees on the shoreline of the Randsfjord. Brandbu Mountain, a round butte and a prominent landmark, is nearby.

Thick evergreens and treelined roads atop the ridges and hills north of Oslo reminded me of Alaska and northern Minnesota. Traffic included lumber trucks. Norwegian farms are small but diversified, and lumber is an important cash product.

What To See in Oslo

No one could become thoroughly acquainted with Norway's beautiful capital in a few days. But several days will provide an interesting look at a capital city of half a million which has one of the largest geographical areas of any capital in the world.

The view of Oslo and Oslofjord from the mountaintops within the city is only one of many spectacular scenes for the tourist in Norway.

A day spent on the Bygdoy Peninsula will give you such highlights as a glimpse at Thor Heyerdahl's Kon-Tiki raft, the Polar exploring ship Fram and the Viking ships which were dug up in Oslofjord late in the 19th century.

The Folk Museum on the Bygdoy Peninsula is large, and has many buildings typical of farm and town homes from throughout Norway. There is a splendid Stave Church in the museum, similar to the one at Rapid City.

A visit to the Sonja Henie museum on the western outskirts of Olso was disappointing. The museum was a gift to the city from Sonja Henie and her husband, Niels Onstad. It features contemporary art, and showed Miss Henie's trophies.

I had hoped to see some large scale photographs depicting the highlights of the career of the late Norwegian skating star. But presumably, such a display may have to wait a long time—until the grief over her death from cancer in 1969 is eased.

Memories of Occupation

Anyone who's interested in recent world history should make it a point to see the Resistance Movement Museum at Akershus Castle, on the waterfront in Oslo and not far from downtown.

The Norwegian government through murals, dioramas and displays of documents and war material tells the story of the 1940-45 period when the Germans occupied Norway.

Photographs show the German parachute landings, the valiant but unsuccessful effort of the Norwegians and the British to counteract the invasion and many other facets of occupation days.

There are exhibits of Allied, Norwegian and German military orders, displays of German propaganda posters by which the occupying troops hoped to win support from the Norwegians for their war against the Russians and many articles of material. The latter include German rifles, machine guns, Norwegian short wave radios, etc.

Dioramas depict the British bombing attack on the heavy water plant in Norway, which the Germans used in their atomic development, and other highlights of the Norwegian resistance to the occupation.

The exhibit ends with photographs of the Germans marching to leave . . . and the Allies in a liberation march in Oslo. The flags of Norway, the United States, Britain and the U.S.S.R. are depicted in the final exhibit.

The ski enthusiast will find a museum devoted to his sport at Holmenkollen. on the mountain overlooking Oslo.

Plan your next step

Oslo is the place to make arrangements for further travel, such as reconfirming air reservations, checking on ferry reservations on the fjords and the like.

Although it is well to do some checking on ferry schedules, reservations probably won't be necessary in most cases for inland Norway. Your travel agent can advise you.

If you arrive in Norway by auto ferry from England, Denmark, or Germany, your planning should take such reservations into account. They should be made in advance.

TOURING NORWAY BY AUTO SHOULD BE DONE AT A LEISURELY PACE

Argus Leader, Aug. 3, 1971

OSLO, Norway—The South Dakotan who tours Norway by car shouldn't expect to do four or five hundred miles a day.

A trip of that length should be spread over several days to allow a leisurely pace on mountain roads, time to stop and look or snap pictures and to eat a mid-day lunch in a road-side cafeteria.

Anyone setting out from Oslo or Bergen for a tour in the country will find several differences right away in touring, Norwegian style.

Distances are in kilometers. Your rental car will have a speedometer marked in kilometers. Multiply by .6 to convert to miles.

Gasoline is sold in liters (about one quart). More gas stations are self-service than in the United States. Wiping your windshield is not a regular thing for attendants. It's mainly do-it-yourself for the motorist

Road maps, which Americans are accustomed to obtaining free, are sold in Norway. The most complete maps are found in book stores. The large scale of these maps will help the motorist enjoy his trip.

If the Yank in Norway happens to be looking up relatives, a topographical map may be useful. These are either Norwegian maps, or U.S. Army maps from Norwegian data. They are available for the locality in most bookstores in a particular region.

These topographical maps show, among other things, farm homes and their names. If your relatives came from a particular part of Norway, and you know the general area, you may be able to pinpoint the family farm or area on a map.

Another aid to the traveler seeking relatives is the telephone book. If you find a familiar name, your next step is to find someone who can interpret for you.

Many a hotel manager or other businessman in Norway has helped an American traveler find kin and homeground by interpreting.

Europe 68 from Oslo to Bergen.

The traveler in a tour group finds that his time to locate relatives is limited. They may be in an area not readily accessible to car or telephone. Taking the time to tour Norway on your own is an advantage.

Another assist for the motorist in Norway is a book "Motoring in Norway," published by the Norway Travel Association. This book was sold out in Oslo, but I was able to pick up a copy in Gjovik.

The book has brief, pertinent comments on interesting places and stops for the American traveler. The strip maps are excellent.

Europe 68 to Bergen

One interesting way to see much of the variety of Norway is to take Europe 68 from Oslo to Bergen.

This Oslo-Bergen route will provide the traveler with a look at the rolling plains near Oslo, foothills, mountains, countless waterfalls, fjords and ferry passages.

Europe 68 takes the traveler north and west from Oslo, past another large inland lake, Sperillen, and on to Fagernes, a scenic mountain town. The numerous lakes along Europe 68 enhance the drive.

A mountain hotel at Tyin, on Europe 68, is a delightful stop. Here, at an elevation of 4,800 feet, the vegetation is sparse. The mountain lake is a mirror for the surrounding peaks.

Traveling west from Tyin, the South Dakotan will be especially interested in the Borgund Stave Church, built in 1150, of which the Dahl Memorial Stave Church at Rapid City is an exact replica.

Europe 68 utilizes a ferry from Revsnes to Gudvangen. This trip, along the magnificent Sogne Fjord and its tributaries, is another spectacular in my travel notebook.

Lake Tyin provides sharp reflections at midmorning. A mountain hotel at Tyin is an interesting stop on Europe Route 68 from Oslo to Bergen. Reflections at midnight were similar but eerie in the twilight. It never really gets dark in Norway during the summer.

This is one of numerous car ferries which ply the Sogne Fjord and give the interior of the boot of Norway access to the Atlantic. Travelers on Europe route 68 have a 2½-hour ferry ride from Revsnes to Gudvangen.

Aboard the ferry you may see an ocean-going liner in the nooks and crannies of these fjords, 75 miles northeast of Bergen as the crow flies, but much farther by ship or car.

Near Gudvangen is the Stalheim Hotel, perhaps the most renowned tourist hotel in Norway. Stalheim was a favorite of British tourists at the turn of the 20th century.

The present hotel was built in 1960, replacing one lost by fire in 1959. There's a spectacular view of Stalheim's sugar-loaf mountain and Naeroy Fjord, 1,000 feet below, from the hotel's flower gardens at the top of the cliff.

Voss—A Tourist Delight

Closer to Bergen on Europe 68 is the mountain town of Voss. A town of 13,000, it has a lot going for the tourist. It's on the main line of the Oslo-Bergen Railway. Eight through-trains, plus 13 local trains a day, provide ready access for the traveler who uses the rails.

Voss, on the Oslo Bergen main rail line, gives the tourist ready access to mountain hotels, hiking trails, and nearby fjords. The Voss Cathedral (spire at center right) was built about 1270. The town has a scenic site for campers on Lake Voss.

Voss has developed its skiing attractions in recent years, giving the area a much needed extension of its tourist season.

There's a lovely site for campers on the lake at Voss. The shoreline, incidentally, is free of construction of any kind. This is typical of Norwegian zoning regulations.

Bergen—Gateway City

Bergen is 167 kilometers or 100 miles west of Voss by a circuitous road and is the terminus of Europe-marked Route No. 68.

Bergen was the home of Edvard Grieg, the great Norwegian composer. His home is a tourist attraction. Bergen is an ocean port . . . and its waterfront displays a wide range of water taxis, ferries and big ships to excite a landlubber from South Dakota.

There are parks, shipyards and lovely views for the tourist to see in Bergen. The funicular, which carries travelers up the mountain 1,000 feet above Bergen to Floien, provides a breathtaking view of Norway's second largest city.

During the Middle Ages, Bergen was a gateway city for Hanseatic League trading. Today it's a world port, and in recent years has had sailing direct to Chicago via the St. Lawrence Waterway and the Great Lakes.

Bergen's Flesland International Airport puts Norway only eight hours and 10 minutes from Chicago, including a stop at Montreal.

More Americans are likely to find something of what they're looking for in a vacation in Norway. Bergen is a good place to start or finish a trip to Norway.

A LARGER 747? NOT FOR THIS TRAVELER

Argus Leader, July 24, 1971

News Item—Boeing Company says it has plans for a new 747 jetliner with a capacity of 1,000 passengers, more than twice as many as the largest 747 jumbo jet now flying is designed to carry.

Today's 747 is a magnificent flying machine, but the 350 passengers it carries at capacity across the Atlantic are a bit much for many travelers this season, including me.

The woes of the airlines with all kinds of capacity and not enough passengers have been pointed up by empty seats 31,000 feet above the North Atlantic.

The Pan American 747 which I took from Chicago to London June 22 was about half full. The return trip on Air France July 15 found its 747 almost full. But Air France is a nationally-owned airline, and can draw on passengers from the world's largest overseas network and its own domestic operations. Pan American has the problem of having no domestic routes, in addition to being private enterprise.

The world's airlines have started a fare revolution with their $220 transatlantic tickets for persons under 30. But they're going to need another kind of innovation to fill their airline seats today, let alone a 1,000-passenger 747.

The airlines may yet find their answer to increasing business in lower transoceanic fares applicable to all travelers, not just the young. If they do, the 1,000-passenger 747 may be what's needed to put it over.

But I'm convinced that it will be a pain to fly seven hours with so many people. The unstretched Boeing 707 and the McDonnell Douglas DC8 are 50 miles an hour slower than the present 747, but they feel more comfortable than Big Daddy.

Great French Parade

Some random observations from three and a half weeks in Europe:

The French know how to put on a parade. Their marching men and women were a sight to see in Paris on Bastille Day, July 14. President Georges Pompidou stood in his car as he passed the troops lined up on the Champs Elysees before they passed in review for him. Gendarmes took no chance with security; they were on the avenue and on rooftops. Mirage jets, helicopters, troop transports roared overhead. Tanks and jeeps rumbled along, and the Frenchmen swung their arms to the lilting march music.

The French Concorde, seen from a distance at Orly Field, looks impressive. Its needlelike configuration may be the first supersonic transport in passenger service.

Norway is importing, not exporting, labor. Skilled workers are coming in from England to work in shipbuilding, other trades. There are some Spaniards in restaurant service, some Pakistanis and other Europeans and Asiatics coming into Norway. Spaniards come to Norway alone first, send for their families later. Norwegians say the in-migration is bringing some social problems, but they consider it part of a booming economy.

Medium-sized cars are as popular in Europe as they are in the United States. The Volkswagen is No. 1 in Norway. But its larger models, and the medium-sized cars of American firms doing business in Europe and the United Kingdom are gaining in popularity. The full-sized American car is a rarity on European roads.

"Gunsmoke" is a popular TV offering in Norway. Some of the newscasters on Norway's sole TV channel, operated by the government, are women: beautiful, sophisticated Nordic types that look like they came out of the latest fashion pages.

The language barrier is still tough in non-English speaking countries. In Norway, youngsters now start English in grade school. Older clerks who can't handle English quickly refer tourists to the younger clerks.

Norway makes many of its signs bilingual; invariably, the second language is English. The French still have ideas about their language being the world's universal tongue. They don't take the trouble to go bilingual to the extent found in some other European countries.

The British retain their matter-of-fact patience and aplomb, despite changing fortunes of empire and industry. They queue up today as they did in World War II, whether it be at a bus stop or information counter. Their patience index level is high.

Although there are some supermarkets, the individual store dealing in one or related categories of items still seems to be the rule in Europe.

Norwegians, who are outdoor-minded, close up shop about 2:30 every Saturday afternoon, and head for a weekend in the mountains. Every Norwegian seemingly has a summer home of some kind, at a higher elevation, regardless of whether his regular house is in a mountain setting.

The French, too, are great for a home in the country.

Sioux Falls Role

Sioux Falls' role in the jet age is something to think about. We're an hour from Chicago, 30 minutes from Minneapolis. From either city, you can be in London in about seven or eight hours. Or in Bergen or Paris in the same time from Chicago.

As air travel develops even greater volume in international routes, Sioux Falls will help many more passengers to a happy start and a pleasant homecoming in the jet age.

U.S.A. CONJURES THAT OLD FEELING

Argus Leader, July 22, 1971

This American never fails to appreciate getting back to home soil after a trip abroad.

I had that same old feeling about the United States upon returning last week from three and a half weeks in Europe.

The feeling began in Montreal, touch-down for a transatlantic crossing from Paris. Although Quebec Canadians are bilingual and the accent in Montreal's splendid new air terminal is French, the food and service were more American than European.

This American becomes frustrated at some of the interminable waits in placing a food order with a European waiter, be he Norwegian or French.

Serving food has its special niceties in Europe, including personal service and the waiter's pause for the diner's approval or disapproval of the food he is about to serve.

Trying to speed up most Norwegian or French waiters in dining room settings is a lesson in frustration. And the final wait for the check, with the seemingly interminable parleying at the maitre d's station, appears to be unnecessary to this Midwestern traveler.

I felt more comfortable in Norwegian and French restaurants that had adopted some of the basics of American service.

American gasoline companies operating in Europe have opened many dining rooms or cafeterias in connection with their gasoline business.

Service in these filling station restaurants in Norway, for instance, was quick and easy. Service in a cafe in the Lido Square on the Champs Elysees in Paris retained some of the French niceties, but with a difference. The waitresses—they were pretty—did their serving at almost a run. They provided excellent French food with some American speed.

Arrival back in North America—at Montreal—brought with it quick service in the airport terminal. The waitress recommended a veal dinner and served it promptly. It satisfied a traveler after a transatlantic crossing—and would have appealed to a South Dakotan on a hay crew, too.

Motels and $10,000 Mustangs

Oil companies which have expanded their filling station and restaurant operations have also put motels into European cities. Americans find them much easier to use than the old-style hotel.

The freeway system started in Germany with Adolf Hitler's autobahns. The United States picked it up in a big way with the Interstate System. The Europeans are marking their main routes with a Europe number and they are a boon to the auto traveler.

Around Oslo, Norway, for instance, there is a new and efficient ring of multi-lane highways. The Norwegians have been busy in recent years in widening and improving the main routes between cities. Their new roads are blacktopped, well done and cut a smaller swath through the green Norwegian countryside than the new primary roads do in South Dakota.

I noted a marked improvement in Norway's new roads during this visit, compared to what I saw during a trip to that country in 1961.

Norwegians pay more than twice as much for gasoline as we do in South Dakota—and the difference is tax. Their new automobiles also carry a sales tax of more than 100 percent.

A new Ford Mustang in Oslo, for instance, costs $10,000. The car salesman said that tax system is "killing" business. The auto and gas taxes go for road construction, but their severity acts as a brake on the purchase of new cars.

Popular smaller cars, such as the Volkswagen or the European products of American firms, cost about twice as much in Norway as they do in the United States.

Political scientists in South Dakota who debate the ethics of putting the sales tax on food would throw up their hands at the approximate 20 per cent sales tax paid on most food in Norway.

Despite discontent over high taxes, however, Norwegians are happy in their country's booming prosperity. Everyone is working. The continuing diversification of the country promises new prosperity. One of the most significant developments is the oil find in the North sea, off the Norwegian coast.

Little Things Welcome

Getting back home to the U.S.A. was an overnight stay in the Ramada Inn near Chicago's O'Hare International Airport.

Baggage handling, checking in and leaving a call with the operator, all seemed simpler than in Europe. There was no passport information to put on the hotel register. The staff moved at a quicker pace, from the telephone operator to the courtesy car driver. The language was no barrier—crisp, snappy, American.

Europe is nice to see. . .but the U.S.A. has its own little welcomes for the traveler home from some globetrotting.

FATHER, SON SEEK GERMAN FAMILY ROOTS

Argus Leader, July 2, 1986

Many Americans have stayed home from Europe this summer because of the threat of terrorism.

Charles Sorensen. **Tom Sorensen.**

But not Charles M. Sorensen of Sioux Falls and his son, Tom, of Flandreau.

They had no hesitation about flying in May to West Germany to retrace their 1984 trip and renew their quest of family roots.

Both were impressed by American Airlines' security precautions in checking passports and inspecting luggage for the overseas flight.

An 8 1/2-hour flight overnight by DC10 from Chicago to Frankfurt, West Germany, was uneventful. They rented an Opel, a General Motors car produced in West Germany, and took the Autobahn northward to Hamburg.

Americans who chafe at the U.S. 55-miles-an-hour speed limit should try Adolf Hitler's highway legacy. There's no speed limit for cars in the two left-hand lanes unless the roadway is marked. Trucks and cars with trailers are limited to 80 kilometers per hour (50 miles an hour) and restricted to the third and right-hand lane.

Tom said, "I stayed on the right side with all the trucks. They must have been going at least 100 miles an hour in the left-hand lane. You really drove hard. There was no time for sightseeing. I just followed the road. Dad navigated."

Traffic was heavy, like eight hours of driving Interstate 494 around the Twin Cities in Minnesota. Tom said his speed varied from 60 to 70 miles an hour. A driver must give cars approaching from the rear right of way when their operators blink their lights to pass.

What drivers miss with their eyes on the road ahead and the rear view mirror is rolling, forested land between Frankfurt and Hamburg. Northward from Hamburg the terrain is much like eastern South Dakota, except there are more trees.

The Sorensens stopped at an archive in Schleswig to see whether there was any information on Charles' mother, Frieda Grube, who emigrated from Germany to Chicago at age 19 in 1893. However, they found none.

They headed for Denmark, met some acquaintances from the 1984 trip and also made some new friends. Near Viborg (pronounced Veeborg), for which the South Dakota town is named,

Charles met for the first time two first cousins—Sigried, 88, and Soren, 94—whom he hadn't known about.

They revisited the village church at Orum, where Charles' father, Hans Frederick Sorensen, was baptized Jan. 1, 1873. He went to Chicago when he was 19, and to South Dakota with his wife in 1908. They farmed near Lily in Day County, where Charles was born. Charles said it was nice to see the farm where his father was born, his church (built in 1150) and the original baptismal record.

After a visit with another cousin of Charles' in northern Denmark, the Sorensens returned to West Germany and entered East Germany, which they had also toured in 1984.

They went behind the western wall near its northern end on the Baltic Sea. The wall's purpose is to keep East Germans inside the Soviet bloc country. The Sorensens said the East German boarder guards were courteous and efficient.

There wasn't as much traffic as in West Germany and Denmark, which looked prosperous. East Germany appeared dated—like the 1940s—and colors were more subdued. People were friendly. In two instances East Germans got in their car and led the Sorensens to their destination.

They toured the Lutheran Church (built in 1250) at Bruel where Charles' mother was baptized. There were no old records at the church, but the deacon told them that copies were in another East German town and the originals were in Ratzeburg, West Germany.

Charles said: "You always think that isn't true. They have services every Sunday in my mother's church. I feel for the people in East Germany....You don't know what a pleasure it is to talk to these people. They are so happy to meet you."

His wife, Delores, who made the trip in 1984 but not this year, recalled the joy of a wedding party in the hotel at Wismar where they stayed.

Tom said: "If I got anything out of the trip, people are the same all over. They just make different noises when they talk."

Stopping in Ratzeburg, father and son found original copies of the church records of Charles' mother. They recorded her birth date, the names of her parents and learned where their homes were. They also discovered that all these records are microfiched and available in genealogical records maintained by the Mormon Church in Salt Lake City.

Back home in Sioux Falls, the Sorensens look over pictures from this year's trip and think about another journey in pursuit of their roots. Tom, who is a pharmaceutical salesman, will probably check Mormon Church records first.

His father, a former Internal Revenue Service agent, retired eight years ago.

AMERICANS MEET THEIR ENGLISH COUSINS

Argus Leader, Oct. 3, 1987

Another plus of retirement, American style, is that you and your spouse have time to travel to faraway places.

Our September trip to England was an opportunity for Ada May to explore her roots and for me to visit again one of my favorite countries.

This flight to London had an interesting beginning. We are members of the Bidwell Family Association, a group of 400 families in the United States who trace their ancestry to Richard Bidwell and his son John, who landed near Boston in 1630 from the ship Mary and John. They emigrated from England, embarking from Plymouth. My wife is the Bidwell in our family.

The association meets yearly in the United States. Two years ago at the reunion in Rochester, N.Y., Robert and Maxine Bidwell of Arpin, Wis., posed a challenge: why not hold a reunion in England, and meet modern English cousins? Response was positive. The couple made a pathfinding flight to England a year ago.

As a result, on a bright September morning Ada May and I checked our bags at Joe Foss Field through to Heathrow Airport in London. That night we flew out of Chicago on a British Airways 747 and seven hours later landed at London.

It was a much quicker trip for us than it was for Richard and John Bidwell in 1630. They boarded their sailing ship March 20 and disembarked in New England on May 30. There were 120 passengers on the ship. There were approximately 380 aboard our flight.

Our journey triggered memories for me of two previous flights to England. One was another Chicago to London flight on a 747 in 1971. My mother and I were en route to Norway to explore her birthplace alongside the Randsfjord north of Oslo.

My first trip to London was in February 1944 as an Army lieutenant and passenger aboard military air transport planes. It was a circuitous journey of about 27 hours flying time in propeller-driven planes from New York via Newfoundland, the Azores, Casablanca and Prestwick, Scotland. Over England you could spot many military airfields.

There was scarcely a glimpse of the countryside as my wife and I flew into Heathrow on a cloudy morning with flight 296 under radar control. Industrial buildings on the west side of London suddenly appeared alongside the aircraft as we approached touchdown.

Two days later, after sightseeing in London, we were on our way by motorcoach to the plains of East Anglia northwest of London. At Thetford, the 1987 Bidwell pilgrims to England explored 18th and 19th century graveyards of two churches, seeking a connection between Bidwells buried in those cemeteries and Richard and John. They had lived in Devon (southwestern England) before they sailed for North America. However, the family was believed to have come originally from Thetford.

The link wasn't positively made, but rubbing flour on old gravestones to bring out 200-year-old names and dates may provide some clues when compared with genealogical charts.

In any event, there were many Bidwells in 18th and 19th century Thetford. Five Bidwells served as mayor between 1809 and 1930. There was a Bidwell brewery in Thetford in the last century. A sign advertised a contemporary Bidwell Construction Co.

Eighty U.S. Bidwells—parents, children, siblings and spouses—met about 60 British Bidwells in a two-day reunion at Newmarket. Many of the Brits joined the U.S. family association and organized a branch of it. A number of the British Bidwells plan to attend the association's 1988 reunion next July at Manhattan, Kan.

Like their distant American cousins, British Bidwells have done genealogical research in recent years. They were impressed by the work of Joan Bidwell, of Tama, Iowa, a vice president of the association. She and her husband, Virgil, spent 12 years compiling the "Bidwell Family History 1587-1982." The 1,094-page book traces 15 generations of direct descendants in the United States of Richard and John.

More about the tourist's impressions of Britain in the next column.

IOWA WOMAN INVESTIGATES HER FAMILY TREE, WRITES BOOK
Argus Leader, Sunday, July 21, 1991

Families interested in finding their roots should emulate Joan (pronounced JoAnn) Bidwell, Tama, Iowa, farm wife.

Joan Bidwell, addressing a family reunion.
—Anson Yeager photo

She became so interested in husband Virgil's British roots that she compiled a 1,100-page family history. It lists 15,000 American descendants of Richard and John Bidwell, father and son, who landed near Boston in 1630.

The book, *Bidwell Family History 1587-1982, Vol. I*, has 1,094 pages. It was published in 1983. Her printers were incredulous at her insistence on putting Volume I on the title. She told them Volume II would surely follow.

It had to wait, however. Bidwell received laments from her side of the family that it had been ignored in her pursuit of her husband's family tree. So she began researching the history of her mother's father's family. It chronicles ancestors and descendants of Ernest Uhrhammer, born in Germany, who migrated to the United States in 1904. The book spans 11 generations back to the 1600s. It will list several thousand descendants. Bidwell will give the book to the printers on Nov. 1. She will then resume work on Volume II of the Bidwell family.

Joan and Virgil Bidwell's search started more than 20 years ago with a telephone call to son Bob from another Bob Bidwell in Iowa whom they didn't know. She tracked him down through census and other records and found both families were related. Initially, they could not pinpoint Virgil's ancestors beyond his grandparents. They found the link to Richard and John Bidwell in an old family Bible on one of their trips.

Their quest has taken them to numerous courthouses, cemeteries and archives in 28 states. Old records in basements or attics often yielded clues. There were also many trips to the Mormon genealogical library in Salt Lake City and a check of Census archives in Kansas City.

Bidwell flew to Germany to pursue her roots. She took a taxi to a farm neighborhood north of Hamburg in Schleswig-Holstein where her grandfather had lived. She found his name in various records and a picture of the ship on which he crossed the Atlantic.

Contacts with other Bidwells, among them the late Dwight Bidwell of Nasvhille, Tenn., and the late Dale Bidwell (my wife's brother) of Arp, Tex., resulted in establishment of the Bidwell Family Association in the 1970s. The association started holding annual reunions, reviving a family practice that had been followed periodically between 1899 and 1940.

The association held its 19th meeting June 29-30 in Lynnwood, Wash., a suburb of Seattle. Reunions have become conventions, with a mix of fellowship, tourism and a continuing search for more family members. This year's reunion was attended by 209 from 21 states and provinces; 48 of them took an add-on cruise to Alaska. The association met in England in 1987 and will return there in 1993. Next year's reunion will be in Midland, Ont., Canada.

Bidwell at 57 still enjoys her pursuit of family ties which has turned into two labors of love. She is a vice president of the Bidwell Family Association. Virgil is the association's historian. She appears regularly on Bidwell reunion programs. She has an uncanny knack of referring questioners to the genealogical chart that shows their family line. Joan and Virgil know hundreds of Bidwell cousins throughout the United States and Canada.

She has organized flights from Iowa to Salt Lake City in recent years for genealogical enthusiasts to check their family records at the Mormon center. Her advice to individuals seeking their roots is to be persistent: there are records out there for everyone. "Sometimes it takes a lot of hunting," she said. "There is something somewhere. People haven't lived a life without leaving tracks. You need proof. It's in the record of births and other information.'

THE YEAGER FAMILY

Charles Franklin Yeager, father of Anson Yeager.

I was fortunate to know one of my grandparents: Anders Thingelstad (1852-1940), a carpenter and cabinet maker in Norway and a homesteader in western South Dakota. He and I once walked four miles together from near Cedar Canyon to Maurine, S.D. He made Christmas skis for me and my brother Iver in the early 1930s. On a trip to Norway in 1971, my mother and I visited her family's parish church, the Neskirke, near Roikenvik on the Randsfjord north of Oslo. My grandfather had helped with the reconstruction of the 18th century church when he was a young man.

My grandparents on both sides were not lucky in family circumstances. My grandmother Kjersti (Iverson) Thingelstad died in Colfax, N.D., in 1907, two years after leaving Norway. My grandfather and his brother-in-law, Thorwald Iverson, kept the young family of four children—two boys, Hans and Iver, and two girls, Elise and Mony—together. They moved to Sturgis and then homesteaded near Maurine.

Elijah Fisk Yeager (1844-1890), a Waxahachie, Tex., lawyer and owner and editor of the weekly Enterprise, and my grandmother Minnie (Rainey) Yeager both died within three years and two months of each other. Elijah died in May 1890, leaving his widow with six young children, two boys and four girls, Charles Franklin, Anson, Fannie Lu, Mary, Lilian Lee and Winnie Davis. My father, Charles Franklin, was 14 and the oldest child. Minnie became owner of the Enterprise and published the paper. My dad became manager. My grandmother died after a long illness in July 1893. My grandmother's brother, Judge Anson Rainey, became guardian and took care of the family. My dad and his brother Anson worked on the family newspaper for several years.

Later my father moved to Greeley, CO., where he was advertising manager of the newspaper and then to Colorado Springs where he was president and manager of the Telegraph from 1906-1910. He met my mother, Elise Marie Thingelstad, in Wyoming. I was born June 5, 1919, in Salt Lake City. My dad published the Goshen Hole News, a weekly at Yoder, Wyo., in 1922-23.

The family then moved to Denver where I attended the first five grades. My dad worked in advertising sales. In 1930 my mother moved their three sons (Anson, Iver and Robert Lee) to Maurine, S.D., and divorced Yeager. I completed grade school at Red Top two miles west of Maurine on the site where my mother and other children of homesteaders attended school. My mother married Nels Afdahl, a neighbor and native of Voss, Norway. They had three sons: Nels Richard, George and Larry.

My mother encouraged me to learn typing by lamplight in our ranch home. My father was killed in an auto accident in Texas in 1934. My mother encouraged me in my ambition to be a newspaperman like my dad. She helped me get a job as printer's devil at the Faith Independent.

39

Anson Yeager, 1 year old, in Denver.

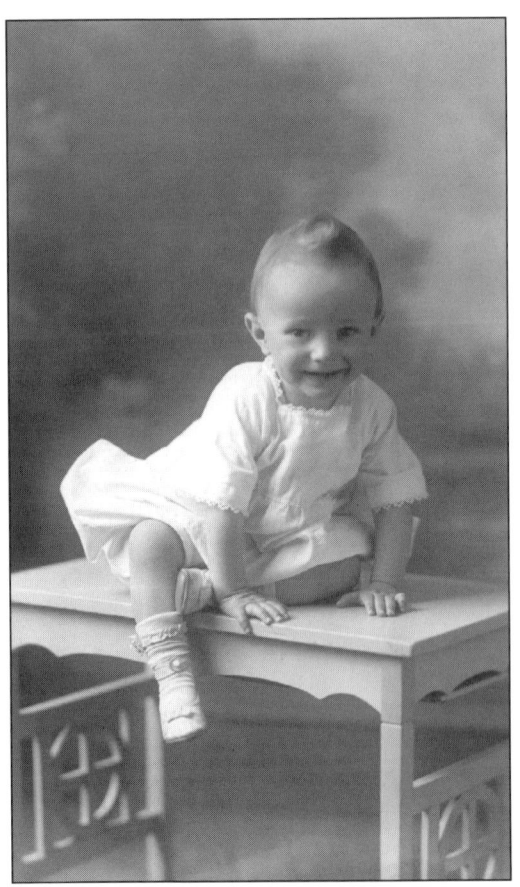

Anson, two years old, in western South Dakota.

THE YEAGER FAMILY

This was Thorwald Iverson's, a half mile north of Maurine in 1930. Iverson and his brother-in-law Anders Thingelstad built the sod house (left of white house) in 1910. The author lived in the white house from 1930-1934. Hay corral, barn, grainary and chicken house are at far left.

Anson Yeager, three years old, in Denver.

Frank and Elise Yeager, Denver 1926.

Anson Yeager, 5, and brother Iver, 2, in goat cart, in Denver.

C.F. Yeager's Ford Model T, Deadwood, S.D., about 1927.

Anson, 10, in Highlander Boys uniform, Denver.

THE YEAGER FAMILY

"The Boys," Anson's four youngest brothers at Nels Afdahl ranch, Maurine, S.D., in 1945. From left: Larry Afdahl, Robert Yeager, George and Richard Afdahl. —Elise Afdahl photo

Iver, left, and Anson Yeager on Afdahl ranch, at Maurine, S.D. Richard Afdahl is at lower right.

Anson Yeager, 1937 graduate, Faith, S.D., High School. —Black Hills Studios photo

2nd Lt. Anson Yeager, commissioned 1943.

Ensign Ada May Bidwell, commissioned 1943.
—Merin-Baliban photo

1st Lt. Anson and Lt. J.G. Ada May Yeager, married, September 10, 1944. —Chase-Statler photo

Anson and Ada May Yeager, married 50 years, 1994.

Left: Lt. Col. Anson Yeager, Battalion commander (1961-1964) 3rd Battalion, 147th Artillery Group, S.D. Army National Guard. Right: Private Anson Yeager, Camp Shelby, Mississippi, summer 1942.

A Black Hills family tour followed Anson and Ada May's return from Alaska in 1952.
From left: Nels, Elise and Larry Afdahl, Ada May Yeager and Karen. —Anson Yeager photo

Lilacs were in full bloom at home of Nels and Elise Afdahl in early 1960s.
From left: Elise, Nels, Ada May Yeager and her mother, Lydia Bidwell of Colman. —Anson Yeager photo

THE YEAGER FAMILY

Five sons honor their mother, Elise Afdahl, at the celebration in Faith, S.D. of her 80th birthday. From left: Iver Yeager, Larry Afdahl, Anson Yeager, Richard and George Afdahl.

Captain Anson Yeager, Headquarters Battery commander, 147th Field Artillery Battalion, called to active duty, 1950-1952.

Robert Lee Yeager.

The manager, Ival Wilson, taught me the linotype. I then worked for the Faith Gazette for two years. Later, operating a linotype helped me attend S.D. State College.

My first German ancestor in America was Nicholas Yager. He and his wife Anna Marie Sieber, son Adam and daughter Mary disembarked in Virginia in 1717 after leaving their home in Wickersbach, Germany. They were Alsatian Germans. Their descendants moved west in Virginia and beyond. Elijah was born in 1844 in Johnson City, TN. Minnie Rainey was born in Eldorado, Ark., March 21, 1852. Her family moved to Alabama and then to Texas in 1874. Elijah enlisted in the Confederate Army of Tennessee in 1861 and served until the Civil War ended in 1865. He was pardoned by the United States.

He graduated from Tusculum College in 1869. He and most of his family moved to Texas after the Civil War. Elijah's older brother Abraham, also a Confederate veteran and a lawyer, was a newspaper publisher at Cleburne, Tex. He died at the age of 98 on Nov. 3, 1940, the last surviving Confederate veteran in Johnson County, Texas.

THE ENDING OF A SUCCESSFUL LIFE

Argus Leader, Jan. 20, 1980

There's a memory tape recorder in each one of us which has some vivid flashbacks to yesteryear.

There is also a circle in which individuals and families find themselves returning to a place or locale that was a part of them long ago.

The death of my uncle, Iver Thingelstad, at Sturgis last Tuesday started me thinking about memory tapes and the circle.

He was the last of my Norwegian uncles and that is something you have to expect when someone reaches 84, which he did last June.

Uncle Iver came to this country in 1905 with his parents, brother and sisters and his uncle, Thorvald Iverson. They left a beautiful area on the Randsfjord north of Oslo out of economic necessity. My Great Uncle Thorvald, who had emigrated earlier to North Dakota, had gone back to Norway to bring his sister and family to a new land.

Iver, his brother Hans and my mother found themselves going to school in Colfax, N.D., where English was in and Norwegian was forbidden. They learned fast. The youngest daughter—my Aunt Mony—wasn't old enough to start school there.

My grandmother died in North Dakota about two years after leaving Norway. In 1908 the family moved to Sturgis, S.D. That was only a brief stopping point until my Grandpa and his brother-in-law could file on homesteads between what would become Faith and Newell.

Sturgis was part of the circle for my Uncle Iver. On a recent visit with him during the last year or so, he told about living in an apartment on the west side of Sturgis while waiting for spring and the trip to the claim.

He and some other boys played at Fort Meade, then a cavalry post, on the eastern side of Sturgis.

A big event for the stay in Sturgis was the time Uncle Thorvald took Hans and Iver on a day-long expedition to climb Bear Butte.

From the top of Bear Butte they could look northeast and see the ridge of hills 50 miles away, beyond which would be their new home.

By coincidence there is a prominent landmark in their neighborhood in Norway: the Brandbu Kampen (mountain). There's a beautiful view from its nearly 1,700-foot summit. Like Bear Butte, it had to be climbed.

Bear Butte is a bigger, steeper challenge: its elevation is 4,422 feet above sea level and it rises 1,400 feet above the plains.

The recounting of the Bear Butte climb made an indelible impression on me. But frankly, I couldn't or didn't do anything about it until one cloudy and fairly cool day in the summer of 1978. My wife Asie and I climbed Bear Butte and enjoyed the view.

Home for the new homesteaders was near Cedar Canyon, once a post office on Highway 212, which took its name from canyon breaks dotted with cedar. Both Hans and Iver proved up on land near their dad's and started farming and ranching after World War I service. Great Uncle's homestead was near what would become Maurine, about two miles away.

Iver and his wife, Helen, were on their ranch 40 years. There were many happy visits at their home. This was an opportunity for me as a young boy to wear his chaps, see his saddle horse and help Aunt Helen get the cows.

Some visits turned into exploring trips—walking the length of the canyons surrounding their place. When it rained, diversion turned to rummy. There were some whist games, too, in wintertime.

Some trips to Iver's and Helen's place were to cut a Christmas tree. Uncle Iver often helped me or my brothers select a nice young cedar from a stand alongside the canyon.

In later years some of my youngsters were fascinated by the traveling Mexican crew which was at his place to shear sheep during one of our visits.

Iver and Helen retired to Spearfish almost 20 years ago. They had a nice home facing one side of the Black Hills State campus. Retirement was enjoyable for both of them. And part of Uncle Iver's routine was going downtown for a friendly card game.

Many times on quick trips through Spearfish we'd stop at the house first—and then go downtown to pick up Iver at his "office." That was the cardroom in the backroom of a barber shop or in an otherwise unused room in a garage building.

Iver didn't do any driving in later years, because of a vision problem. But that didn't bother his card game.

On a trip to the Black Hills last March, we visited Iver in his hospital room at Fort Meade, a Veterans Administration Hospital since World War II. He entered the hospital for diagnosis, which turned out to be cancer.

When Iver lived in Sturgis as a boy, the fort was only 30 years old. Fort Meade was started about two years after General George Armstrong Custer and his troopers died at the Battle of the Little Big Horn in 1876.

It would be another 30 years after Iver first saw troopers rein their mounts over hill and valley at Fort Meade before the U.S. Army decided it didn't need horses for World War II. Fort Meade was one of the last cavalry posts. Its cavalry was mechanized.

Uncle Iver's last year wasn't that bad. He and Aunt Helen moved to an apartment. He didn't have to stay in the hospital until near the end. He enjoyed seeing visitors. He died the day after their 59th wedding anniversary.

Seeing Aunt Helen and other family members at the service Friday seemed like stopping at a familiar spot on the circle.

Uncle Iver was back in Sturgis where he had lived long ago. His service was at a Sturgis church where other family funerals have been held. Uncle Iver's nephews were pallbearers.

Burial was at Black Hills National Cemetery, south of Sturgis, where my younger brother, Robert, and Uncle Hans are buried.

When all's said and done, who can argue with 84 good and successful years? Most of them were happy years, lived outdoors. Helen was his constant helper.

His was one of the world's most independent occupations: ranching in the American West. Naturally, he kept wearing cowboy boots and a Stetson hat in retirement.

Uncle Iver saw the auto, aviation and nuclear ages unfold in turn before the present electronic and computer era. He liked baseball, especially the New York Yankees. When Maurine's baseball team played the Sunday circuit in the early 1930s, he cheered them, too.

You can't argue with such a lucky life. But Aunt Helen, his sisters and the rest of us are going to miss him.

RIDE IN 18-WHEELER OFFERS A DIFFERENT PERSPECTIVE
Argus Leader, Dec. 13, 1981

The quarters and dimes tinkled into the pay phone at Murdo before my brother Richard Afdahl of Faith, S.D., came on the line a week ago yesterday morning.

Would I like to ride with him to Holstein, Iowa, to deliver some feeder calves?

I would—for a couple reasons. I had never ridden in an 18-wheeler. And I wanted to see the Iowa feedlot destination of a load of South Dakota cattle.

Richard, who drives a truck when he isn't ranching, had known for a long time that I wanted to hitch a ride and see his world from the cab of a big truck.

He had been through Sioux Falls many times when his schedule and mine didn't coincide.

He thought the Saturday trip would be ideal. It was. He pulled into the Mobil station's lot on North Cliff Avenue at Interstate 90 about noon.

I clambered up the ladder into the cab and we were off for Holstein, with 88 steers from this year's calf crop in the trailer behind the tractor.

The day before, a buyer at Philip's Livestock Auction thought the steers met the requirements of a feeder at Holstein.

A neophyte on a stock truck reflects a bit on the ultimate destination of range stock. The steers averaged 560 pounds a head. The feeding process will nearly double their weight.

Sometime next year Iowa corn will have done its job—and the steers will become nice steaks and roasts for consumers somewhere in the United States.

✦ ✦ ✦

The view of the road from the cab was appealing. My perch was higher in the Kenworth than in my Itasca mini motorhome.

It was a much better look than you get from the front seat of an automobile.

We headed south on Interstate 29. I quizzed Richard on the 1977 rig's over-the-highway mileage: it was 471,000 plus—and the number of forward gears: 13.

The load was about 49,000 pounds—and the steers represented a value of $30,000 or more tracking us behind the cab.

We stopped at the North Sioux City truck stop for coffee. A short time later, we were driving through Sioux City on the Interstate and heading east on Highway 20.

Iowa's countryside, like South Dakota's, wears a somber, grey look on a December day.

A passenger can scan the horizon from the right hand seat in a cab, sizing up neat Iowa farm houses, red barns and feed lots—most of them filled with cattle.

Snow on terraced fields and hills and dark-limbed trees stripped of leaves were reminders of Christmas card etchings.

In late summer similar Iowa countryside scenes were a brilliant green with lush corn crops reaching skyward.

About three hours or so after leaving Sioux Falls, we were in Holstein where Richard got directions to the feeder's farm. It was about 4 miles away.

The farmer was ready for the load—and apologized because some gravel hadn't been spread all around the yard.

It didn't matter but I was glad I had brought along overshoes. The area near the feedlot was muddy.

Richard backed the trailer toward the gate to the feedlot. The farmer and his hired man hooked up a loading ramp.

Soon the first steers were starting down the chute, a step at a time. The steers looked us over—the farmer was counting—and decided to continue their way toward the feed lot.

Richard Afdahl.

Once on the ground, they speeded up and broke into a run. Soon all the steers were off the truck.

Safe on solid ground, the steers looked across a fence at some other cattle already on feed—and started bawling for feed of their own.

The farmer didn't say that he was pleased with the new feeders—but he looked like he was. As Richard told him before we left, "I hope you make a mint on these."

That depends, of course, on beef prices at the grocery counter next year.

✦ ✦ ✦

We drove back toward Sioux City in the dusk, stopped at a truck stop for supper and then continued north on Interstate 29.

Richard dropped me off at the Mobil truck stop in Sioux Falls about 8 p.m.—and headed for Faith. He reached home the next day after a snooze or two at a rest stop along the way.

It was a nice day for both of us—a chance to catch up on visiting. For me it was an opportunity to do something different.

Eighteen-wheelers had always held a fascination for me. Now I knew what it was like to be in a cab watching car traffic go by.

I had a new appreciation for truckers.

They're on the American road day and night, delivering raw products to factories or feedlots and finished products to department stores or grocery counters.

In about eight hours on a Saturday I had a fascinating look at another part of the cycle that is repeated many times for South Dakota livestock.

Someday, if South Dakotans' plans and hopes for water development reach fruition, this state will feed more of the livestock it grows on western rangeland. That would be a plus.

There would also be a large enough market for finished beef, I believe, to keep both Iowa feeders and new ones in South Dakota busy doing something at which they excel.

A LETTER TO A DAUGHTER FROM A PROUD DAD
Happiness for parents is seeing the future in the faces of graduating offspring

Argus Leader, Sunday, May 29, 1983

Dear Ellen:

Having missed Washington High School graduations for a number of years, I saw some changes at the Sioux Falls Arena last Wednesday night that I liked very much.

There was that sea of orange caps and gowns: a blaze of color that fit a beautiful spring night in Sioux Falls. The effect was much more exciting that the prosaic grey, silver and black of yesteryear. Can this be Sioux Falls? I asked myself that when you and your classmates started tossing your caps into the air, with all the abandon of cadets at graduation ceremonies at West Point or Annapolis.

Yes, it was Sioux Falls. Spinning those caps toward the ceiling, Robert Caselli, Washington High's principal, told me, is a tradition that began with the class of 1975. It shows spirit—a willingness to meet tomorrow.

Never mind the caps. Unlike those of the past, these are made of paper and intended to be expendable.

Another change that appealed to me were the speeches by two students: Heidi Batz and Todd Warren. They were sharp, to the point—summations of what most of you in the graduating class must have been thinking about in leaving Washington High.

In a few minutes each speaker said something vital, nostalgic and pertinent about the spirit of your class and your school and what it means to graduate.

That is much better than having graduates and the audience endure a well-meaning politician's delivery of a speech that might run an hour or longer. That has happened in the past.

I suspect that the Board of Education and school administrators some years ago decided enough was enough—and opted for short speeches and sticking to a time schedule.

The double lines by which your graduating class received diplomas have been a fixture of Washington High commencements for many years. The lines seemed faster, however.

It takes careful planning and execution to graduate a class of 517—with appropriate music and other ceremonial details—and have the audience outside in the parking lot within an hour and 20 minutes from the time the program began.

✦ ✦ ✦

A graduation program is like spring. It's renewal. There is boundless energy, hope and enthusiasm exhibited by graduates about their transition from high school and life at home to what is in prospect now.

This parent has the feeling that each young person in that graduating class holds the big, wide world in his or her hands—and that the road ahead is practically interminable. And it is. The realization that the years go faster as you grow older comes sometime after middle age. That, fortunately, is a long time for someone who is 18.

Back to graduation night.

Your mother and dad spotted you in your seat at the end of one aisle, and glanced at you more times than you'll ever know during the program. I'm sure that other parents in the audience played the same game, alternating their attention from their graduate to the stage, band, chorus, etc.

THE YEAGER FAMILY

Ellen Elise Yeager.

The pleasant glow felt by parents and relatives at the Arena continued at receptions held at many graduates' homes that evening. In some families, the receptions had been held last Sunday afternoon.

The receptions were a reflection of a cross section of an important part of life in Sioux Falls. Parents, grandparents, aunts, uncles, nephews, nieces and friends offered congratulations to the graduates in the friendly spirit so typical of South Dakota and this part of the nation. Cards and gifts were happily offered and displayed.

Your mother and I enjoyed meeting parents of your classmates we had not known before, and seeing others with whom we had been acquainted. There were friendly greetings at each door, earnest questions about what each graduate would do now and a buoyant, happy attitude about tomorrow.

There are many happy moments in a lifetime—and none equals the thrill of graduation from high school.

❖ ❖ ❖

And what about tomorrow?

The future should always be approached with optimism and the kind of high spirits and confidence that your mother and I saw in the faces of Washington High School's class of 1983.

This was the 101st class graduated by Washington High School—which says a couple of things to me. The school, with its fine traditions, has been an operating entity for more than a century. The school and the city are older than the state—which won't observe its centennial until 1989.

Your class benefited from Washington High's heritage.

Nationally, you and your classmates of 1983 have benefited from living in the United States. No other country enjoys the measure of freedom, wellbeing and opportunity that are part of life in America.

I feel confident that will continue to be America's outlook and future.

The years ahead belong to you and your classmates throughout the nation. Your parents and those of your friends all want your generation to have the best life yet in the USA.

Generally, your generation is better fed, better clothed and better informed than any of your predecessors. There are some anxieties, to be sure, about how well today's high school graduates will be able to compete with Japanese and Western European counterparts in the high technology future that is already here.

Those problems, I'm sure, will be met. I'm also confident that the larger challenge of finding a way for superpowers and their allies to live in peace for the foreseeable future will be solved.

I hope that you and your classmates will always keep your keen regard for each other, your confidence in yourselves and your typically American attitude summed up so well by your quip, "I can handle it, Dad."

♦ ♦ ♦

Your mother and I have some special feelings about you—because you're the fifth and last Yeager youngster to graduate from Washington High.

I'm going to include a note in this letter for Caselli and all your teachers and other instructors we've known through the years.

Thanks, Washington High, for the pleasant memories involved in these parents seeing two daughters and three sons graduate from your halls—and for giving them such a good start.

It makes us both feel a little bit older. And we are.

That's happiness. And so is seeing the future in the faces of you and your friends.

—Your Dad

COMING TO THE END OF LIFE'S ROAD

Argus Leader, July 4, 1987

This is a chronicle of four weeks in June for a South Dakota family which buried a brother and uncle at Colman last Monday.

He was Dale L. Bidwell, 75, a retired U.S. Soil Conservation Service engineer and my brother-in-law. He had lived in Texas since 1933, except for three years of U.S. Navy service in World War II.

Someone once said it's better to check out while you still have some things to do. It beats months or years of immobility in a nursing home.

Dale still had some things to do. One was looking out for 11 head of cattle and calves he had just purchased to feed on the lush grass on his 29 acre farm southeast of Tyler. Another was a summer of playing golf. In September, there would be a program to dedicate a plaque to a deceased colleague who had played a key conservation role. Dale was an initiator of the recognition and was helping with arrangements.

Ila Mae, his wife of 49 years and ill with cancer in a nursing home where she had been a patient for three years, would be expecting his biweekly visits.

♦ ♦ ♦

June 2. Dale woke up in a sweat. He couldn't get his breath. He was choking on fluid in his lungs. He telephoned his neighbor, Tommy Harris, who saved his life by getting him to the emergency room of the hospital 12 miles away in fewer minutes than that.

A hospital representative phoned his sister, Mrs. William Richter, in Colman. Hospital personnel worked on Dale several hours before his condition stabilized. The diagnosis: a massive heart attack. There was some improvement the next few days.

June 5. My wife and I flew to Tyler; she and her sister were prepared to split their stays to help their brother when he came home from the hospital. Harris and his wife met us at the airport.

Dale was in intermediate care when my wife and I walked into his room. We had the first of several good visits. I returned to Sioux Falls after the weekend.

My wife was encouraged that there had been no subsequent heart attack. The doctor was cautious in his outlook, but said Dale probably could be released about two weeks after his entry. My wife flew home June 10. The Richters made arrangements to leave Sunday.

June 14. Sunday. Dale had a cardiac arrest early that morning. Hospital personnel were at his bedside at the first alarm on his heart monitor. A doctor got his heart started again.

Dale Bidwell, ca. 1950.   Dale Bidwell, Anson's brother-in-law.

Someone called the Richter farm home in South Dakota, but there was no answer. They either didn't hear the phone or were already on their way to Tyler.

June 15. Monday afternoon. The Richters arrived to learn about Dale's latest heart attack. There would be a week of short visits to his bedside in intensive care, and near week's end, to an intermediate care room. Dale's chest pain was eased by morphine.

June 21. Sunday Morning. The second cardiac arrest was fatal. Mrs. Richter called her sister. The funeral would be in Overton Tuesday.

June 22. My wife and I flew again to Tyler. The Richters met us at the airport. There would be lots to do. Dale's wife, unable to leave the nursing home, had been told about his death.

June 23. Tuesday. The Rev. Jack Strickland, former pastor, and the Rev. Ray Eastridge, pastor, were comforting in their conduct of Dale's service.

June 24. Wednesday. The lawyer told the sisters to sell the cattle; this was done the next day. Dale's body was shipped by air to Joe Foss Field. Elapsed time from Dallas. about six hours.

June 26. Friday. The Richters and Yeagers started for South Dakota via the interstate, arriving home late Saturday.

June 28. Sunday. Relatives and friends visited at Skroch Funeral Chapel in Colman and viewed Dale's body.

June 29. Monday. Dale was buried in the Colman Cemetery, about two miles from where he was born. Charles Richter, a nephew, recalled impressions of his uncle: how he started playing golf on a homemade course on his parents' farm, how he encouraged the nephew's children to achieve in school, how he always checked the crops on his quarter section when he visited South Dakota.

This writer said the dams Dale and his colleagues built changed the face of Texas for the better—and that no farmer would object to being buried in the rain. It didn't rain on the committal service, but the prospect for showers was good. Dale would have liked that.

A SON'S MORTALITY COMES INTO FOCUS FOLLOWING THE DEATH OF HIS MOTHER

Argus Leader, Oct. 17, 1987

When a person is young—from small child to 50—he or she believes that life will go on forever.

There is so much future ahead that you give little thought to the mortality of man, especially yourself. Time seems to stand still.

Sometime after a person reaches 50 time speeds up. Every year seems to go faster. As life goes on, a person loses close relatives. My brothers and I cherished the 1970s and 1980s because we still had our mother, Elise Marie Afdahl. She died at age 88 Sept. 26 in Rapid City. Her services and burial were Sept. 30 in Sturgis.

She was tiny: 5 foot 2 and only once or twice weighed more than 100 pounds. She was also strong—a real tough lady, as one of my half brothers described her.

It was a toughness of spirit and endurance that enabled her and other western South Dakota ranch women to help their husbands cope with drought, low livestock prices and the Depression in the 1930s, and wartime shortages in the 1940s.

She raised bum lambs, which grew into a small herd, and turkeys, which she and my stepdad, Nels Afdahl, shipped dressed to Chicago. Her garden supplied vegetables, strawberries and potatoes. She made her own butter and sometimes shipped cream.

Her goals in life were to help her second husband and look after her six sons, three of them from her first marriage to my father, Charles F. Yeager. She had helped him publish a small weekly newspaper in Wyoming in the early 1920s. She moved back home to South Dakota from Denver in 1930 and married Nels in 1933.

There was very little money, but a lot of inspiration for her boys to obtain an education. This was not the easiest thing to do when you live 30 miles from town and boarding during high school poses an economic problem. She had worked her own way through high school at Deadwood.

One son had to forgo a high school education to stay on the ranch and help his dad (my stepfather), who had incurred arthritis. Five sons completed high school and four were graduated from college. Five sons survived her.

Our mother found time to be a school board officer and served as clerk of the Fox Ridge School District for 25 years.

The 1950s and 1960s were easier. REA brought electricity to the ranch in 1951. For 14 years our mother enjoyed being postmistress of the Maurine Rural Station, housed in a trailer in the yard. She and Nels became eligible for Social Security. He sold the cattle and retired on the ranch. Nels died in 1970.

Elise Afdahl, Anson Yeager's mother.

Our mother was proud of her Norwegian heritage. She especially enjoyed a trip to Norway in 1971, where she visited her birthplace at Brandbu and met several first cousins and other relatives. At Voss she met Nels' sisters and brothers and many of their children.

I was astounded when she easily understood Norwegian conversation, although speaking in her native tongue was too much of a challenge. She had left Norway in 1905 at age 6. She started school and a new language in North Dakota. The family homesteaded near Maurine in 1908.

She celebrated her 80th birthday at an open house in Faith in March 1979. In November 1980 she moved from her ranch home at Maurine where she had lived more than 46 years to a new mobile home in Faith. In late 1984, a tired, weakened heart and a blood clot led to several weeks in a hospital and a pacemaker. She entered a Rapid City retirement center in the summer of 1985.

Her life and a part of mine swept in review the first week of October. My wife and I helped sort a lifetime of her treasures: photo albums, grandma 'brag' books picturing her 19 grandchildren and seven great-grandchildren, souvenirs, letters, greeting cards and household possessions.

The realization hit me that now I was the older generation. Only our mother's sister, Mony Lehman of Sturgis, nearly 84 and also born in Norway, remains from the generation older than mine.

Our mother was proud to be a naturalized American and considered the USA the land of opportunity. But to me, she'll always be my Norwegian mother.

PRECAUTIONS, NICE PEOPLE HELP IN ON-THE-ROAD EMERGENCIES

Argus Leader, May 30, 1993

What do you do when you encounter an emergency health or medical problem on an extended trip?

Try local sources first.

This writer will always have kind thoughts about the friendly people who live in Raton, N.M., a stop on the Old Santa Fe Trail where townspeople still look after travelers like their predecessors did in frontier days.

Nearly 28 years ago when this writer was younger and so was our family, we were enroute to Philmont, N.M. One of our boys needed medical attention for a rash. We stopped at Raton and consulted Dr. John J. Smoker at the medical clinic. The diagnosis was quick: impetigo. Treatment and medicine quickly solved our nine-year-old boy's problem.

The doctor also prescribed something else: be sure this boy gets plenty of malted milks with his hamburgers. We promised he would.

Returning home from Texas and New Mexico this spring, we stopped overnight in Raton. When my wife awoke, she couldn't see our of her right eye. What had been tiny, irritating pinpoints for several days had become clots of black. After finishing breakfast in our motorhome, we decided to see an optometrist.

We walked into Dr. E.K. Ragsdale's office shortly after he opened at 9 a.m. He looked at my wife's right eye and told us that she had "floaters" (specks or "bugs") and he couldn't see the back of her retina. He advised us to stop in Pueblo, 110 miles away, and see an ophthalmologist. He said emergency treatment was necessary. He gave us detailed directions off Interstate 25 to an eye clinic in Pueblo. He wouldn't accept any money for his help.

As it happened, the eye doctor was not in his clinic that day. A nurse referred us to another doctor at a different location in Pueblo and phoned that we were on our way. Dr. Benton Murphy, a young ophthalmologist, determined there had been a slight tear in the retina of my wife's right eye. There was some hemorrhaging. He called in a colleague for a second opinion. Treatment involved freezing the retina near the tear.

We stayed overnight at Pueblo so the doctor could look at the eye the next morning, which was a Friday. There was some improvement. We arranged to return to Pueblo from Denver on Tuesday for a second look. That was also favorable. The doctor's assistant gave my wife her paperwork and arranged an appointment with Dr. Charles W. Mohler, a retinal specialist with Ophthalmology, Ltd., in Sioux Falls.

My wife saw Dr. Mohler in Sioux Falls a week later. Treatment in Pueblo had solved the problem.

The concerned assistance of Dr. Ragsdale steered us to the right solution. Dr. Murphy and his staff members at Rocky Mountain Eye Center in Pueblo knew what they were doing. Confirmation at home was reassuring. It's great to have friendly help every step of the way.

We think our experience makes a strong statement about the excellent medical care that's available in the United States. We hope that First Lady Hillary Rodham Clinton and her husband, President Bill Clinton, will succeed in their efforts to make excellent care available to all Americans.

My wife and I travel a lot. Perhaps the following tips will be helpful.

Ask your doctor to give you basic prescriptions for diarrhea and stomach upsets or other conditions that require an antibiotic before an invasive procedure; take a dose along with a note from your doctor.

Carry enough of your regular medicine to last the trip. Pack an extra pair of prescription glasses.

LESSONS ON HEARTS, HOUSEKEEPING

Argus Leader, Sunday, Jan. 22, 1995

Hi! It's nice to be back in the Argus Leader after a hiatus of nearly three months spent looking after my wife of more than 50 years.

Ada May received a pig's valve at North Central Heart Institute at Sioux Valley Hospital on Nov. 2. Two weeks later she was fitted with a pacemaker. She is making an excellent recovery.

Her experience and what I learned about hearts, housekeeping and other things changed our lives.

Her health problem started with a slight heart murmur in 1991. Her doctors watched it closely while she continued her favorite pastime of lap swimming at the YW. Her swimming would result in a great bonus: she didn't require any bypasses.

When Ada May started tiring last summer, doctors indicated that surgery in November would be timely. She didn't want anything to interfere with our 50th wedding anniversary which we celebrated Sept. 10.

Preparations for her hospital stay included prepping me on cooking, laundry and other household chores. It's strange what a husband doesn't know about the house he's lived in for more than 42 years.

THE YEAGER FAMILY

Our son, Anson Jr., a doctor, and our youngest daughter, Ellen, a physician's assistant, arrived to be with their mother during the operation—and with me. They also consulted by phone with our other three children.

Waiting rooms at the Heart Institute reflected many of life's dramas: kin and friends sweating out procedures on their loved ones.

A nurse telephoned us about the progress of Ada May's operation: the opening of the chest cavity, when the surgeon began sewing the new valve to her aorta and when he began closing the chest. Later, he told us the operation had gone well.

Tomorrow's technology was dramatically evident in the recovery room: digital readouts provide all pertinent data on heartbeat rate, blood pressure and other vital figures. We had witnessed a modern medical miracle, commonplace in Sioux Falls' burgeoning health industry.

It helped this husband greatly when daughter Ellen returned from Denver to help her mother at home for two weeks. But soon, I found myself looking after Ada May alone.

Anson and Ada May in their home.
—Greg Latza / Argus Leader photo

Driving is forbidden for at least six weeks. Lifting more than 10 pounds is a no-no. Cardiac rehabilitation three times a week at the hospital helps strengthen the patient. Walking in the home is essential; so are daytime naps.

Breakfasts and lunches were no problem for this housekeeper. Evening meals were a challenge. Freezer hot dishes from friends and the children helped.

Shopping for groceries was no longer as simple as pushing a cart for my wife. Selecting meat, finding spices and getting the right cheese took some doing.

Sorting laundry, spraying shirt collars and selecting the right temperature soon became second nature. One hint Ada May passed on was using hair spray on ink spots on my shirt pockets.

My wife ran the household for years. I couldn't remember the last time I balanced the family checkbook. Resuming that chore was a pain. Writing checks was laborious. The day she reclaimed the checkbook was a welcome sign. Another tipoff was the morning she made up her bed. She has started cooking again.

Ada May's talks with her cardiologist and surgeon at six weeks were encouraging. I watched her heart beating and her new valve functioning perfectly on ultrasound.

We're now discussing plans for traveling to the Sunbelt in mid-February. I have resumed writing my column.

This husband is thankful for the dishwasher, washer and dryer in the laundry and microwave oven.

But I'm still learning how many things my wife did before her surgery. Now, I truly believe a housewife's work is never done.

TRAVELING PROGRESSION LANDS IN TEXAS
Argus Leader, Sunday, March 22, 1998

ALAMO, Texas—Nope. The small city of Alamo has nothing to do with Texas' historic Alamo at San Antonio some 215 miles north of the Rio Grande Valley.

Alamo is our new winter home—a natural change in the lives of a couple of senior citizens. Ada May and I are in a two-bedroom mobile home in a recreational vehicle park in Alamo. We wound up winter's travels a year ago with a mild case of claustrophobia while living in our motor home.

Alamo is a city of approximately 12,000 located six miles east of McAllen, population 100,000. Texas cities embrace surrounding rural areas, so Alamo's boundaries include citrus groves and numerous strip malls along U.S. Highway 83 and the freeway which runs east and west in the Rio Grande Valley. The Rio Grande and Mexico are approximately 4 miles south of our new home

There have been many pleasant delights and old experiences revisited in moving into a different home. This move was easy. The mobile home was completely furnished. A previous owner had installed all kinds of convenient kitchen and other aids. Also, the lady had a green thumb.

The last thing Ada May and I did in the valley in April 1997 was buy a winter home. Since arriving in January both of us have enjoyed doing some of the little things we used to do around our home in Sioux Falls.

For example, Ada May supplemented silverware and gadgets in the kitchen with some new utensils and china. I put in a couple of rose bushes and spent a lot more time raking up leaves from an oak tree that is green the year around.

One thing I found appealing is the saguaro cactus on the sunny side of the home. There are flower buds on several of its spines this month. I like the small concrete burro with a kindling harness on its back. It's a suitable guard for a circle of flowers. A dwarf palm in front and a tall palm at the back add to the semi-tropical flavor. And a neighbor said to help ourselves to his grapefruit tree in a backyard that faces ours.

One of last year's problems in close quarters was that when I used my computer on the kitchen table, there was no room left in the motor home for Ada May. That's solved with my office set up in the second bedroom.

We also find it easier to stay in one place, instead of driving day after day.

Looking back, the experiences of this happy camping couple followed a progression. First, there was the tent and station wagon with three boys using their Scouting lore to set up camp and take it down on a trip to California. Next were tent campers which we rented for trips to California, Florida and New England.

There was our first motorhome, a Class C with a bunk over the cab. It was only 21 feet long and we could park it nearly anyplace a station wagon would fit. We drove the motorhome 11 years and more than 125,000 miles, including trips to Key West, Fla., and Alaska and the Yukon. Its engine and coach never failed us.

Our second motorhome is a 31-foot Class A. We like the big, buslike windshield. We've enjoyed it on trips to Mexico, Canada and most of the West. We finally got a tow bar to pull a

Anson and Ada May live in this mobile home in Alamo, Texas, during fall and winter. —Anson Yeager photo

car. I got tired of driving the rig in heavy traffic in the Sunbelt and left it home this year. We plan to use it on summer trips in the West.

But back to Alamo. When a couple of senior citizens decide to stay in one place, it's easy to find something you like. Couples or singles like to sell their mobile park homes at the end of a season.

Many buyers who've stayed in a campground with a motorhome or fifth wheeler often spot a mobile home they like. Used homes, completely furnished, may sell from $20,000 to $30,000. Brand new mobile homes cost more. Renting your lot may cost $2,000 a year. Some refugees from northern winters opt to live here year round.

When one of the partners dies, the survivor often sticks around. Some partners find new companions for whom they really care a great deal and with whom they may live together without remarrying. If they did, the woman partner would lose Social Security and other benefits derived from her late husband.

Campground residents often discuss the problem and solutions that some friends may choose.

Something seems unfair about our tax and pension customs in which females are denied vesting and lose their Social Security and company pension from their husband if they remarry.

Most Winter Texans think there probably won't be any change in this policy.

Residents of a mobile home and RV park really care about each other. They try to help older friends cope with physical and other problems. There are many good turns from helping somebody catch a plane to keeping a doctor's appointment or shopping for groceries. A wheelchair-bound resident gets extra helping hands from spouse and friends.

There's a good feeling about being a Winter Texan and enjoying a new community.

Many women volunteer to help local grade school students—90 percent are Hispanic—with English and other courses. Many RV parks have their own church services. Memorial services are often conducted for camp residents at their park. One pianist said she had played for five memorial services this year.

There are many nice things for senior citizens to enjoy in a mobile home park. Flowers, a fine winter climate, jam sessions, dancing, swimming, shuffleboard, cards and other diversions will satisfy nearly everybody.

Variety in yards is unbelievable. There are homes with rocks and cactus, flower gardens and grass. Statuary includes small angels and lifelike deer, pigs, dogs, chickens, cats, rabbits and eagles. One homemaker put a bonnet on a stone goose.

Nameplates of home states and flags are part of many homes. When campgrounds are full in winter, one wonders if there's anybody left back home in the Dakotas, Iowa, Minnesota or Nebraska. Companionship, new friendships and leisurely pursuit of life's everyday pleasures make a full table for residents in retirement communities.

COLUMNS ABOUT YEAGER

MAKING OF AN EDITOR

E.L. Schetman, West River Progress, Personal Column "SO and SO", Oct. 20, 1955

On the front page this week we are printing the announcement that Anson Yeager has been advanced to Editor of the Sioux Falls Argus Leader Sunday Edition. This is a very important position—a position we believe Mr. Yeager will fill to the satisfaction of the approximately 100,000 readers of the Sunday Edition.

As we have mentioned Mr. Yeager before, it is no surprise to tell you that Anson, a West River boy, grew up among the howling coyotes out at Maurine.

We first came in contact with him at Faith while he was attending high school there and, like so many other high school students, had to work as a flunky on the Faith Independent. He showed brightness for newspaper work even at that time. I remember that while I had the job of printing the ballots for Ziebach County—but at time had no power press—Anson assisted me one night printing the ballots on the Independent's press. It was five o'clock in the morning before we finished the job.

After finishing high school Anson entered State College at Brookings and further increased his knowledge of printing by taking a course also in journalism. That summer he worked on the Progress as Linotype operator and also wrote some articles, one of them being about the late Tom Holt of Isabel when his car ran into a lake up there and had to have a mule team pull it out.

After graduation he joined the Argus Leader as a reporter and, his first assignment, we believe, was to cover a common farm auction sale—no doubt a practical joke since farm sales are so common, but Anson came out with a nice account of it.

He served as a reporter for a couple of years, but the next time we saw him we asked in what particular he was covering at that time and after some hesitation he had to acknowledge that he specialized in—of all things—obituaries. He must have been kind to the "dear departed" as his next assignment was to cover the South Dakota State Legislature at Pierre. He again did a fine job and was sent back the next time, too.

During the last year he has written some of the finest political articles ever printed in South Dakota, and these apparently were the reason for assuming the editorship of the Sunday Edition of the Argus Leader.

We salute his advancement!

BEHIND THE BYLINES

James D. Ashley, Argus Leader, Sunday, Aug. 16, 1959

Cowboy "Ans" Yeager left the cool comfort of the Argus-Leader newsroom this weekend to go back to the range country.

Not to Maurine, S.D., where his parents live, but to Wyoming; and not as a vacationing Sunday editor but as Maj. Anson Yeager, intelligence officer of the 147th Field Artillery Group. He'll be with the South Dakota guardsmen at Camp Guernsey for two weeks.

Anson is a westerner all the way—born at Salt Lake City, reared in Denver, in Wyoming and at Maurine, in the sheep and cattle country of western South Dakota, and a graduate of South

Dakota State College. He herded livestock as a youngster, loves the western land, and finds occasion to wear Stetson and western tie, especially when he's covering Legislature at Pierre.

Yeager, whose early education was in a country school and Faith High School, was influenced toward journalism by his father, who was a newspaperman. Anson worked as a printer's devil at Faith when finishing high school and then enrolled in printing and rural journalism at State College.

There was a time when Yeager had to make a choice between an army career and newspaper work. After four years at State College he left for the Army in 1942, gained a commission in OCS (1943) and emerged from World War II as a captain. Completing his college course in the next six months, he joined the Argus-Leader in January, 1947, but was recalled to active military service in August, 1950, with the national guard.

He commanded Headquarters Battery at Camp Carson, Colo., and on Operation Totem Pole in Canada and Alaska. It was then that he debated returning to civilian life, but he took his discharge in August, 1952, and came back to the Argus-Leader. His promotion to major came in 1953 after he had become plans and training officer in the reorganization of the 147th in 1952.

Yeager, August 1959.

Anson's main beat as a reporter was Federal Building and schools but he has covered all beats; started dealing with politics in 1948 and has gone to Pierre to report S.D. Legislature sessions since 1949, with one exception caused by army service.

Besides his columns, pictures and news reports from Pierre, Anson has caught the readers' attention with outstanding special series.

His "Loopholes for Murder," an exciting study of the antiquated coroner system in South Dakota, won him the South Dakota Sigma Delta Chi award as the outstanding editorial contribution of 1956.

He followed with an investigation of the investment of idle funds in state and local government, which led to the passage of a law allowing counties to put funds in interest-paying accounts.

"Our Unknown Neighbors," a statewide survey of the Indian problem, in 1957 won acclaim from Indian leaders and state officials as a realistic and fair appraisal of conditions.

Anson has served as Sunday editor for nearly four years, planning special pages and organizing the layout of the weekend editions.

Today's photo, made last week, may not accurately picture how he will look when he returns from camp. The 5'11", 170-pound Yeager does keep in military trim with some golf, some swimming and a lot of scampering with four children, but a mustache seems to come and go.

Mrs. Yeager is the former Ada May Bidwell of Colman, whom he first met in chemistry class at State College and whom he married in Washington, D.C., in 1944 when she was in the Navy (Waves) and he was in the Army. Karen Ann, the only daughter, was born in Anchorage, Alaska in 1952. Anson Jr. is 5, Harry 3 and Terry 2. They play cowboys at 2204 West 28th St. when they can't get out to the Maurine ranch.

YEARS AS A NEWSMAN FAIL TO SPOIL ANSON'S OPTIMISM

Kim Ode, Argus Leader, Sunday Oct. 19, 1980

Anson Yeager was born to be a newspaperman.

"I can honestly say I never wanted to be anything else," he says, removing his glasses and pondering that thought. To say that ink flows in his veins is a forgivable exaggeration.

Consider: His most memorable story is a church explosion that killed six people; his most famous story one that uncovered loopholes for murder in the coroner system. His favorite night is election night.

He is a stickler for detail, a perfectionist who makes corrections many of us would deem unnecessary.

For instance, in the brief biographical sketch that accompanied the announcement of his being honored with the Distinguished Alumni Award at South Dakota State University this weekend, Anson corrected a statement that read "from 1961 through September 1977" to read "from 1961 to September 1977."

With that in mind, he'll probably disapprove of my calling him Anson in this column. Journalistic style prefers that surnames be used, but no one around here calls him Yeager. Anson is, well, Anson.

At 61, he's the veteran of this Argus Leader newsroom, a guide for us young punks just out of J-school, and a reference library on legs who favors deck shoes with suits and Hawaiian shirts in the summer.

Even his wife, Ada May, calls him a walking history book.

He is no Lou Grant.

No, all the news about Anson is fit to print. He wonders "where the devil" things are and believes in the basic goodness of all people, especially those who live in his beloved South Dakota. He's not a pushover, though. When sports editor John Egan came to the Argus in 1955, he remembers that everyone in the state knew Anson for a series he did "on the horrible way the coroner system operated. It caused some dramatic changes."

That series went on to win the South Dakota Sigma Delta Chi outstanding editorial contribution award in 1956, just one of the many honors he's won since joining the Argus Leader in 1947—January 1947, to be totally accurate. It was his first job out of college and, so far, seems destined to be his only one.

Surprisingly, to those who have heard him expound on the glories of this state, Anson was not born in South Dakota, but in Salt Lake City, Utah, the eldest son of Charles F. Yeager, a newspaperman, and Elise Thinglestad, a Norwegian immigrant.

Anson lived on a ranch in western South Dakota while attending school near Maurine.

His first practical newspaper experience came while attending Faith High School, where he worked for a year as a printer's devil at the Faith Independent, the local Democratic weekly, then later worked as a printer for the local Republican weekly.

Those years are marked in his memory, for Faith, just north of dead center in western South Dakota, was in the depths of the Dustbowl. Yet his references to that time are typically forward-looking. He talks not of the dust and the heat, but of how things look so good these days.

"The Main Streets of some towns have sort of folded up, but the homes are nice," he says. "Sioux Falls, of course, has changed drastically, and some cities have really sparkled."

He sounds almost too optimistic to fit the stereotype of the hardened and cynical newsman. Indeed, his newspaper philosophy reflects opportunity rather than antagonism, a feature increasingly common as advocacy journalism gains popularity.

"I think it represents a freedom to read, a freedom to know," he says of a newspaper. "This freedom doesn't belong to me—and certainly not to the company—but it's a privilege the American people have for getting more information without the government telling what can be printed and what can't be.

"I think a newspaper has to mirror Sioux Falls and South Dakota and the world. You've got to tell it straight, present the real world."

Anson's forte is his sense of perspective. He reminds us that things don't really change that much; that students were marching on campus, protesting the draft—in the 1940s.

Concerning journalism, it's become more analytical, but "I'm not sure there's any more interest in the issues today than there was years ago."

Anson is a reserved man of rare emotion, his sense of concentration at times lending him an air of absent-mindedness. He's always willing to share an anecdote, especially if it's political, but is more of an observer than instigator.

Unlike a lot of former soldiers, he does not offer great tales of his days in World War II, of his service during "that Korean business," of his 17 years in the National Guard.

Instead, he drops little bombshells to casual conversation, unaware of their impact. Only those of us who have pegged him as a lifelong son of the prairie express surprise at his continental view.

For instance, several staffers and editors recently drove to Rapid City for a press convention. Photographer Lloyd B. Cunningham, a World War II buff, was reading a history book and wondered out loud about the kamikaze pilots of that era.

"Oh," Anson said, turning around in his seat, "I sat next to one of those guys on a train between Tokyo and Yokohoma."

Jaws dropped. What was he like? Why were you there? What were your impressions?

"Oh, he was quite a guy," Anson said, and turned around. That was all he had to say

Anson returned to school after the war, graduating in 1947 and getting a job at the Argus Leader where he wrote obituaries for almost a year.

"I jumped into politics in 1948 and went out to the legislature in 1949. Was to go out there for a 10-year period and always enjoyed that very much."

Fred C. Christopherson, the man who hired Anson, says the fledgling journalist turned out well and better than expected.

"I have tremendous respect for Anson Yeager," said Christopherson, who retired as a contributing editor in 1972. "He is a man of integrity, ability and vitality."

Anson was named Sunday editor in 1955 and executive editor of the editorial page and news staff in 1961, serving in that capacity until the Gannett Corporation bought the Argus Leader in September 1977 and Anson was named associate editor.

There were those who viewed that as a step down for the veteran, since the move lessened his participation in the daily process of making a newspaper. Not so, however, says Egan.

"I think a lot of us felt sorry for him but I know from talking to him that it was the greatest thing that ever happened. He used to do everything, from worrying whether the copy boy came in to doing the hiring. And if the copy boy didn't come in at 4 a.m. or whatever that hour was, Anson was the one they'd call."

These days, Anson writes most of the editorials, a job that leaves him a bit more time for roaming the state and camping in the Black Hills as often as possible. Having bounced around enough in the Army, from which he retired as lieutenant colonel, he's never wanted to move again.

"I wasn't interested in commuting in Chicago and I have no yen at all for Washington," he says, his face creasing with his wide grin. "I like the wide open spaces."

The same goes for his wife, Ada May, whom he met in chemistry class at SDSU and married in 1944, their 36th anniversary having passed in September with each of them forgetting it. They've lived in the same house for 28 years and have raised five children.

"I don't know if you'd call him a workaholic," Mrs. Yeager says. "But he works a lot."

Like many people, she says, he spends a lot of time reading, yet he rarely gets to read for sheer enjoyment; his mind always is geared toward work.

Of his future, Anson chuckles and says he'll stick around for a while. He's got enough laurels to rest on: South Dakota Associated Press Newsman of the Year in 1978, winner of the state award for best editorial in 1978 and 1979 and other journalistic and civic honors.

Perhaps John F. Cannon, an editor of the Rapid City Journal, summed it up best. Although having been in the state for 25 years himself, Cannon said distances have prevented him and Anson from becoming close friends.

"But I respect him for his abilities," he said, then paid him the highest compliment a journalist can receive: "And I read him."

ANSON YEAGER, ARGUS LEADER EDITORIAL PAGE EDITOR, TO RETIRE JUNE 1

Mel Antonen, Argus Leader, May 5, 1984

Anson Yeager, who has been commenting on South Dakota news in the Argus Leader editorial pages since 1961, will retire June 1.

Yeager, an associate editor who will be 65 in June, writes most of the editorials for the Argus Leader and a Sunday column. Yeager will take the summer off to travel. His Sunday column will resume in the fall, Publisher Larry Fuller said.

"Anson is recognized as one of the great journalists in the history of South Dakota," he said.

"He is an important part of our daily newspaper operation, and we will miss him. But we feel fortunate that he still will be writing the weekly column."

After graduating from South Dakota State with a degree in printing and rural journalism, Yeager joined the Argus Leader in January 1947. He worked various news beats and was the paper's legislative correspondent in Pierre for 10 years starting in 1949.

Yeager was named Sunday editor in 1955 and executive editor in charge of the news staff in January 1961. He also became editor of the editorial page in 1961.

Yeager was born in Salt Lake City, Utah, and his father, Charles, was a newspaperman in Texas and Colorado. But he grew up on a ranch in western South Dakota between Faith and Newell. His mother, Elise, who came to the United States from Norway in 1905, lives in Faith.

"I have lived in Colorado and Wyoming, but South Dakota is my home," Yeager said. "I'm hooked on the state."

Yeager said he always wanted to be a newspaperman; he said he could read the news wires for hours.

"I am fascinated by news in South Dakota and Sioux Falls," he said. "It's a passion....Writing is my favorite pastime. I like reading the news and offering a comment on how it affects South Dakota."

Yeager's news career started in 1935 when he worked at the Faith Independent and then at the Faith Gazette, both weekly newspapers. That was when everything was done by hand.

Today, newspapers are telling readers what's going on better than they ever have because of a technical revolution, he said. "Linotype is dead at 100....There are computers now. No copy paper, no typewriters....There's instant communication with better pictures and better printing."

Yeager served four years in the Army during World War II. He joined the South Dakota Army Air National Guard at Sioux Falls in 1947; he was a battery commander, and the unit was called to active duty in Colorado and Alaska during the Korean War. He is a retired lieutenant colonel in the U.S. Army.

A 1979 Yeager editorial, titled "A Helping Hand for Our Indians," won a first-place Editorial Excellence Award from the Inland Daily Press Association.

Yeager won first place in the South Dakota Press Association's annual contest for best editorials two years in a row. In 1978, his winning editorials called President Jimmy Carter's attention to South Dakota's stake in the Oahe Irrigation Project and the half million acres that the state gave up for the four Missouri River dams. The 1979 honor came for his writings on an anti-obscenity proposal.

Yeager was named South Dakota Associated Press Newsman of the Year in 1978.

Yeager said he will travel during his retirement; he already has plans to attend the Summer Olympics at Los Angeles.

ANSON YEAGER
A CLASS NEWSPAPERMAN: 1947-1987

John Egan, Argus Leader, Sunday, May 27, 1984

Anson Yeager has written thousands of editorials.

Opinions as to the best ones must be as divergent as there are points of view on dozens of subjects.

But the least effective one—that would have to be in the spring of 1942.

Even the author refused to take the advice offered.

"I was editor of the Collegian at South Dakota State and World War II was on," Yeager says. "I had written an editorial telling the kids it was best to stay in school. Then a week later I quit school to be drafted."

Discharged from the Army a captain, Yeager returned to SDSU in the summer of 1946. The next January he began a 37-year association with the Argus Leader.

Retirement, which begins officially Friday, will be punctuated starting this fall with a continuation of his Sunday columns. As usual they will deal with Yeager's random observations. "I consider my work at the Argus to be an opportunity to look out the show windows of the world," he says.

What about the man who peeks out that window?

Rotarian, retired National Guard battalion commander, Methodist, Republican, devoted husband, concerned father, and hardworking editor, Yeager is a true product of environment.

Anson Yeager: 'I consider my work ... to be an opportunity to look out the show windows of the world.'
—Argus Leader photo by Lloyd B. Cunningham

The journalese originated with his writer father. A homespun philosophy was given wings in northwestern South Dakota by his ranch-woman Norwegian mother. His dedication to purpose took firm root in the hardpan country of Perkins and Meade Counties where he grew up.

The conglomerate that emerged—soft spoken, keen-eyed observer and reporter—is singularly Anson Yeager.

The boy who scurried through Cedar Canyon on the back of his pony became the man riding herd on a succession of South Dakota politicians. In that refining process, Fannie Lu Yeager, an aunt who taught school in Houston, Texas, played a significant role.

"She bought me a subscription to Time magazine when I was about 14 years old or so," Yeager says. "She kept paying for it after that, and I kept poring over it every week."

Aunt Fannie Lu's present was transformed into volumes of material floating about in Yeager's active mind as he went about achieving his boyhood goal. He was determined to become a newspaperman.

Profile
- Name: Anson Anders Yeager.
- Date of birth: June 5, 1919, at Salt Lake City.
- Education: Faith High School, 1937; South Dakota State University, 1947, printing, rural journalism, history, political science.
- Honorary degree: Doctor of letters, Dakota State College, 1972.
- Occupation: Associate editor of the Argus Leader.
- Family: Wife, Ada May; daughter Karen Ann, 32, graduate of Sioux Falls College, Sioux Falls resident; son Anson Anders Jr., 30, a doctor in Boston; son Harry H., 28, Santa Clara, Calif., electrical engineer; son Terry D., 26, headed for medical school out of University of Nebraska graduate program in chemistry; daughter Ellen, 19, sophomore-to-be at the University of Colorado; mother, Elise Afdahl of Faith.

His father, Charles Yeager, was a Texan whose world revolved around a printing press.

Anson's mother, Elise Thingelstad, who came to the United States from Norway in 1905, returned to South Dakota from Denver with her three sons and got a divorce.

That sent Anson and the family to a ranch owned by his mother's uncle, a half mile from the tiny community of Maurine.

Yeager finished grade school in Maurine, then, about when his mother married rancher Nels Afdahl, traveled 28 miles east on U.S. Highway 212 to high school in Faith.

"My dad had owned a paper. I always would hang around newspaper offices. I thought I could just get started in it by working at one of the weeklies, and go on from there," Yeager says.

Picture used on an invitation to "a community reception honoring Associate Editor Anson Yeager upon his retirement from the Argus Leader." Starlite Room, Holiday Inn City Centre, 5:00 to 7:00 p.m., May 24, 1984.

"But there was a man named H.S. Hepner. He was a persuasive professor from South Dakota State. He traveled the state recruiting students. That's how I got there."

Yeager coupled history and political-science majors with his printing and rural journalism studies. Upon graduation in January, 1947, he joined the Argus Leader.

"My first recollection of the Sioux Falls paper was in Maurine," Yeager says. "A storekeeper there had lived in Tea. He kept the Argus at his place and I could read it there.

"When I started on the staff it was writing obituaries for six or seven months. I had no idea what the start would lead to. All I ever wanted was a chance to be on a newspaper. Throughout, I have just enjoyed what I was doing."

What Yeager did, among other things, was leave trail marks in the lives of countless South Dakotans.

One remembers an original crossing of paths: "My first meeting with him was many years ago when I was a young 4-H'er in Humboldt. Unknown to him, Anson has had a meaningful influence on my life. I have very much enjoyed reading his historical perspectives.

"Owners have come and gone at the Argus Leader, but Anson has remained as a steady influence of South Dakota integrity and fairness. A newspaper with the tradition and reputation of the Argus Leader has extensive files of clippings and pictures, but nothing can replace the informed judgments of an editor with a background like Anson's.

"Anson's vast knowledge of South Dakota history gave him insights on current events. This benefited the paper's readers and reporters both. He maintained high journalistic standards. He will be missed."

That 4-H'er became Sen. Larry Pressler. His thoughts echo the sentiments of many who have brushed up against this prairie journalist.

South Dakota-born Al Neuharth, chairman and chief executive officer of Gannett Co. Inc., and founder of USA TODAY says: "From the time that I was a journalism student at the University of South Dakota to my two years with the Associated Press in Sioux Falls and Pierre, and my two years at SODAK Sports, I envied and was in awe of Anson.

"I considered him Mr. South Dakota. I watched his gentle and yet his firm judgments on people and things—covering the broad spectrum from academia to politics to just plain people.

"He is a helluva guy who leaves a helluva legacy to South Dakota journalism and South Dakotans. One of my great satisfactions has been the direct association with him since Gannett's ownership of the Argus Leader since 1977."

Yeager's personal version of shorthand, his battered manual typewriter of yesterday, and now a green computer tube have created light from darkness during the last five decades.

Two memorable examples of Yeager's investigative style came along in the mid 1950s.

The first a brainchild of Fred Christopherson, then the newspaper's editor, was called Loopholes for Murder.

The series started: "You can get away with murder in South Dakota.

"State law will help you do it.

"You just have to be smart enough to outwit the coroner."

Several months of travel, conversation and research, coupled with Yeager's skillful writing, produced a classic of journalism. The series which exposed the state's antiquated coroner system won the South Dakota Sigma Delta Chi award as the outstanding editorial contribution of 1956. It was the first time the award had been made.

Awareness, though, is not always followed by action.

"I don't think there'd been anything quite like that story yet. Some people in Sioux Falls got pretty nervous as I remember. But sad to say, the system still isn't what it should be," Yeager says.

The other example was the brainchild of Howard Chernoff, associate publisher. Chernoff's idea concerning a story depicting the lives of South Dakota Indians was transformed from suggestion to series during 3,000 miles of arduous travel by Yeager.

What resulted was an intimate discussion called The Sioux—Our Unknown Neighbors. It examined, in 13 in-depth installments, Indian life from reservation to city, from joy to despair, from history to future, from hope to reality.

It concluded: "South Dakota's Indians are caught between two worlds.

"There's the Indian world and the old Sioux virtues of sharing, worrying only about today, and not thinking of tomorrow....

"There's the white man's world of work, worry, save. Hit the ball and be on time. Work 50 weeks and take two for vacation....

"The Indian is on the outside looking in."

The series brought a touching situation, as well as a journalist, to the forefront in South Dakota.

Yeager covered all of the traditional beats for the Argus Leader. Individual personalities flash through his memory: the thoughtfulness of Harry Truman, the rapidfire speech of Hubert Humphrey, the can-do spirit of Joe Foss, the oratorical magic of Karl Mundt, the old-shoe earthiness and practicality of Gen. Omar Bradley.

Yeager became editor of the editorial page in 1961.

His editorials have won countless citations. Recognition has come in the form of the Ralph D. Casey Award from the University of Minnesota, plus honors from the Inland Daily Press Association, the South Dakota Press Association and other organizations.

When possessed by an editorial message, he went after a keyboard in the manner of an excited bareknuckle prizefighter.

Frank Harrington of the American Red Cross, who worked with Yeager for 15 years as wire editor of the Argus Leader, says: "I had never seen a newsman literally attack his notes and typewriter with the vigor and resolve that Yeager showed. Out of that full-speed-ahead system rolled a torrent."

Sixteen years of Yeager's Argus Leader duty was double-barreled in nature. He directed the editorial pages. As executive editor, he did the hiring, firing, budgeting, supervising and motivating in the newsroom. Those long days came to an end in 1977 when the editorial page became his primary function.

"I was happy to be shed of the burden of hiring and firing," Yeager says. "I have no regrets but there were times when the work was maybe a bit too much."

The first 17 years of his association with the Argus Leader was coupled with service in the Army National Guard.

Yeager sees many similarities in his roles in the service and newspapering—planning organization, leadership, and the focusing of various operations on a single goal.

Of his three sons and two daughters, only one, middle son Harry, ever entertained thoughts of following in his father's footsteps. "And that was very brief," Yeager, who will be 65 June 5, says.

Yeager's love of Sioux Falls led him into civic involvement of several kinds, including the Boy Scouts and Boys Club.

He's lectured at the University of South Dakota.

He retired from military service saying it was a young man's business. He believes the Argus Leader will do just fine without his fulltime attention.

There are, Yeager says, new hills to climb, new roads to travel, new sights to see.

That may be true.

But an old newspaper is going to prove an old British Army ballad wrong, even though the thought was stolen later by Gen. Douglas MacArthur. It isn't going to let this old soldier fade away.

Anson Yeager didn't get his discharge. He's only on leave.

THERE'S ANOTHER SIDE TO THIS STORY, AND YEAGERS ALL OVER THE COUNTRY...

Jodie Egan Flolid, Argus Leader, Sunday, May 27, 1984

For the last 37 years Ada May Yeager has been able to keep track of her husband by picking up the daily newspaper.

She's the wife of Anson Yeager, the journalist who has helped South Dakotans get a better understanding of the news and how it affects their lives.

She's been involved in her husband's work as an observer of life in South Dakota, the United States and the world.

She's traveled with her husband, proofread his stories and arranged the family life around his long hours and split shifts.

"Mostly, I'm Mrs. Anson Yeager, and I don't mind that," she says. "Maybe it's because I grew up in a different generation."

She wouldn't have had it any other way.

"I grew up on a farm where the whole family was involved. It would be hard for me if my husband had a job I wasn't allowed to know anything about. Some women ask their husbands what he did at work and maybe get a grunt—or if he tells them, they might not understand anyway."

Reading the Argus Leader and discussing the news has been a part of life in the Yeager household.

Couples think alike who have been married as long as she and Anson, Ada May says. But there have been times when she's disagreed with positions her editor husband has taken.

Ada May Yeager.
—Argus Leader photo

"Oh yes, I tell him. I just don't write any letters to the editor."

Through the years, Ada May has had to take criticism of her husband's stands. "I just don't take it personally. It's just a complaint about what he wrote."

But his job at the paper was harder on the couple's five children. During their years at Washington High School, they were chided about sports scores that didn't get in the paper or coverage of school events. "The kids have all had to suffer through it."

Anson was a journalist when she met him, Ada May says. "He never wanted to do anything else."

Ada May Bidwell, a farm girl from Colman, met Anson Anders Yeager in chemistry class at South Dakota State University. She went on to get a history major and English minor, graduating in 1943.

The couple married Sept. 10, 1944, during World War II. He was stationed in South Carolina in the Army and she was a lieutenant in the WAVES, stationed in Washington D.C.

After the wedding, the couple went back to their posts.

"That's the way it was then, that's all. You couldn't get out of the service for something so minor as not being with your husband,"

After 2½ years in the WAVES, Ada May began taking library science classes at the University of Chicago. After one quarter Anson was discharged, and the couple moved to Brookings so he could finish college.

After they moved to Sioux Falls, Ada May worked at the Washington High School library, the public library and as a stenographer for a law firm. She never went back to work after Anson was called back into the Army in 1950.

"When you have four children in five years, you think that's enough," she says. There were few hours in the day that at least one child wasn't home. Through the years she attended football and basketball games, horse shows and swim meets. She was a Girl Scout leader.

When the children were young, Ada May and the wife of an Argus pressman took swimming lessons to get out of the house two nights a week. Now she swims four times a week, and participates on a competitive swim team. She is a member of the WCA board of directors and the women's group at Asbury United Methodist Church.

Ada May and Anson encouraged all of their children to go to college. Although none chose journalism as a career, the children are all good writers, she says.

The children were Anson's regular critics. "It was always a joy to them to find an error in the Argus when he was editor," she says.

Anson's busy schedule at the Argus, as well as his part-time work with the National Guard, affected family life.

"At one time or another, each of the kids asked me when they could start playing the stereo after 10. I'd always tell them, 'As soon as your father gets a job where he doesn't have to get up at 6 o'clock in the morning.'"

Anson is ready to retire, she says. They have travel plans, starting with the Olympics this summer in Los Angeles.

The Yeagers camped in tents for years. Now there's a motor home waiting to take them across the country.

Most anywhere they travel in the United States, they'll be able to visit a Yeager. After the trip to the Olympics, they'll stay in California for the birth of their first grandchild. Son Harry, 28, an electrical engineer who lives in Santa Clara, and his wife, Stephanie, are expecting a child in August.

The oldest of their children, Karen, 32, lives in Sioux Falls. Anson Anders Yeager Jr., 30, is a doctor in Boston, finishing the fourth year of a five-year residency in surgery. Terry Yeager, 26, a graduate assistant in chemistry at the University of Nebraska, is headed for medical school. Ellen Yeager, 19, has completed her freshman year at the University of Colorado, Boulder.

Anson's retirement will give the couple a chance to travel in style. And allow Anson time to search out stories for his Sunday column that will resume in the fall.

"We won't have to be back in X number of days, and start crossing things off because we run out of time," Ada May says. "Usually we start out exploring every little nook and cranny and have to come back full speed ahead."

ANSON YEAGER, A CITY JOURNALIST WHO STILL LOVES TO COME HOME TO FAITH

Linda Hipps, The Faith Independent, April 21, 1982

Most Argus staffers are sitting in front of computers instead of typewriters and such was the case when we stopped by the news room and found former Faith Independent staff member Anson Yeager hard at work editing copy at his computer.

Anson Yeager has been employed at the Argus Leader for 35 years. He is presently serving the huge daily as Associate Editor. His roots in the newspaper industry are deep, and his love of the profession is even deeper. He enjoys writing about his boyhood in Faith country, but also writes many editorials and covers the political scene extensively.

Anson writes a Sunday column for the Argus and has done the editorial page for 16 years. He was executive editor for the daily publication for 16 years. He has been active in civic affairs and was enlisted in the National Guard in 1964 with the rank of Lt. Col. He served active duty during the war for six years.

Yeager's newspaper career began while he was attending Faith High School. He worked for Ival Wilson at the Independent in 1935 and for Mr. and Mrs. George King from 1936 through 1938.

Anson graduated from Brookings in 1947, and after that he began his work at the Argus Leader. With the exception of a few years serving in the reserves, Anson Yeager has been at the Argus ever since.

In his early newspaper career, Yeager covered most beats in Sioux Falls, including the political scene. He covered the legislative session at Pierre for several years and has won a number of honors for writing. A recent award, added to his long list of accomplishments, was presented in 1981. Yeager was the 1981 recipient of the Ralph D. Casey Award from the University of Minnesota School of Journalism and Mass Communications. The UM awarded this prestigious award for Yeager's contribution to the profession of journalism.

Yeager is the son of Elise Afdahl, Faith. He enjoys returning home whenever he can. The 1982 FHS graduating class asked him to speak for their commencement this year, but Yeager had other commitments on the graduation date. He said that he felt very honored to be asked to speak to the graduates and was sorry that he could not make the date.

Yeager recently wrote an article on Highway 212 which The Faith Independent will be reprinting in the near future. Yeager said he received many comments from Faith country on the article he wrote for the Argus, which was reprinted last year, about western South Dakota history.

When asked how he felt about all the newfangled equipment used these days in the newspaper business, Yeager said he wouldn't want to go back to the letterpress days. The computers have made the job much easier and less time consuming. He enjoys newspapering in the big city but still misses home. Yeager said, "There is something very special about the people of Faith. I have never returned home once that people didn't greet me as if I had been away only a few weeks. It's probably the greatest place on earth!"

50 YEARS OF NEWSPAPERING WAS HIS WINDOW TO THE WORLD

Linda Hipps, The Faith Independent, June 27, 1984

He began his career in the newspaper business as a "printer's devil" at the Faith Independent in June 1935 for Ival S. Wilson. He learned the linotype operation procedures at age 18 and other backshop chores under Wilson. He worked two years for the Faith Gazette under Mr. and Mrs. George King (1936-38). For one summer he worked for E.L. Schetnan on the West River Progress at Dupree. One day a week Schetnan and Anson Yeager would take the Milwaukee train to Eagle Butte to print the Eagle Butte News, returning at night on the westbound train.

Anson Yeager retired last month from 50 years in newspapering. His 37½-year association with the Argus Leader in Sioux Falls ended May 24 when the state's largest circulation newspaper threw a big party for their retiring associate editor. Friends, relatives and business associates gathered to wish him, and his wife, Ada May, well in their retirement.

Anson is one of South Dakota's most respected and admired journalists. His career has led him to many challenging and rewarding experiences over the years. He has hobnobbed with the most influential and powerful people in the state. People from every walk of life have read his stories and editorials. He has written about all segments of society. Each time he came away with a story or editorial which his peers respected and recognized.

Anson's journalistic trade mark is his vast knowledge of the history, heritage and culture of his state. He has covered a broad spectrum from academia to politics to just plain people.

Yeager's personal version of shorthand, his battered manual typewriter of yesterday, and now a green computer tube have created light from darkness during the last five decades.

His investigative reporting has been substantial. Two memorable examples of Anson's investigative style came along in the mid-1950s. The first, a brainchild of Fred Christopherson, then the Argus editor, was called "Loopholes for Murder."

The series began: "You CAN get away with murder in South Dakota. State law will help you do it. You just have to be smart enough to outwit the coroner."

Several months of travel, conversation and research, coupled with Yeager's skillful writing, produced a classic of journalism. The series which exposed the state's antiquated coroner system won the S.D. Sigma Delta Chi award as the outstanding editorial contribution of 1956. His editorials have won countless citations for editorial excellence. One of his most cherished awards was the Ralph D. Casey Award, presented by the University of Minnesota School of Journalism and Mass Communications. An incredible understanding of the state of South Dakota and its people inspired a 13 (in-depth) part series titled "The Sioux—Our Unknown Neighbors." The series examined Indian life from reservation to city, from joy to despair, from history to future, from hope to reality.

It concluded: "South Dakota's Indians are caught between two worlds. There's the Indian world and the old Sioux virtues of sharing, worrying only about today, and not thinking of tomorrow.

"There's the white man's world of work, worry, save. Hit the ball and be on time. Work 50 weeks and take two for vacation.

"The Indian is on the outside looking in."

The series brought a touching situation, as well as a journalist, to the forefront in South Dakota. The depiction of the lives of South Dakota Indians was transformed from suggestion to series during 3,000 miles of arduous travel by Yeager.

How could you sum up a lifetime of writing about the Land of Infinite Variety and the people who make this state so grand? Anson said, "I consider my work at the Argus to be an opportunity to look out the show windows of the world."

Retirement, which began officially Friday, May 25, will be punctuated starting this fall with a continuation of his Sunday columns in the Argus. As usual, they will deal with Yeager's random observations.

Anson is the son of Faith pioneer Elise (Thingelstad) Afdahl who came to the U.S. from Norway in 1905. Elise lives in Faith and receives a call from her journalist son every week.

THE ARGUS LEADER

THE WAY IT WAS IN 1947

Argus Leader, Aug. 2, 1981

There is a special feeling about being 100 years old, which the Argus Leader is today.

It has been my good fortune to be a part of the Argus Leader since Jan. 6, 1947, a warm winter day in Sioux Falls. At 8 o'clock that Monday morning, I started as a reporter.

The Argus was published at 109 N. Main Ave., a location now occupied by Time Loan Plan and Land Title Guaranty Co. in a building that has the same shade of light brick of yesteryear.

The Argus Leader's clock on the front of the building carried the connotation of the race against time newspaper people associate with the business.

Then, of course, the Argus was an afternoon and Sunday morning newspaper. The switch to all morning publication, accomplished July 9, 1979, was many years away.

What did a beginning reporter do on the Argus staff of 1947? The obituaries. I was to write many of them before turning to other beats.

The city was smaller then. That and the longevity of South Dakotans who had many years ahead of them meant fewer obituaries in the paper. There were only two funerals that day—a marked contrast to the number—15 or more—sometimes carried today.

There's a mortality lesson for news people in chronicling obituaries. It's softened by the realization that the daily listing of new births is evidence in print that life goes on.

It also reinforces this writer's lucky feeling about the privilege of writing about a day nearly 35 years ago when my peers and I were younger—and the Yeager children hadn't been born.

◆ ◆ ◆

The Argus Leader's front page that day carried a black streamer, TRUMAN CALLS FOR STRIKE BAN, and another headline across the page saying that a Rapid City state senator would step out of the race for president pro tem of the South Dakota Senate.

Herb Qualset, photographer at the time, had a front page picture of ice skaters at Covell Lake, enjoying good ice from colder weather the preceding week.

Spence Sandvig, now of the Chicago Tribune, was Argus Leader sports editor. His column related how bad Brookings looked in defeating Watertown and how the Warriors of Sioux Falls "stunk" in vanquishing Yankton's Bucks. Winning was complicated by the Christmas holiday blahs.

Herb Bechtold (whose untimely death in 1970 at age 51 would be a future shock) was columnist and No. 1 local reporter. Herb used a letter from a Sioux Falls housewife, a military dependent on Saipan, to lead off his Round Robin column. The letter told about the changes in that island—once a Japanese base—since our forces captured it in World War II. Peacetime routine was much better.

In 1947, the entire country was caught up in the process of enjoying life, liberty and the pursuit of happiness after the war—and returning to normal. The Argus Leader reflected this national preoccupation in its news columns.

There were six city reporters on the staff. They had desks in the middle of a newsroom that wasn't much larger than the Argus Leader's copy desk and an aisle today.

Jim Ashley, then the city editor, took me under his wing and carefully edited my obituary and other stories.

This was the newsroom of the Argus Leader in 1954, first year in the building at 10th Street and Minnesota Avenue in Sioux Falls. —Argus Leader photo

THE ARGUS LEADER

The Argus Leader moved into its new building at 10th and Minnesota in February 1954.

Many pieces of paper hit an editor's desk, including newspaper contest entries which Anson Yeager looked over in his second floor office. He was executive editor for 16 years and associate editor for seven years. Concurrently he was editor of the editorial page for 23 years and wrote most of the editorials. He also handled readers' letters.

William H. Leopard, left, publisher of the Argus Leader, and Anson Yeager, right, executive editor, visit with columnist Drew Pearson. He was in Sioux Falls to address a convention. —Argus Leader photo

Three friends enjoy a capitol visit at Pierre during a session of the South Dakota Legislature. From left: Rep. George Kirk, Executive Editor Anson Yeager and Publisher William H. Leopard.

Anson enjoyed reading the Argus Leader and other newspapers
—a much easier chore than judging contests.

NORTHERN PLAINS ADVENTURES

Anson Yeager, 1956 centennial beard came off before National Guard camp.

Bow ties were a favorite while covering Legislature in the 1950s.

The 1960s were fun, too.

The 1970s had key adventures in my newspaper work.

There were more new vistas in the 1980s and 1990s. Older former editors like to think of themselves as reporters again.

Writing features was more fun. My first one—for the Sunday paper at the end of my first week—was about the unfolding of the farm sale season in the area.

Ashley sent me and Qualset to the Cliff Meves' farm sale 12 miles west of Sioux Falls. Al Erskine, a veteran Sioux Falls auctioneer, was one of three who cried Meves' sale.

Used farm machinery brought a premium price. Wartime shortages still persisted. A boy at the sale started the Model M Farmall. The motor roared. When it cut out, the auctioneer said, "It runs." He started at $1,500 and in a matter of seconds the bid was $2,000. The 1942 tractor sold for $2,210. Comparable new equipment was $1,852 FOB, if you could get one.

Buying a new car was equally difficult. My first car was a 1946 used Plymouth which I liked, but soon sold to buy a new 1947 Kaiser. It was the first of two Kaisers I owned. The second had overdrive and gas left in the tank after a trip across South Dakota.

Apartments were difficult to get, too. Bill Leopard, then classified manager and later publisher, helped me find an upstairs apartment through his want ad contacts. My wife, Ada May, soon joined me from Brookings.

That first day on the job I recall "Chris" (Fred Christopherson, the editor and the man who hired me) stopping in the newsroom on the first floor to check with the staff. He said hello and headed upstairs, a bundle of papers under his arm. He looks almost the same today and at 85 retains his keen interest in news of Sioux Falls and the world.

❖ ❖ ❖

Fortunately, other beats soon followed the obituary assignment. That old newsroom, which was destroyed by fire in 1951 (I didn't set it—my alibi is that I was back in the Army), reinforced my conviction in news as a career.

That newsroom was a window to Sioux Falls, South Dakota and the world beyond—a view that I have enjoyed and appreciated.

The typewriters, copy paper and pencils, linotypes and presses of yesteryear are long gone. There are video display tubes in the newsroom and computer—connected typesetting machines which speed the process—and make it much easier.

The last two decades have brought a bigger revolution in daily newspaper production—thanks to photocomposition, computers and offset presses—than Ottmar Mergenthaler's linotype did in the 1880s.

The revolution, perhaps, is mainly refinement in the art of communicating with the printed word.

I say that because the magic of a newsroom and a newspaper in its many business and production facets is unchanged. The Argus Leader, now as in 1947, is a window to the world for the men and women who produce it.

There is still adventure—in the business—and daily wonder about all the world, its stage and many players, as William Shakespeare wrote centuries ago.

I hope it's still that way for the paper's bicentennial in 2081.

ARGUS-LEADER EDITORIAL WINS FIRST PLACE AWARD

Argus Leader, Feb. 23, 1976

WILLIAMSBURG, Va.—The Sioux Falls Argus-Leader was named first place winner in its circulation category today in the 1976 Editorial Excellence Award contest.

The contest is sponsored by the William Allen White Foundation for the Inland Daily Press Association. The late Mr. White was the renowned editor of the Emporia, Kan., Gazette, noted for his editorials which were reprinted over many years by the nation's largest newspapers.

Del Brinkman, dean of the William Allen White School of Journalism at the University of Kansas and a director of the foundation, presented an engraved plaque and award certificate to the Argus Leader during this morning's session of the Inland group's spring meeting in Williamsburg.

The Argus Leader's editorial, published Jan. 8, 1975, encouraged Gov. Richard Kneip in his challenge to South Dakota to solve its Indian jurisdiction problems responsibly and in a mature way. The editorial was written by Anson Yeager, the newspaper's executive editor.

PRIZE-WINNING EDITORIAL
ONE OF 101 INLAND CONTEST ENTRIES

Argus Leader, Monday, Feb., 23, 1976

This Argus Leader news story was published on February 23, 1976, in the issue announcing that the editorial, "A Helping Hand for Our Indians," had won first place in the William Allen White Foundation contest.

The Sioux Falls Argus-Leader's editorial which won first place in its category in the Inland Daily Press contest was one of 101 entries from 23 states and the Canadian provinces of Manitoba and Ontario.

The editorial, which commented 13 months ago on the Indian jurisdiction problem in South Dakota, is reprinted below. It won first place in the contest's 25,001-50,000 circulation category.

Anson Yeager, executive editor of the Argus-Leader who wrote the editorial, said that the problems confronting South Dakota and its Indian population with respect to the jurisdiction situation still remain.

"However, I am hopeful that the goals of Gov. Richard Kneip and others who are seeking to resolve this problem and lend a helping hand to our Indian people can be attained in the wake of the Wounded Knee and the Custer and Minnehaha County Courthouse trials. This is South Dakota's most pressing 'people problem,'" Yeager said. He said he was very pleased by the recognition for the Argus-Leader.

Free Press Top Winner

The Detroit Free Press was named the top winner in the 1976 Editorial Excellence Award Contest. The Free Press entry also was judged best among newspapers with a circulation of more than 50,000.

Other winners of the best-of-class awards, by circulation groups are:

Grand Junction, Colo., Sentinel, 10,001-25,000 circulation.

Parsons, Kan., Sun, under 10,000 circulation.

Ten other finalists also were announced in the contest. The finalists in the Argus-Leader's category are the Hutchinson, Kan., News, the Port Huron, Mich. Times Herald and the Marion, Ind., Chronicle-Tribune.

The contest was the fourth annual editorial competition for Inland Press members. The contest is sponsored by the William Allen White Foundation.

Selection of the top entries in each circulation category and the Free Press as sweepstakes winner was made by faculty members of the William Allen White School of Journalism at the University of Kansas, where the foundation is housed.

Contest Criteria Given

The contest is designed to honor editorials that best exemplify the standards of the late William Allen White, Emporia, Kan., editor. The criteria for citation in the contest require clarity of thought, pungency of phrase, understanding of a need of expectation in specific terms for concrete action and appreciation of man's limitations, his capability for folly and his potential for glory.

The Free Press editorial said that a Michigan State Department of Natural Resources plan to drill for oil in forest lands of that state did not safeguard the area sufficiently and should be rejected.

Joe Stroud, the Free Press editor, wrote that the Pigeon River Forest in Michigan "is a major treasure of the state....It ought to be dealt with now not on the basis of legalisms of expediency, but as it has been for these many years—on the basis of public interest." Following publication of the editorial and a companion interpretive article, drilling was delayed and, Stroud believes, may be stopped altogether.

The Grand Junction Daily Sentinel warned in its editorial that the expansion of gag rules by the courts is judicial abuse that threatens the rights of defendants.

Editor Clyde Reed of the Parsons Sun commented on an attempt in a neighboring town to reform the Ku Klux Klan. It made him think of the 1920s, he wrote, when "the ranks of white sheets" were all over Kansas. "Surely we must be wiser now . . . but we need to remember what took place in Kansas a half century ago before we are ready to be swallowed up in our own complacency."

A HELPING HAND FOR OUR INDIANS

(Reprinted from the Jan. 8, 1975 Argus-Leader.)

Gov. Richard Kneip has challenged South Dakota to solve its Indian jurisdiction problems responsibly and in a mature way. He wants the state to become a model for the world in its solution of complicated legal, political and social problems in the state's relationship with nine Indian tribal governments.

Kneip says the other alternative is to make South Dakota's name synonymous with intolerance. Barring some ill-considered action by the federal judiciary or U.S. government which would further confuse or upset the present jurisdictional problem, South Dakota can do much to help the situation.

Certainly, the time is here and now for South Dakota and its people to attempt solutions within the state that will help the relationships between whites and Indians, between state government and tribes.

Out Of Sight, Mind

No other people in America have been so apart from the mainstream of life as the first Americans and their descendants. Their problems have been many since the federal government compelled them to live on the reservations. Until recently, Indians have been mostly out of sight and out of mind. The hopeful sign has been the emergence of some Indians into the white man's cities and working world.

Yeager receiving the 1978 Newsman of Year award from Roger Kasa, of the Huron Daily Plainsman, retiring president of the South Dakota AP editors group. —Pierre Daily Capital Journal photo by Jeff Owens

There are some well-meaning but misguided citizens in this country who think that the way to solve the Indians' problem is to perpetuate their way of life on the reservations. Most Indians, we believe, would trade the old ways for a paycheck. The old ways do not fit today's times. White and Indian ranchers alike have a difficult time making do with limited land resources.

Kneip said that his approach will be to resist any effort to diminish state authority, or the authority of South Dakota subdivisions to enforce laws fairly and firmly where the state has that authority. He said "just as we enforce the law, we shall obey it." He welcomes a re-awakening of pride among Indian people and wants them to play a greater role in the life of the state. He sees a need for respect for the integrity and dignity of each other, and learning from mistakes of the past to build understanding for the future.

There is no more important task that South Dakota could undertake than to achieve understanding among its people and to build for a better future for all.

They Got Our Attention
Recent events, including Wounded Knee and the courthouse disturbances at Custer and Sioux Falls, have served to set back the cause of good relations between Indians and whites, to the detriment of thousands of Indian citizens who had nothing to do with those incidents. They did, however, gain the state's and world's attention to some real problems.

The future for all South Dakotans should not be limited by the color of an individual's skin or by his or her ancestry. Each South Dakotan should have an opportunity to share in the state's good things and way of life, in return for his or her efforts. There is a real opportunity for South Dakotans to do some missionary work within the state's borders to help the first Americans.

It is time to seek understanding and resolution of old ills, for a better future for all. Helping hands and tolerance are needed. Gov. Kneip, starting an unprecedented third term as South Dakota's chief executive, has no more important job in the next four years than finding some answers to a common problem shared by Indians and their fellow citizens. We wish Kneip well in his resolve.

ARGUS WINS AWARDS; GROUP HONORS YEAGER
Argus Leader, Sept. 11, 1978

PIERRE—The Argus-Leader won eight awards—including four first places—in the annual South Dakota Associated Press writing and photography contest Sunday.

At the same time, it was announced that Anson Yeager, associate editor of the Argus-Leader, was named Newsman of Year by his colleagues. The annual award is for contributions to journalism and community service.

Argus-Leader members Chuck Raasch, Tim Schreiner, John Bannon and Lloyd Cunningham all were announced as first-place winners at the luncheon Sunday.

ANSON YEAGER'S DESERVED HONOR
Dean C. Smith, Argus Leader, Monday, Sept., 11, 1978

This space on the editorial page has been frequently used to commend individuals who have won recognition for serving their profession and community well.

Today's editorial is one of those pleasant occasions. It is our intention to salute an individual who has devoted a lifetime in serving his fellow man, in making Sioux Falls and South Dakota a better place to live.

The man is Anson Yeager, associate editor of the Argus-Leader.

Anson was selected Associated Press Newsman of the Year at a gathering in Pierre over the weekend. He was cited for his more than 30-year devotion to South Dakota journalism and was also praised for his enormous contributions to his community and state.

Anson needs no introduction on the streets of Sioux Falls, and he is equally comfortable and well-known in many corners of the state.

Anson was raised on a ranch near Maurine, S.D., giving impetus to his vast knowledge of agriculture on the state, national and international levels.

Dean C. Smith, Argus Leader Publisher.

Ralph D. Casey Minnesota Award Medal.   **Ralph D. Casey Minnesota Award.**

He graduated from Faith High School, then South Dakota State University with a degree in printing and rural journalism. He went to work for the Argus-Leader in 1947 as a reporter. He reported the legislative sessions in Pierre from 1949-59 and was named to his first editor position in 1955.

Anson is a World War II veteran and also commanded the Sioux Falls' Headquarters Battery of the 147th Field Artillery Battalion in Colorado and Alaska during the Korean War. He later served as a lieutenant colonel in the South Dakota Army National Guard commanding an artillery battalion before retiring in 1964.

Anson is a member of the American Society of Newspaper Editors; past director of the Sioux Falls Chamber of Commerce; past director of the Sioux Falls Development Foundation; a former member of the executive board of the Sioux Council of Boy Scouts; past chairman of the Associated Press Managing Editors Association in South Dakota; and past president of the Eastern South Dakota chapter of Sigma Delta Chi. In 1975, he was named an ambassador in the South Dakota Diplomatic Corps.

Other awards include being selected the first annual Boss of the Year in 1970 by the National Secretaries Association; a Sigma Delta Chi citation for outstanding editorial contribution to professional journalism; and the American Business Women's Association Boss of the Year selection in 1972.

And probably one of the professional highlights of his career came when Anson was selected for the prestigious William Allen White Foundation award in 1976 for editorial excellence, which was given by the Inland Daily Press Association.

The Argus-Leader salutes one of its own, Anson Yeager. He has been a reflective thinker, a high achiever, a devoted family man and a gentleman always. Sioux Falls and South Dakota should be proud to call Anson their own.

CONGRATULATIONS, ANSON

Advertisement, Argus Leader, Friday, Oct. 30, 1981

We're proud that our associate editor, Anson Yeager, was selected for the prestigious Ralph D. Casey-Minnesota Award by the School of Journalism and Mass Communication at the University of Minnesota.

Named for the late Dr. Ralph Casey, regarded as the chief architect of the School of Journalism, the award is presented annually to an editor or publisher who, in the judgement of the senior SJMC faculty, has given distinguished service to the community, state and nation.

The award was presented in Chicago at the annual meeting of the Inland Daily Press Association on October 19, 1981.

Anson Yeager joined the staff of the Argus Leader in 1947 and shares, what Larry Fuller, publisher, calls an "incredible understanding of our state."

ARGUS LEADER'S YEAGER WINS CASEY AWARD

Murphey Reporter, University of Minnesota, November, 1981

Larry Fuller, publisher of the Argus Leader, nominated Anson Yeager for the prestigious Ralph D. Casey Minnesota Award. Following is an article from the University of Minnesota publication announcing the award by the School of Journalism and Mass Communications.

Anson A. Yeager, associate editor of the Argus Leader of Sioux Falls, S.D., has been selected for the Ralph D. Casey-Minnesota Award by the School of Journalism and Mass Communication.

The award is named for the late Dr. Ralph Casey, director of the School of Journalism from 1930 to 1958. Casey is regarded by many to be the chief architect of the School. The award is presented annually to an editor or publisher who, in the judgement of the senior SJMC faculty, has given distinguished service to the community, state and nation.

Yeager received the award at the annual meeting of the Inland Daily Press Association in Chicago, Oct. 18-21.

Yeager joined the Argus Leader staff in 1947, serving as a reporter until he was appointed executive editor of the paper in 1961. During his career with the Leader, he has written about every facet of South Dakota life, from reports on its legislature to observations on its citizenry, sharing what Larry Fuller, publisher of the Leader, calls an "incredible understanding of our state."

In a letter nominating Yeager for the Casey Award, Fuller wrote, "Anson's journalistic leadership through the years has produced a reasoned viewpoint that pierces issues and overrides parochialism. He has, for example, championed the rights for American Indians, sought statewide cooperation on water development, and from time to time, taken on the governor when he felt that his comments or actions were not in the best interests of the state."

Apparently bearing no grudges, South Dakota Governor William Janklow also wrote to support Yeager's nomination. "I can be very critical of the press when I know that printed or broadcast information is inaccurate or misleading," he said. "Politicians and reporters should strive to achieve the highest levels of excellence in their professions....Anson Yeager of the Sioux Falls Argus Leader has attained that level of excellence and deserves special consideration."

Larry Fuller.

♦ ♦ ♦

In 1975, Yeager was named an ambassador in the South Dakota Diplomatic Corps. He is a member of the American Society of Newspaper Editors and has served as chairman of the Associated Press Managing Editors Association and as president of the Eastern South Dakota chapter of Sigma Delta Chi, the professional journalism honor society. He has been a director of the Sioux Falls Chamber of Commerce and the Sioux Falls Development Foundations and was a member of the executive board of the Sioux Council of Boy Scouts.

Yeager has been honored as Boss of the Year by the National Secretaries Association (1970) and the American Business Women's Association (1972). He received the Sigma Delta Chi award for outstanding editorial contribution to professional journalism and the William Allen White Foundation Award for editorial excellence (1976). He was named South Dakota Associated Press Newsman of the Year in 1978.

♦ ♦ ♦

Yeager's writing awards include state awards for best editorial in 1978, 1979 and 1980. He received a Distinguished Alumni Award from South Dakota State University at Brookings, from which he was graduated in 1946.

He served in the armed forces during World War II and was a member of the South Dakota Army National Guard for 17 years. He retired as a lieutenant colonel in 1964.

Yeager is the 35th recipient of the Casey Award. Other recipients in recent years have included B.H. Ridder Jr., Ridder Newspapers; Robert J. Burrow, Danville (Ill.) Commercial News; James Kerney Jr., Trenton (N.J.) Times and Times-Advertiser; the late Joe W. Seacrest, Lincoln (Neb.) Journal; Philip D. Adler, Davenport (Iowa) Times Democrat; Richard L. Blacklidge, Kokomo (Ind.) Tribune; Peter MacDonald, Harris Enterprises, Hutchinson, Kan.; John F. Dille Jr., Elkhart (Ind.) Truth; Otto Silha, Minneapolis Star and Tribune; Byron C. Vedder, Linday-Schaub newspapers, Decatur, Ill.; and last year's recipient, John R. Finnegan, St. Paul Pioneer Press and Dispatch.

IT'S TIME TO DO SOMETHING DIFFERENT

Argus Leader, May 27, 1984

Thoughts while shaving—after more than 37 years of working for the Argus Leader in your favorite city and state—and mine.

There's something comfortable about Sioux Falls.

It yearns for all the attractions and advantages that go with being the largest city in the state.

But it also has a genuine small town interest in everything that happens locally and in South Dakota and the Sioux Empire.

You see civic ambition in such local projects as the Arena and Howard Wood Field, the continuing renewal of downtown Sioux Falls and the spread to malls, big and small, throughout the city.

Costello Terminal and Joe Foss Field epitomize the city's link to the jet age.

City residents rightfully take equal pride in commercial airline schedules that put you anywhere in the 48 contiguous states in half a day or less and in the South Dakota Air National Guard's savvy ways and topnotch record.

Thanks to a civic leadership that works together and the initiatives of Gov. William Janklow in bringing in Citibank and other firms, the city's economic base today is much broader than it was in 1947 when this writer started with the Argus.

Actually, the broadening process has been under way since the end of World War II, when Sioux Falls became attractive as a regional headquarters to many national firms. Their managers were determined to put their sales staffs closer to their public.

This kind of thinking and variety of the city's retail, wholesale, medical, educational service and other offerings—has made most post World War II years come up roses for Sioux Falls.

There has also been some good luck, part of it helped along by the city's leadership in reaching out and asking for help from the state's political leaders of both parties, whether governors or members of the congressional delegation.

Fortunate decisions in the 1950s enhanced the city's transportation opportunities. These included the choice of South Dakota instead of Minnesota as the route of Interstate 29 and Western Airlines' urge to stop in Sioux Falls instead of overflying the city between Minneapolis and Denver. More recently United Airlines' entry in Sioux Falls was a major step ahead for Joe Foss Field.

There have been other landmark decisions, too, like the support the business community gave to obtaining the EROS Data center, the expansion of industry and business in industrial parks and the way everyone helped to save the Brockhouse animals and incorporate them into the Delbridge Museum at the Great Plains Zoo.

The most unselfish decision this writer has seen in a working lifetime in Sioux Falls was the vote by Local 304A of the United Food and Commercial Workers in September 1982 to take a wage cut and save 900 jobs at John Morrell & Co.

✦ ✦ ✦

One advantage in South Dakota's small population—somewhat more than 700,000 people—is that it's easy to cultivate a statewide acquaintanceship.

That applies to many lines of work. Every endeavor—whether professional, business or trade—has an organization or association that looks after the group's interests.

Sometimes those diverse interests collide in Pierre—where the South Dakota Legislature annually puts on the best and most interesting show in the state. It's easy to know your legislator—and just as easy to know the governor and other officials of the Coyote State.

South Dakotans take an intense, personal interest in local and state government. One of the bonuses of working for the Argus Leader has been knowing so many people from across South Dakota.

There have been dramatic changes in South Dakota: all-weather roads, rural electrification, the Great Lakes (dams) of the Missouri, better homes and remarkable improvements in most county seat towns have characterized progress since Dust Bowl days of the 1930s.

Newsroom personnel say goodbye.

Mel Antonen presents the Argus Leader's gift to Anson Yeager.

This writer is convinced that the best is yet to come for South Dakota and its people.

✦ ✦ ✦

If you want some interesting, easy to digest South Dakota history lessons this summer, tune in on public television.

South Dakota Adventure, produced by Richard Muller for the 5th and 6th grades and previously shown on instructional television, will be screened at 10 o'clock on Tuesday nights, starting June 5.

The series will run for 16 weeks, showing two 15-minute history lessons on each telecast. The programs will be repeated at 2 o'clock each Thursday afternoon, starting June 7.

Muller and his colleagues in South Dakota Public Television spent four years producing the series for the State Division of Elementary and Secondary Education.

The programs were filmed at many different locations. Classroom teachers and pupils benefit from excellent study outlines—a chore that adults may forgo. Just sit back and enjoy the series!

✦ ✦ ✦

This column marks a transition with my retirement from the Argus Leader this week. I've enjoyed my work immensely—but it's time to do something different.

My Mrs. and I will be journeying along the American road to see some new scenery and enjoy camping in the national parks. There's also the happy prospect of seeing the Olympics and becoming grandparents for the first time. The latter event also has a California locale.

We'll be back in the fall, when resuming this column will be a pursuit of retirement. My thanks to a readership I've grown to like and enjoy through the years.

Author's Note: Larry Fuller hosted a community reception for Yeagers at the downtown Holiday Inn on Thursday, May 24, 1984. It was a nostalgic evening and a wonderful way to say goodbye to my Argus Leader readers and community friends.

My Argus Leader newsroom colleagues wished us a happy retirement, too. Mel Antonen presented the paper's gift, a nice print of a Black Hills Gold Mine.

ANSON YEAGER CITATION FOR THE HONORARY DEGREE DOCTOR OF PUBLIC SERVICE

Anson Yeager has been awarded two honorary degrees during his newspaper career. The first was an honorary doctor of letters from Dakota State College of Madison. The second was an honorary degree, doctor of public service, on May 4, 1991, from his alma mater, SDSU. Following is the citation from SDSU:

ANSON A. YEAGER
HONORARY DEGREE DOCTOR OF PUBLIC SERVICE
AWARDED MAY 4, 1991
SOUTH DAKOTA STATE UNIVERSITY
BROOKINGS, SOUTH DAKOTA

Mr. Anson Yeager is one of the most respected journalists and editors in South Dakota. Most of his life's work has been with the Sioux Falls Argus Leader daily newspaper. Although he retired in 1984, he is still an important voice in South Dakota in a weekly column.

He has been an extraordinary alumnus of South Dakota State University. He was selected as Distinguished Alumnus in 1980. He was selected by the Associated Press as the South Dakota Newsperson of the Year in 1978 and cited for community service. He was selected in 1981 by the University of Minnesota School of Journalism for the Ralph D. Casey Award that is given annually to the Midwestern journalist who has given distinguished service to the community, state, and nation. He was named Distinguished Alumnus by the Department of Journalism and Mass Communication at SDSU in 1985. He chaired the SDSU Foundation Board of Directors in 1988.

Mr. Yeager has distinguished himself as a columnist of great perception and insight and as an editor whose opinions and viewpoints were not only avidly sought by leaders in many capacities, but also provided important direction to the public in examination and resolution of issues, concerns and problems. He has been an editor and journalist with extraordinary vision. His stories and editorials have focused on helping South Dakotans know South Dakota. He has written broadly on Native American affairs when few others were doing so.

Dr. Robert Wagner confers honorary doctor's degree on Anson Yeager. —Jolesch photo

In recognition of his enthusiasm for promotion of good journalism in South Dakota, his encouragement to all newspapers and educators, and the honor he has brought to his alma mater, South Dakota State University confers on Anson A. Yeager the degree, Doctor of Public Service, honoris causa.

HERB BECHTOLD, ARGUS-LEADER CITY EDITOR, STRICKEN AT AGE 51

Lloyd Noteboom, Argus Leader, Thursday, Aug. 6, 1970

That can't be right!
Check those facts again, because there must be some mistake.
But, the facts check out. There is no mistake.

Herb Bechtold, the Argus-Leader's Round Robin columnist for nearly 25 years, has tapped out his last column.

Herb Bechtold, the Argus-Leader city editor since 1950, has left the city news room for the last time.

Herb Bechtold. that mild-mannered man who kept his fingers on the happening of a growing city since 1940, has put his last edition to bed.

Herb Bechtold is dead at 51.

Felled by a massive heart attack against which he continued to fight for 18 hours after he was stricken Tuesday afternoon, Herb died at McKennan Hospital at 10 a.m. Wednesday.

He had been on vacation since July 27. He was attending a meeting of the Sioux Falls Board of Adjustment in the commissioner's room at City Hall when he collapsed. The hearing concerned a property use matter in his neighborhood; he lived at 110 N. Summit Ave.

First aid was administered at the scene. A Fire Department resuscitator unit responded to the call at 4:25 p.m. Oxygen was administered. A team of doctors at the emergency room at McKennan Hospital administered further treatment and he was moved to the hospital's coronary care unit Tuesday evening.

The Barnett Funeral Home is in charge of arrangements.

Herb was THE city editor of the Argus-Leader.

But Herb was not the type of city editor too often portrayed in comic strips, in movies or on television.

The rough, tough, gruff, hard-drinking, free-swinging, narrow-thinking, constantly smoking prototype of a city editor never came through with Herb.

Because he just wasn't that kind of man.

Working with Herb for nearly 20 years, the past 3½ as his assistant city editor, I learned to know him as a mild, considerate, kind, non-drinking. non-smoking, broad-minded, gentle and thoroughly unflappable newspaperman.

You, had to know Herb to understand just how unflappable he was.

If he got excited or tense as big news broke, or deadlines arrived too soon, he didn't show it.

As sometimes happens in this business, more news breaks suddenly than can be comfortably covered by the available news staff.

But Herb remained calm, juggling his reporters and photographers to produce the maximum effort in a minimum of time.

Deadlines were met.

While he was not the type to come out and say, I like my work, he must have liked it.

If he missed a day because of sickness (which was seldom), you know he was sick.

When he was on vacation as he was when he was stricken, you knew he could be reached at home if he was needed.

Herb Bechtold.

Nor was it unusual to find him at his desk in the evening or on Sundays, typing out his column for the following day or checking his mail or doing any of the countless things that would give him a headstart on the news breaks of the next day.

Today, Herb is part of that news.

Herbert Miles Bechtold was born in Sioux Falls on Jan. 2, 1919. His parents were the late Mr. and Mrs. F. H. Bechtold.

Herb attended Cathedral School and was graduated from Cathedral High School in 1936. He attended Trinity College in Sioux City from 1936 to 1938, at which time he went to Marquette University in 1938. In 1940 he received his bachelor of philosophy degree in journalism at Marquette and he began working for the Argus-Leader on July 15, 1940.

On Nov. 12, 1945, Herb's first Round Robin column was printed in this newspaper. He continued that column five days a week up until the time of his death. He was named city editor in 1950.

Herb was married to Catherine A. Roche in Sioux Falls on June 24, 1946.

Mrs. Bechtold survives him as do two sons, Daniel, who is a newspaperman at Winner, and Michael, who graduated from O'Gorman High School last spring, and a daughter, Bridget Anne, who attends Nettleton College.

Other survivors include two sisters, Alta Marie of Brookings and Mrs. William Rumpza of Huntsville, Ala., and three brothers, Charles of Brookings, Thomas of Albuquerque, N.M., and Robert of Minneapolis.

Herb entered the military service March 2, 1942, and served in the U.S. Air Force in North Africa, Sicily, Italy, India, Egypt and Burma. He received a field commission in North Africa in 1944 and was discharged as a first lieutenant on Dec. 8, 1945.

He had served as a director the Junior Chamber of Commerce and as a director and treasurer of the Chamber of Commerce. He was a member of the Advisory Board at Marty College in Yankton and had served as deputy grand knight and grand knight of the Knights of Columbus.

Herb reigned as King and the Mardi Gras of the North in 1965.

A NOSTALGIC RETURN TO 1927

Argus Leader, Sunday, Nov. 11, 1979

Walter A. Simmons, who delighted Argus-Leader readers of another era with his "Maybe You Heard" column, still has his intriguing way with words.

He couldn't return last month for the mini-reunion of his Washington High School class of 1927 and promised, "Maybe next time I can come."

He sent a letter instead that pleased his classmates. His comments provide a nostalgic look at the Sioux Falls of his boyhood. Here are some selected excerpts:

"I must be getting younger (Simmons is 71), since I can remember things that happened last year much better than 1927 as it was in Sioux Falls. But I remember the street cars that were so convenient and cost only a nickel.

"In the summer there were open cars that ran to Sherman Park and back. On Halloween, when we were kids, we used to grease the car tracks on the hill south of Lowell School on Summit Avenue. It was very satisfying to see how exasperated the motorman became as he tried, in vain, to get up the hill....

"There was also a jitney that ran on Minnesota Avenue as far south as 26th Street. Beyond 26th Street lay the Great and Mysterious World, peopled no doubt by strange and funny people.

"On the streets ran all manner of cars that have long disappeared from our ken—the princely Packards, the Studebaker, Franklin, Marmon, Saxon, Maxwell, Moon, Hudson, Reo, Willys-Knight, Graham-Paige, Jordan and many others.

"In those days any boy could identify any of those cars from blocks away. Little old ladies ran about in quiet dignity inside electric cars now rediscovered.

"At the Orpheum Theater Pierre Watkin, Alney Alba and Lyle Talbot were playing in stock, and we saved our Indian head pennies, buffalo nickels and Liberty head dimes so we could see as many of their shows as possible.

Olympia Theater had stage show

"At the Olympia Theater, 10th and Phillips, the Powderpuff Girls were prancing in a stage show. At the State, farther up the street, Jack Malerich prevailed at the mighty Wurlitzer organ.

"The Strand had a woman piano player who would let a few favored ones in the side door when she went outside for a smoke.

"Just south of the Strand was the Coney Island Red Hots place, where for a nickel a hungry high school boy could get a mouth-watering hot dog with everything, including a heavy load of chopped onions. Three of them on the side made a splendid lunch.

"Who said we had no gourmets in Sioux Falls in those days? The roast beef hash at the YMCA was also heavenly.

"It is hard to bring back the images of the stores on Phillips Avenue in those days, but I remember the Bee Hive, Fantle's, Weatherwax and several drug stores—Dunning's, Bernhardts and Lynn's....

"On Saturday nights there was always an unending procession of cars on Phillips Avenue, driven by boys on the lookout for girls, not quite knowing what to do if the girls consented to being picked up. I thought of this with a pang some years ago when I read that Phillips Avenue had been closed off for a mall.

Those nasty notes

"We did not have sex education classes in those days. I Learned about Life—with a big capital L—from the notes that certain girls passed in the big assembly hall at Washington High School. This shocked me out of my socks, but I manfully recovered, even if it was never the same again.

"Most of us boys were very timid when it came to girls. We admired them from a distance as splendid and inaccessible creatures, beyond our reach.

"Our equivalent to Playboy magazine was the women's underwear section of the Sears catalog....

"Our world was a pleasing and orderly one. In Washington, wise old Cal Coolidge was steering the ship of state.

"Once I had occasion to write the secretary of commerce for some material to be used by our debate team. He sent everything requested and also a polite note, signed Herbert Hoover.

"In later years, nobody could ever tell me that Hoover was not a nice man.

"Our newspapers—the Sioux Falls Press in the morning and the Argus-Leader at night—were not filled with recitals of disasters and triumphant exposures of man's frailty as today's papers are.

"It hurt when the Press closed up (in 1928). The Argus, for which I was later to work for a dozen years, used to have great crowds massed in front (of the location on North Main) to hear election returns or the outcome of the World Series.

Only the women knew

"Unless they were a bit queer, people smoked Chesterfields, Lucky Strikes or Camels. Men wore things like garters, stiff white collars, plus fours and caps. God knows what women wore. We heard allusions to corsets and step-ins....

"Postage was 2¢ and if you didn't get a letter in the morning you could still look for one in the afternoon. Lots of houses still had outside toilets.

"The ice man was followed by a cry of children in summer and delivered coal in the winter, putting it into the basement through a chute....

"It was an era of heady progress. We had entered the era of wrist watches—called strap watches then. You could buy electric irons, toasters, percolators—even grills and waffle irons. Electric washers made Monday a sunnier day. We had phonographs and radios...

"A good pair of shoes cost $5. A man's three-piece tailored suit in Sioux Falls cost $29. I remember it well, for my Dad splurged on that suit for me....

"A double dip of Skoug's ice cream in a cone cost one buffalo nickel. Fenn's ice cream was the smoothest I ever encountered in a lifetime of aggressively searching out and eating all the ice cream I could find....

"Beyond this, memory flags and it's just as well....But I'll always remember the years at Washington High School as ones of important personal growth. All of us entered as big children and emerged as almost-adults, our characters largely formed for life.

"Affectionate good wishes to you all,

—Walt Simmons."

✦ ✦ ✦

Simmons was back in Sioux Falls in July 1977 for his 50th class reunion. That's the one that no one wants to miss.

He was on the Argus-Leader news staff from 1930 to 1942, as reporter, columnist and city editor.

His column appeared the last four years he was in Sioux Falls. Simmons went from the Argus to the Chicago Tribune and was assigned in 1944 as war correspondent in the Southwest Pacific.

After the war he was based in Tokyo as the Tribune's Far Eastern correspondent. He spent 10 years in Asia and reported the Korean War before returning to Chicago in 1955.

His later assignments with the Tribune included service as Sunday Magazine editor and Sunday editor.

He retired in 1973 and lives in Kenilworth, Ill.

THE LEPRECHAUN OF LAGUNA BEACH

Argus Leader, Feb. 17, 1980

The death of Hubbard Keavy at 77 last month in Laguna Beach, Calif., brings to mind some anecdotes about his reporting career which began in Sioux Falls in the early 1920s.

Keavy was a lifelong crafter of words. His emphasis on a brief, easy style of writing led years later to assignment as head of The Associated Press' campaign for better writing.

Keavy for 10 years starting in 1929 chronicled the ups and downs of Hollywood stars in a daily column for the AP. It was titled "Good News." He always liked the "good news" better than the other kind.

He became a confidante of movie greats and advised many fledgling stars who asked him what they could do to further their careers.

In 1939 he pleaded for a return to the news desk in the Los Angeles bureau. He became its chief in 1942 and directed news from that busy bureau for the next 25 years. He retired in 1967 and moved to Laguna Beach.

His newspaper career started at age 12 as a carrier boy for the Argus-Leader in Sioux Falls. Keavy was a graduate of Cathedral High School, the predecessor of O'Gorman, in Sioux Falls.

Hubbard Keavy.

Fred Christopherson, then managing editor of the Sioux Falls Press, hired Keavy as a reporter. He left the Press after 18 months for $2 more a week at the Argus-Leader. That brought his salary to $20 weekly.

Keavy's work at the Argus-Leader included reporting and writing a humor column. After about a year and a half he moved on in 1923 to Des Moines.

Keavy told Jerry Korbin, columnist of the Santa Ana Register, that the managing editor at Des Moines wasn't appreciative of his work and refused him a $5 raise.

Keavy, being a blithe spirit and with $100 in the bank, went to Milwaukee, then Cleveland, Toledo and Bloomington, Ill., where he wound up as managing editor of The Pantagraph.

Keavy wrote so many critical letters to the AP that the wire service hired him.

Keavy in the late 1950s was put in charge of the AP campaign to improve writing. He conducted seminars and wrote a booklet "Writing for the AP." More than 40,000 copies are in circulation. His writing style featured terseness. To him, that meant keep the copy short and easy to read.

In a sentimental visit to Sioux Falls in 1962—his first in 30 years—he renewed old acquaintances and was impressed by the city's growth.

He also enjoyed seeing the countryside and going to Waterville, Minn., where his mother once owned a farm. His mother is buried in Sioux Falls.

He kept up his interest in writing after retirement. He put together an occasional bulletin of news about AP alumni in a publication he called "Cleartime." He recounted the big stories and wartime experiences of many AP byliners, but was modest about his own happenings. He called himself "coordinator" instead of editor of Cleartime.

He contributed several articles to the Argus-Leader in 1976, including a St. Patrick's Day dispatch on his visit as a third-generation Irishman to the Emerald Isle.

That article was classic Keavy: interesting, tightly written and to the point. He dealt with the ramifications of Irish humor, which he found occasionally sly, "never cutting or sarcastic, nor does it ridicule. It is often absurd and preposterous, tongue-in-cheek satire. In a word, it is soft—and wonderful."

Keavy included several examples in his article, which, of course, was datelined LIMERICK, Ireland.

❖ ❖ ❖

Only an Irishman would have answered this way when I asked which of two hotels in a small town in County Galway was the better:

"It's like this, whichever one ye stay in ye'll wish it was the other."

Occasionally their humor is sly: when the landlord asked a tenant what his farm produced to the acre, the reply was: "In the summer it might raise enough to feed a hare, but in the winter she'd have to run for her life."

A classic example of the preposterous (as related by an Irishman whose job was to greet visiting journalists):

"When I went into a pub, the sun was shining and as I started to leave, these two Dublin guys came against me. I don't know what made me say it, but seeing a fine film of rain on their coats, I asked, 'Is it raining here?' And this fellow, who must have been waiting for years for someone like me to come along, answered: 'I don't know. I don't come from here.'"

No matter how often they've heard it, the Irish roar with laughter over this one:

Customs officer to old lady: "What have we here?"

"Only holy water."

"But it says '86 proof whisky!'"

"Holy Mother, another miracle!"

❖ ❖ ❖

Korbin called Keavy's long stint on the Hollywood daily column assignment "a great tribute to his cast-iron stomach as well as his ability to stomach actors...

"Several times I urged him to write a book about the behind-the-scenes stories which never made the wires—the off-beat tales he regaled us with during the past decade. 'I couldn't do that,' he said. 'Most of them were given to me off the record.'"

Keavy had a reputation in the AP for helping young writers develop their skills—an interest he retained virtually to the end of his two-year battle with cancer. He died Jan. 20.

Keavy encouraged Korbin's 17-year-old son, Jeffrey, in his ambition to become a humor writer. Despite a 60-year difference in their ages, they were on the same wave length.

Keavy and his wife, Jane, were the first to call with congratulations when Art Buchwald sent Jeffrey a check for a funny column idea.

Keavy also gave frequent tips to Korbin, who started his daily column several months ago. That figured, too, as a mark of Keavy's continuous quest for an interesting story.

Korbin wrote: "He came through with so many items, that many simply were attributed to The Leprechaun of Laguna Beach."

HOW A DAY IN S.F. CHANGED INDUSTRY'S COURSE

Argus Leader, Sunday, Jan. 11, 1981

"A Bad Day in Sioux Falls," related by Fortune in its Jan. 12 issue, tells in capsule form the national significance of a $2,500 contribution rejected 25 years ago by Sen. Francis Case of South Dakota.

That episode, of course, led to President Dwight Eisenhower's veto of a bill deregulating natural gas. Fortune's comment is carried with this article.

Case's action in going public with a questionable contribution sparked one of the biggest news stories Sioux Falls and the Argus Leader have experienced in modern times.

The incident involved the newspaper, then called The Daily Argus-Leader, and posed an ethical question that was promptly answered by the then publisher and editor-in-chief, John A. Kennedy, and the editor, Fred C. Christopherson.

The ethical question derived from the role of Ernest J. Kahler, then the paper's manager, and the newspaper's having supported editorially the deregulation of the natural gas industry a few days before the story hit the nation's front pages.

Unknown to Kennedy and Christopherson, Kahler had accepted $2,500 from a Nebraska lawyer, John M. Neff, to pass along to Case, who faced a re-election campaign that year.

The ethics question was quickly resolved when Kennedy announced Kahler had not acted for the newspaper.

The incident also brought a Senate investigation that the paper carried for weeks on its front pages. For the first time in the memory of Sioux Falls residents, two of its citizens were principals in a congressional investigation.

Case never called the proffered $2,500 contribution a bribe and he acknowledged that it was offered with no strings attached and he had first been inclined to accept the money for his campaign.

However, the amount was so much greater than the $5, $25 and $50 contributions the senator was accustomed to in $50,000 campaigns of those days that he told the Senate there must be "inordinate profits" for somebody in the bill. So he announced his vote against the bill.

The news story unfolded in stages. Christopherson told his friend, John Griffin of Lewis Drugs of Sioux Falls, that he wouldn't want to be the individual who had handled the money for Case. Griffin, who was area campaign chairman for Case, told Christopherson, "It might be closer to you than you think."

A few days later, Kahler announced the money had been left with him in his downstairs office (subsequently used by publishers) at the newspaper and he had later turned it over to Griffin at Case's request.

Griffin, Kahler and Neff were promptly subpoenaed by a special Senate committee.

Kennedy said he was "shocked at these disclosures" and said "Mr. Kahler has no authority to commit the Argus-Leader on any issue. His job is that of business manager. The policy question of the Argus-Leader is supervised by Fred. C. Christopherson, its editor.

"In connection with the Harris bill (to deregulate gas), Mr. Christopherson wrote that editorial favoring it with my approval.

"I am amazed that Mr. Kahler would accept unsolicited campaign contributions from a stranger at any time or any place while he is still an executive of the Argus-Leader."

Christopherson in a signed front page editorial a day later reiterated an editorial stand of a few days earlier saying all aspects of the incident should be made public.

Christopherson also wrote that the paper's stand on the natural gas bill was a reflection of the judgment of the editor. "Wrongly or rightly," Christopherson said, he had "always advocated a policy of opposition to governmental regulation of any phase of the economy unless it seemed absolutely essential."

Kennedy sent Christopherson to Washington to represent the newspaper and to testify in case that would be required. Christopherson, however, was never called to the stand. Kahler and Griffin did testify. Griffin produced the 25 $100 bills and turned the money over to the committee.

The investigation showed that the $2,500 donation came from the personal funds of Howard B. Keck, president of Superior Oil Co. in California, who passed them to Elmer Patman, a Washington lawyer. Patman had recently hired his friend, Neff, as a lobbyist in the Nebraska Legislature.

Neff subsequently was employed to help with passage of the natural gas bill in Congress. Neff in about four months covered five states and sought out the attitude of 10 U.S. senators on a single piece of legislation.

The report said, "A sum of $10,000 was at least considered and spoken of by Mr. Neff as a contribution and $5,000 of this was actually contributed. He exercised incredibly poor judgment. Mr. Patman was responsible for the direction of Mr Neff's activities and directed this activity either expressly or impliedly."

The Select Committee for Contribution Investigation found that there was neither a bribe nor an attempt to bribe Case, but condemned the attempt to influence a vote of a member of the U.S. Senate. There was no reflection by the committee on Case.

The committee severely censured Patman and Neff and said Keck could not escape responsibility for what the lawyers did with his money.

During an appearance in Sioux Falls that spring Case praised Kahler and Griffin for their integrity and their testimony before the committee.

Griffin said last week, "I still think Francis Case was the most honest politician I have ever known." Case died in office in 1962.

Both Griffin and Christopherson recall the front page news of 25 years ago vividly. Griffin said he couldn't remember what happened to the $2,500. A news story said the committee would return the money to Keck.

Christopherson said that when Griffin told him the incident was close to him, he thought it might be a lawyer whom Neff had contacted. It was really a big surprise, Christopherson said, that it was Kahler.

Neff had come to Sioux Falls to talk to friends of Case, and asked for Christopherson. However, he was in New Orleans for an editor's meeting so Neff saw Kahler.

Christopherson said, "Ernie was completely innocent." Kahler retired from the Argus-Leader in 1958 and later moved to Rapid City. He died in April 1979.

Neff, 72, retired about a year ago from his Lexington, Neb., law practice. "I have no comment to make," he said of Fortune's article, which he hadn't seen and didn't care to hear read to him—after the first paragraph. "I don't care to have my life ruined again."

Neff didn't lobby after the expose. "The big boys don't always tell the truth," he said.

As to Fortune's comment that if he had only gone to the race track instead of visiting Kahler, Neff said: "I never went to a race track in my life until a year ago."

The rejected $2,500 contribution would be small by today's campaign standards. But its telling embarrassed the U.S. Senate, changed the course of an industry and eventually resulted in tighter election laws for campaign contributions.

Two million dollar Senate campaigns in South Dakota followed 25 years after that "bad day in Sioux Falls."

A BAD DAY IN SIOUX FALLS

Argus Leader, Jan. 11, 1981

Editor's note: The following article by Daniel Seligman appeared in Fortune on Jan. 12 and is reprinted by permission Copyright 1981 Time Inc. All rights reserved.

The news about natural gas is suddenly rather good. There is apparently now a congressional majority for speeding up the decontrol of gas prices, and the prospect of decontrol has got the production totals rising, following years of shrinkage. In 1980, more than 15,000 gas wells were drilled in the U.S.—close to double the level of the mid-1970s. After a quarter-century of subsidizing consumption, penalizing production and guaranteeing that gas would be used wastefully, we may actually be recovering from the damage done by John M. Neff.

We are, in fact, approaching the 25th anniversary of the day on which Neff made his fateful move. It was on January 16, 1956, that he visited Ernest J. Kahler, business manager of the Sioux Falls Argus-Leader, then and now the leading publication in that South Dakota city. If only Neff had gone to the racetrack instead of visiting Kahler, the U.S. would have had a sensible natural gas policy all these years. Unluckily, however, there was and is no horse action in Sioux Falls.

In fairness to Neff, it must be said that his visit to the Argus-Leader offices was not the sole reason for our screwed-up gas policies. Some responsiblity also devolves upon the U.S. political establishment, including President Eisenhower and numerous members of Congress, many of whom appear to have suffered severe mental reversals upon learning of Neff's day in Sioux Falls.

What the man did was to leave 25 hundred dollar bills in Kahler's care. Kahler was a friend of U.S. Senator Francis Case, a South Dakota Republican, who was supposed to get the money—characterized as a "no strings attached" campaign contribution. Neff was working for Superior Oil, which liked Case because he was presumably supporting a bill to decontrol gas moving in interstate commerce. The bill was needed because the Supreme Court said the Federal Power Commission, which yearned to control gas prices, was free to do so.

What Superior hadn't counted on was the predilection of professional pols for the grandstand play. When Case learned that an oil company had given him green money, he announced the fact and then, turning his profile to the audience, said the episode proved there would be "inordinate profits" if that bill got through. Case's dramatics did not prevent the Senate from passing the bill, but by this time there was so much static about wickedness at the wellhead that Eisenhower felt obliged to deliver a veto.

So if you're wondering why we have uneconomically burned natural gas in industrial boilers all these years, it's because Ike felt that signing the bill would "risk creating doubt among the American people concerning the integrity of governmental processes." And because of that Thoroughbred shortage in Sioux Falls.

SDSU MISSES GETTING NO. 1

Argus Leader, March 29, 1981

Too bad South Dakota State University didn't have a new building to dedicate to President Ronald Reagan.

SDSU might have persuaded him to fly to South Dakota in May to be commencement speaker.

Like some other state institutions including the Argus Leader, South Dakota State University this year is celebrating its centennial.

SDSU kicked off its centennial with a Founders Day birthday party in February. The next big event will be commencement on May 9.

The centennial committee went right to the top. They tried to get Reagan as the speaker, but he had a schedule conflict.

In an earlier era, SDSC (it was a college then) had more success. President Calvin Coolidge dedicated the outdoor Coolidge Sylvan Theatre and Lincoln Memorial Library in 1927. That was the year Coolidge spent the summer in the Black Hills.

Candidate Dwight Eisenhower spoke from the Sylvan Theatre stage on the campaign trail in 1952 about a month before he was elected president.

Vice President Hubert Humphrey was commencement speaker on the same platform in 1967.

Humphrey and President Lyndon B. Johnson won big in South Dakota in 1964. In this case, however, SDSU wanted No. 2. The late Minnesota senator and former vice president attained the highest office ever won by a native South Dakotan.

Well, there's nothing like trying for No. 1.

Centennials come only once in 100 years—and if you can give them a top level presidential aura, so much the better.

Recognition of the roles of SDSU's presidents is an appropriate part of the centennial observance.

The first issue of a special SDSU Centennial newspaper features the school's history. The paper carries brief biographies and pictures of SDSU's 14 presidents.

Hilton M. Briggs had the longest service—more than 17 years until 1975 when he was succeeded by President Sherwood Berg.

Charles W. Pugsley, who served from 1923 to 1940 had the second longest tenure, also 17 years.

George L. Brown, beloved dean of men and several times acting president, had the shortest term. He was appointed president for a brief time in 1940, at age 70, to recognize his long service.

Briggs, who is president emeritus, and David Pearson, who is vice president for administration professor of economics emeritus, are the leaders of centennial activities at the Brookings campus. They have the help of a 22-member steering committee.

Special events are planned for summer and fall, to be climaxed by a centennial theme for Hobo Day.

◆ ◆ ◆

This week's Argus Leader comic section marks a milestone for the newspaper. The comics were printed on the Argus Leader's offset press—a first for the newspaper in producing its own Sunday color comic section.

Production personnel prepared the pasteups from progressive proofs supplied by the syndicates from which the Argus Leader buys its comics.

There are four proofs—one each for black and red, yellow and blue for the three primary colors. This results in four press plates for each page.

Printers, engravers and press personnel at the paper took considerable pride in the effort. It followed a test run made several months ago.

This weekend's section and the one for next Sunday were printed on Friday night, March 20. Previously, the Argus Leader contracted for printing the section at a specialty plant in Buffalo, NY.

✦ ✦ ✦

KELO-Land TV has a memorable weekend too, in a different facet of communication history. The station dedicated its new earth receiving station late Friday afternoon, ushering in a new era of satellite communications for South Dakota's pioneer TV outlet.

Congratulations, Joe Floyd, Evans Nord, Joe Floyd the younger and staff of Midcontinent Broadcasting Co.

KELO has used the facility in recent weeks to transmit news stories from Washington. Its first extended program use was set for this weekend for reception of the Pat Boone and Marvin Hamlisch Easter Seal telethon.

KELO's dish antenna pointed skyward from 13th Street and 1st Avenue is one more sophisticated step in communication. It's the same principle as the EROS Data Center's antenna at the facility 11 miles northeast of Sioux Falls.

EROS' dish antenna began operation in February 1979. It receives digital (numbered) data for the center's simulated aerial photographs.

Cameras on Landsat satellites high in space transmit the data to ground stations in California, Maryland and Alaska. The next step is transmission to the Goddard Space Flight Center in Maryland. After some preprocessing, the material is transmitted via the domestic satellite system to EROS' antenna in Sioux Falls.

The original concept was for the EROS data center to receive direct transmissions from Landsat satellites. In practice, the intermediate steps have proved more feasible.

"EXTRA"—AN UNCOMMON OCCURANCE

Argus Leader, Sunday, May 17, 1981

Wednesday, the day that Pope John Paul II was shot, was an eventful one in the Argus Leader building.

The newspaper published its first extra in many years. That became an exciting event in itself.

It was also the first extra since the Argus Leader switched to morning publication in July 1979. Normal publication time was about 13 hours away—early Thursday morning.

The assassination attempt in Rome made everyone from Publisher Larry Fuller through the ranks in the newsroom, circulation and production departments think about the challenge of publishing an extra.

In the process, our newspaper people subordinated their own feelings of grief and concern about the pope to the task at hand.

It was quickly done.

The shooting in Rome occurred at 10:25 a.m. CDT. The news story started as a trickle on the video display tubes—which have replaced teletypes and typewriters in the Argus Leader newsroom—and grew to a flood as the details of the shooting poured in.

Fuller was informed promptly. Editors Joe Novotny and Jeff Thomas started working on an extra with the understanding it might end up only as an interesting newsroom experiment.

There was a major difference, however, from the shooting of President Ronald Reagan on Monday afternoon, March 30.

The attempt against the pope happened in the morning, Sioux Falls time. The basic facts about the shooting in St. Peter's square became known more quickly than the circumstances about Reagan and the other three persons who were wounded outside the Washington Hilton Hotel.

In midafternoon on March 30, there was contradictory information about whether Reagan was wounded, whether press secretary Jim Brady had died (fortunately, he is recovering), etc.

What started as an experiment in watching an unfolding story in Rome of another assassination attempt against a famous person quickly became a mission for the Argus Leader: to publish an extra.

William Bogert, production director, quickly shifted his day crew in the composing room into preparing for the extra and called in a press crew. Gary Ruhberg, circulation director, needed paper sellers. Several reporters, a photographer and a couple editors volunteered.

Originally, the plan for the extra was simply to replace the top story from Wednesday's paper with the story from Rome about the pope.

However, The Associated Press wire brought so many stories so quickly that news editors were able to develop a completely new front page, including a story about Sioux Falls children praying for the pope.

The extra was off the press at 12:45 p.m.

Ruhberg sent his selling force of about 20 persons—newsroom staffers and people from the circulation department—to downtown streets, shopping centers and two of the hospitals. They enjoyed it—and purchasers were interested.

Fuller had high praise for Argus Leader employees in a memo the next day. He praised their "professionalism and spirit." He said the extra "was an important part of our commitment to provide people in South Dakota information as fast and accurately as we can."

The extra sold about 2,000 copies—not a profit, but not a large expense, either. The extra edition was 10 pages—the new front page, a madeover page 2A plus the rest of Wednesday morning's section A.

It was the kind of experience that afternoon newspapers frequently experienced until the era after World War II, when extras became less and less frequent.

✦ ✦ ✦

The Argus Leader's last extra, published on an impromptu basis, was on Sunday morning July 26, 1953, when Gen. Mark Clark, the supreme United Nations commander in the Korean War, obtained an armistice from the Communists.

The regular Sunday morning edition had been printed when The Associated Press in Minneapolis called the paper's editor, Fred C. Christopherson, and told him the news story announcing the armistice would move at 3 a.m. Sioux Falls time. He decided to publish an extra.

A small staff, including this writer, was quickly assembled. The extra carried the details of the armistice agreement under a headline: KOREAN WAR WILL END MONDAY.

There were also several extras published during the nights of general elections in the early 1960s to provide morning service, but those were scheduled well in advance and did not stem from unexpected events.

One of the most memorable Argus Leader extras of the last half century was published Sunday evening, Dec. 7, 1941—to chronicle the Japanese attack on Pearl Harbor. The extra had eight pages—a new front page and page two about the attack, plus six other pages from that Sunday morning's regular edition.

Other World War II extras included one June 6, 1944, when Gen. Dwight Eisenhower launched the invasion of Normandy, and Aug. 14, 1945, when President Harry S. Truman announced that the Japanese had accepted unconditional surrender terms.

Christopherson said that extras were a common occurrence for the Argus Leader and its onetime morning competitor, the Sioux Falls Press, before the advent of radio and television. (The Press ceased publication in 1928).

The Press published an extra and scooped the Argus Leader Nov. 11, 1918, when the World War I armistice was signed. Both papers knew the armistice was coming and took precautions to watch the single Associated Press wire into the city.

The Argus Leader and Press pressrooms were practically back to back across the alley from today's city hall. The Press used a buzzer system to tell its pressmen to change plates. Argus Leader editors had someone watching the Press building about 2 o'clock in the morning to let them know if anything happened. Unfortunately, the Argus' spy fell asleep—and no one woke him up.

Christopherson was in military service at the time. His friends on the Press, for which he worked before joining the Argus Leader, told him about their scoop when he returned from the war. It became a legend in Sioux Falls newspaper circles.

❖ ❖ ❖

There simply aren't any national statistics available about publication of extras during the years since World War II. The Audit Bureau of Circulation, a newspaper industry organization, didn't have any. Neither did the American Newspaper Publishers Association.

A spokeswoman for the latter organization said the Fort Myers, Fla., News Press published an extra in January when the hostages were released and another one when Reagan was shot.

The Bakersfield Californian printed an extra about the shooting of Reagan. Cocoa Today, which serves Cape Canaveral, Fla., published an extra on Sunday, April 12, after the space shuttle Columbia lifted off at 7 a.m.

According to a Gannett Co. spokeswoman in Rochester, N.Y., the Huntington, W. Va., Herald-Dispatch and the Idaho Statesman of Boise also published extras for the hostage release. The Herald-Dispatch issued an extra on the shooting of Reagan. The Burlington, Vt., Free Press printed an extra on the pope.

The Chillicothe, Ohio, Gazette published a Reagan extra.

Professor Ed Emery of the School of Journalism at the University of Minnesota recalled his reporting days in California when Los Angeles papers published extras about tennis great Bill Tilden winning the Davis cup.

Emery also recalled the old San Francisco News, an afternoon paper, getting an extra on the streets the day President Franklin Delano Roosevelt died at Warm Springs, Ga. That was April 12, 1945. Emery worked for United Press at the time. California papers, of course, have always had an advantage in being in the Pacific time zone.

The News fed the UP bulletins directly to the composing room—a practice the Argus Leader and many other daily papers followed in the days of Linotypes.

It's different now. Editors press a button on their video display tubes to convert news stories into type much faster than before—thanks to computers and a new generation of typesetters.

There's no longer any paper copy to rip off a teletype machine. Reporters and editors see the story on the tube's screen.

The methods have changed—but the thrill of an extra brings the same kind of excitement today that it did in an earlier era.

My own hunch is that extras will continue to be few and far between. Our friendly competitors in radio and television day in and day out long ago took over immediate coverage that once was provided by the extra.

But extraordinary events, involving world leaders or governments or the appeal of a space shuttle mission to a particular locale, likely will inspire newspapers to produce a few more extras in the near future than in the past.

"CHRIS" WATCHED, GUIDED CITY THROUGH 93 YEARS OF CHANGE

Argus Leader, Friday, June 16, 1989

Fred C. Christopherson.

Fred C. Christopherson saw many changes in his lifetime, but he seemed to change little as the years rolled by.

"Chris," as everyone knew him, was bald, slightly plump and liked his pipe and a martini before dinner. He enjoyed excellent health; nearly all his 93 years were good ones.

Chris wrote as he talked: calmly.

He was an extemporaneous speaker and easily chaired news conferences for headliners such as Adlai Stevenson or meetings of the South Dakota Press Association, of which he was president.

Christopherson was a sharp observer of the local, state and world scene. As editor of the Argus Leader for 33 years, he translated that interest into hot pursuit of stories and thousands of daily editorials.

He marshaled editors and reporters to cover breaking stories in The Front Page tradition.

He prodded reluctant public boards into telling more than they wanted. He visited daily with Phillips and Main Avenue friends over coffee. He and they were Sioux Falls' movers and shakers.

He was a Republican and espoused generally conservative economic policies. During the 1930s, he assailed many of President Roosevelt's New Deal programs.

But on trips to Washington, he wrote in a friendly vein about FDR and his press conferences. When Roosevelt died in wartime in 1945, Christopherson hailed his leadership, saying the commander-in-chief had sacrificed his life like a soldier for his country.

He covered Soviet Premier Nikita Khrushchev in Iowa in 1959. When big news broke, such as the "Baby Face" Nelson gang's bank robbery in 1933 and the New Year's Eve powderhouse explosion in 1936, Chris was in the newsroom.

Christopherson and Yeager, London, 1971.

His editorials spurred change and debate. Readers often disagreed with him, it took several bond issues before Sioux Falls finally approved the Arena, which he favored.

Chris was an active participant in civic affairs. He liked to write about and encourage the city's spectacular growth following World War II.

As editor and publisher of the Sioux Falls Press during the 1920s, he competed with the Argus Leader. The Press, Sioux Falls' pioneer morning paper, suspended publication in 1928. He then joined the Argus Leader at the invitation of Charles M. Day, editor and principal owner.

Christopherson sought to focus on news that was interesting and vital to Argus readers. During his editorship, the Argus usually carried two banner headlines across page one. He told his staff members that at least one of the two main articles had to be about a local or state story.

He and his wife, Marie, who was his inseparable companion until her death Jan. 25, enjoyed traveling in South Dakota, visiting Washington and touring the world. Their travels became topics of innumerable "Notebooks," which he continued as contributing editor for 11 years following his 1961 retirement.

Christopherson, born in 1896, saw the vast political and technological changes of this century.

He was a star high school baseball player in his hometown of Toronto. He was an Army pilot in World War I, and learned to fly a plane before he drove a car.

His newsrooms were in the era of typewriters, copy paper, editors' blue pencils and Linotype machines that put stories into type. He found today's newsroom with video display terminals and other electronic changes vastly different.

Throughout his lifetime, Chris considered the world his oyster. News was his passion.

❖ ❖ ❖

Anson Yeager, Argus Leader executive editor from 1961 to 1978 and associate editor until 1984, was hired by Christopherson in 1947.

PHOTO KEEPS WINNING HONORS

Ann Grauvogl, Argus Leader, Saturday, June 15, 1996

Photographer Ray Mews doesn't get too excited that the New York Times Magazine chose his photograph of a Vietnam vet returning home as part of its celebration of 100 years of pictures.

"It was all right," he says of the latest honor for the Aug. 13, 1966, photograph shot in Sioux Falls.

But the former Argus Leader photographer is used to honors for the picture of Marine Lance Cpl. Perry Shinneman embracing his wife, Shirley, crutch fallen at his side, as he returns from war.

The picture is in the Eastman Kodak museum and was a finalist for the Pulitzer. It won awards from Sigma Delta Chi and was named the National Press Photographers Association picture of the year.

"I think it'll live on forever," Mews says from his home in Hawaii. It's a striking photo that tells the entire story as soon as people see it, he says.

Ray Mews.

The New York Times Magazine published its picture essay as part of the 100th anniversary of Adolph S. Ochs' purchase of the newspaper.

A century ago, "there was little, even in the giant newspapers, in the way of music—the photographs that convey the beat, rhythm and thrill of the news," the magazine reports. Ochs invented the Sunday magazine to marry writing and photography. The magazine celebrated that marriage in its June 9 issue when it ran 68 photographs, chosen to reflect changes in news and visual taste.

From a canine courier in World War I and Jewish men, women and children lined up for execution in World War II to portraits of celebrities such as Denzel Washington, Barbra Streisand and Mark Twain, the magazine takes a look at the last century.

"The history of photojournalism over the past 100 years is the history of photographers learning to say more than simply This Is What It Looked Like," magazine photo editor Kathy Ryan writes.

New technology has given photographers more freedom and more choices, she writes. But the real change is in photographers who now say, through their pictures. "This Is How I Saw It. They're able to accomplish this because they see what others don't."

Mews told the magazine he shot four or five frames as Shinneman crossed the tarmac: "When he got to his wife, his crutch suddenly fell as he reached out to embrace her. I knew that was the image."

As he developed the film that night, the AP photographer working next to him said: "You've got something here."

Mews says he's worked on bigger stories since taking his most celebrated photos, including the Fisher quintuplets and the accident that opened up the side of Flight 811. "But you don't come across one of those photos every day."

Prize-winning photo — Perry and Shirley Shinneman

CHRISTMAS NOSTALGIA

REFLECTION ON A BYGONE CHRISTMAS ERA
Some western S.D. families spent yuletide in wagons while watching flocks

Argus Leader, Sunday, Dec. 20, 1981

This is the week that the nation goes home for Christmas.

Flyover people bound inland from the coasts have no trouble spotting lonely lights in the mountains of the West or the hills of Appalachia from 30,000 feet.

However, airline passengers miss a close glimpse of the countryside and Christmas lights until they land at Joe Foss Field or other airports which are the last stops before home.

Families who take the Interstate miss the Christmas decorations on South Dakota main streets. Travelers whose routes are on other highways have the best opportunity to see hometown U.S.A. in Yule dress.

So do bus passengers. Their Jackrabbit Greyhound or other coaches usually take them into a city or town.

If your car or bus windows aren't frosted over, you can see America getting ready for Christmas from town's edge to city center.

Street decorations, store windows wrapped up like gift packages and colored lights on homes, in windows or yard displays herald the Christmas season.

South Dakota during the last week has had subzero weather, snow and icy breath to match.

❖ ❖ ❖

The week conjures memories of Christmases past and a bygone era—like the sheepwagon in which herders, sometimes with families, watched their flocks on rangeland in northwestern South Dakota.

Some of my boyhood friends spent Christmas in the early 1930s in a sheep wagon, sometimes at their ranch buildings and sometimes not. Christmas was a good time for variety in the menu—a switch from mutton to beef.

On a cold winter night, KFYR in Bismarck, WNAX in Yankton and a Mexican station across the Rio Grande from Del Rio, Texas, came booming into the Zenith or other battery-operated radio in the wagon.

The Christmas season moderated December's chill in a sheepwagon. Visiting a sheep camp was more fun on a warm summer day when boys could go swimming in the Moreau River in Perkins County.

A sheep wagon had a bunk across the back, cupboards, a kitchen stove for wood or coal that doubled as a heater and a white canvas top. The stovepipe protruded from the top of the canvas. There was a door on the front and a window in the back. The table was hinged to the bed and there was room underneath to stow a herder's gear.

There were many sheepwagons in western South Dakota as late as the 1930s and into the 1940s. They have long since all but disappeared.

Part of the reason is that herds are not as large—a herder often looked after a couple thousand head. Another reason is that sheep now run entirely on fenced range. Western South Dakota sheep growers years ago turned to sheds for lambing, a better idea than nursemaiding ewes and their offspring in tiny tents on the range.

Jim Thompson, extension livestock specialist in Rapid City, hasn't seen an oldstyle sheep wagon in actual use in western South Dakota, but has observed a few sitting around a ranch.

He says there are more likely to be sheep wagons in Wyoming and Montana, where herds are larger and the range is more open. Even so, today's sheep wagons are a different type.

Mobile quarters for a sheepherder in Wyoming or Montana are towed trailers. They come with gas stove, refrigerator and other comforts of today's recreational vehicle age.

Sheep numbers have changed, too. There are 810,000 sheep in the state, down from 20 years ago when there were more than 1,200,000. Numbers declined in the 60s and 70s.

South Dakota has enjoyed a slight increase in sheep numbers in the last two years and today has about 6 percent of the U.S. total. Texas, California and Wyoming are the top three sheep states. South Dakota moved ahead of Utah and is now tied with Colorado for No. 4.

I don't know whether any American museum has a western sheepwagon—but I hope so.

❖ ❖ ❖

Skiers should be happy about the snow. And if you want ultimate winter happiness and driving comfort, try a Saab or a Mercedes Benz.

Seat warmers have been standard equipment on Saabs since 1979. The electric heaters are thermostat controlled, come on with your ignition switch and provide warm front seats to a maximum of 80 degrees, when the heaters shut off.

Saabs are made in Sweden. Swedes, of course, have centuries of savvy in making cold weather tolerable.

Mercedes Benz, a West German make, offers heated front seats as an option at $180 each for the driver and front passenger seats, or $360 for the back seat.

You can program your Mercedes Benz seat heaters with the radio. Instructions fed into your radio on a 380 SL roadster will start your seat heaters, your car engine and do all kinds of interesting things.

As a onetime colleague, ski enthusiast and Saab owner told me Friday, his bun heater is a comfort in weather like South Dakota's.

Some inventor, I believe, should try for a limited, affluent market with portable bun heaters for skiers, sheepherders and well diggers, whose posteriors we all know are as cold as can be.

Merry Christmas!

CHRISTMAS AND OTHER MAIL

Argus Leader, Sunday, Dec. 27, 1981

Happiness after Christmas is not having to worry about mailing cards after Dec. 25. You can keep score on your family's revised mailing list—and also on the U.S. Postal Service.

How much money does a postal worker in Aberdeen save the system when he stamps a Christmas card envelope "Return to sender, no such number?" The address, so help me, was one digit off—probably three houses from one block to the next.

The same mail man undoubtedly delivers to both blocks—and as the Mrs. told me, he would know the name of our addressee as a longtime resident of Aberdeen.

I quickly agreed that this was darned foolishness—and something that she should take up with the Aberdeen postmaster or his general in Washington. After all, it takes 20 cents to mail the card again. And why can't the Postal Service look up the addressee?

However, I had a second thought about raising a fuss—thanks to the courtesy of someone in the Sioux Falls Post Office.

The Christmas card from cousin Ole in Norway arrived at our house despite a Sioux Falls Post Office stamp that originally was checked "No such number." The number was 20 blocks off the right address for our house. The envelope was also stamped, "Return to sender," which was scratched out.

Fortunately, someone in that busy Federal Building at 12th Street and 2nd Avenue took a second glance at the envelope, looked us up and stamped it "Directory service given."

Maybe the Norwegian stamps did it, or a holiday impulse by a mail handler to make delivery without sending it back to Norway. Ole pays more to mail a letter than we do. And it arrived before Christmas!

Thanks very much, Sioux Falls.

◆ ◆ ◆

POTPOURRI: Random observation about things that come in the mail:

• It must be loss of face. Every biographical sketch or personal history that I've seen in publicity about Japanese government leaders or businessmen recently jumps from the mid 1930s to about 1947 or 1948. There is no mention of where they were during World War II. Japanese Army? Navy? Kamikaze Corps? The gap between graduation from a college and a civilian job is very conspicuous. They lost the shooting war, but they're doing very well in the trade battle.

• The ingenious Chinese on Taiwan (Republic of China) have developed a system to transfer Chinese calligraphy to computers. After 10 years of research and experimentation, a system that can digest complex Chinese characters is ready to be marketed. Our alphabet has 26 characters; the Chinese language has some 50,000 words with about 10,000 in common circulation. The first computer system will handle about 30,000 characters; the entire 30,000 character vocabulary should be coded within the next few years.

• It's not gasohol in the Philippine Islands—it's "cocodiesel." It's a mixture of 80 percent coconut oil and 20 percent diesel oil, used in Filipino government vehicles. It takes advantage of low coconut and high oil prices.

Happy New Year!

IT'S TIME FOR FAMILY, HOME AND CHURCH

Argus Leader, Dec. 21, 1985

Today's column is a compilation of selections from several of the writer's Christmas columns of recent years.

◆ ◆ ◆

Christmas present and Christmas past blend into a happy collage of memories for older Americans and excitement for the youngsters. For many South Dakotans those memories have wide variety, reaching two or three generations back to life on the frontier in Dakota Territory and only one generation to the tough times of the 1930s and World War II.

Christian missionaries of several persuasions—Catholic, Episcopal and Presbyterian were the main ones—brought the white man's Christmas to South Dakota Indian reservations.

Army families at frontier posts up and down the Missouri River in the Dakotas and Nebraska celebrated Christmas with the young, unattached cavalrymen and infantrymen—the GIs of their times.

Cowboys on large ranching spreads in the western half of South Dakota saddled up for a half day's ride or more for Christmas dinner at the main ranch. That was long before the Model T, dirt roads and Detroit V-8 pickups that carry the modern cowboy's saddlehorse.

Christmas in east river South Dakota in pioneer and early statehood days had more amenities. This came mainly from settlement by farmers and townspeople in communities bound together by ambitious railroads anxious to build a new economic empire on the Plains.

Most South Dakotans have ties to farms or small towns in this or other states. Their observance of Christmas becomes a blend of family custom with modern nuances brought by television and other gadgets of more affluent times.

This is the week that the nation goes home for Christmas. Flyover people bound inland from the coasts have no trouble spotting lonely lights in the mountains of the West or the hills of Appalachia from 30,000 feet.

However, airline passengers miss a close glimpse of the countryside and Christmas lights until they land at Joe Foss Field or other airports which are the last stops before home.

Families who take the Interstate miss the Christmas decorations on South Dakota main streets. Travelers whose routes are on other highways have the best opportunity to see hometown U.S.A. in Yule dress.

So do bus passengers. Their Jackrabbit, Greyhound or other coaches usually take them into a city or town.

If your car or bus windows aren't frosted over, you can see America getting ready for Christmas from town's edge to city center.

Street decorations, store windows wrapped up like gift packages and colored lights on homes, in windows or yard displays herald the Christmas season.

Have you ever noticed how stately and comfortable Sioux Falls evergreens look when they're the centerpieces of snowdrifts in city parks or homeowners' lawns?

And how bright the reds and greens are in Christmas decorations downtown and in shopping malls and centers around the city?

Christmas trees, red bells and other lighted decorations framed in home picture windows offer cameo glimpses of Yuletide.

In yesteryear as today, Christmas is family, home and church. Some of the fixtures are different, but the idea is the same.

It comes from the Prince of Peace and his love for fellow man. Americans of all creeds or none at all demonstrate their affection for relatives, friends and occasionally a stranger at Christmastime.

Merry Christmas!

CHRISTMAS SEASON TAKES US BACK TO ONE-ROOM SCHOOLS

Argus Leader, Dec. 20, 1986

Christmas is the season when South Dakota senior citizens turn on memory's tape recorder.

Many of us will recall with fondness the one-room rural school's Christmas program of yesteryear. The one-room school has vanished from the South Dakota scene and with it the one-room Christmas program.

It was a climactic event for all the boys and girls. It was also a labor of love for the school teacher, customarily called the school ma'am.

Christmas skits, poems and songs were prepared with care. Nearly every youngster in the school—from grade one through eight—had an individual part.

The teacher made arrangements for a school patron or acquaintance to play Santa Claus. Older students found it a challenge to penetrate his cover—and tell some of their classmates that Santa Claus was really their neighbor.

His "Ho, ho, ho" was usually a dead giveaway to the older kids, but the youngsters who still believed in him were more interested in seeing the jolly old gent than discovering his identity.

Amidst the squeals of youngsters in the primary grades, some of the neighbors commented to each other that Santa needed only one pillow around his middle instead of two he'd worn the year before.

Santa appeared for the climax of the school program with a big sack of candy treats and popcorn. The proprietor of the country store donated the candy.

Pupils exchanged gifts from names they had drawn early in December. Their homemade gifts were practical and fit the tough times of the 1930s.

Today's school children have neat Christmas programs whose teachers devote the same kind of care and attention that yesteryear's school ma'am gave to the event. But it's not quite the same for today's senior citizens who were school children in the country half a century ago.

Memory triggers a vivid recollection of one school program. It was a cold, snowy night several days before Christmas. There was a star on the Christmas tree and a warm stove in the schoolhouse. It was packed with parents, toddlers, grandparents and friends.

One of the neighbors—a lady who had a beautiful voice—usually sang several carols for every Christmas program. Her rendition of "Silent Night" that year left many moist eyes in the schoolroom.

Parents that night watched their youngsters perform with the same kind of pride and happiness that today's parents see mirrored in the eyes of children at Christmas school events this month.

Yesterday's child has long since become today's parent or grandparent and finds the role change enjoyable.

✦ ✦ ✦

There's a sequel to this story. Maurine, South Dakota's Red Top School of the past, is gone. Its site today is just a wide spot two miles west of Maurine alongside Highway 212. Happily, there's a successor to Red Top in a two-room school at Maurine.

Many other South Dakota one-room schools have also vanished. A few remain—boarded up against the weather, and never to be used again. If walls could talk, there would be reminiscing about Christmases past and what happened to the youngsters who played in the schoolyard so long ago.

Local and former residents in South Dakota's countryside know where their old schools were located. They think about school days and the good times when they pass the site. These passersby recall Christmases past the way many younger people someday will think about Christmas 1986.

Merry Christmas!

CHRISTMAS PRESENT MORE ENJOYABLE THAN CHRISTMASES PAST

Argus Leader, Dec. 19, 1987

Christmas present or Christmas past?
What's your choice?

You can't have one without the other. This Christmas will be the sum of Christmases past and present.

It's a season when nostalgia, sentiment and the ties that bind kith and kin make nearly everyone more tolerant of fellow man.

For adults, there are recollections of Christmases past that start memory's data bank rolling.

For children, these are the days of anticipation before Christmas. Waiting is half the fun.

For young parents of small children, there are new experiences ahead.

The prelude to Christmas puts a heavy burden on many parents, particularly mothers, in ensuring a happy time for a family. But who complains about shopping? Or spending to provide gifts for loved ones?

Generosity by the giver cannot be measured by price tags. Families give to their own what they can afford. But more importantly, they give part of themselves.

Some of us are lucky enough to have direct links to European Christmas customs. It's nice to remember how a parent or grandparent recalled Christmases past in the old country.

Other Americans also have links to Europe in Christmas cookie, candy or meal recipes passed down in the family.

The Americanization of Christmas is sometimes attacked as being too commercial. But the motive in giving is unselfish. There's no difference from one generation to the next in what prompts generosity. Gifts have changed with the times.

The writer recalls one Christmas in the early 1930s in western South Dakota. My grandfather, who had been a cabinet maker in Norway, made skis for me and a younger brother.

The skis had a hand-carved Viking emblem at the tip, and a leather strap in the middle for overshoes. All they cost were four pieces of new lumber and Grandpa's time. It was a labor of love.

My brother and I enjoyed making ski trails in the yard and on hillsides in the pasture. The skis were much simpler than today's sleek skis, bindings and boots that my children use on elaborately built ski runs.

Christmas fun for a boy on a ranch in the 1930s sooner or later involved a new .22 caliber rifle and a box of shells. There was time to hunt cottontails or jackrabbits during Christmas vacation.

Today, thanks to television and general economic well-being, Americans can enjoy football, basketball and countless other diversions. Many older South Dakotans flee south or overseas to enjoy flowers and sunshine at Christmas time.

One of the great sights of today's America is seeing young servicemen and women flying home in peacetime to visit loved ones. You can catch the excitement of these reunions at Joe Foss Field almost anytime now in the days before Christmas. You may hear someone say, "I was lucky to get on."

These comments remind the writer of jam-packed passenger trains in the U.S. during World War II. Nearly every male passenger was in uniform; many young mothers with a baby or a toddler were headed home or to their GI's camp for Christmas. They, too, were lucky to get a seat.

Like yesterday, family, home and church take key roles at Christmastime on the Northern Plains. South Dakotans and their neighbors enjoy the warmth of home and hosting relatives and friends.

And they are renewed each year by regular and special services in their churches.

They see a reflection of themselves, their children or grandchildren in the faces of youngsters in a choir or Christmas pageant.

They listen anew to the story of the babe born in a manger in Bethlehem, and his message of love and thoughtfulness for fellow man that made him the savior of much of the world.

It's a heart-warming feeling to drive home from church after singing "Silent Night" on Christmas Eve and see the lights of Sioux Falls.

Christmases past are nice, but the one to enjoy is Christmas present.

CHRISTMAS TRADITIONS LIVE ON TODAY DESPITE SUBTLE CHANGES

Argus Leader, Sunday, Dec. 25, 1988

Christmas past, Christmas present, Christmas future. The first two are a part of the thinking of most adults. Future Christmases evoke little thought, mainly because the current Christmas demands all our attention. Nonetheless, a senior citizen should be excused for pondering the shape of Christmases to come. Will Christmas in South Dakota during the 21st century resemble our contemporary Christmas?

Hopefully, church services and emphasis upon family will be much the same. School programs have changed through the years. This stems partly from consolidation and, to a lesser extent, from constraints placed on schools to keep religious themes out.

South Dakotans who attended one-room schools fondly remember programs of Christmas past. There were skits and songs that gave most children an opportunity to recite. Santa Claus appeared for the finale, shouting a merry "Ho, ho, ho" and distributing small sacks of candy and nuts often donated by the owner of the area's general store. There was an unspoken pact among seventh- and eighth-graders not to reveal Santa Claus' identity to younger children. But occasionally, Santa's familiar voice gave him away.

Some parts of the one-room school program, of course, have been transferred to today's Christmas programs. But they're not the same as yesteryear in rural areas.

During drought and depression years in western South Dakota, farm and ranch families made the most of simple gifts. Gifts have changed with better times and electronic technology. Who knows how sophisticated gifts for children may become by the year 2000?

South Dakota rural families probably will travel farther to church for Christmas services in the next century. More South Dakotans will be living in cities.

Jesus Christ never had a Christmas tree. He never saw printed advertisements or watched a TV program. He never heard a radio. Nevertheless, his precepts fit today's times as well as those of Biblical days.

He surely would not object to Americans' thoughtfulness and love for family and children, as shown by gift-giving at Christmastime. His message of love and consideration for fellow man has survived to this day. It will be a part of tomorrow, too.

CHRISTMAS MEMORIES AMONG OLDER SET ARE FOND

Argus Leader, Sunday, Dec. 24, 1989

Christmas is a skein of memories that warm the heart and make home the place to be for this holiday.

CHRISTMAS NOSTALGIA

Someone has said, "Christmas is for the young." So it is.

But it is also for the old among us, whose memory bank spans several generations.

These senior citizens see Christmas in the eyes of children at school or church programs. They also see themselves, when they were young in South Dakota and homesteading and frontier days were much closer in time than now.

South Dakotans with a farm or ranch background can recall the country school at Christmastime, when children in grades 1 through 8 staged their Christmas program. Parents, grandparents and many neighbors showed up to see the kids play parts carefully assigned by the teacher. Santa Claus arrived with a "Ho- ho-ho" and candy for the kids as the night's finale.

Country church on Christmas Day was special, with sermons devoted to "peace on earth, good will toward men." "Silent Night" and other carols made everyone feel at peace with the world and themselves.

There were some Christmases in ranching country when the landscape was brown and temperatures were on the balmy side. But the Christmas of memory usually has snow cover, lights in the window and a plume of smoke rising from the chimney.

College days produced another set of Christmas memories, with trips of several hundred miles across the state from campus to home. Half a dozen of us piled into a Chevie four-door sedan and endured the trip from Brookings to Faith. There was usually a lunch stop at Miller. That was long before highway bypasses. You got to see Christmas decorations on every Main Street along the way. Today, most small town main streets still reflect cheer at Christmastime. Sadly, many once thriving towns have sunk into oblivion.

Every journey home conjures thoughts of yesterday's neighbors and the smaller ranches and farms that have disappeared in the changing economy of South Dakota. Nevertheless, one should be optimistic about South Dakota and its future.

Surely, our wide open spaces, our comparatively small population and the need for food that South Dakotans produce so well can be used to advantage in tomorrow's world. Today's computers and communications make doing business in South Dakota easier than ever.

Sixty years ago children found under their Christmas trees books of fiction (like the X Bar X boys in the West or the Bobbsey twins) and biographies, like one on Charles Lindbergh, the Lone Eagle. His solo crossing of the Atlantic in 1927 opened the aviation age to stunning development.

Changes since Lindbergh's trailblazing have been profound. Jet planes have shrunk the world. The United States has landed men on the moon and brought them back. There's more to come.

Today, electronic gadgetry makes toys better than ever. Nintendo games from Japan hype the interest. They're so good that congressmen (shame on them) are talking about a law to limit imports.

But the biggest change at Christmas time is the prospect that eastern Europe and its people will be drawn into friendly trade links with the West, that barriers to political and religious freedom will come down and the United States and Soviet Union will really end the Cold War.

This veteran of World War II and the Korean War finds today's news from Europe almost unbelievable. May it continue in that vein.

Smile at your minister today. Who else remembers you and your family, remembers the sick, and preached love and understanding before it became internationally acceptable? And savor your Christmas carols. "Peace on earth, good will toward men" has its best chance of fruition in years.

IT'S TIME TO SORT MEMORIES OF CHRISTMASES IN S.D. PAST

Argus Leader, Sunday, Dec. 19, 1993

This is the week that South Dakotans sort out their individual skeins of Christmas memories.

Family, home, school and church are the threads that tie together recollections of Christmases past.

One of my most memorable Christmases was in the early 1930s when my Norwegian grandfather built skis for me and a younger brother. Each ski carried a carefully carved Viking symbol at the tip. Yes, there was snow Christmas Day.

Grandfather and Great Uncle talked once in a while about their home area in Norway: Roykenvik and Brandbu alongside the Randsfjord about 35 miles north of Oslo. The region is hilly and covered with evergreens. Skiing has been part of Norwegian life for hundreds of years. No residents of that region then could have foreseen that in 1994 the Winter Olympics would be held in Lillehammer, only 50 miles north of Brandbu.

Books and clothing were the usual Christmas presents for many South Dakota families during the Great Depression. Books were relatively inexpensive. Clothing was a necessity.

Christmas Day dinners were home-raised turkey or beef. Vegetables from summer gardens, chokecherry and buffalo berry jam and Christmas cookies and cakes were part of my Mother's menu. Fudge and divinity were homemade, too.

Rural school Christmas programs included recitations and Santa Claus. All the kids tried to determine his identity by voice—and few were fooled. Treats were sacks of Christmas candy from the Maurine, S.D., store. A neighbor who had a beautiful voice sang "Silent Night" at Red Top School programs.

The coincidence of Sunday and Christmas Day resulted in a big crowd for morning church services. There was something heartful and sentimental about the congregation's chorusing favorite Christmas hymns.

It was fun during Christmas vacations to help one of my uncles with chores at his place. Sleeping in the sheep wagon and listening to yuletide songs on KFYR-Bismarck and WNAX-Yankton enhanced the visit.

Whist parties, oyster stew dinners and ice skating on dams built by one of President Franklin D. Roosevelt's alphabetical agencies (like WPA for Works Progress Administration) were among Christmas vacation diversions.

Christmas 1941, only 18 days after the Japanese bombed Pearl Harbor, was especially cherished by American families who were still together. I was lucky: I was home for Christmas. There would be three more wartime Christmases.

A couple of years after the war Ada May and I spent Christmas at my folks' home at Maurine. We drove five miles to Cedar Canyon and searched its snow-covered cliffs and hills for a Christmas tree on another uncle's ranch. He helped us find a nice, small cedar at the bottom of a canyon.

One of our memorable Christmases was 1951 at Fort Richardson at Anchorage, Alaska, with the South Dakota Army National Guard. Many members of the 196th Regimental Combat Team and 147th Field Artillery used their GI skis on Christmas Day.

Trying to line up four Yeager children (and eventually five) for Christmas pictures was a big challenge for this Mom and Pop. Sometimes it took several rolls of film to get a decent family shot. Today, one of the boys who fought it the most has adopted an annual Christmas picture as his own family's custom.

Technology has given us better pictures, the world in living color on television, and all kinds of improvements in the home, workplace and playgrounds.

This is a vastly changed country today. Even so, Christmas and its hymns heralding "peace on earth, good will to man" are unchanged. The message of the Man of Galilee to love thy neighbor and do unto others as you would have them do unto you is still good for the world at Christmastime 1993.

CHRISTMAS CARDS, PHOTOS DENOTE SPECIAL TIMES, PLACES

Argus Leader, Sunday, Dec. 22, 1996

Here's a tip for young couples who want a Christmas card and pictorial history in one package.

Make your Christmas card a family picture of some significant event during the year. Continue with a new card every year as your children grow up and you become grandparents.

My wife and I last week mailed our 44th picture Christmas card since 1952.

We remember one ordeal about a week before Thanksgiving in the 1960s when I shot three rolls of film to get one suitable black and white picture of four lively youngsters.

We announced the session in advance, which was probably a mistake. Our oldest boy made faces as Dad tried for a picture of all four. Strangely enough, he has adopted the same tradition for his family. So have another son and a daughter.

There's many a smile for a parent in reviewing five decades of Christmas pictures. Our oldest daughter, Karen, was the only subject on our 1952 and 1953 cards when she was almost one and two. She was joined by Anson Jr. in 1954.

There was no 1955 Yeager family Christmas card. Harry, our second son, was born Dec. 27. He complicated our picture taking schedule and his mother's daily routine. Our third son, Terry, was born in the summer of 1957.

When the children were small, there was no open revolt against our picture taking session. That came later. So did long hair.

Our cat, Grey Ghost, a fine large light orange-colored male, sat contentedly on Anson Jr.'s lap while all four smiled. Christmas trees and socks were backdrops during the last three years of our first decade of Christmas cards.

Our boys started wearing suit coats as the 1960s began. We switched to our new fireplace for a backdrop. Our youngest daughter, Ellen, made her debut on the 1965 card. She was in the middle of her siblings. She was smiling and standing on the fireplace ledge under Christmas stockings. Two years later, she and Karen were seated on Miss Topsy Stonewall, Karen's American Saddlebred, with her brothers standing in front of the horse.

There was a definite shift of boyish hair styles as the 1960s merged into the 1970s. Male hair became progressively longer as the boys neared college age. In 1971, my wife and I made our first appearance on the card.

About this time college made family schedules more complicated. So we resorted to two or three pictures in a montage to show all the children.

We switched from black and white to color pictures in 1980. There were graduations, weddings and new faces—of daughters-in-law—on the cards. Grandchildren followed. The 1994 card pictured an event from our 50th wedding anniversary. Other cards have pictured reunions in the Black Hills, Colorado, North Carolina and Hawaii.

Alex, a daughter-in-law's 10-year-old Golden Retriever who thinks he's a person, made his first appearance on our card in 1987.

Our tribe donned western gear—from frontier Army uniforms to dance hall girl costumes—during our 1990 summer reunion at Palmer Gulch KOA Campground near Mount Rushmore.

This year's card is a montage of six color pictures.

Picture taking has become easier. My automatic Japanese camera rarely misses a good shot. Through the years, the men and women at Harold's in Sioux Falls have processed our Christmas cards efficiently and well.

They send you out the door with a box of envelopes, so you can get them ready for mailing while you wait for the cards. A computer list at home makes addressing labels easier.

Our Christmas cards are displayed in a hallway of our home. One recent Christmas Ada May gave each child a photo album of cards. They said it was one of their nicest gifts ever.

COLUMNS ON S.D. LIFE

DAKOTAS' LOW MURDER RATE

Argus Leader, Sunday, Jan. 28, 1979

The people who live in the two Dakotas have a hard time understanding the latest manifestation of odd behavior in more crowded areas: killing the other driver.

In California in recent years there have been two freeway shooting incidents near San Jose due to road congestion. Two men killed another near Sacramento because of a detour in the road. In Texas there have been similar incidents in Dallas and Houston, where angry motorists got even for a slight or being pushed to No. 2 in traffic by killing the other driver.

This would be unthinkable in North and South Dakota—firing a shotgun or other weapon at some hapless individual because he cut into traffic or cut you off.

North Dakota, according to 1977 Uniform Crime Reports by the Federal Bureau of Investigation, has a murder rate of only 0.9 per 100,000 population, the lowest in the nation. Vermont is second with 1.4. South Dakota is third with 2.0. Iowa is fourth with 2.3; Maine, fifth, 2.4; and Minnesota, sixth, 2.7.

Nevada is the most dangerous state in the nation when it comes to your chance of being murdered. The rate there is 15.8 per 100,000 persons. Louisiana is in second place, with 15.5. The murder rate in Texas is 13.3; in California, 11.5.

There is something about both the people and the territory that contributes to the low murder rate for the two Dakotas.

The people of the two Dakotas are much alike. Generally, citizens of both states take changes in weather, farm prosperity and other circumstances of living in an uncertain climate in stride.

Their stoicism is both a reflection of the territory and their heritage. Much of the present day population is descended from Scandinavian or Northern European immigrants whose problems of wresting a living from the Northern Plains were much more basic than a traffic irritation.

There is still time in the Dakotas to think about getting along with your neighbor. On California and Texas freeways, the neighbor is impersonal. To some luckless out-of-their-mind drivers who can't cope with the problems of traffic, the man in the other car is the enemy.

In contrast to urban congestion elsewhere, there is plenty of living room in this part of the Northern Plains. Both Dakotas have relatively small populations (under 700,000) and lots of wide open spaces between Minnesota and Iowa on the east and Montana and Wyoming on the west. There's open space to the south, too, in Nebraska.

Before all South Dakotans pat themselves on the back, they should remember that some thoughtless drivers use highway signs for marksmanship practice. Such behavior isn't hostile, but it's juvenile. A stray bullet kills just as dead as one fired in anger.

North Dakotans are the ones to beat in competition showing regard for fellow man.

BEST DAYS OF THE YEAR

Argus Leader, Sunday, Sept. 9, 1979

Sun-splashed days.

Cooler nights.

A strong hint of fall in the air.

And a gorgeous countryside and beautiful city. Have you ever seen Sioux Falls in a lovelier green?

South Dakota, the Land of Infinite Variety, has autumn days ahead that promise bountiful corn and soybean crops for farmers and a delightful season for all to savor and enjoy.

For many, including this writer, the days of fall are the best of the year.

Trees change from green to the mellow, golden hues of Indian summer. There are adventures in driving country lanes to observe the progress of row crops. Later on, the quest of the ringneck beckons hunters to corn rows.

Lawn chores and tending the roses, if accomplished during fall days and not put off because of other pursuits, give promise of a better stand of grass and nicer blooms a year ahead.

Young cross-country runners brighten the local scene after school. Joggers enjoy their daily challenge.

Fall nights are special, too. Football under lights complements the zest of breathing in that crisp night air. The snap of the ball and do-or-die on the playing field are center stage.

❖ ❖ ❖

For farmers who had late plantings last spring of corn and soybeans every warm day is a plus. There's a race against the calendar and frost.

Some lucky farmers will win the race in another two weeks. For others it will take another three or four weeks of sunny days and hot weather to bring corn and soybean crops through to maturity. No frost before Oct. 10 would help just about every late blooming field in Minnehaha County.

The weatherman's outlook is upbeat.

The September long range forecast said that temperatures would be below normal north and west of a line from Aberdeen to Rapid City. But below that line, normal temperatures are in prospect, with the south and east near normal.

For Sioux Falls the average first freeze comes on Oct. 3. Along the extreme southern and south central part of South Dakota including Yankton and Vermillion the first freeze on the average arrives Oct. 15 or after. A narrow 30-mile band just north of that southern strip has freeze dates bracketed between Oct. 10 to Oct. 14.

Mid-state east of the river the area on a line roughly from Brookings County to Chamberlain and northward to a point between Mobridge and Pierre looks at frost on Oct. 5.

The beautiful Black Hills can't do any bragging about late frosts. Their date is before Sept. 25. Across the northern tier of counties the frost date is Sept. 30 to Oct. 4.

There's comfort in local folklore predictions, too. One says that the first frost comes six months after the first thunderstorm. That would be Oct. 9 or 10 in the Sioux Falls area.

Try another man in the street or farmer's estimate. Freezes or coldest nights come on a new moon or full moon. First the good news.

This autumn the Harvest Moon falls on Oct. 5. That's the full moon nearest to the autumnal equinox. This phenomenon gives farmers extra hours of light in which to harvest their crops before frost and winter come. Harvest Moon ushers in a period of several successive days when the moon rises soon after sunset.

Now the bad news. The new moon rises on Sept. 21. Let's hope for a warm night.

Just in case you didn't know it, Hunter's Moon, the next full moon after Harvest Moon, will be on Nov. 4. As in October, there will be several successive days when hunters will have extra hours of light, but less marked than for Harvest Moon.

✦ ✦ ✦

The calendar says fall arrives on Sept. 23. Its approach is the best heralded and most consistent of any season in South Dakota.

The signals of cooler breezes, brighter days and man's seasonal pursuits in fields and town are unmistakable.

Autumn in South Dakota is also an excellent time to visit state parks and recreational areas. State Game, Fish and Park leaders and the tourist industry would like to encourage more autumn travel and year round use of the parks. It would smooth out some of the peaks and valleys in tourism especially after this summer's decline because of the energy crisis.

If you're of a mind to roam and can't wait for frost in South Dakota, try northern Minnesota. There's another plus in its north woods and lake region: fall colors to rival the best in New England.

The variety offered by South Dakota's winters is something else. Snowbirds know that they can leave Sioux Falls in a blinding blizzard in December and find a warmer clime between Sioux City and Yankton.

THE MOURNING TIES THAT BIND

Argus Leader, Dec. 16, 1979

What do friends do when their neighbors are overcome by grief in a tragedy?

They do what what was done last week in Sioux Falls, Letcher and Mitchell where funeral services were held for the eight victims of the collision north of Mitchell a week ago Saturday night.

They turn out for the funeral. They sign the guest books. They sympathize while relatives—and even the minister—are overcome with emotion.

They become a part of the friends and relatives whom they are comforting. And they develop a new kinship, too, with the departed. For most of them, since early years, have also sat in the mourners' rows reserved for relatives.

There's a streak of fatalism in most people that makes them think, "There, but for the grace of God, or a lucky break on the highway, I could be, too...."

They file out of the church or auditorium after the mourners. And they make the trip to the cemetery if that is part of the public ceremony.

When Alfred, Lord Tennyson, the beloved poet laureate of England, wrote these lines, he was thinking of living out a long and useful life (his span was 83):

> *Sunset and evening star,*
> *And one clear call for me!*
> *And may there be no moaning of the bar,*
> *When I put out to sea.*

Even so, his requiem has relevance for the mourners if not the eight victims who were struck down before their time.

The four Letcher boys and the Mount Vernon girl who was with them were high school students in their teens: Daniel Lucid, Troy Von Walleghen, Randall Ruml, Joseph Northrup and Sally Hohbach. They were the victims in one car.

The dead in the other car were Mr. and Mrs. Verlynn Nelson, both in their early 40s, and their son, Michael, 13, of Sioux Falls.

South Dakotans and their neighbors on the Northern Plains show unusual concern and regard for friends and relatives at a funeral service.

In Sioux Falls, for instance, it's reflected in police escorts from church or funeral home to the cemetery for the mourners. Most motorists throughout the state pull over to the side of a road and stop as a gesture of respect to cars—headlights on—in a cortege.

It's evident when the adult children come home to South Dakota to bury a parent, say farewell to a favorite uncle or aunt or comfort a brother or sister and family in the loss of a loved one.

Small-town churches fill up with relatives and friends, some of whom haven't seen each other for years. The town's best vocalist has a couple of selections that are comforting.

The minister or priest has words that fit the departed, and also the occasion. He knows what is appropriate, and expresses it in the hour of grief that comes to all.

Pall bearers—ruddy-faced farmers, or young nephews, or the friends in town or next door—file in and out with the casket.

On a winter day, a small-town frame church where a funeral is in progress is a study in period art from anyone's youth.

You note the shoveled sidewalks and white paint outside; inside, the belfry, the painting of the Saviour on the wall and the attendance or collection figures on the board behind the pulpit.

Hymns, the sermon, the recital of a brief biography (sometimes) are played out during the service.

The trip to the cemetery on the edge of town has familiar fixtures: a country road, maybe two ruts in the snow or grass inside the gate for cars to make their swing in and out.

At graveside: the canopy on days either mild or cold, the "ashes to ashes, dust to dust" tribute by the minister, the touch of a handshake, the nod of a friend.

If the decedent was a veteran, the U.S. flag is passed to the widow or parent. A Legion, VFW or military squad fires a salute.

Back in a church basement, restaurant or club room, a lunch or a meal continues the scenario that makes the unbearable bearable.

For a brief hour or so the son or daughter from the East Coast or the West, from overseas or a neighboring state compresses years into minutes in catching up on what's happened to friends and relatives in intervening years.

Later, guest books that show who attended the funeral are put away and treasured. The oldest son or daughter closes out Mama's or Papa's house. A mother or a close relative sorts the possessions and clothing of the youngster or teenager no longer among the living.

Everyone wipes away a tear and life goes on.

Winter's snow cover on prairie cemeteries in South Dakota fades with spring. A daughter, granddaughter or other relative—usually from the distaff side—makes sure that come Memorial Day there'll be flowers on green graves and that her family's beloved ones are remembered.

BEATING THE HEAT
Swimming hole was a great place for kids to cool off in '30s

Argus Leader, Sunday, August 7, 1983

These hot days of August are an inspiration for reflections on days of yore—before air conditioning.

This writer found delight during the early 1930s in cooling off in the Moreau River in northwestern South Dakota or in a stock dam in the summer time.

There was a memorable week spent with boyhood friends at their sheep wagon, staked out on a hill east of Bixby, S.D. Midafternoon was the time for a dip in the Moreau River.

Another summer, there was a week spent with a friend west of Bixby. The Moreau River ran through the place.

Luckily, there was water in the Moreau those two summers. There was exhilaration in jumping into the swimming hole—and plenty of horseplay in splashing water on each other. The same kind of fun was available on stock dams, too.

One of the big events on Main Street in Faith during one hot summer—I think it was 1935—was when Reginald Pickard, the owner of the Wapazo Theatre, installed air conditioning.

It was a big attraction and helped at the box office. Needless to say, the Wapazo's advertising emphasized the joys of cooling off while seeing Hollywood's latest attraction.

There were other simple things that made summer heat bearable—like a cold drink when stacking Russian thistles for hay—and nightfall. Sundown usually brought relief from the heat in the wide open spaces of western South Dakota.

A bottle of ice cold pop at a Sunday ball game cost a nickel. So did an ice cream cone—with generous one-dip dimensions.

Today, air conditioning is by no means universal in homes. But its use in stores, businesses, offices, automobiles, etc., gives many South Dakotans a break.

Any kid who drove a farm tractor 50 years ago couldn't have dreamed of today's air conditioned, glassed-in cabs—some with radio, too.

The old thrills, however, still feel good.

Like swimming in August.

Swimming holes or pools never fail to satisfy, especially when the sun is burning down and there are cumulus formations, like big white cotton powderpuffs, in a blue sky over South Dakota.

Try it again.

You'll like it.

QUARTZITE POSTS LASTING MARKERS OF STATE BOUNDARY

Argus Leader, Sept. 10, 1989

It's August, 1892.

U.S. Surveyor Charles H. Bates of Yankton has arrived in Sturgis. He has just completed one of the most remarkable surveys in U.S. history. He and his crew during 1889 and 1892 surveyed and marked the border between North and South Dakota.

They set 720 quartzite monuments—one every half mile—to mark section and quarter lines along the border from Minnesota to Montana.

As he customarily did on survey trips, Bates talked to the local newspaper. He gave Charles C. Moody, publisher of the Sturgis Weekly Record, a national scoop. Moody was the first to publish the exact length of the boundary between North and South Dakota: 360 miles and 45.35 chains (or 360.56 miles).

Ada May by a quartzite marker on the South Dakota-North Dakota border, 330 miles west of the Minnesota border and one mile west of Highway 85. —Anson Yeager photo, Sept. 11, 1989

Bates also jokingly told Moody that he planned to apply for membership in the Humane Society of the U.S. He said he had just set 720 "of the most superb scratching posts for cattle that were ever seen."

The posts or markers were 7 feet long and 10 inches square and were embedded in the ground at half their length. Each weighed approximately 800 pounds. They were quarried and marked in Sioux Falls for specific mile and half-mile locations from the Minnesota line.

Gordon Iseminger, a University of North Dakota professor, chronicles Bates' achievement in *The Quartzite Border*, published by The Center for Western Studies of Sioux Falls.

Iseminger, born on a farm near Carthage and a 1959 graduate of Augustana College, tells Bates' story in the context of the quest for statehood and political intrigue when the two Dakotas were fledgling states.

Iseminger has walked most of the boundary between the states several times. He estimates half the markers remain and fears they are endangered.

His book was inspired by a chance encounter in 1979 with Ole Breum, a Rutland, N.D., resident and former state legislator. Breum took Iseminger and other members of a Chautauqua troupe on a tour of the state line and showed them the quartzite monuments; some were in disrepair and some were missing. Breum had tried without success to pass legislation in North Dakota to protect the markers.

Iseminger includes a history of Sioux Falls' durable building stone and how U.S. Sen. Richard Pettigrew of Sioux Falls urged its use to mark the boundary. Pettigrew wanted the contract for the project awarded to a Sioux Falls friend who was not a surveyor.

Pettigrew became highly piqued when Bates' bid ($200 less than his friend's) was accepted and inferred that Bates' bid had been changed. Pettigrew sought to get even by gaining the appointment of George G. Beardsley, a North Dakota surveyor, to check Bates' work before payment.

Beardsley, however, reported after field inspection that Bates' performance was excellent. Bates received $21,300 for the contract, of which $4,300 was for the stone monuments.

Iseminger puts you in the border area with Bates, his crew and survey wagons—as they fight heat, rain and cold. He documents rail or Missouri River steamboat shipment of the markers to near the border.

Iseminger's book is one of the most interesting centennial year offerings. The 123-page book, illustrated with the author's photographs of boundary markers and several of Bates' survey sketches, is available for $10.95 at Cover to Cover in the Empire or from The Center for Western Studies, Augustana. College, Box 727, Sioux Falls, S.D. 57197. Call the Center for shipping charges.

LIFE OFF STATE'S MAIN HIGHWAYS WORTH PRESERVING
Argus Leader, Saturday, Sept. 14, 1985

There's a lot to see away from the interstates and along the byways of South Dakota.

There's a fine corn crop headed for maturity in the southeastern corner of the state.

A friendly service station attendant said: "We needed those August rains. Now we need sunshine."

Soybeans are looking good. New hay abounds.

In the quiet of a Sunday morning you'll see another crop, too: South Dakota's rural people. And you'll wonder if they're an endangered species in a countryside that's becoming depopulated.

Look ahead on your blacktop road to a water tower set above a grove of trees on a hillside. Turn into town and see change.

Drive past a mix of stores—a few still operating, many closed—toward the grade school at the end of the street. The school is well-kept, but the high school is long gone.

Observe stately white frame church buildings. Catch the refrain of hymns through open front doors on a September morning.

Drive slowly back to Main Street. Ponder the days when the town hall was new and business was good. Check the dates from early statehood when Main Street's most imposing brick building was erected.

Today's most prosperous business is the bank, housed in a fairly new and functional one-story brick building. There's no date on the building. Nearby, the Post Office shows signs of wear.

Drive into another small town. Its crown jewel is a retirement home. Pretty flowers line the sidewalk. The facility is obviously well cared for and tenders loving care toward its elderly residents.

Although the hour is early, there are already half a dozen visitors' cars parked in the lot. It's easy to imagine callers talking to a father or mother, sister or brother. Their conversations typically would center on family and occasionally include reminiscing about an era when the community had more people.

Parking is heavy around several churches in other parts of this small town. Main Street? As dead as it can be on a Sunday morning. Business? It's all at the nearby intersection, where the proprietor is pumping gas and his customers, most of whom drive pickups, are shooting the breeze over beer or pop.

Resume speed along the highway. Glance left. An abandoned farm house has turned from white to an aging grey. The house seems to melt slightly sideways into the background. The barn is also sinking into oblivion. Where have the people gone who called this farmstead home?

Count successes in farming in the remaining farm homes along the road. Many are of recent construction, well cared for and substantially built. But unlike yesteryear, there are no longer farmers on every quarter or half section.

Drive into another town. It has a pretty park and a classic Civil War statue erected in memory of the Grand Army of the Republic. That was the society of Union veterans of the Civil War. They helped populate the frontier when this was Dakota Territory.

Today someone in family gatherings may incidentally mention a grandfather or great-grandfather who fought in the Civil War. Contemporary military service organizations include the American Legion and Veterans of Foreign Wars. They have aging members whose wars of this century also are fading into the past.

At midmorning, families and their young are visiting outdoors between church and Sunday school.

Luckily, this town still has a newspaper to record community life and achievements of its young people in service or away at college. Buildings that once housed auto or farm machinery firms stand idle along Main Street. Many smaller shops have closed their doors too. Happily, this and most small towns have many newer homes built in recent years.

Farther along the highway, church attendance was good in a village intersected by the road. Otherwise, there was nothing going on, about like a residential neighborhood in Sioux Falls on Sunday morning. Afternoon for some village families would mean a trip to the malls in Sioux Falls.

Like yesteryear, most young people in small towns will leave after high school for training or careers elsewhere. There are fewer opportunities than ever in small towns or in farming.

Life in the smaller towns and on farm or ranch has much to do with raising children, the state's best crop.

One can only hope that South Dakota has seen the worst of depopulation of the countryside.

The way of life that you see off the main highways of South Dakota is worth saving for the 21st century.

S.D. LIFE—PEOPLE

FOUR BALCERS SCHOOLED UNDER THEIR DAD

Argus Leader, Sunday, May 25, 1980

When Dr. Charles Balcer handed out Augustana diplomas last Sunday for the last time as president of the college, he might have reflected a bit on three graduates in particular who received their certificates from him.

They are his three oldest children: Mary, wife of Pastor Dennis Tranberg of Minot, N.D.; Mark of Sioux Falls, and Beth, Mrs. Greg Amble, of Rochester, Minn.

Brian, the youngest son of Dr. and Mrs. Balcer, will be a senior at Augustana next fall.

Fifteen years ago when the Balcers moved to Sioux Falls, their four children were all of pre-college age. This made for exciting times in the household of the college president and his First Lady, Elizabeth. Her role also will change in a few weeks to being the wife of a visiting professor at the University of Arizona in Tucson.

One extracurricular duty which Balcer will probably miss in his new career will be writing a column for Bob Binger's "Augustana Today," a quarterly publication which goes to the college's 17,000 alumni and several thousand other individuals.

Binger will carry the text of Balcer's commencement address, which appears on the opposite page, in the next issue as the departing president's last column.

❖ ❖ ❖

One of the most exclusive organizations in the United States these days is the "Silver Wingers of World War I"—men who served as military pilots in 1917-1918.

Fred C. Christopherson, retired Argus-Leader editor, made a trip to Omaha in 1917 to enlist as a balloonist. At the time he was working on the Sioux Falls Press.

The Army told him they didn't need any more balloonists, but there were openings for pilots of winged aircraft. He signed up.

He qualified as a military pilot at San Diego in July 1918, flying the Curtis Jenny, a biplane with an open cockpit. He took advanced training as a bomber pilot in England, training on the British two-engine Handley-Paige aircraft.

"Chris" missed bombing German lines in France due to a shortage of planes.

"Are you sorry about that?" I asked him.

"Yes, it was a disappointment," he said, "that I didn't have a chance to go on one bombing raid after preparing for it for all that time."

Memories of his World War I duty came crowding back on a recent weekend in May, when the Order of Daedalians at Ellsworth Air Force Base sponsored their annual "Silver Wings" event.

The Daedalians are a national order of military pilots which lists the "Silver Wingers of World War I" as their founding members.

As it happened, "Chris" was the only "Silver Winger" to appear at Ellsworth this year. Two other chapter members, Glenn Levitt of Clark, the South Dakota wing commander, and Emil Loriks of Oldham, missed the trip because flying weather was bad.

"Chris" and his wife, Marie, had driven from Sioux Falls to the Black Hills, combining a visit to the South Dakota Press Association convention at Spearfish with the event at Ellsworth. They enjoyed being on the Air Base.

"They (Strategic Air Command personnel at Ellsworth) treated us royally," "Chris" said. "They put us up in VIP quarters at Ellsworth and had us as guests at dinner."

Time did not permit a flight in today's B-52s or other aircraft at Ellsworth which would dwarf the planes that World War I pilots flew.

"Chris" likes to recall another sidelight about his flying days. "Incredible though it may seem, I flew an airplane before I drove an automobile."

That's another bonus of a busy lifetime that spans two centuries. Chris celebrated his 84th birthday May 13.

✦ ✦ ✦

Mrs. Roy D. Burns, wife of the longtime Sioux Falls judge who died May 13 at 83, told me she encouraged her husband to be the gardener at their home at 28 Riverview Heights.

She thought it would be a good diversion from working with his mind all day long as a lawyer. This pleasant outdoor diversion lasted almost half a century. Their lot was a bare hillside when they bought it in 1932.

He planted the evergreens and shrubs and looked after them so well that people would ask Mrs. Burns who their professional gardener was.

Burns appreciated other outdoor activity, too. He liked the Black Hills and Lake Okoboji best for vacations. "He loved to swim," Mrs. Burns said.

Another favorite locale was Cedar Pass at the Badlands, where he enjoyed staying.

Many family trips were surprises, cooked up by Burns and sprung on his family in an impromptu way.

The happy times of 60 years in Sioux Falls were chronicled in six scrapbooks. Mrs. Burns has one tip for other families: date your material as you go along. The dates were missing from some of the pictures and mementos.

Burns, so highly regarded by his peers and all who knew him, also looked the part he played in real life as a judge. Hollywood couldn't cast a better type: white hair, dignified and quiet manner, fair—and firm.

HISTORY STUDENTS SHOW THAT THEY KNOW THEIR STUFF

Argus Leader, Saturday, May 3, 1986

It's our public shame that South Dakota pays its teachers less than any other state in the union. But don't use that statistic to judge the quality of instruction in South Dakota schools.

Consider, instead, what a remarkable job some of the state's teachers are doing by their students' performance.

As demonstrated in State History Day competition at Pierre April 26, South Dakota's best history students know their subject. Their expertise showed in dramatizations, history papers, exhibits and video or slide shows that wound up as the best in the state.

Students chose local, national or global issues to develop a theme of "Conflict and Compromise in History." First and second place winners at Pierre will be eligible to compete in the National History Day contest at College Park, Md., in June. Stephen Ward, professor of history at the University of South Dakota, who directed the state contest, expects to take up to 40 winners by plane to Washington.

Judges furnished by the South Dakota State Historical Society were impressed by students' grasp of issues, thoroughness in research and ability to communicate.

For instance, four senior high school students from Vermillion (Sarah Dahlin, Debbie Miller, Kitty Bartels and Alison Hunter) portrayed the Roaring Twenties. In scarcely 15 minutes, they depicted very well the nation's experiment with Prohibition and provided a glimpse of flappers, jazz and America's preoccupation with business.

Four junior high students from Patrick Henry in Sioux Falls (Traci Harvey, Julie Driver, Calie Afdahl and Emily Norris) in their skit traced highlights of women's rights and the suffrage movement in the last century. They did it easily by having one student take the role of editor Horace Greeley to interview suffragettes of the period.

One judge of individual papers written by students said that he couldn't recall doing anything that extensive or involved, during his own high school days in the 1930s. This was very evident to adults who looked over dioramas constructed by the students.

Tandi Swift, a Sully Buttes seventh-grader, had an outstanding exhibit on Hitler's Holocaust. It included a scale model of the Auschwitz death camp, striking news pictures of Hitler and camp victims and concise explanatory texts.

Tonya and Troy Swift, a sister and brother of Sully Buttes High School, depicted The Alamo: A Bloody Fortress. They, too, used a scale model in their diorama, which showed the conflict that led to Texas' independence from Mexico 150 years ago.

There were many other remarkable exhibits on such national and world controversies as the U.S. bombing of Hiroshima, abortion, the Civil War and capital punishment.

Students appropriately used local examples and sources for their dioramas, like Lisa Solvie, Duane Kolb, Kristi Kolb and Danny LaDue of Bison. Their exhibit, "Capital Punishment," featured South Dakota's last hanging, at Bison in 1913. A homesteader was executed for the murder of a neighbor woman and her daughter near Bixby, once a post office and stage stop on the Moreau River.

Two hangman's knots caught viewers' initial attention. But what was most remarkable was the students' display of copies of original source material.

Two eighth-graders from Buffalo, Kristi Price and Tammy Piantino, depicted in an exhibit the conflict between cowboys and Tipperary, a Harding County bronco that has been characterized as the greatest bucking horse that ever lived.

The competition showed a wide and keen interest by today's students in issues that affect them. But more than that, it demonstrated inspiration and close attention by history teachers in South Dakota classrooms.

These students will leave their hometown schools well prepared to take on the challenge of education after high school. Students who develop bibliographies and write brief summaries on controversial subjects and then present them effectively in exhibit or skit form have a head start.

If more South Dakotans could see classroom results like these, there would be new backing for better salaries for teachers.

As a starter, South Dakotans should boost teacher's salaries enough to overtake Mississippi and let that state regain last place.

HISTORIC BRIDGE COMES HOME TO CENTERVILLE

Argus Leader, Sunday, May 12, 1991

Sometime in early June Don and Mary Ann Hart will look out the window of their home and witness the arrival of the historic bridge they've adopted.

Mary Ann will have her camcorder ready. Don will direct the truck driver into their pasture where the bridge will be placed. It will span a creek which splits the acreage of their home 7 miles south and 1.75 miles east of Centerville.

Their bridge is almost 98 years old. It is one of South Dakota's two oldest highway bridges. It was built by the only 19th century South Dakota builder of iron and steel bridges.

The bridge is 41 feet long, 16 feet wide, 10 feet high and weighs 20,000 pounds. For almost a century the bridge has carried a local road over Mud Creek near Groton.

The bridge was saved from demolition by a South Dakota Department of Transportation program which permits sponsors to acquire an historic bridge. A saving in demolition costs and a nominal payment of $400 from the Harts partially offset costs of moving the bridge approximately 230 miles from Groton.

Graves Bros. Inc. of Sioux Falls which has the contract for the new bridge will move the old one to its new home. The Harts will provide abutments, approaches and upkeep.

As Mary Ann jovially said last winter, "We had to agree to care for the bridge, hug it and kiss it and talk to it once a day so it doesn't get lonely." Her interest in old things stems partly from her job as secretary of the State Historical Preservation Center in Vermillion.

The bridge is a single-span, pin-connected Pratt pony truss structure built for the Brown County Commission in 1893 by J.G. Bullen of Ashton, S.D., for $476. Graves' contract for the continuous concrete, 68-foot bridge which will replace it totals $135,008.

The historic bridge will help the Harts in their second 10-year plan. Their first was to restore and rebuild the old farm home. Phase II involves growing trees on their 14-acre pasture to resemble Don's native Arkansas.

"When we moved here 10 years ago there was nothing here but Chinese elms. Every time we cut down one, we planted 50 trees," he said. So far they have planted more than 900 trees and shrubs.

He believes terracing in the pasture will help trees the couple were planting on a blustery Saturday morning in April. They've set out 250 trees this spring and hope the pasture will be covered in 10 years.

"I like trees. I don't think South Dakota could have enough trees," Don said. Evergreens are high on their planting list.

The Harts' home started in the last century as a two-story frame house with two rooms down and two up. There have been seven or eight additions since. "We're in the process of making it look like one house," Don said. They recently finished the north side.

Some artifacts from the pioneer home include square-headed nails, one of them 5 inches long. A graveled driveway, lawn and flower and vegetable gardens enhance the home's setting.

Don has been in carpenter work in the Centerville area for 15 years and operated Hart Construction Co. He started work last month as a carpenter at the University of South Dakota.

The Harts are believed to be the first South Dakota couple to adopt an historic bridge.

This is the second bridge Graves Bros. Inc. has helped preserve. The first was the nation's first reinforced concrete arch highway bridge. Tom Graves said his firm some years ago moved it several miles from Highway 9 to a city park in Rock Rapids, Iowa.

The South Dakota Department of Transportation's final report on "Historic Bridges in South Dakota" last November listed 140 bridges including Harts' as eligible for nomination to the National Register of Historic Places.

REUNION BRINGS VICTIMS, RESCUERS BACK TOGETHER

Argus Leader, Oct. 20, 1991

"I never did spend any time saying, 'Why me?'" Karla Kay said of her life today at age 50.

Half a lifetime ago when she was 25 she kept her 10-week-old daughter alive for two days in the wreckage of her father's airplane on Mount St. Helens in Washington state.

Since then she has kept in touch with two of the men who rescued her and her daughter, Laurie Little. Their survival was front page news in the Argus Leader and nationwide.

Mother and daughter were trapped in the back seat of the small white plane. It was almost indistinguishable against the snow. Karla's parents were dead in the front seat. Despite a broken back, collapsed lung and frost-bitten legs, Karla managed to nurse Laurie and change her diapers. She was conscious when rescuers reached them on June 25, 1966.

Karla was the wife of Loren Little, a medical student at the University of Washington in Seattle. Both were 1959 graduates of Washington High School in Sioux Falls and 1963 graduates of Macalester College. Karla's father, Grant Erickson, was the pilot; his wife Dolly (Karla's stepmother) was the other passenger. Erickson was vice president and general manager of Warren Radio Supply Co. in Sioux Falls.

The Ericksons were en route to Los Angeles to attend the 50th wedding anniversary of his parents. Erickson radioed for help about an hour and a half after leaving Seattle for Portland. Two days later an Army helicopter pilot spotted the plane's wreckage at about the 5,500-foot level of Mount St. Helens, which was then 9,671 feet high.

An Army lieutenant reached the crash and radioed that there were survivors. Air Force reservist Evan Hale, 26, and M/Sgt. Gene Ingram, 41, regular Air Force, parachuted to the site. Karla's first words were: "The baby." She had only a small bruise.

Karla was in shock. Hale administered first aid. Her rescuers carefully moved her litter to the helicopter. Three hours after the sighting, the pair were in the hospital at Longview, Wash., about 40 miles west of St. Helens.

When Karla woke up, Loren was at her side. He had participated in the search. He told reporters his wife's courage and initiative saved their baby's life. Karla was transferred to the university hospital in Seattle. She didn't sit up for six months; she was either on her back or stomach in a Foster frame.

Karla in a telephone interview said, "I still wear a leg brace, and I'm still weak on the left side, still classified as handicapped." She said she should always wear shorts so bystanders could see her brace. If they look incredulous at her fitness while using a handicapped parking space, she simply smiles.

Life has changed for her and Loren. They were divorced about 12 years ago after they moved to Las Vegas where he's an eye surgeon. She changed her last name to Kay, her middle name.

In 1980, Mount St. Helens erupted, blowing the top off their mountain and destroying the spot where the plane crashed in 1966.

A family highlight last summer was the marriage of Richard, 22, Karla's and Loren's son and University of Nevada/Las Vegas student. Karla teaches remedial reading in the Clark County School District. Laurie works as an ophthalmic surgery assistant for her father. His mother, Maxine Little, formerly of Sioux Falls, lives in Las Vegas.

Last summer's other big event was a weekend reunion in Las Vegas with Hale and Ingram. Karla said they had a wonderful time. "I had kept in touch with both of them. But Gene had not seen Laurie since 1980. This was really a thrill. They are exceptional men."

WIDOWS FIND THRILL WITH B&B ON STRAWBERRY HILL

Argus Leader, Sunday, Jan. 14, 1996

Two widowed sisters—one 61, the other 64—have found new happiness in the bed and breakfast they built on Strawberry Hill.

When they first saw the site three miles south of Deadwood in January 1994, it was covered with five feet of snow.

Marrilynn Lehman and Darlene Fees wouldn't get a good look at the terrain on the residential acreage until two months later. They bought it in March 1994, moved in on the 15th and worked on making the house livable. In May they started on the units and began their race to open by Aug. 1. Their goal was to be in business during the Sturgis Motorcycle Rally.

They made it, thanks to a lot of sweat, a few tears and much more laughter. They raised rafters, pounded nails in bedroom floors and shoveled 13 tons of sand to insulate wiring in the rocky outcropping on Strawberry Hill. They hauled sand in a small trailer behind an all-terrain vehicle.

The prospect of running a bed and breakfast brought the Thomas sisters, born and raised in Faith, S.D., to the Black Hills in the fall of 1993 to look for a site.

Lehman had found herself at loose ends. Her husband, Paul, owner and operator of Coast to Coast Hardware at Fort Benton, Mont., had died in 1990. Marrilyn, the mother of seven children and grandmother of 12, wanted a new career—something different. She had taught crafts and ceramics and had done tole painting on wood and made porcelain dolls during 34 years at Fort Benton.

Lehman thought a bed and breakfast would be fun for her and Darlene, an older sister. So she broached the idea to her in September 1993. Darlene is the widow of Byron Fees. He was superintendent of public utilities at Chamberlain, S.D., where she had lived for 37 years. Her husband died in 1979. She was in a somewhat stressful job as a group leader at the Missouri River Adolescent Center at Chamberlain.

"We trooped all over the Black Hills," Lehman said. And then they found Strawberry Hill. Its 8.5 acres was enough land to expand.

The sisters hired a Fort Benton contractor who had built Lehman's husband's store. The contractor could stay only a month, so they hired a second contractor to finish the job.

They built a unit with two rooms and a single room. They remodeled an existing building to gain their fourth unit.

Ronald Bohnet of Hill City, Fees' son-in-law, helped with the painting. Lehman said, "When our kids came to visit us that summer, they all pitched in to help: pounded nails, put up wall paper."

Fees found no pressure, only pleasure in the hectic seven-day work schedule of getting their business ready.

The sisters sold out during the 1994 Sturgis Motorcycle Rally—and promptly filled their reservation book for the 1995 event. All space for the 1996 rally has been reserved for months. Lehman said recent snow gave snowmobiling a boost. They expect more winter business.

Fees, mother of five, has 14 grandchildren and four great grandchildren. Like her sister, she loves the beauty of the Black Hills and the peaceful forest surroundings.

Deer and two fawns frequent their yard this winter. There are many birds. Fees said, "We plan on just continuing to do more business as we become known. We meet lovely people from all over."

Sisters pose on a porch of their Strawberry Hill Bed-N-Breakfast south of Deadwood. From left, Darlene Fees and Marrilynn Lehman.

Strawberry Bed N' Breakfast is located on Strawberry Hill three miles south of Deadwood on Highway 385. It is a tenth of a mile off the highway. There are four rooms, nicely furnished, each with private entry and bath. Continental breakfast is served in the house. There's a TV room and a hot tub on deck. Write HCR 73, Box 264, Deadwood, S.D. 57732. Phone 605-578-2149.

SNOWBIRDS HELP KEEP PARKER VANS ON MOVE

Argus Leader, Sunday, Oct. 20, 1996

Moving affluent snowbirds' automobiles and household goods to the Sun Belt and back is not a big part of Parker Transfer & Storage's annual business.

But Jeff Parker, president of the Sioux Falls firm, thoroughly enjoys it. He said, "It's one of the fun things we do."

It started about 10 years ago when a customer asked to move car and goods to Arizona. Parker said he'd have to fill a truck—and placed a small ad in the Argus Leader seeking customers. He wound up with three truck loads.

This month and next there are four scheduled van trips to Arizona and other destinations. California is often an add-on for vans going to Arizona. Vans also go to Florida and Texas.

Affluent senior citizens, "grey panthers" and business people are spared driving to their winter home and lifting all those boxes in and out of the car. They take a plane and have car and goods delivered to their Sun Belt home.

For $800, you can send your car to Mesa or Sun City, Ariz., on a Parker van. It's expected that you'll have some odds and ends in the trunk or back seat. For $100 or $150 more, you can

John Parker. —Anson Yeager photo

Jeff Parker. —Anson Yeager photo

send household goods to furnish a room or two. And if there's a special piece of furniture for a daughter along the way, you can send it along, too.

Shippers are spared the risk of losing personal belongings from a car parked at night while enroute south.

The firm puts together van loads in a heated dock at its building at 1700 F Avenue on the south side of Joe Foss Field.

Cars go in the van first; household goods go on a deck above the car. Some van loads carry as many as four automobiles.

A homemaker can put canned goods in her car with no worry about their freezing before arrival. A northbound snowbird can ship home a crate of oranges or grapefruit the following spring.

Parker said that one of the first things a newly-arrived snowbird does in the Sun Belt is to set dates for the return move to the Sioux Empire. Most return trips are in April.

A typical van trip to Phoenix and return takes four days; drivers leave Monday morning and are back in Sioux Falls Thursday night. Drivers rotate: four hours driving and four hours off. Each day is counted as 20 hours on the job (sleeping included). The trip is a coveted one because drivers put in 80 hours in four days (for two weeks' pay) and get a three-day weekend.

Parker said each van has a cellular phone so drivers may call ahead with arrival times and reach their contact at the destination. Drivers get a computer printout which describes turns and other directions within a city in detail.

Usually, there are two computer printouts: one, the easiest, utilizing all interstate routes and the other, the quickest, via some two-lane highways.

The easiest all-interstate route to Phoenix follows I-29 to I-80 across Nebraska, I-76 to Denver, I-25 to I-40 in New Mexico, thence to Flagstaff, Ariz., and I-17 to Phoenix-Mesa.

The quickest route cuts across the Oklahoma Panhandle to Dalhart, Tex., and continues on U.S. 54 to I-40 in New Mexico.

Parker van. —Anson Yeager photo

Parker said one customer had them move him within a metro area in the Sun Belt. Another customer changed her mind after one winter in Arizona. She had her goods moved home. But another winter in the Upper Plains convinced her that was a mistake, too. So she moved back to Arizona.

If you move your car by van, don't worry about half a tank of gasoline in your car. But don't fill the tank, either. Parker said cars are strapped down and pose no transit problems. Today's wide bodied vans—102 inches—give movers a break. There's room to open the car door. Don't worry, either, about loading decks in the van. Strong sidewalls bear aluminum girders which carry the weight of household goods placed on the deck floor above the automobiles.

Jeff Parker, who began his career at the family firm in 1968, is the third generation of his family to direct Parker Transfer & Storage.

His grandfather, Walter Parker, founded the firm in 1927 by purchasing a dray line. His son, John D. Parker, who will be 82 on Oct. 23, worked part-time while attending Washington High School. Upon graduation in 1932, his father offered him a choice: going to college or driving a brand new International truck. He chose the truck. On his first trip to Detroit, a trucker there asked him: "Hey, kid, do you have roads out there?" (in South Dakota)

When his father died in 1941, John Parker faced two challenges: the prospect of being called up for military service and the loss of the firm's lease in its downtown location. He had a tentative deferment because the firm had moving contracts with the federal government. A friendly banker helped him borrow the money to buy the building; other government work kept him on the job at Parker Transfer. He was 27 at the time.

He recalls moving miners from the Homestake Mine, shut down by the War Manpower Commission in World War II because gold was considered non-essential. Parker went to Lead and Deadwood. His vans carried miners' household goods to Idaho, Montana and other western lead mines.

Parker still comes into the office to do some work, like checking driving and fuel logs. He enjoys it and shows up every working day. But son Jeff says there's an understanding that Dad doesn't have to come back to the office tomorrow, unless he wants to.

The senior Parker has seen many changes in the moving business. The firm's modern office has glowing computer screens—and an old-fashioned wall clock with the legend: "Parker Transfer." The clock came from the firm's downtown building which was razed for urban renewal. It is now the site of the city's bus terminal.

S.D. LIFE—TOWNS

THE PRAIRIE OASIS MALL, BUILT BY THE FAITH-FUL

Argus Leader, Sunday, Feb. 6, 1977

FAITH, S.D.—The little town of 600, whose businessmen are as self-reliant as the northwestern South Dakota stockmen they serve, never looked better.

There's a new enclosed mall on the east side of Main Street, which softens winter's blows out of the northwest for shoppers who can do the stores in a block without going outside.

There are 50 parking spaces on the mall's Main Street frontage.

The Prairie Oasis Mall, a $450,000 project, was completed in approximately 18 months from the time in March 1975 that three Faith businessmen got the idea of doing something about their building problems and for the future.

No Urban Renewal

They did it without an urban renewal program, federal matching funds or revenue bonds. They did have the help of the Small Business Administration (SBA), two area banks and the cooperation of the community.

—A new apartment house, with 18 units for the low income elderly, will open in Faith in March. It is a HUD (Housing and Urban Development) project, conceived and pushed along by three other businessmen.

—The Church of Christ has a new edifice under construction, the first new church building to go up in Faith in years.

—There are several new homes in the city, and more in prospect.

Faith is the town which gained national attention last year when its independent-minded civic leaders turned down a $250,000 grant and the federal help that went with it for the new grandstand that Faith needed.

The residents didn't like putting in $50,000 of their own money, paying $30,000 for architect fees and putting up with the paperwork necessary to make it a federal project.

The grandstand became a community project. Farmers and ranchers joined townspeople in donating help. They put up a new 3,000-seat grandstand for $40,000, which went for materials and one carpenter. The grandstand opened in time for the annual Stock Show in August.

Civic Sparkplugs

The officers of Prairie Oasis Mall, Inc., were the civic sparkplugs who got the mall project going. They are Carv Thompson, druggist, president of the corporation; John Fisher, vice president, and Lynn Feist, secretary-treasurer, now of Lemmon, who owns the grocery store in the mall.

Thompson is the former state legislator who, as the Republican candidate for governor, challenged Gov. Richard Kneip in 1972. Thompson lost his political bid, and Kneip won re-election to a second term. Thompson came home to look after his drug stores in Faith and several other area towns.

Thompson said the idea of an enclosed mall developed in March 1975, and that he and his colleagues thought it might make the difference in "whether or not this little town would survive. It was really a turning point in our future."

Thompson Drug needed a new building; the store was located in Faith's first building, erected in 1910 when the town started. Feist needed new quarters for his grocery store: Lynn's Super Valu. Fisher wanted a new building for his laundromat.

NORTHERN PLAINS ADVENTURES

The Prairie Oasis Mall, an enclosed shopping center, dominates the east side of Faith's Main Street.

Druggist Carv Thompson, president of the corporation.

Everyone Involved

"By the time we got ready to build, the whole block was involved," Thompson said. "People cooperated."

The three looked at five other locations, but came back to the block on the east side of Faith's Main Street where their businesses were located.

Their eventual plan involved cutting off the backs of the old buildings, so the new mall could be erected behind Main Street while they stayed in business. When the new structure was completed, the old buildings were razed and the land was converted to parking.

They decided on an Armco steel building, to be erected on a cement slab. The building would be 275 feet by 70, and provide 19,250 square feet of space. Footings were poured in October 1975, erection started late in November and construction was completed March 16, 1976. The project was completed Oct. 1, 1976.

The Faith Country Development Corp., a local, nonprofit development corporation organized in 1970, is the parent corporation which obtained the financing and owns the building.

SBA Loan Included

The financing includes an SBA loan of $182,700 for 25 years at 6 and 5/8 per cent; two loans of $91,350 each for 25 years at 8 per cent, obtained from the Farmers State Bank of Faith and the Bank of Lemmon, and a $40,600 loan for 25 years at 8 per cent from development corporation members. Loans totaled $406,000; Fisher, Feist and Thompson put in $44,000 in cash and real estate to bring the project's total to $450,000.

Approximately 40 local residents loaned money to the development corporation for the project. Principal and interest is paid to them annually. These are direct loans. The 40 hold a third mortgage, plus personal, cross guarantees of repayment by Fisher, Feist and Thompson.

The Faith and Lemmon banks hold the first mortgage; the second mortgage is held by the Small Business Administration.

As stockholders in Prairie Oasis Mall, Thompson, Fisher and Feist have a 25-year lease purchase agreement for the real estate, building and parking lot. The three have personally guaranteed repayment of all loans and at the end of 25 years, Prairie Oasis Mall, Inc. will own the building.

The city of Faith gave the project a tax break under state law, by which the structure is assessed for 25 per cent of taxable value the first year, 50 per cent the second year and 75 per cent during the third and fourth years.

Voters of Faith, which has a municipal liquor store, also gave 75 per cent approval for a liquor license in the mall's cocktail lounge which adjoins the restaurant. Both are operated by Fisher, who also has the laundromat and some rental space.

The Faith Post Office is located in the center of the mall. The Frontier Theatre, which is owned by Mr. and Mrs. Thompson and managed by her, has 140 portable seats. The theatre gives the town a meeting place it badly needed.

Theatre a Problem

The Thompsons' problem of the moment is that the theatre is losing approximately $50 a week, which they have to subsidize. Thompson said he believes a theatre is an essential part of the Faith scene, and that this problem will work itself out. The theatre operates on Saturday and Sunday nights.

Other businesses in the mall include the town's newspaper, The Faith Independent, and the grocery store. There are seats in the mall's corridor, where shoppers can rest or visit, and public rest rooms in the building. There's a landscaped patio at the front of the mall.

The mall has made a big difference in Faith already. The "cando" spirit which the mall project exemplifies has given the town an upbeat feeling. The mall is the topic of some bragging by area residents who say it shows what a small community can do.

Opening of the 18-unit apartment house scheduled for March 15 will ease the housing situation somewhat for the low-income elderly. This project was put together by Andrew Fishbach, Virgil Nesland and Duane Thomas, who are the owners of the Faith Lumber Co.

Faith, unlike some small South Dakota towns, has always been fortunate in having a doctor. A medical service pilot project of the federal government and the Northwest South Dakota Rural Health Corporation is a recent development.

Under the project, Faith has a doctor and a physician's assistant. The Faith Memorial Hospital building has reopened as a clinic. The project is staffed through an arrangement with the Massa, Berry clinic in Sturgis.

A $190,000 federal grant, which also provides service to Buffalo, S.D., is involved.

As elsewhere in South Dakota this winter, Faith area residents are talking about next spring's moisture and the promise of a better year. It's a part of the optimistic "tomorrow will be better" spirit so typical of residents of the high plain country.

AMERICA'S SMALL RURAL TOWNS WILL HAVE TO FIGHT TO SURVIVE

Argus Leader, April 13, 1985

What will rural cities and towns in America's midsection look like 15 years from now in the year 2000?

There's a mixed answer to that question.

Larger small cities, particularly county seats and locations along well traveled primary highways or interstates, reflect America's prosperity.

They're certain to share in the country's growth.

But in between cities that are thriving are smaller towns and villages that are standing still or fading away.

Progress has passed them by in the age of shopping centers, television and fast food restaurants.

A winter trip to the Southwest and Texas and return to Sioux Falls via the High Plains provided many examples of change.

Generally, they reflect what is happening in South Dakota's middle where population in the countryside is declining. There's a relentless continuation of the shift to larger farms and ranches.

As the countryside loses farms and homes, yesteryear's smaller towns shrink, sometimes to villages.

Small businesses that once served a trade area are either boarded up or drastically changed.

Some towns have lost their businesses but kept their homes in bedroom communities that are satellites of nearby county seats.

New houses that reflect a share in America's prosperity sometimes are only a block away from old, larger homes of another era.

Some of the big homes sit idle. They were locked up when the last family member who remained in the small town died.

Rerouting of highways has resulted in abandonment of many country stores, gas stops and restaurants. Before interstates and depopulation of the countryside, they offered a service. Today, it isn't needed. Entrepreneurs who want to stay in business have had to move to the interstate.

There's a snowball syndrome for many small towns in coping with the shift of population to larger towns. Every time a business closes on Main Street, the remaining firms may expect a decline in traffic because of services no longer offered.

Fewer farms and the drop in the birth rate have meant fewer pupils in small town schools. Some of them have been closed—another difficult problem for the residents.

There are other echo effects for the small town or rural community that loses population. Churches close. Local organizations lose much of their effectiveness.

The problem for small communities in the Northern and High Plains is aggravated by the depressed farm situation.

Greater worldwide demand for American crops—as in the days before the Russian grain embargo—would help. That will be difficult to achieve, given the impact of the strong U.S. dollar on foreign trade.

Farmers and livestock producers have both a price and volume problem. It's graphically illustrated along American highways by abandoned farm homes whose owners walked away from a no-win situation.

✦ ✦ ✦

There's little in today's outlook that indicates population decline in the countryside will be reversed in the Northern Plains.

For South Dakota, growth in population likely will continue in the eastern tier of counties and in the Black Hills.

Smaller, non-county-seat towns in the middle of the state will have to fight hard and well to stay even—if they're not located on main highways.

The outlook for smaller towns is not much different in the Sunbelt, with a couple of exceptions. Their climate encourages a population boom. Living is easier where there are no blizzards.

The deserts of Arizona and New Mexico will continue to attract new residents so long as there's adequate water and air conditioning.

The woods in East Texas and the Hill Country north of San Antonio lend themselves to country living. They are also close to large population centers.

✦ ✦ ✦

Something vital will be lost if rural America fades away in the 21st century.

Where else can you find citizens so concerned and thoughtful about their neighbors as in a small South Dakota town or in farming and ranching communities?

They never forget their friends. They share in the joy of achievement by native sons and daughters who left home for fame and fortune. They ease the grief of hometown friends who return to bury their relatives. They unhesitatingly resume friendships interrupted by years of absence from hearth and home.

These people and their counterparts elsewhere in rural America have been the foundation of the nation.

Their numbers are bound to be fewer in the next century. Retaining their ideals and hopes for the future is an important priority for mid-America.

FAITH SMALL BUT BIG IN CELEBRATING

Argus Leader, Aug. 19, 1985

FAITH, S.D.—While small towns are battling to stay alive in most of South Dakota, Faith, population 576, has shown once again how to get things done.

The town wrapped its annual Stock Show and Rodeo and an all-school reunion into its Diamond Jubilee celebration.

It attracted Faith's migratory sons and daughters—some of them children of 1910's homesteaders—from many parts of the nation.

Faith's 75th birthday party, like the 1984 Olympics, should set a record in anyone's league of how to stage an event very well.

• Item: The schedule said that Johnny Holloway's rodeo broncs, trailed 50 miles from Eagle Butte, would arrive in Faith at 2 p.m. on Friday, Aug. 9. They did, on the minute.

Outriders ran some 70 of the meanest bucking broncs this rodeo fan has ever seen along Highway 212 in Faith without incident or jeopardy to spectators who lined the streets. Broncs and cowboys repeated the spectacle for the parade.

• Item: The program said that the South Dakota Air National Guard would fly over at 10 a.m. Saturday (Aug. 10) to start the parade. Four planes thundered over Faith right on time, turned and made another pass and zoomed back to Sioux Falls.

• Item: A three-hour rodeo program moved along smartly without delays at the chutes or in the ring. Some South Dakotans call Faith's rodeo the state's best. Many cowboys are local talent. All are the real thing.

• Item: A superbly cast Faith group staged two performances of Irving Berlin's musical "Annie Get Your Gun" after more than a year's work. Two out-of-state college drama professionals with ties to Faith were the directors.

Faith in 1985 celebrated its diamond jubilee with a parade, stock show, and rodeo. —Anson Yeager photo

S.D. LIFE—TOWNS

Three jets of South Dakota's Air National Guard salute Faith. —Anson Yeager photo

A rider tests a steer at the rodeo. — Anson Yeager photo

Indian dancers perform on the main street stage during the 1985 Stock Show. —Anson Yeager photo

• Item: A computer kept track of registered visitors. Callers at jubilee headquarters could locate friends alphabetically by name or maiden name, by class year, or address and where they stayed in Faith.

The result of all this was a celebration that will be hard for Faith to top next year—or even for its centennial in 2010.

Like the Olympics' Peter Ueberroth, the Faith Stock Show and Rodeo has its own sparkplug: Carv Thompson, local druggist, former legislator and a Republican nominee for governor during the 1970s.

Thompson's promotion of Faith, its Chamber of Commerce and the Stock Show has spanned many years. He and his wife Margaret were co-chairmen of the Diamond Jubilee Committee and were honored as king and queen of the event. In addition, Margaret was associate director and organist of "Annie Get Your Gun."

Faith's leaders, like the 1984 Los Angeles Olympics Committee, relied mainly on volunteers and existing facilities. Some 60 committees with more than 400 volunteers—many of them ranchers and homemakers from the countryside—produced the celebration.

Faith High School, the Legion Hall, several local churches and the Masonic Hall were used for various events. There was a wide variety of Main Street entertainment, including Indian dancers from Red Scaffold and area musicians. Shuttle buses ran a loop around town to the fairgrounds.

The Stock Show through the years has presented some of the biggest names in country music at two performances in the 2,500-seat grandstand. Mel Tillis and Jeannie C. Riley were this year's stars.

Faith has won renown in recent years for constructing the grandstand without federal aid and for a shopping mall built by local entrepreneurs. The mall replaced some of the town's earliest buildings.

The next major civic improvement will be a new airport with a 3,400-foot hard-surfaced runway. The project will cost almost $600,000, nearly all of which will come from federal funds.

The Stock Show committee was embarrassed several years ago when the country music star's personal jet couldn't land at the present shorter grass airstrip. Stock Show officials gallantly drove the star from Bison's airport to Faith.

Despite the reason why Faith wants a new airport, there's ample justification for better facilities. Faith serves a wide area in northwestern South Dakota as a livestock market and retail center. Its second generation leadership, as exemplified by the Thompsons and others, has been aggressive and pays attention to the area's needs.

Faith likes to maximize its opportunities, like inviting Cathy Bach, the "Dukes of Hazzard" star, back to her hometown. Faith's most famous celebrity gave spectators a real thrill.

Some towns are much larger than Faith and can tap a wider range of leaders and volunteers. Some cities never capitalize on what they have. Faith does—and no one can do it better.

FUTURE WILL BRING BETTER TIMES

Argus Leader, Dec. 24, 1985

Year's end brings more reviews and predictions than anyone can digest.

Most analyses and forecasts are based on a time frame that is too tight.

The process compels comparison of 1985 with 1984 and the new year. It's easy to be pessimistic in dealing with the short term.

A better approach is to relate 1985 to longterm change.

South Dakota in the mid-1980s is struggling with a farm crisis just as it did in the 1920s and 1930s.

This year has been one of anguish on farm and ranch. The problem turns on price, costs and weather and new competition for world markets.

There's a further complication in the depopulation of the countryside.

The loss in numbers of farms and ranches in the last decade has seen many small towns fade away and the remaining ones endangered.

What rural South Dakota has to do is hang on for several years in the hope that American agriculture can regain export markets that made farming so profitable in the 1970s.

Hopefully, the new farm act will help American agriculture regain export business with its gradual reduction of price supports. Export and other subsidies will ease the transition to price levels that more nearly reflect the world market.

The farm act is the most expensive in the nation's history: $52 billion worth of help for various crops through 1988. Under the circumstances, the act is about the best that was attainable.

South Dakota farmers who want to survive the 1980s will have to manage better than ever. Too many farmers got hurt in recent years in betting the family farm on appreciation of land values. More of them should have said no to their friendly bankers.

Murals on Faith Municipal Building depict area's heritage. —Anson Yeager photo

Gov. William Janklow's program to assist farmers who want to retrain and to obtain advice and help from state government is a helpful step. The Extension Service's change in its programs to fit the computer age is another significant move.

South Dakota should continue to press for water development projects. Irrigation projects will help South Dakota feed and finish more livestock. Delivery of Missouri River water to more rural users and to cities and towns will help the state's economy.

South Dakota in the last 15 years has seen diversification that has brought many manufacturers and Citibank and other national credit card firms into the state.

These acquisitions have eased the impact of agriculture's misfortune on the economy, particularly in Sioux Falls, eastern tier counties and in Rapid City and the Black Hills.

Thanks to steps taken during the Janklow administration, the future of fishing has been assured by new or acquired fish hatcheries. Improvement in recreational facilities along the the Missouri River has been accomplished through cooperative steps with the U.S. Army Corps of Engineers.

What is needed now are new ways to attract tourists to South Dakota's recreational areas.

South Dakota took a giant step forward in the 1960s in the development of its educational television system. There has been significant expansion in the last year or two of the state's public radio stations to make the system statewide. Both TV and radio networks offer possibilities for creative steps in expanding educational opportunities for the general public in the years ahead.

Fifty years ago most state roads were gravel. Cement or blacktop was the exception. There was no TV set in the living room. Many school pupils attended one-room country schools.

South Dakota homes of today are much nicer than those of 40 or 50 years ago. Some of the larger county seat cities are thriving.

Perhaps the travel index is an excellent barometer of longterm change. The jet age has shrunk the nation and the world. The holidays have seen hundreds of parents, grandparents and children arriving at or departing from Joe Foss Field.

In South Dakota of yesteryear it was a treat for a country kid to ride to the county seat with his parents or for Sioux Falls youngsters to go to Minneapolis.

Changes that came during the 1970s saw Augustana College students flying to Kenya on an African interim study trip, or a Sioux Falls College music major spending January in London. All for college credit.

It would be easy for any writer to offer doom and gloom as the South Dakota scenario for the years immediately ahead. That ignores the characteristics of a population that has met challenges of drought, depression and war in stride.

The future will bring change. Based on the past, it will be for the better.

S.D. LIFE—CITIES

WHY CITY HAS "GOOD THING GOING"
Argus Leader, Oct. 23, 1983

Sioux Falls has a way of emphasizing the positive and recognizing the time and effort that civic leaders give to their organizations.

It was demonstrated anew at the annual dinner meeting of the Sioux Falls Area Chamber of Commerce Thursday night at the Ramada Inn.

Dr. Richard Friess, the outgoing president, got a plaque for his wall. During the last year, he's spent countless hours representing and leading the chamber and putting its schedule ahead of his own.

His wife, Barb, received a big rose bouquet.

M. L. "Murph" Murphey, the new president, noted the contributions Friess had made.

Another nice touch to the event was the introduction by Friess and Murphey of members of their families and their colleagues at work. Both acknowledged that their civic efforts were made easier by understanding at home and the office of what such a leadership role entails.

◆ ◆ ◆

Out-of-state speakers, like Michael H. Annison who addressed the chamber's event, customarily receive gifts that remind them of South Dakota and Sioux Falls pluses.

Annison, who lives in Denver, took home Black Hills gold cufflinks and an aerial photograph of Sioux Falls. He'll get another aerial photograph later of Denver. Both photos are a product of the EROS Data Center.

Annison should find EROS' high technology especially interesting as a facet of the information society about which he talked. Annison is associated with author John Naisbitt of Megatrends fame.

◆ ◆ ◆

It takes a lot of planning and some showmanship to stage a dinner for 700.

Annual meetings like the chamber's event have made increasing use in recent years of colored slides and graphic presentations.

Chamber officers and directors were pictured bigger than life on a screen as their roles were described briefly. A slide show narrative, entitled "Hidden Giant", depicted the increasingly larger part the medical community plays in Sioux Falls.

It was a surprise to this writer, for instance, to learn that today's 300 doctors represent a three-fold increase since 1971.

Donald A. Isaacson had the job of annual meeting chairman. This year it was a bigger challenge than ever, with events, including the Health and Business Fairs, spread over three days.

And just in case you're interested, last week's annual meeting was the 77th for the Sioux Falls Area Chamber of Commerce.

Appropriately, the program carried the names of past presidents from 1907 to this year. The first president, W. L. Baker, served in 1907-1908. The roll call from Baker to Friess includes many names familiar to today's residents of Sioux Falls.

Today's props—with public address systems, slide shows, etc.—probably would surprise chamber presidents and audiences of an earlier era.

The basics, however, probably haven't changed in three generations.

Each annual meeting is both a look backward and a glimpse toward the future.

Presidents and speakers of yesteryear must have dwelled on their hopes and aspirations for your favorite city and mine as their successors do today.

Sioux Falls has had a good thing going—as the chamber motto says—for a long, long time.

CITY HAS MUCH TO OFFER PASSING MOTORISTS
Argus Leader, Sunday, March 26, 1989

"Why would anyone come to Sioux Falls?"

That question makes Teri Ellis' blood pressure rise.

But more than that, it triggers a persuasive rejoinder. Ellis loves to tick off many assets that she believes make your favorite city and mine a nice place to visit.

She's director of the Sioux Falls Convention and Visitors Bureau (CVB) of the Sioux Falls Area Chamber of Commerce.

"My job is to increase the number of visitors to Sioux Falls, whether they're attending a convention, coming as tourists or to seek medical care," she says. Her main effort is developing new convention and tourist business.

Ellis' frustration about why many people discount Sioux Falls as a tourist destination has sparked a determination to change things.

"We're not known as a destination. In the past, we have been satisfied with seeing drivers go by on the interstate. Now we want them to stop, to see our historic districts, go shopping, go on the water slide or Karts West. We want a piece of the action.

"We may not be a destination for 10 days, but we can be for two or three days. There is a market out there and we are actively seeking that market.

"Part of our problem is educating people. First, we have to educate our local people as to why Sioux Falls is a great place to visit. We have to educate people more on our own state—let them know what we have to offer. Then we can sell Sioux Falls on the regional and national level. Once we get people in here, we can get them back."

Ellis said that Sioux Falls' increased interest in tourism has brought recognition from the industry in the state that Sioux Falls is serious about developing future tourist business.

That interest was publicized in a full page ad by the CVB in the Argus Leader last May. The ad asked: "What does tourism have to do with Sioux Falls? Plenty."

The ad said every year more than half a million parties travel the interstates on vacation and one-third of them stop overnight in Sioux Falls. (That would be half a million tourists a year, based on three persons per car).

The ad said that more than 100,000 convention goers in 1987 chose Sioux Falls, patronizing local motels, restaurants and stores.

The ad also said that in 1987, more than 10 million people visited the Empire, making the city shopping mall South Dakota's biggest tourism attraction. Mount Rushmore National Memorial attracts 2 million tourists a year.

Mary Kiley, general manager of the Empire, said that the mall is still using 10 million as its annual visitor total. The number is derived from daily checks of electronic traffic counters. The formula uses 2.2 people per car.

Ellis says, "Granted, we are not Mount Rushmore. We respect the national memorial highly. But we still have something worthwhile here."

Some attractions that Ellis believes will make Sioux Falls a desirable stop are: Great Plains Zoo and Delbridge Museum of Natural History, Falls Park, Old Courthouse Museum and Pettigrew Home and Museum, several historic districts and individually recognized historic sites, EROS Data Center, Sioux River Greenway, Augustana College, Sioux Falls College, Civic Fine Arts Center, full-scale reproductions of Michelangelo's David and Moses and the Center for Western Studies.

Ellis believes that other cultural attractions, such as the South Dakota Symphony and Community Playhouse, enhance Sioux Falls' tourism offering.

PIERRE ATTRACTIONS INCLUDE CAPITOL, HERITAGE CENTER
Argus Leader, Wednesday, June 7, 1989

Be sure to see Pierre, the state capital, and its sister city, Fort Pierre, before the centennial year ends.

History's trail is well marked in South Dakota's twin cities on the Missouri River. They've never looked better!

Getting there is half the fun. The West begins at the Missouri Hills; buttes and grassy expanses embrace the river and unfold before you.

South Dakota's Capitol, completed in 1910 and beautifully restored, is a treat. You'll enjoy seeing the rotunda and dome, white marble grand staircase, murals and displays.

The new $6.5 million South Dakota Cultural Heritage Center is destined to become the capital city's No. 2 attraction. It contains, among other things, state archives and the Robinson State Museum. Its changing gallery currently features The Way They Saw Us, illustrations of territorial and early statehood days from eastern newspapers.

Hilger's Gulch Park, set between the Capitol and the Center, is a jewel. You can walk, jog or cycle its path. Nearby are the State Library, Kneip Office Building and the Department of Transportation Building.

Parents may find it inspiring to walk Capitol steps with their youngsters. There's a nice view of Capitol Lake and Anderson and Foss office buildings. The South Dakota Korean and Vietnam War Memorial is on the northwest shore of the lake.

There are stately old homes from the late 19th and early 20th century only blocks from the Capitol. Historic St. Charles Hotel, where politicians decided many state issues in smoke-filled rooms, has been renovated as an apartment dwelling. Many old storefronts have been refurbished in the Pierre Mainstreet program.

Pierre will open the South Dakota Discovery Center and Aquarium July 4 in the former municipal power plant. The center will feature a hands-on science center for adults and children. The aquarium will display Oahe Reservoir fish species.

Steamboat and Griffin Parks, located along the Missouri River, offer many activities. A new causeway has been built to La Framboise Island. It and Farm Island State Recreation Area, four miles east on Highway 34, have excellent walking trails.

Cross the river from Pierre to Fort Pierre. The Verendrye Monument marks the site where Louis Verendrye and his brother planted a lead plate in 1743 to claim the land for France. School children discovered the plate in 1913.

The Verendrye Museum in Fort Pierre has excellent collections of South Dakota pioneer relics. The Cowboy and Western Heritage Hall of Fame honors notables in South Dakota history.

See blue water backed up in Oahe Reservoir, at the dam approximately seven miles northwest of Pierre on highways 1804 and 1806. Highway numbers stand for the years explorers

Lewis and Clark ascended and descended the Missouri River. There's a visitors center at the power plant.

See restored Oahe Chapel, located on the eastern side of the dam, just above the power plant. The Rev. Thomas L. Riggs, pioneer Congregational minister, built the chapel at Oahe Mission in 1877. It was given to South Dakota in the 1950s. Since 1966, Fort Pierre and Fort Pierre Ministerium has provided Sunday services starting at 8 a.m. during June, July and August.

Four miles south of the chapel on Highway 18M there's a monument at the center of South Dakota and the approximate center of North America.

Adjacent to the marker is South Dakota's Centennial Acre. Buy a square foot for $19.89 and receive a special historical deed. Then check it out when you visit Pierre. For more information, contact Roxie Danilko, State Centennial Office, 773-4036, or write the office, 500 E. Capitol Ave., Pierre, S.D. 57501.

S.D. LIFE—SIGHTS

A GLIMPSE INTO THE MILITARY PAST
Restored fort shows ingenuity of frontier troops
Argus Leader, Sunday, May 28, 1989

One hundred years ago on June 1, Capt. Joseph Hale signed an order closing Fort Sisseton in Dakota Territory.

For one year Hale and 39 men of the Third Infantry had been preparing the post for abandonment. When they marched away to Browns Valley, Minn., the post was turned over to the territorial government. There was no longer any need for an army post in the northeastern corner of what would become the new state of South Dakota.

Today, Fort Sisseton State Historic Park preserves 15 of the original 45 buildings. Visitors can roam the grounds, walk through some buildings and imagine what life was like on the frontier from 1864 to 1889.

This step back in time is an interesting one. Fort Sisseton is a national historic landmark and one of the nation's best preserved frontier forts.

Step into the Visitors Center in the North Barracks. You'll be handed a History and Tour Guide which you can follow on your own walking tour. But first, look over the excellent historical exhibits. They give highlights of Fort Sisseton's role, how soldiers constructed its brick and stone buildings and their difficult life on the Plains.

Step into the barracks room and see new wooden, double-decked bunks built without nails by the park staff during the winter. Step outside onto the new boardwalk which borders buildings fronting on the parade ground.

Walk to the flagpole in the center. A plaque says a time capsule buried July 25, 1964, will be opened at the bicentennial of Fort Sisseton on July 25, 2064. It was placed there 25 years ago by the Northeastern South Dakota Lake Region Association's centennial committee.

Another plaque notes that Fort Sisseton was rebuilt by the state of South Dakota and the Works Progress Administration in 1939 as WPA Project Number 3384. The WPA was one of many alphabetical agencies that President Franklin D. Roosevelt used to combat the Great Depression.

The WPA restoration and the 1959 South Dakota Legislature's designation of Fort Sisseton as a state park are the main reasons there's a restored fort today.

Restoration has been continued by the Department of Game, Fish and Parks, with assistance from legislative appropriations and the State Historical Preservation Center. The 1989 Legislature appropriated $127,000 to start renovation and restoration of the commanding officer's quarters.

Visitors will marvel at the ingenuity of frontier troops in constructing the fort with available material, such as lime, lake clay for bricks and field stone. They kept a sawmill busy.

There wasn't enough wood to erect a stockade, so they built earthen breastworks, dug a ditch and put log blockhouses on northwest and southeast corners. The blockhouses provided fields of fire on all four sides. The northwest blockhouse replica was built from original War Department plans.

Fort Sisseton was never attacked in its 25-year history. But its strategic location on the Coteau des Prairies (hills of the prairie, which rise 600 feet above the Plains) helped keep the peace. It was built following the Sioux uprising in Minnesota in 1862.

Fort Sisseton, originally named Fort Wadsworth, was erected during the last year of the Civil War by Wisconsin volunteers and "Galvanized Yankees." The latter were enlisted Confederate prisoners who chose to serve out their time in the West rather than in military prisons.

Fort Sisseton is 22 miles north of Webster or 10 miles southwest of Lake City off Highway 10. Hills and lakes are beautiful in late spring.

The Fort Sisseton Historical Festival June 3-4 offers a fascinating glimpse at yesteryear. It includes a rendezvous of muzzleloaders, infantry and cavalry drills, horse pull, fiddlers jamboree, Indian cultural demonstrations and a military costume ball.

DESMET PRESERVES FRONTIER HISTORY OF LAURA INGALLS WILDER

Argus Leader, Sunday, June 11, 1989

History's trail is well marked in DeSmet, "The Little Town on the Prairie" immortalized by Laura Ingalls Wilder.

Her children's books, written after her 65th birthday, relate her family's travels to the West and joys and trials of homesteading near DeSmet.

Her books have been dramatized on the popular television series *Little House on the Prairie*, now in reruns.

Six of Wilder's 10 books have their setting in the DeSmet area, where she lived from 1879 to 1894.

The Laura Ingalls Wilder Pageant Society stages an annual pageant one mile east of DeSmet on Highway 14.

The pageant will be presented at 9 o'clock each evening on three successive weekends: June 24-25, July 1-2 and July 8-9. Tickets are $4 for adults, $2 for children. There are no advance ticket sales.

The pageant grounds overlook the homestead site of Charles and Caroline Ingalls and their daughters Mary, Laura, Carry and Grace. A plaque marks the spot. Nearby, cottonwood trees planted by Pa Ingalls still stand.

Laura was 12 when the family spent fall and winter months of 1879-80 at a railroad construction camp near DeSmet.

She described this period in *By the Shores of Silver Lake*. Her father worked for the railroad and they lived in the Surveyors' House

The family lived in several homes in DeSmet and on the homestead. After an October blizzard, the family moved back into DeSmet.

She characterized the ordeal in her book *The Long Winter (of 1880-81)*. Early to bed and two meals a day helped settlers' families get through the winter without starving.

Self-guided tours include 18 places in DeSmet mentioned in the books. Guides staff the Surveyors' House and the Pa and Ma Ingalls Home and Museum, the residence they built in 1887. Tours are from 9 a.m. to 5 p.m. daily through Sept. 15.

Tours begin at the Laura Ingalls Wilder Memorial Society's Headquarters and Gift Shop located three blocks east of the city library. Admission is $3 for adults, $1 for children.

Laura taught a rural school one mile south of the Ingalls homestead site. Her book *These Happy Golden Years*, on which the pageant is based, chronicles her romance and marriage to Almanzo Wilder and their life in a claim shanty two miles north of DeSmet.

There's a historical marker along Highway 25 near the Wilder homestead site.

The couple's daughter, Rose Wilder Lane, who became a well known novelist, journalist and essayist, was born on the claim. Wilder's book, The First Four Years, tells of farm life at this location from 1885-89.

The Wilders also lived at a tree claim a mile and a half north of their homestead. There the Wilders experienced a fire which destroyed their home, the death of an infant son and other natural disasters which were a part of frontier life. She wrote, "No one who has not pioneered can understand the fascination and the terror of it."

In 1894 the Wilders moved to a farm in the Ozarks near Mansfield, Mo. She died there on Feb. 11, 1957, at age 90.

DeSmet displays other historical links with the past. The town is named for Father Pierre Jean DeSmet, a Roman Catholic Jesuit missionary who devoted his life to American Indians. There's a statue of him in DeSmet's Washington City Park.

Several original paintings of prairie artist Harvey Dunn, who was born near DeSmet, are displayed in the city library.

DeSmet converted its railroad depot, completed in 1906, to a museum. Exhibits include a wildlife display and a country print shop. The latter is a memorial to the late Aubrey Sherwood, longtime DeSmet editor and publisher.

Located across the street from the Headquarters and Gift Shop is a one-room country schoolhouse restored in 1976. Former Gov. Sigurd Anderson taught in the school in 1927-28.

DeSmet, population 1,237, is one of South Dakota's neatest small town county seats. DeSmet's depiction of its heritage has to be one of South Dakota's best efforts.

FAULKTON'S ON THE MAP

Argus Leader, Sunday, Aug. 20, 1989

FAULKTON—"Just because you are not on the interstate doesn't mean you can't be on the map!"

So says Jody Moritz of Faulkton. She's president of the Faulkton Historical Society and co-editor and publisher of the Faulk County Record.

Faulkton in this centennial summer is very much on the map thanks to some remarkable community cooperation and promotion.

Faulkton is a neat, county seat town of 981 people on Highway 212 in north central South Dakota. Faulkton is 75 miles west of Interstate 29 and 96 miles north of I-90. The town has maintained Main Street vitality and made the most of its civic attractions.

Moritz credits promotion efforts by Shirley Pritchard for much of Faulkton's visibility.

Pritchard coordinates group tours of the century-old, 20-room mansion built by John Pickler, South Dakota congressman from 1889 to 1897.

Part of Pritchard's efforts are reflected in the visitor's guide of the Glacial Lakes Tourism Association.

Faulkton lists 17 attractions in the guide, compared with 14 for Aberdeen, the largest city in the region, and 18 for Watertown, the region's second largest city.

Pritchard said she came away from a centennial planning meeting in Miller convinced that "we don't promote enough." So steps were taken to promote some unique local assets.

"Everyone just pitched in," she said. Eight retailers paid for an ad in the South Dakota Vacation Guide.

She credits Moritz' leadership in the Historical Society for the opening a year ago of the Pickler home, and other historic preservation efforts. The Historical Society is using $5 admission fees to restore the home. While it is now Faulkton's major draw, there are other keen attractions.

Wauneta Holdren, like Pritchard, a senior citizen, started her labor of love on a flower garden about five years ago. Her Hillside Garden is near her home above the Nixon River in the north part of Faulkton.

The site was an old city trash dump. Holdren hauled out debris by pickup loads and persuaded contractors to dump surplus dirt on old tires that she used to terrace the hillside.

Visitors view flower beds and walk tree-lined paths in the acre-and-a-half garden.

Between May 2 and Aug. 10, 1,100 visitors toured the garden. Last year the garden drew 1,286 visitors by mid-September.

Holdren's centennial good turn is a flower garden on Main Street, on a vacant lot between the post office and her daughter-in-law's flower and gift shop. The garden replaced a weed patch.

The "Happy Times Merry Go Round" offers free rides several times a week in a park across from the Courthouse. The late Bob Ketterling, a cement contractor, bought the carousel at an auction in 1981 and reassembled it piece-by-piece. He opened the park in 1982.

Since his death in 1988, volunteers have helped his wife continue the free rides.

A sign on the Courthouse lawn says, "Happy Birthday South Dakota." No community has enjoyed the centennial more than Faulkton.

DON'T SKIP THE DAKOTADOME WHEN YOU VISIT VERMILLION

Argus Leader, Sunday, Feb. 25, 1990

When in Vermillion, tour the DakotaDome and get a feel for the ambience of the stadium that a University wordsmith has termed "an acre of June 12 months a year."

Actually, the DakotaDome has 3.2 acres under its roof—a translucent fiberglass coated with teflon and strung to steel cables. It's held aloft by air pressure from fans.

A visitor comes away with a different perspective after viewing the DakotaDome from its playing field below stands seating 9,000 fans and 100 feet below the rooftop.

DakotaDome's astroturf replaced the green sward of Inman Field almost 11 years ago and started a new way of life on the University of South Dakota campus.

Gone were the days late in the season when fans braved snow and cold at Inman to see the Coyotes battle football foes. Gone, too, was crowding 2,500 basketball fans elbow to elbow in the New Armory.

Attending athletic events at the DakotaDome became easy; a fan could go in shirtsleeves or dressed for dinner. The Dome also gave University students a stadium full of intramural and recreational opportunities.

A couple of years after the DakotaDome's first use in September 1979, state high school football playoffs bloomed in Vermillion, with the University acting as host.

When blizzards blow on game weekends, South Dakota, Iowa and Nebraska high school football teams find it easy to switch games to the Dakotadome. Students play touch football and frisbee football on the artificial turf.

When the turf is rolled up, there are basketball, volleyball, baseball/softball, track and other game courts available. Or space for farm and dog shows, high school band competition and other expositions. There are also areas for weights, aerobics, batting practice and other diversions.

The DakotaDome is unmistakable, rising from the plain on the north side of Vermillion. You can see it from miles away, especially when driving east toward Vermillion on Highway 50.

Jack Doyle, University athletic director, calls the Dome "a tremendous facility" and said that "all citizens in the state feel proud that South Dakota has a dome.

"When people come to visit Vermillion, a trip to the city is not complete until they have gone through the Dome. People from all over the United States come in to look it over. Many are amazed that a town the size of Vermillion would have such an attraction.

"A survey was made of freshman students at the U about six years ago. They were asked: When you hear USD or decided on a school, what was the first thing you think about? The greatest percentage said 'DakotaDome.' It has become synonymous with USD."

Doyle said that before the DakotaDome was built, people worried that only athletic teams would have access to the Dome. One promise made to the students at the time was that they would have use of the dome. Students are pleased that they can use these facilities.

One estimate is that 1,000 students (about a sixth of the student body) use the building every day. It is open from 6 a.m. to 11 p.m. Monday through Thursday; until 9 p.m. on Friday; from 9 a.m. to 9 p.m. on Saturday and from 1 p.m. to 10 p.m. on Sunday.

Recreational hours are scheduled morning, noon and night around physical education classes during the daytime. Recreational hours are also scheduled on the weekend.

The six-lane, 25-meter swimming pool has hours for lap and recreational swimming, in addition to regularly scheduled instruction. The pool is also used for canoe classes.

Faculty, staff, students, spouses and dependents can all use the facilities; so can families and individuals in the community and visitors on a fee or daily pass basis. Adults are charged $2 for a daily pass. Registration is at the Dome's southeast entrance.

The Dome was the brainchild of Carl Miller, who was athletic director in the early 1970s. His goal—in response to alumni who sought an all-weather facility—was a structure which could incorporate the entire health, physical education and recreational activity program into one building.

The Board of Regents approved funds for a feasibility study in 1972 and approximately a year later, the University of South Dakota kicked off its national fund raising project. The late Joe Robbie, USD graduate and owner of the Miami Dolphins, was the chairman.

Cost of the DakotaDome was $7.9 million, of which $5.X was appropriated by the Legislature, which authorized the project in 1974. Gov. Richard F. Kneip signed the authorization.

There was some campus turbulence. Some students attacked the plan. There were detractors off the campus, too. When the DakotaDome's roof collapsed in snowstorms early 1979 and again in 1982, detractors said, "I told you so." But the Dome's overwhelming success, from its initial financial backing to extended use, has made the early criticism something less than a footnote in South Dakota history.

This weekend brought the North Central Conference track meet to the Dome.

A three-phase improvement program will add facilities within the Dome. Phase I has been started, to install a new volleyball court and basketball court on the west side of the Dome, along with bleachers for approximately 1,200. Eventually, the building will open on the west.

A visitor walking through the Dome can feel the beat. It's fun.

MUSEUM OFFERS FASCINATING LOOK AT OLD WEST

Argus Leader, Sunday, July 2, 1995

CHAMBERLAIN-OACOMA, S.D.—Gene Olson's passion for collecting pioneer artifacts started with the 13 notches on a Remington revolver auctioned at a sale in the late 1950s in western South Dakota.

Olson, who with his wife Alice and son Greg operate the Old West Museum at Oacoma, had to have that revolver.

What do the notches count? Dead cowboys or coyotes? Gun fights? No one knows.

Olson and his wife collected artifacts 10 years before they opened the museum in 1969, This is their 27th summer of operation.

The revolver is one of more than 100 pistols, rifles and shotguns. All told, there are more than 100,000 separate items displayed in the Old West Museum's five buildings. The relics provide a remarkable glimpse of pioneer life.

Main Street stalls show facets of small town life: the law office of former Gov. M. Q. Sharpe and John Larson, the Pukwana drug store soda fountain and Post Office boxes from Dalesburg.

Olson grew up at Pukwana where his Swedish grandparents farmed. When the drug store fixtures went on sale, Olson had to outbid several others.

There's an excellent collection of steam and other farm engines. Car fans will like the neat red 1926 Ford Model T roadster, a 1917 Oldsmobile V-8, a 1923 Dodge sedan and a 1952 Kaiser Virginian.

Olson acquired an 80-foot miniature steam train, scale of 1-1/2 inch to the foot, from the builder, who was the husband of Olson's cousin who lived in Rochester, Minn. The Union Pacific locomotive weighs more than 2,000 pounds.

Salesmen's models of plows, farm gates and other equipment illustrate how frontier merchants sold big ticket items. There's a tobacco cutter from Sioux Falls and numerous crockery jars from pioneer grocers.

There's an extensive exhibit of horse-drawn vehicles. Live exhibits include a Texas longhorn and a buffalo. The senior Olsons once ran 100 longhorns on their ranch near Chamberlain. An iron lung used by the Chamberlain hospital during the polio epidemic of the 1950s is a reminder of Alice Olson's years as a nurse. The claim shanty was moved from Olson's grandfather's farm.

Other attractions include Rowena's wooden jail, Garretson's two-man metal cage lockup and Indian beadwork.

The Old West Museum is open from 7:30 a.m. to 9 p.m. seven days a week. Hours change Sept. 1 to 8 a.m. to 6:30 p.m. The museum is closed Oct. 31 for the winter and opens April 1, weather permitting. Admission is $5 per adult and $2.50 for children 6 to 14. Take exit 260 at Oacoma.

Other attractions: The Akta Lakota Museum at St. Joseph's Indian School in Chamberlain. Paintings, sculptures and artifacts of Indian life and culture are outstanding. The museum is a learning center to provide Lakota children with visions of the past and future. Admission: free. Summer hours: 8 a.m. to 6 p.m. Monday through Saturday; Sunday, 1 a.m. to 5 p.m. Take exit 263.

World Wildlife Adventures Museum in Oacoma. Trophy game specimens from North America and Africa, bagged by Lou and James Klaudt of White Lake, are featured. They are the museum owners. Admission. Exit 260.

Separate Travel Tip Item

The South Dakota Department of Transportation expects to have the Chamberlain rest area on Interstate 90 open to both lanes of traffic by mid-September. A paving project is under way on the I-90 hill near the rest stop.

Clyde Pietz, director of operations, said that about mid to late July the rest area will be opened to east bound traffic and closed to west bound traffic. The rest area is presently open to west bound traffic and closed to east bound traffic.

The rest area overlooks Lake Francis Case, Chamberlain, Oacoma and the hills to the north. It is one of South Dakota's most dramatic viewpoints.

EXHIBITIONS ARE SPECTACULAR AT SHRINE TO MUSIC MUSEUM

Argus Leader, Sunday, July 30, 1995

There's a treat for music lovers at the Shrine to Music Museum in Vermillion that begins in the Townsley Courtyard.

A bronze statue of an immigrant fiddler playing for three adoring children grouped around a water fountain greets visitors. The courtyard memorializes John B. and Emeline C. Townsley. He was the longtime editor and owner of the Dakota Republican, former weekly newspaper in Vermillion.

Step inside the University of South Dakota's recycled former Carnegie Library building and enjoy the exhibits. They showcase musical instruments and their manufacture and development from the 1600s to the present.

Whether you play an instrument or simply enjoy tunes, you'll find something of interest. Exhibits are spectacular.

- Several grand pianos more than 200 years old look like they just came off a showroom floor.
- Stradivari violins from Italy; Hardanger fiddles from Norway and a quarter-size violin made in London in 1856 for midget Tom Thumb which showman Phineas T. Barnum attempted to hype as a Stradivari.
- Six show cases of Conn cornets and other band instruments. The bust of Charles G. Conn, of Elkhart, Ind., who became the world's largest manufacturer of band instruments, is on display.
- The museum's holdings of brass, woodwind and stringed instruments by 17th- and 18th-century Nuremberg makers, is unique outside of Germany, Andre Larson, the museum's director, said.

You'll like the museum's technique of using mirrors to show backsides of violins and other instruments.

The industrial revolution added intermediate notes to wind instruments by use of valves that were perfected in the 19th century. Instruments had elaborate decorations, like figures of serpents or floral designs.

There are approximately 6,000 musical instruments in the museum. It opened in 1973 with the 2,500 piece-collection of Arne B. Larson as its nucleus. Larson became professor of music at the University of South Dakota in 1966 after USD agreed to house his collection. He moved from Brookings, where he headed the music department in the public schools, to Vermillion. He and his wife donated his collection—valued at more than $1 million—to the state of South Dakota in 1979. His son, Andre, has directed the museum since it opened. Arne Larson died in 1988.

The Shrine to Music is governed by a 25-member board, of which Joan Holter, Vermillion, is chair. The University's Department of Music offers graduate study in conjunction with the Shrine to Music and Center for Study of the History of Musical Instruments.

The Shrine had 35,000 visitors last year. Its backers would like more.

Opening of two galleries this spring completed the Shrine's building layout. The Cutler Gallery features musical innovations of the Industrial Revolution and instruments used by European folk musicians. Richard and Sharon Cutler of Sioux Falls underwrote construction costs. The Everist Gallery introduces the American music industry and how it grew. Margaret Ann and Hubert Everist of Sioux City sponsored the gallery.

Shrine to Music hours are 9 to 4:30 Monday through Friday; Saturday, 10 to 4:30; Sunday, 2 to 4:30. Free.

Also on the USD campus: The W.H. Over State Museum, with 26 original paintings by Oscar Howe. A new Indian exhibit will be ready by early fall. Hours: 8 to 5 on weekdays, 1 to 4:30 on weekends. Admission: $3 for 18 and older; under 18, free. The museum is adjacent to the DakotaDome.

WALL DRUG OPENS ITS PHOTO-FILLED BACKYARD TO TOURISTS

Argus Leader, Sunday, Aug. 13, 1995

WALL, S.D.—Wall Drug Backyard, a 14,000 square foot expansion, is another step in the evolution of Wall Drug Store.

Free ice water and five-cent coffee have long been Wall Drug's attractions for tourists. William Hustead, president and chief executive officer, believes the free museum attractions in the Backyard will help keep tourists coming.

Wall Drug Backyard opened in a new concrete block building across the alley behind the Drug Store in late May. The Backyard has 1,500 historical and pioneer pictures from the 1870s to the 1920s. A life-size diorama of an Indian village, an art store with Western and Indian paintings and a new cafe are in the addition. Wall Drug Christmas paintings are displayed on cafe walls. Color photographs of South Dakota flowers are shown in a hallway. Another gallery shows 250 articles from a total of 780 about Wall Drug Store that have appeared in newspapers and magazines.

Traditional picture-taking sets, like the mounted bucking horse, team and wagon, six-foot rabbit and replica of Mount Rushmore, have been regrouped outside in a Backyard corner. Picture taking is free.

The historical pictures are remarkable. They include photographs from the collections of historian Leonard Jennewein and six photographers. Many prints are from glass negatives. They capture the faces of soldiers, Indians, cowboys, settlers and men, women and children who came to a territory and built a state.

Bill Hustead (1923-1999) stands before the new backyard of Wall Drug Store in summer of 1995. —Anson Yeager photo

Colorful Indian exhibit is first of many displays in Wall Drug Backyard. —Anson Yeager photo

Hustead, whose hobbies include Western and South Dakota art, has shown the Wall Drug Christmas paintings at Federal Reserve Banks in Minneapolis and Billings. He likes the "Grandma Moses" quality of some western paintings in the Backyard's galleries. Wall Drug has nine Harvey Dunn paintings and many life-size statues of frontier figures.

Hustead said the Backyard expansion is the biggest one undertaken by Wall Drug in recent years. It follows by several years the grouping of Western-interest stores in the Western Mall on the south side of Wall Drug Store. One major attraction is the Travelers Chapel, designed like one in Dubuque, Iowa, and fitted with stained glass windows from an early church in Pierre.

Wall Drug Store has built its reputation on worldwide advertising using signs giving the mileage to Wall Drug. South Dakota GIs have put up Wall Drug Store signs practically everywhere the U.S. military has served. Other travelers have placed signs, too.

Hustead said Wall Drug Store had record sales grossing $11,186,462 in 1994. He said the store was down 2 per cent in June and 1 percent in July. "If we didn't have the Backyard, we would be down five or six percent."

Wall Drug Store operates with 250 employees, including 150 college students, during peak summer months. The payroll shrinks to 100 in November. Students live in 32 houses in Wall that are operated like dormitories. A swimming pool is a store perk.

Wall Drug Store has become a legend. Ted Hustead founded it in 1931. His wife Dorothy came up with the free ice water idea in 1936. Both Ted and Dorothy are in their early 90s. Son William started as pharmacist and store manager in 1951. His sons Rick and Ted are store managers. A Backyard photo gallery features the Hustead family.

VISIT MURDO FOR GREAT SHOW OF CARS

Argus Leader, Sunday, Sept. 10, 1995

MURDO, S.D.—You'll find many chapters of America's love affair with automobiles at the Pioneer Auto Museum and Antique Town in Murdo.

There are more than 300 classic and old cars in one of the nation's largest privately owned collections. There are Ford Model Ts, As and V-8s, nostalgic convertibles from the 1950s and muscle cars. A 1948 Tucker, a 1951 Henry J. (Kaiser small car) and a 1925 Stanley Steamer are among exhibits.

Antique Town portrays Murdo in 1906. Stop at the railroad depot, press a button and hear a telegraph key clicking out a Morse code message. You can lose yourself in half a dozen large buildings which display old cars. One building is signed Henry's Ford Garage.

If motorcycles are your passion, see Elvis Presley's 1976 Harley Davidson 1200 motorcycle. If you're a movie buff, you'll like the big, white 1931 Packard convertible once owned by legendary movie actor Tom Mix.

There's a Burma Shave jingle posted outside the 1908 country school:
"Past the school house
Take it slow
Let the little
Shavers grow
Burma Shave"
The school house is one of 39 buildings of exhibits on the grounds.

A street in Pioneer Auto Museum and Antique Town in Murdo captures yesterday's automobile and gas station row in small towns. —Anson Yeager photo

An Antique Town historic site sign recalls Murdo's beginning as the northern head of the Texas Cattle Trail in 1880. —Anson Yeager photo

There are interesting reminders of Murdo's past. A restored historic sign marked the northern head of the Texas cattle trail near Murdo in 1880. A 1909 Auburn touring car was used to drive homesteaders overland to their claims when roads didn't exist.

Dave Geisler, Ford dealer in Murdo from 1962 to 1980, is owner-manager of the museum and Antique Town. It is a family project. Wife L. J. does restoration work. Son David M. and daughter Vivian help in the business. Some of brother John's cars are on exhibit.

The museum had its start when Dave Geisler's father, A. J. "Dick" Geisler, Murdo Chevrolet and John Deere dealer, displayed old cars to attract tourists to his filling station. Geisler and sons Dave and John built the first museum building in 1954.

The "Orange Peel," a three-wheel, one-passenger car manufactured on the Isle of Man in 1964, attracted much attention this summer. It is on loan from Dusty and Gayl Rhodes, Colville, Wash., and will be at Murdo for two years. The car, built of high grade fiber glass, has a one-cylinder motorcycle engine and transmission which weigh 23 pounds.

Other attractions include old toys and games and a rock and gem collection.

Museum hours during September, October, April and May are 8 to 6. Hours June through August are 7 a.m to 10 p.m. Admission charge. Winter hours depend on the weather but the gift shop and food service are open.

While in Murdo, stop to see the dolls at Camp McKen-Z Doll Museum. Some 300 dolls are displayed; also paintings of Edna McKenzie, local artist and campground operator. Admission charge. Free to campground patrons. Camp McKen-Z closes Sept. 30 and reopens May 1.

INDIAN-PIONEER MUSEUM IS SPIRITED

Argus Leader, Sunday, Sept. 17, 1995

There's a new spirit at the Friends of the Middle Border Museum of American Indian and Pioneer Life in Mitchell.

Much of the drive for change comes from Stacey Vanden Heuvel, a 29-year-old international economist, and a revitalized board.

Vanden Heuvel quickly admits that museums were not her field, but she obviously enjoys applying economic principles to the job she's held since April 1994.

What does an executive director do when she is the only staff person on the payroll?

She uses friendly persuasion in doubling the number of volunteers to 90, promotes sponsorships by businesses and community organizations and pushes maintenance, painting and fixup.

There is also renewed attention to the exhibits, which include South Dakota and other treasures.

The two-block site on the eastern side of Dakota Wesleyan University, with which the museum is affiliated, has seven buildings.

The Italianate home built by Louis Beck with a co-founder of the Corn Palace, has had many coats of paint in its 109 years. Original sage green and oxblood red trim are being applied as restoration continues.

The 1900 railway depot, moved from Dimock, has a life-size model of a telegrapher. The Milwaukee Road donated the depot.

Church services are held every third Sunday from May through September in the 1909 Farewell Methodist Church moved from near Artesian. Classes were held in the one-room Sheldon School from 1885 to 1945.

The Indian and art exhibits are comparatively small, but choice.

The Indian exhibit concentrates on people on the Pine Ridge, Rosebud and Cheyenne River reservations between 1890 and 1929. Exquisite bead work by Indian women fascinates European tourists. They want to know where the glass beads came from—mainly Central Europe and England.

The Missouri State Capitol at Jefferson City has James Earle Fraser's bronze sculptures of explorers Lewis and Clark. His original plaster castings from which Missouri's statues were made are exhibited in the Case Art Gallery.

His original carving of the Buffalo nickel—which he designed—is also there.

Other original works by Oscar Howe, Gutzon Borglum, Harvey Dunn and Charles Hargens, a Hot Springs native who became a magazine illustrator, are exhibited.

Leland D. Case, a co-founder of FMB in 1939 and benefactor and for whom the art gallery is named, is memorialized by a replica of his retirement office and library in Tucson, Ariz. He was editor of Rotarian and Together magazines and a brother of U.S. Sen. Francis Case.

The sheep wagon in which Archer Gilfillan lived and wrote his book, "Sheep," in Harding County is shown.

Vanden Heuvel, a Rock Rapids, Iowa, native, graduated from Augustana College in 1988. She did her master's work in economics at the National University of Malaysia. She worked and taught in economics and was married to Rashid Kadir before returning to the United States. He is employed as a mechanical engineer in Mitchell.

The museum is open 9 a.m. to 5 p.m. weekdays and 1-5 p.m. Saturday and Sunday in September and May. June-August hours are 8 a.m. to 6 p.m. Monday through Saturday and 10-6 Sundays.

October to April hours are by appointment; phone (605) 996-2122.

There is an admission charge. Call for group and bus discounts.

S.D. LIFE—VARIETY

NORTH DAKOTA FOLLOWS LEAD IN TOURIST STOPS
Argus Leader, Sunday, Sept. 24, 1989

Compared with its sister state of South Dakota, North Dakota is a Johnny-Come-Lately in tourist attractions.

In South Dakota, Wind Cave became a national park in 1903; Jewel Cave, a national monument in 1908; Mount Rushmore, a national memorial in 1927; and the Badlands, a national monument in 1939.

North Dakota obtained Theodore Roosevelt National Park in 1947; Fort Union Trading Post National Historic Site was established by Congress in 1966 and Knife River Indian Villages became a national historic site in 1974.

North Dakota has gained two major park improvements—one federal and one state—as lasting legacies of its centennial year. They are:

• The replica of the home of Lt. Col. George Custer and his wife Libby, which opened at Fort Abraham Lincoln State Park in Tune. A $3 million project (including about $2 million in federal funds), the house was rebuilt from original designs Custer helped draw.

• The fort and visitors center of Fort Union Trading Post National Historic Site, dedicated in August. Fort walls and two blockhouses were completed during summer 1989; the visitors center was erected in 1987 and replicates the lavish Bourgeois House (manager's home). This is a $4 million project (mainly federal money).

Fort Lincoln is the post from which Custer and the 7th Cavalry marched away May 17, 1876, to the Little Bighorn in Montana. Custer and about 225 men under his immediate command were wiped out June 25, 1876, by Indians whose leaders included Sitting Bull.

Fort Union was established in 1829 by John Jacob Astor's American Fur Co. near the junction of the Missouri and Yellowstone rivers. It soon became headquarters for trading beaver furs and buffalo hides with Indians in a large area. The fort was dismantled in 1867.

Extensive archeological digs preceded construction at both Fort Lincoln and Fort Union.

The Fort Abraham Lincoln Foundation plans to build replicas of a commissary, barracks and other buildings found at the original fort. The Custer home is near other state park attractions, including infantry post blockhouses, a museum and Mandan earth lodges. The park is five miles south of Mandan. The Custer Home will be open through Sept. 30 from 1 to 4 p.m., and by appointment with the foundation office (phone 701-258-0203) until reopening next May 1.

Fort Union, which is 24 miles southwest of Williston, is just inside the state line. The parking lot is in Montana.

Fort Union's nearby twin attraction is Fort Buford State Historical Site, open May 16 through Sept. 15. It has a museum, stone powder magazine and a military cemetery. The U.S. Army established a military post at Buford in 1866. Sitting Bull and Nez Perce Chief Joseph were among Indian leaders imprisoned at Fort Buford.

The Custer home and Fort Union join North Dakota's premier tourist attraction—Theodore Roosevelt National Park and historic Medora—in increasing the Peace Garden State's appeal to visitors. The park includes North Dakota Badlands where the nation's 26th president ranched during the 1880s.

The Chateau de Mores State Historic Site at Medora features the restored home of the Marquis de Mores, a flamboyant Frenchman who founded the town in 1883. His packing house and other ventures failed.

Completion of a new visitors center for the Knife River Indian Villages National Historic Site is planned for the fall of 1990. The site is three miles north of Stanton.

South Dakotans will enjoy late spring or summer trips north of the border to view their neighbors' improved tourist sites.

LEGENDS ENHANCE S.D. IMAGE
Argus Leader, Sunday, June 13, 1993

Knowing the product is essential for any successful salesperson.

No one in South Dakota knows more about its geography, facts, figures and history than the creative staff of the state Department of Tourism. There's also a bonus in the department's compilation of legends that enhance story telling about the Mount Rushmore state.

I hope you'll enjoy these legends and facts reprinted from the department's booklet, "Escort Essentials."

• The Feline Legend: Before the railroads came to South Dakota, all freight was hauled to the Black Hills in wagons. One of the most famous freight wagons was filled to the brim with...you guessed it, cats! Crates and crates of them.

It seems back in 1876, the city of Deadwood had no cats, and the dance hall girls and "working girls" of the town yearned for the fluffy little creatures for pets and as mousers.

Eyeing a potential gold mine in cats, mule skinner Phatty Thompson set off for Cheyenne, Wyo. Phatty paid the youngsters of the town two bits for every cat they brought him. It wasn't long before Phatty's wagon was filled with 50 yowling, scratching passengers.

Back in Deadwood, Phatty garnered $10 a cat, $30 for the fat ones, and 30 minutes later Phatty Thompson was without a cat to his name and $1,000 richer.

• The John Philip Sousa Legend: "March King" John Philip Sousa had been engaged to play for the 13th annual Corn Palace Festival in 1904. Festival organizers sent a telegram to New York asking what the bandmaster's fee would be for 12 performances. Sousa's manager returned a reply asking if the Dakotans were aware of Sousa's fee for just ONE performance.

Again Mitchell asked the fee for 12 concerts. When Sousa's manager replied the fee would be a whopping $7,000, Mitchell jumped at the deal. But Sousa was not so easily swayed. When he arrived in the city, he insisted that he be paid in cash before he would let his band members off the train. Sousa was paid and his 12 concerts are now part of the great history of the World's Only Corn Palace.

• The "Scotty" Philip's Bison Legend: James "Scotty" Philip watched with misgivings the disappearance of the once mighty buffalo. At the close of the 19th century, nearly all the bison in existence were gone, except for a few herds on private ranches. One such ranch was that of Pete Dupree. When Pete died, "Scotty" Philip bought his herd of five buffalo. Over the years before the carving of Mount Rushmore, the buffalo were the most popular tourist attraction in South Dakota. Today, Custer State Park's buffalo have "Scotty" Philip's bison ancestry. They now make up one of the largest publicly owned herds in the world.

• The Lawrence Welk Legend: In 1928, a young accordionist from Strasburg, N.D., arrived in Yankton with his novelty band. Hoping to restock their dwindling cash reserves, the band sought out the local radio station (WNAX) and asked if they might perform.

After feeding the hungry group, the station's manager arranged to put them on the air. Listener reaction was so great that the manager offered to add the band to the station's roster of regular entertainers. The leader of the band realized that though the pay was sparse, the gig could help the band attract better paying bookings.

As a result that "brief stop" in Yankton lasted almost nine years. Thus began the illustrious career of the great Lawrence Welk.

- Did you know?: The four faces of Mount Rushmore National Memorial tower 6,000 feet above sea level and are scaled to men who would stand 465 feet tall....Korczak Ziolkowski's gigantic sculpture Crazy Horse is the world's only mountain carving in progress.

WINTER TRAVEL OPPORTUNITY GREAT CLOSE TO HOME
First Bundle Up then slow down and enjoy S.D.

Argus Leader, Sunday, Feb. 6, 1994

Here are things to think about during white knuckle days of what is beginning to be an old-fashioned winter.

Driving during a weather alert will require all your attention. Let your traveling companion describe the picture post card scenes that unfold along the roadway.

Wind blowing snow across the highway makes it difficult for the driver to take his eyes off the road. Another distraction is the whirlwind of snow served up by the tires of an 18-wheeler passing your vehicle. Sometimes there are three or four trucks in a row. That makes it white knuckle time all over again.

That's when this driver says a quiet thank you to the South Dakota Department of Transportation for its generally excellent job of keeping highway lanes and roadways striped. Seeing the white stripe on the highway's right edge helps a lot when weather outside is frightful.

Driving on snow-covered roads when wind chills and temperatures are below zero is no fun—but sometimes it's necessary. Pay attention when highway reports include snow and ice-covered roadways, scattered slippery spots and plunging wind chills. Slow down!

South Dakotans rightfully have bragged about outdoor scenery, especially since Kevin Costner's "Dances With Wolves" showcased our western land and sky.

The same landscape under winter snow has many settings that could be the backdrop for winter adventure movies. The expanse of white, snow-covered plains and hills would easily fit story lines set in Alaska, Canada, Russia, Norway or New Zealand. Our outdoors is an authentic setting for skiing and snowmobiling that South Dakotans enjoy so much.

There's no guarantee that a South Dakota winter will provide enough deep snow for a script that requires it. However, there would probably be sufficient snowfall in the Black Hills to make up for lack of snow on the plains.

A big snow brings out old-fashioned friendliness in Sioux Falls. Individuals you haven't seen for months will stop their car in the middle of a residential street and holler to you about the weather while you're shoveling your sidewalk. Neighbors with snow blowers have a nice way of helping out neighbors.

There's no need to travel far during white knuckle days to take your own pictures. Your neighborhood, city parks, churches and schools offer picture opportunities. If you live on a farm or ranch, you'll probably want some snapshots to send to the kids in California or snowbirds in the South.

When your friends in Florida, the Rio Grande Valley or Phoenix call home to jab you about our big snow, tell them what they're missing: sparkling white snow, skiing, skating, snowmobiling and nice nights at home by the fireplace. Send them a card with a winter scene and scribble a note: "Wish you were here. Ha-ha!"

Meantime, South Dakota's greatest show—the Legislature—is in session in Pierre. See it if you can. Lawmakers will take off Monday, Feb. 21, for President's Day and wind up regular work Feb. 26. They'll return March 15 to consider any vetoes.

If you visit Pierre during the session, try to see exhibits at the Cultural Heritage Center. A room in the State Archives section features former Sen. James Abdnor's career from boyhood at Kennebec to service in the U.S. Senate and House. Memorabilia, photographs and a video tape are included.

For one of the best panoramic views of winter in South Dakota, climb the stairs (they're not steep) to the observation room of the Cultural Heritage Center. You can look southwest to the State Capitol and across the Missouri River to the hills that overlook Fort Pierre and the Bad River.

There are no white knuckles in the observation room. You're behind glass and climate is controlled according to museum standards.

CYCLISTS HAVE ROOM TO ROAM IN S.D.

Argus Leader, Sunday, Aug. 6, 1995

QUESTION: What does population density have to do with the Sturgis motorcycle rally which attracts Harley Davidson and other fans?

ANSWER: Everything. Motorcyclists can roam free in South Dakota.

The population density in South Dakota, the Coyote or Mount Rushmore State—take your pick—is 9.37 persons per square mile.

Population density in California is 197.9; Illinois, 209.2; New York, 383.7, and New Jersey, 1,049.9.

Motorcyclists would risk life and limb riding their bikes in populous states. Even with Rapid City's Central States Fair coinciding with the rally, motorcyclists still have lots of room on South Dakota's highways.

The Sturgis Rally and Races open Monday and run through next Sunday. However, the vanguard of motorcycle fans has been in South Dakota for days now.

Whether a South Dakotan drives a car, pickup or motorhome, he or she can help motorcyclists enjoy their visit.

Gene Abdallah, state superintendent of the Highway Patrol, and Maj. Tom Dravland, assistant superintendent, have some tips for you.

"The main thing is to be aware that there are a lot of motorcyclists out there," Dravland said.

"Although we encourage motorcyclists to drive with their headlights on, there is no law that requires it. Anytime you make a lane change, watch for both cars and cyclists."

Abdallah said: "Although motorcyclists have the same rights on the road as other drivers, they stand to lose more in event of an accident." He said all drivers must drive more defensively.

There is no estimate for attendance at this year's event, although requests for information are up 23 per cent, Francie Ruebel-Alberts, executive director of Sturgis Rally and Races, said. Attendance figures for the yearly event are based on traffic counts.

A crop duster heads for takeoff at Hayes International Airport, Hayes, S.D. —Anson Yeager photo

She said last year's attendance was between 175,000 and 200,000. The 50th anniversary event in 1990 set the record with attendance estimated at between 200,000 and 400,000.

Grain harvest, the big hay crop and a persistent green hue should enhance touring for all. South Dakota's "big sky" scenery, August sunshine and white clouds are part of the mystique.

Couples astride motorcycles can have a great adventure as they enjoy the hills and buttes of western South Dakota where much of the landscape looks like the locale of "Dances with Wolves."

There's a lot to see along the way.

For instance, the big hangar on a hill at Hayes, 34 miles west of Pierre on Highway 34, carries this sign: "Hayes International Airport."

"We wanted to have some fun with that," August Houston Rose, president of Rose & Son Spray Service, said.

"We are international, you know. A pilot from Canada stopped to refuel once," Rose quipped. He's 73, a transplanted Texan and a World War II U.S. Navy fighter pilot. He had finished his training in the summer of 1945 and was waiting assignment to a carrier when the U.S. dropped the atomic bombs on Japan. The Navy sent him and fellow officers home with a blunt "We don't need you fellows any more."

Rose said he flew his last spraying run earlier this year, completing 48 years in the business. He counts himself lucky to have flown for 50 years.

LET SOUTH DAKOTA LURE FAMILY FOR MORE VISITS

Argus Leader, Sunday, Jan. 7, 1996

South Dakota offers travel and enjoyment opportunities in all seasons for senior citizens- and for younger people, too.

Grandparents can plan now to double the number of family reunions and leisurely get-togethers throughout 1996.

This is the time of year to plan summer reunions in the Black Hills, along the Missouri River or in other vacation spots. Follow up by making campground and motel reservations. Some of the choice spots go quickly months before the summer season.

Grandparents with motorhomes can plan now to drive their rigs to the summer reunion, and put up children or grand-children in motel, tent or other campground space.

There are opportunities galore in the Black Hills and elsewhere in South Dakota to ride horseback, go sightseeing or participate in a variety of other sports during a reunion of several days or a week.

A week allows adult children flexibility in arranging their schedules to take family members home to South Dakota to see Grandma and Grandpa.

Summer reunions are a good time to discuss Thanksgiving and Christmas plans for the year. The result may double the number of times you will see your extended family during 1996.

Many snowbirds have already fled to the Sunbelt to avoid winter's snow and ice. Those who linger in South Dakota can enjoy skiing, snowmobiling, ice skating and fishing. This depends on the right mix of snow and temperature.

Here are some pleasures that seniors can anticipate during the year.

• Cooking a western breakfast of eggs, potatoes and meat on a campout or sitting down to one on a trail ride.

• Fishing on a summer day below the falls in Sioux Falls. Take your grandson. Talk to the regulars about catfish and other big ones they catch there or near downtown Sioux Falls.

• Watching sailboats at the marina at Gavins Point Dam at Yankton.

• Driving west of Pierre on Highway 34 and north on Highway 63 to Eagle Butte. This was the locale of big cattle ranches in pioneer days and is still prime grazing land today. Green grass on hills and buttes will make your day.

• Roaming the lake region and viewing a three-state area from atop the Nicollet tower west of Sisseton.

• Picnicking in Custer National Forest in Harding County. Visiting 1876 Battle of the Slim Buttes sites near Reva Gap east of Buffalo.

• Climbing Bear Butte near Sturgis. Take in all 360 degrees: Black Hills, range land and distant hills to the northeast and east.

• Touring the Cultural Heritage Center at Pierre. Look through its observation windows to the Missouri River and Fort Pierre. Walk the halls of the State Capitol, beautifully restored, and see legislators during the 1996 session.

• Become familiar with wildlife at home. You'd be surprised how many deer, small animals and birds live in Minnehaha County's hills and rural areas.

• Learn more about your hometown and local attractions. Visit museums and artists' studios. Enjoy close-in day trips in Sioux Falls or wherever you live. Reconnoiter the sights you'll show to grandchildren next summer.

SOUTH DAKOTA CENTENNIAL

DAKOTAS BOAST STRONG TREASURY OF HISTORY

Argus Leader, March 12, 1989

Hey, Minnesota, Iowa and Nebraska—look us over!

Celebrating 100 years of statehood gives South Dakotans a bit of newly-found maturity in talking to their neighbors.

Minnesota is nearly 131 years old. Minnesotans have always acted much older in gazing west at the upstarts on the prairie. Iowa is 142 years old and Nebraska, 122 years old. None of the three states seems as venerable as before.

Now South Dakotans can tell their good neighbors that with nearly 100 years under our belt, we, too, can brag about tradition.

South Dakotans can also point out that our wide open spaces (77,116 square miles, rank No. 16 among the states) and sparse population (709,000, rank No. 45) give us some advantages.

Minnesota has 84,402 square miles (rank No. 12) and 4,246,000 people (rank No. 21). Its population density is 50.3 per square mile. South Dakota's comparable figure is 9.2 per square mile, so Minnesota is more than five times as crowded as the Coyote State.

Iowa's population density is 50.4 per square mile, practically the same as Minnesota's. Nebraska's population density is 20.6 per square mile, more than twice as crowded as South Dakota. Nebraska is only 239 square miles larger than South Dakota.

A color guard marks 100 years of statehood in Pierre's Centennial parade. —Anson Yeager photo

South Dakota beats its sister state of North Dakota both in area and population. North Dakota, with a population of 672,000, ranks No. 46 among states. Its population density is 9.5 per square miles, or 0.3 of a person more than South Dakota.

This slight crowding north of our border results from the Peace Garden State's smaller area, 70,702 square miles, rank No. 17 among states.

South Dakota and North Dakota share a common birthday, Nov. 2, 1889, when President Benjamin Harrison signed almost identical statehood proclamations that created the two states.

By agreement some years later, North Dakota was ranked the 39th state and South Dakota, 40th.

But no one will ever know which state entered the union first because Harrison covered and shuffled the documents before and after signing them.

Harrison proudly declared: "They were born together—they are one and I will make them twins."

People of both Dakotas know all about the twin factor. Eastern newspapers and television networks occasionally misplace the Black Hills in North Dakota or Bismarck in South Dakota.

Both states share a common history from Dakota Territory days and many points of similarity in geography and development.

Lt. Col. George Armstrong Custer detrained his Seventh Cavalry at Yankton, capital of Dakota Territory, in 1873 and marched overland to Fort Lincoln, near modern Bismarck.

Fort Lincoln was his point of departure for his Black Hills exploratory expedition of 1874 and the fateful Battle of the Little Big Horn in 1876.

Theodore Roosevelt as a young man regained his health on a ranch in what is now western North Dakota. The 26th president is one of four faces on Mount Rushmore National Memorial in South Dakota.

Each state has rugged badlands, extensive look-alike western rangeland of buttes and hills and broad wheat fields. Each is cut by the Missouri River. South Dakota has the Black Hills and North Dakota the Red River Valley.

Both state governments experimented with business ventures. North Dakota has had a more volatile body politic.

South Dakota has had greater constitutional change by adopting annual legislative sessions. It was also the first state to adopt initiative and referendum laws.

Each state prides itself on its way of life and institutions. Small populations make it easy to develop statewide friendships.

State borders are big barriers, even to friends. Hopefully, our older neighbors will forgive button-popping and bragging in modern Dakota Territory this year.

FAMOUS SOUTH DAKOTANS COMING TO CITY FOR HOMECOMING

Argus Leader, Sunday, June 26, 1983

June brought Sioux Falls a planeload of Norwegians for the citywide Nordland Fest which winds up tonight.

July will bring Sioux Falls a South Dakota homecoming for 70 or more native sons and daughters whose names sound like a roll call from Who's Who.

If you'd like a glimpse of Al Neuharth, chairman and president of the Gannett Co. which owns USA Today and the Argus Leader, among other newspapers; Joe Robbie of the Miami Dolphins or Daisy Duke of the Dukes of Hazzard, the South Dakota Homecoming dinner on July 23 is for you.

Daisy Duke, of course, is Catherine Bach. Her television name has been shortened from Bachman, her family name when she was a girl at Faith, S.D.

She'll have a table down front at the dinner with another former resident of Faith, Francis Galbraith. He is a former ambassador to Singapore and Indonesia.

Among other former South Dakotans who've been invited and are expected to attend are G. Keith Funston, past president of the New York Stock Exchange; Felix Mansager, former chairman of the board of the Hoover Co.; Kenneth Holum, former assistant secretary of the Interior; Maj. Gen. Robert A. Sullivan, a native of Sturgis, and Walter A. Simmons, an alumnus of the Argus Leader who became a Chicago Tribune foreign correspondent and editor.

✦ ✦ ✦

The South Dakota Homecoming is the brainchild of Jim Meaghan, onetime manager of the Huron Chamber of Commerce who is now retired in Sarasota, Fla.

Meaghan's idea for a homecoming was outlined in this column a year ago. Meaghan envisioned an event in which former South Dakotans who have achieved recognition in various fields and professions would be invited to a banquet and program and receive Honorary Citizen Certificates from the governor of South Dakota.

Meaghan needed a sponsor. Ultimately, he found one in Ray Antonen, Lake Norden, S.D., president of the South Dakota Amateur Baseball Association. They got together and formed a committee for the South Dakota Homecoming. Antonen is chairman.

Harmon Kopperud, Lake Preston, S.D., is vice chairman; Julie Schmitz, Sioux Falls, is secretary; Frank Burch, Lake Norden, treasurer, and Meaghan, promotions director.

Kopperud, Burch and Meaghan all share Antonen's interest in amateur baseball. Any profits from the $25 a plate dinner will help finance expansion of the South Dakota Amateur Baseball Hall of Fame at Lake Norden.

✦ ✦ ✦

Homecoming activities start at 3 p.m. Saturday, July 23, at the Ramada Inn with a program by the South Dakota Old Time Fiddlers. The Sioux Falls Municipal Band will play a concert at 5:30 p.m. during a poolside reception.

Al Schock, Sioux Falls businessman, will be master of ceremonies. Gov. William Janklow and Mayor Rick Knobe will welcome the returnees to South Dakota and Sioux Falls. Former Gov. Joe Foss will be the keynote speaker.

Homecoming committee members will introduce the guests, who will receive honorary citizen certificates signed by Janklow. He is honorary chairman of the homecoming.

Honorees include Helen Mitchell of Minneapolis, who donated $54,000 to build the Baseball Hall of Fame at Lake Norden in honor of her father, Joe Salo, longtime mayor of the town and a baseball fan.

Myron Floren, native of Roslyn, S.D., and the nation's most famous accordionist, will be in the program's finale, featuring "I Left My Heart in South Dakota," to the San Francisco tune.

The entire event is open to the public.

Seating at the banquet will be at tables of 10, according to towns or other groupings. Lake Norden will have three tables. Amateur baseball supporters in various cities around the state will be part of the audience. The committee expects to sell 900 tickets.

The event should provide plenty of nostalgia, both for honorees and South Dakotans who knew them when.

The event is believed to be the first state homecoming of its kind in the United States. Besides that, it's for an excellent cause.

For reservations, write Julie Schmitz, Sioux Falls Area Chamber of Commerce, P.O. Box 1425, Sioux Falls, S.D., 57102, or call 336-1620.

◆ ◆ ◆

Meaghan deserves recognition for persistence. He didn't give up four years ago. That was when Huron civic leaders didn't act on his suggestion to promote a South Dakota Homecoming in connection with Huron's Centennial Celebration in 1980.

A friend in his hometown of Estelline last year sent him a copy of an Argus Leader feature on this page recounting the recollections renowned natives have of South Dakota.

Meaghan was confident that a state homecoming for famous or successful former South Dakotans would have the same appeal as centennial celebrations of recent years in this state.

Meaghan and Antonen decided last November that Sioux Falls, with its airline connections and other advantages, would be the ideal site for the homecoming.

When the idea was first publicized a year ago, I called it a concept that Janklow or Sioux Falls firms could develop on a couple of year's notice to induce more Citibanks and other firms using electronic technology to locate in South Dakota. I also said it would be a great idea for 1989—when South Dakota will be celebrating its centennial of statehood.

The backers, however, didn't want to wait that long. As one of them said, "There's that great umpire in the sky who has something to say about who'll attend reunions, too."

Sooner is better.

Antonen said Meaghan has written more than 200 letters from his Sarasota home to native South Dakotans, inviting them to Sioux Falls. That's typical of Meaghan. Antonen recalls that during his amateur baseball days in South Dakota, Meaghan helped organize 160 teams. He was also an officer in three different leagues at one time.

That's enthusiasm.

A SPECIAL WELCOME FOR SOME SPECIAL PEOPLE...

Argus Leader, Sunday, July 31, 1983

Editor's note: Following are the extemporaneous remarks, slightly condensed, of Gov. William Janklow, welcoming famous native sons and daughters of the state to the South Dakota Homecoming banquet July 23, 1983, at the Ramada Inn in Sioux Falls.

I tonight have really a special privilege being the governor of this state and the 690,000-some citizens who still live here. I say that because we welcome you people, all who have left and gone on to really not only individual achievements for yourselves and your families, but really glory and honor of recognition of your home state, your hometown, this place we call South Dakota.

And I also really am especially privileged because you people have been the ones who really altered many occasions, made a major difference.

You know, when you talk about coming home, it means a lot of different things to a lot of different people. Once a famous writer wrote that once you leave, you could never really go home again. That man didn't know what he was talking about because home is a lot of things.

For some people it's a state of mind. For some people it's just a feeling. For some people it's where you come from, or what you are. For some it's called safety or security. For some it means belonging; but for everybody, it is a welcome.

We in South Dakota have always prided ourselves that people are welcome here—not just those who were born here but those who leave, those that come here to visit.

But you know, South Dakota's a lot more than 400 towns and cities. It's a lot more than 66 counties. And it's a lot more than just 690,000 people. It's a way of life. It's a value system that all of you have taken wherever you've gone in the world. It's called good old common horse sense that you can't learn any place. You're either born and raised with it, or you never acquire it.

It's a system of beliefs—what's right and what's wrong, what your community or what your country means or doesn't mean.

As I looked down that agenda a couple of days ago that they sent me, specifically the index of the people who were coming home to spend probably all too short a time with us for this occasion, I couldn't help but look at the areas of endeavor and achievement that you former South Dakotans have rained honor on the state with.

I find people who are involved in the entertainment world and actors. I find winemakers and contractors and researchers and geologists and educators and soldiers and authors and judges and sports moguls, corporate leaders, labor leaders, U.S. senators, successful diplomats, religious leaders, scientists, business leaders, journalists—and basically, you name it. What you find is there's no one particular field of endeavor where our people are going to excel. It's really across the whole broad spectrum.

We who still live in South Dakota take a tremendous pride, in addition to that, a responsibility to you folks who no longer live here—a responsibility where we recognize that we have the duty to maintain the ideals and standards that you really hold near and dear when you talk about your home state.

For we have a state that has things like the Air National Guard—on several occasions it was selected as the most outstanding Air National Guard unit in the entire U.S. Air Force. We have the 2nd Battalion, 147th Field Artillery. On two occasions and again this year, it was elected as the most outstanding Army battalion in the U.S. Army, active or reserve.

We've got Lincoln High School in Sioux Falls—the national champions of debate in two of the four award categories. On scholastic aptitude test scores, South Dakota at the present time ranks No. 1 in the nation in verbal skills and No. 1 overall, second only behind Iowa, in arithmetic skills.

Of all the reigning rodeo queens in the world today, all five of them—from Miss High School Rodeo to Miss Rodeo World—at the present time come from the state of South Dakota. We in South Dakota are very unique because our queens, unlike some states, are always women. There's Miss Indian America—a beautiful young lady from the Cheyenne River Sioux Indian reservation in South Dakota.

You folks came from a state that currently ranks as No. 2 in the per capita percentage of its population that actively attends some organized church. The literacy rate in South Dakota is No. 1 in the nation; 99.6 percent of all people in this state can read and write. There's no state in the union that approaches that level.

In safety, South Dakota is No. 2. Only one other state in the union is a safer place in overall categories than your home state of South Dakota. South Dakota is No. 2 in the percentage of its citizens who take the time to go vote when they have an election.

And I guess what I'm trying to say is just that we feel that you people who have left the state really bring a great deal of privilege and honor to us. There is nothing more exciting. Dick Kneip will tell you that. Frank Farrar will tell you that.

Joe Foss, Larry Pressler, and Tom Daschle and Jim Abdnor and anybody else who has ever served this state away from South Dakota can tell you there's nothing that makes you feel better than to go someplace in this country and meet people who say, "Oh, yes, I know so and so from South Dakota."

It wasn't very long ago when we were trying to woo a corporation called Citibank to establish facilities in this state. They went before their policy committee, 22 people.

A suggestion had been made that they move a major portion of their business to South Dakota. There was a certain amount of snickering and laughing, and all of a sudden a fellow by the name of Rick Rush who served on that policy committee says, "I was born and raised in Aberdeen, S.D. What's so funny?"

Another guy said, "I don't dare laugh. My wife is from a place called Dell Rapids, S.D." And all of a sudden, once again, we received the benefits of the considerations of these people who used to be a part of our community.

But I guess what I'm trying to say is we're not just an exciting place to be from. We're an exciting place to be part of. You folks who were born and raised or lived in South Dakota and moved on elsewhere, you know as well as I do that when you come back—whether you're going to Flandreau, or Dell Rapids, or Colton, or Red Owl, or Pukwana, or Aberdeen, or Yankton, or Rapid City, or Lemmon or you name it—you're coming back home.

You're coming back home to your families. You're coming home to your loved ones. But more than anything else, you're coming back home to people who appreciate you. So I speak on behalf of all citizens of this state when I say tonight to all of you, "We welcome you back home."

S.D. public figures as close to constituents as nearest phone
(reprinted from the Argus Leader for Sunday, Nov. 22, 1981)

Jottings from an editor's notebook—telephone and other trivia about public figures that may or may not boggle your mind.

South Dakota's First Family—is in the phone book in Pierre. There's a listing for William Janklow—no title—and a separate phone for the children.

Gov. and Mrs. Janklow and the youngsters have kept the same phone numbers for several years, from before the move into that large, white frame home by the lake in 1979.

South Dakota mansion expense, according to a survey by the Minneapolis Star, is the least expensive in the region, or $51,316 for fiscal 1981. Wisconsin topped the list with $338,564; other states were Minnesota, $163,969; Iowa, $129,893, and North Dakota, $77,911.

Mayor Rick Knobe and some other Sioux Falls citizens with top public jobs are like Janklow—they're in the phone book.

Commissioners Harold Wingler and Richard Peterson are listed. So is Senior U.S. District Judge Fred J. Nichol.

M. E. (Mike) Schirmer, chairman of the Minnehaha County Commission and a former mayor, is in the phone book.

So are Richard Bohy, chairman of the Board of Education and John W. Harris, superintendent of schools. There are three John Harrises in the book and two John W's. The superintendent lives at 1620 S. 5th Ave.

School board members, superintendents—and principals—probably get more phone calls than anyone else in South Dakota. State legislators would be a close second, counting telephone calls to the capitol—called "heat from home"—when they're in session.

People who want unlisted numbers shouldn't run for office—or have a public job.

And here's a commercial for Ma Bell and all the independent phone companies in South Dakota. Your public servant is as close as your telephone.

The state's heritage as an open society—with easy access to public officers—makes it that way. Any officeholder who gets lofty ideas about being above the crowd soon finds himself looking for new employment in the Coyote State.

HISTORIAN GETS CENTENNIAL SHOW ON ROAD
Argus Leader, Dec.11, 1983

South Dakota's centennial as a state is less than six years away.

Several weeks ago Joseph H. Cash, president of the State Historical Society, visited with Gov. William Janklow about the things that should be done now to prepare for South Dakota's commemoration of the centennial.

Cash, a former history professor turned dean, said that Janklow showed considerable interest in the commemoration and the form it would take.

Cash said the step needed now is to set up a centennial commission with legal authority and enlist members who can get the show on the road.

"The important thing is to get it going. While it still seems like a lot of time, there really isn't."

South Dakota entered the union Nov. 2, 1889, so the centennial year is scarcely five away.

Cash sees a need for legislation from the 1984 session to set up a centennial commission, or an executive order by the governor which would do the same thing. The commission also will need funding.

Cash said, "I don't anticipate a great big blowout over it. The governor seems to be interested in the centennial as a kind of homecoming for native South Dakotans—a chance to come home."

The Historical Society has been involved in the planning process for three years, since the group suggested to Janklow that preparations should be made for the observance.

"I see it in a historical sense," Cash said. "We have surveyed all the county and local historical societies to determine what they want to do. We're trying to find out what people want on the local level and how to integrate their observances with the state level.

"During the last few years a lot of local and county histories have been published in connection with centennial dates of cities and counties."

Cash said he recently attended a meeting of the Western Historical Association in which members from other states with centennials coming up the same year as South Dakota outlined their plans.

"North Dakota is really going strong. Washington is just going bananas, running on a quarter million dollar a year appropriation already."

Cash said, "I hope South Dakota's observance is done well—with enthusiasm and dignity."

As of now, what South Dakota does is up to Janklow.

"He indicated to me that he is going to get something ready during this session of the Legislature," Cash said.

❖ ❖ ❖

Cash, who is in his sixth year as dean of the College of Arts and Sciences at the University of South Dakota in Vermillion, retains his interest in history, particularly of his home state. He was head of oral history at USD before he became a dean.

Cash occasionally does an oral interview to add to the more than 3,000 interviews which the Institute of Indian Studies and History Department have on file at the University.

"South Dakota's history is really interesting. This is a fascinating state. This is a fascinating state. There's great variety." He said the slogan, "Land of the Infinite Variety," really fits South Dakota.

He's a native of Bonesteel.

❖ ❖ ❖

FROM AN EDITOR'S MAILBAG—

James J. Meaghan writes from Sarasota, Fla., that he and Ray Antonen of Lake Norden, S.D., have started a file for the 1989 South Dakota Homecoming.

The 1989 homecoming will be a followup to the South Dakota Homecoming of last summer which Meaghan, Antonen and others staged as a benefit for the South Dakota Amateur Baseball Hall of Fame at Lake Norden.

Meaghan said in his letter, "For the South Dakota birthday party in 1989, I would like to see every town and city in the state plan a homecoming celebration, including family and school reunions. The celebrations could be scheduled on or about the same weekend, thereby flooding the state with former residents and capped by one or two big homecoming events like the one staged in Sioux Falls last July 23."

Meaghan said he would be willing to outline steps to follow, free of charge to any interested community. "Planning and tracking down the names and addresses of former residents should begin in 1987, two years in advance."

Meaghan has excellent credentials for advising communities about reunions. He draws on his experience helping his hometown, Estelline, S.D., stage homecoming celebrations in 1973 and 1982, promoting the Huron Baseball Pheastival from 1944 to 1948 and more recently, assisting with the South Dakota homecoming.

STATE'S PRIDE SURFACED THIS SUMMER

Argus Leader, Sunday, October 8, 1989

Our centennial year will go into the scrapbook as the summer we followed different highways and byways in South Dakota.

Those intriguing signs—"Centennial Community"—provided a common thread for many sidetrips off the interstate. Pride showed in Main Streets of villages, towns and county seats.

There are rewards in not being bound by an itinerary and in watching for signs to local attractions: like Summit Lake, a gem, south and east of Summit on the plateau of the Coteau des Prairies (Prairie Hills).

The day I saw it made me wish I had fishing tackle along, even though a senior citizen like myself said fishing was slow that day. Blue water and sky, green cast on the hills and some lazy white clouds made the day picture perfect.

There was another visual treat near Mobridge late in the summer at the U.S. Army Corps of Engineers Indian Creek campground. It offered a marvelous sunset over Missouri River breaks. But, sadly, the Oahe Reservoir was down drastically. Hopefully, that will change next year, given heavy snow in the Rocky Mountains and high plains this winter.

There were many vacant spaces in the campground. The ranger on duty said fishing had been great until the end of July, when walleyes stopped biting. Perhaps what late summer tourism needs most is a way to ensure good fishing.

When in Mobridge, be sure to see Oscar Howe's murals in the city auditorium. The 10 murals have been well cared for. The famed South Dakota Indian artist was paid $60—the regular Works Progress Administration monthly wage—to paint the first five in May 1942. He completed the others during a two-week furlough from the Army. Mobridge has an excellent pamphlet explaining the paintings.

The auditorium has been renamed the Scherr-Howe Arena for Jim and Bill Scherr, Mobridge's 1988 Olympic twin wrestlers, and Howe.

Peaks, buttes and ridges dot the landscape as you travel Highway 63 north from McLaughlin into North Dakota.

Stop at the state line and drive one-tenth of a mile west on a local road to see a Sioux Falls quartzite monument marking the border between the states. Yankton surveyor Charles H. Bates and his crew installed the marker in 1892. It's milepost 205 from the Minnesota border. Drive farther west and see other markers at mile and 1/2-mile intervals.

Enter South Dakota 29 miles north of Buffalo on Highway 85. On the east side of the road at the border you'll find the marker for milepost 329 in a section corner.

There are beautiful camp and picnic grounds atop the pine-covered hills of Custer National Forest north of Buffalo. The campgrounds were unused during the second week of September.

A roadside park on the south side of Buffalo has a memorial marker for Tipperary, "the world's greatest bucking horse." Tipperary thrilled rodeo crowds for nearly two decades before he died in 1932.

Jewel Cave National Monument, 13 miles west of Custer on Highway 16, is a remarkable crystal treasure.

Jewel Cave is the fourth longest cave in the world—and exploration is continuing. It is now 80.01 miles long, the second longest in the United States. Mammoth Cave in Kentucky is 330 miles long and the world's longest.

The Mammoth Site at Hot Springs shows viewers where large elephant-like animals were trapped and died in a sink hole more than 26,000 years ago.

The community recognized it as a world-class dig and built a $1.2 million visitors center over the site. It's open year round but off season hours are limited.

SOUTH DAKOTA CELEBRATED ITS CENTENNIAL WITH STYLE

Argus Leader, Nov. 12, 1989

Thanks, South Dakota, for all the memories that linger from celebration of the centennial.

What happened in 300 communities across the state in the last year offers a legacy for the second century of statehood.

Historical sketches, local guidebooks and other material prepared for the centennial will serve as reference material for years to come.

South Dakotans learned things about themselves, their heritage and their locale that they didn't know before.

Lorna Herseth, South Dakota's First Lady in 1959-1961 and a former Secretary of State, was grand marshal of Pierre's Centennial parade. —Anson Yeager photo

Frank Farrar, accompanied by his wife Pat, was also a grand marshal of the parade. —Anson Yeager photo

Governor George Mickelson and First Lady Linda enjoy the moment. —Anson Yeager photo

Local and state authors, historians and artists came up with some notable books, pamphlets and works of art. The media caught the excitement of South Dakota's first 100 years in news stories and radio and TV programs.

Celebrating the century gained much from South Dakota's experience of recent years in marking historic anniversaries.

The state has a lasting legacy from the centennial in the new Cultural Heritage Center at Pierre. The center houses the South Dakota State Historical Society, state archives and Robinson State Museum. Permanent interpretive exhibits will be prepared during the next two to three years. A fund drive is under way to finance the exhibits.

Restoration of the state Capitol to its original beauty when completed in 1910 is another tangible gain. Restoration efforts extended over a 14-year period. It was a joint effort by four governors and successive legislatures. South Dakotans will enjoy the results for years to come.

The Capitol is beautiful—some say it is one of the most beautiful statehouses in the nation. Viewers enjoy the warmth of original earth tones in the House chamber and the beautifully restored Rotunda. The latter has been enhanced by display of four inspiring centennial statues by sculptor Dale Lamphere of Sturgis.

Hilger's Gulch Park with walking trails, flower gardens and holiday flag display is a notable addition to Capitol grounds.

Pierre has never looked better than it does today. School and public buildings adjoining the grounds enhance the Capitol Complex. Pierre's new Discovery Center in the former light plant and park improvements along the river front are attractive.

The Centennial Finale in Pierre, with its dedication Of the Cultural Heritage Center, rededication of the Capitol, parade and other events provided a splendid ending for the yearlong celebration.

What a thrill it was for South Dakotans to descend the marble staircase in the glittering Rotunda, and have their names announced to the crowd at the Capitol Ball.

For Gov. George S. Mickelson, presiding at centennial events was deja vu. He is the first son of a South Dakota governor to serve in that office. He is also a former legislator. He could recall many anecdotes from living in the governor's home as a boy and from service in the Legislature.

Building plaques will note in an appropriate way what South Dakotans did on Nov. 3 and Nov. 4 to mark the Centennial Finale in Pierre. The historical record, however, should be available in much more complete form for future generations to study.

Presumably, archives in the Cultural Heritage Center will have a record on tape in living color from South Dakota Public Television and commercial stations to supplement the printed word. Perhaps excerpts of the Centennial Finale will be played for bicentennial crowds in Pierre in 2089.

BOOKS

BOOK DESCRIBES POOR FAMILY'S LIFE IN S.D. DUST BOWL DAYS

Argus Leader, Feb. 1, 1981

If you want insight with feeling into what it was like to grow up on the wrong side of the tracks in Mitchell, S.D., during the 1930s, you'll find it in Dolores Barnes Wilson's privately published book.

Her book, "From the Wrong Side of the Tracks," is her story of her family growing up during the Depression.

Most recollections of childhood and youth de-emphasize the less pleasant problems of a large family coping with meager income.

Most chronicles do not recount the feelings poor youngsters have in sitting at the back of the church and observing the well-to-do and their well-dressed children up front.

Or going to the dentist, thanks to government help, to save some permanent molars.

Or shopping at a downtown store with a county relief officer to get clothes for school.

Or the hateful act of a relative who shot the family's pet dog when he found it running loose after he became the city's dog catcher.

The slights and bruises are in Mrs. Wilson's volume—and some of the names have been changed to protect relatives.

However, there is no bitterness in the telling. There is also love and affection for family, friends and acquaintances.

Mrs. Wilson demonstrates understanding of the way things were during South Dakota's Dust Bowl days of the 1930s.

She depicts the gratitude of ordinary citizens that the government acted to ease the effects of the Depression.

She entitled one of her chapters "Tribute to the W.P.A." That was President Franklin D. Roosevelt's Works Progress Administration. It and other agencies made jobs that got many South Dakotans through some bad years.

However, Mrs. Wilson offers much more nostalgia than pensiveness in giving her perspective of life in Mitchell.

She recalls watching the circus unload, taking a spin in Papa's first car and the progress in moving to better rented quarters—still on the wrong side of the track.

Mrs. Wilson uses vignettes to relate both personal impressions and some interesting facets of Mitchell when the town was younger. She employs conversation—her own and others—effectively in telling her stories.

Her recollections of the Mitchell Police Department, for instance, start off with how scared she was as a child about warnings from parents and other grownups about the men in blue:

"'If you kids don't stay off of my property I'm gonna call the cops,' a cranky old man often yelled at us when he caught us picking some lilacs from his bushes that bloomed along the sidewalk. 'Cops take away little boys and girls that don't mind. Cops will put you in jail where they feed you just bread and water.'"

Mrs. Wilson recounts the tall tales of fire fighting exploits told by a hanger-on at the Mitchell Fire Department in a chapter irreverently called "Holy Smoke." She includes historical information about personnel in the fire and police departments.

She portrays the Milwaukee Railroad—from the viewpoint of a youngster who lived close to its tracks at times. Another chapter finds her going to work at Armour's Creamery, where 35 cents an hour was good pay and the work was steady.

Today, of course, the Milwaukee Railroad is out of business in Mitchell and most of South Dakota. Armour's closed in Mitchell in 1968.

Mrs. Wilson, who is 56, dedicated her book "To the memory of my Mother and Father, and to the generation who lived through the Great Depression; the common people who despite their 'blood, sweat and tears' still maintained a faith in God and their hopes for a better tomorrow."

The parents arrived in Mitchell two years apart: Sylvester Raymond Barnes in 1910 from Iowa and Josephine Mary Drees in 1912 from Minnesota. They were married in 1914. Mrs. Wilson was one of the younger of nine children.

She started on her manuscript about six years ago, writing in longhand. She hired college girls to do the typing.

With some help from H. P. Howard, of the Argus Printers of Stickney, Mrs. Wilson completed her book last fall and ordered 2,000 copies. It sells for $9.50 on newsstands or direct from her. It has 438 pages and is illustrated.

Mrs. Wilson says, "I may never make a lot of money but the satisfaction of listening to readers' comments about the book is well worth the time and expense."

Mrs. Wilson's book is engrossing. Her chronicling of an interesting era in South Dakota should enhance Mitchell's centennial celebration this year.

STORY CONSTRUCTS STATE CAPITOL HISTORY
Argus Leader, Saturday, Aug. 17, 1985

Harold H. Schuler has put his knowledge of South Dakota government and its leaders to excellent use in telling the story of the state's capitol.

His book, *The South Dakota Capitol in Pierre*, traces the state's fight in choosing a capital city.

Once Pierre became the permanent choice after several election battles, Schuler relates steps by governors and legislators in constructing South Dakota's beautiful capitol between 1905 and 1910.

Even then, controversy dogged the project. The Sioux Falls Board of Trade insisted that native stone be used for construction. After a two-year delay which brought a determination that Black Hills sandstone and Sioux Falls granite were too expensive, it was decided to use out-of-state stone.

Thus, Ortonville granite and Marquette raindrop sandstone were used at the base course at grade and for the first floor exterior, respectively. Bedford limestone from Indiana was used for the rest of the exterior's superstructure. Boulders for the foundation were the only native stone used in the capitol.

The building was modeled after Montana's state capitol. Gov. Samuel H. Elrod was impressed by a description of Montana's new building and C.E. Bell of Minneapolis, one of the architects. Elrod invited Bell to Pierre to address a joint session of the 1905 Legislature.

Elrod and the State Capitol Commission of which he was a member inspected Montana's capitol at Helena and liked what they saw. The commission made several changes from Montana's plan. They included making the building 41 feet longer, the dome larger and higher

South Dakota's capitol displays centennial banner during the 1989 celebration. —Anson Yeager photo

and differences in the exterior design. South Dakota had to provide space for some officials which Montana did not have.

O.H. Olsen of Stillwater, Minn., in 1907 submitted the winning bid of $528,552 for the general contract, but withdrew it when he discovered he had left out $24,000 for the cost of two elevators. However, Gov. Coe I. Crawford and the Capitol Commission reached a compromise by which Olsen and the state split the cost of the two elevators; this still left Olsen with the lowest bid.

Governors and legislators watched construction progress closely and made some changes. For instance, the commission at architect Bell's urging decided cast iron risers for the grand stairway and dome railings and imitation marble for wainscoting in the interior would look too cheap. Vermont marble was substituted for the stairway and railings and marble also was used for wainscoting.

These and other changes resulted in a cost of $951,000 by 1910 for completion of the capitol. An annex was added on the north side of the capitol in 1932 for $295,857. This brought the cost of the current building to $1,246,857.

Schuler's book is enhanced by historical and modern photographs. There are 86 photographs showing early Pierre scenes, construction in progress and pictures of all South Dakota governors.

Schuler did extensive research in newspaper files and government documents to compile the history of the state's capitol from inception to its recent renovation. He is secretary to the South Dakota Pharmaceutical Association and the Board of Pharmacy. He was an assistant to U.S. Sen. Francis Case from 1954 to 1962 and has lived in Pierre for many years.

BROOKINGS AUTHOR DESCRIBES CIVILIAN CONSERVATION CORPS

Argus Leader, Sunday, Nov. 28, 1993

How 32,471 mostly young men in the Civilian Conservation Corps (CCC) renewed forests and built dams and other public works in South Dakota is well told in a recent book.

Author Lyle Derscheid of Brookings, a CCC enrollee for nearly four years during the Great Depression of the 1930s, is the author. His book recalls a different world—when the unemployment rate was more than 16 per cent and thousands of homeless men and women rode the rails in boxcars in search of work.

Derscheid's book lists the 43 camps that the CCC operated in South Dakota between 1933 and 1942 and gives a history of each. Derscheid includes reminiscences by 24 enrollees who tell what it was like to toil in President Franklin D. Roosevelt's "forest army" and help renew the environment.

Derscheid relates his own experiences from growing up on a Beadle County farm to his career as a professor of agronomy at South Dakota State University following World War II service in Europe. He was an Army officer in the 12th Armored Division.

Most of today's young people will probably be shocked to read that CCC enrollees were paid $30 a month, of which the federal government sent $25 to their parents. Their pay was an irritant to U.S. Army privates of the era who were paid only $21 a month.

Army personnel set up and operated the CCC camps which functioned under several different agencies including the U.S. Forest Service, National Park Service and Soil Conservation Service. The CCC was abolished in midsummer 1942 during the first year of World War II.

Derscheid's first camp assignment was at Pierre, where the CCC developed Farm Island. Derscheid drove a dump truck and courted LaVonne Gustafson of Pierre. When he left the CCC in March 1939, he had a $70 nest egg to find a job and support a wife. His savings quickly dwindled so he enrolled at State College to gain an education. They were married Sept. 8, 1940. He was graduated in March 1943 and entered the Army in April.

Most CCC enrollees were single young men between 17 and 25. Others were World War I veterans and Indians on reservations, regardless of age or marital status. The CCC provided work for South Dakotans as follows: 23,709 enrollees and veterans, 4,554 Indians and 2,834 supervisory and office personnel, for a total of 31,097. Counting enrollees from out-of-state, the total was 32,471. The agency distributed more than $6.2 million in allotments to South Dakota families by the end of 1941.

The CCC helped change the face of South Dakota during drought years. Members constructed dams and lakes, built parks, and thinned and reseeded forests. They renovated Orman Dam and its 654-mile irrigation distribution system near Belle Fourche. CCC enrollees built the stone lookout tower on Harney Peak. They also completed major projects at Custer State Park, Wind Cave National Park, Jewel Cave National Park and in Custer National Forest in Harding County.

A camp near Columbia developed the Sand Lake and Waubay migratory waterfowl refuges under supervision of the U.S. Bureau of Biological Survey. Ralph Herseth, who later became South Dakota's governor (1957-59), was superintendent of the Sand Lake camp for four years.

Thanks to efforts by CCC Alumni and assistance from the South Dakota Department of Transportation, historic roadside markers have been erected near 38 former camp sites. Derscheid wrote the inscriptions for the markers.

The South Dakota State Historical Society plans a permanent exhibit in the Cultural Heritage Center at Pierre. It will depict the work of the CCC.

Derscheid compiled his first history of the CCC in South Dakota in 1985-86. "The Civilian Conservation Corps in South Dakota (1933-1942)" second edition with 366 pages was published in 1991. It's available for $35 plus $3 mailing charge. Write Lyle Derscheid, 1411 2nd St., Brookings, S.D. 57006-2513.

STUNTMAN'S STORY FASCINATES
McElrath covers toils, troubles, thank-yous

Argus Leader, Sunday, Oct. 12, 1997

"The Cowboy Stuntman: Secrets of a Long and Exciting Career"
Author: Buckskin Jack McElrath
Rushmore House Publishing, 157 pages

The parents of Jack McElrath undoubtedly knew they had a dare-devil on their hands when their boy Jack climbed 60 feet to the top of the windmill on their farm near Moville, Iowa, and hung upside down.

McElrath would persist in feats of derring-do as a boyhood cowboy growing up in Sioux Falls and pursuing a career as stuntman, showman and clown on the rodeo trail in the North American West.

His first saddle-bronc ride was on a big horse called Strip at Ben Brune's rodeo arena at the corner of 33rd and Euclid in Sioux Falls when he was 15.

Riding bulls was a natural next step. Those were the days—the late 1940s—when 33rd Street was the boundary between Sioux Falls and the village of South Sioux Falls.

Some years later McElrath would produce rodeos at the Sioux Falls Arena, sailed a motorcycle over nine cars and hit the 10th, and bulldog steers (a catch or two and many misses) from an airplane.

He also would crash cars and ride a scoop shovel down a strip of burning hay. McElrath relates his exploits in short, anecdotal chapters.

There was a lot of toil in trailering his favorite three buckskin horses from show to show, and living on the road. He is frank about his three marriages and divorces. He praises his ex-wives and blames his single-minded pursuit of show business for the breakups.

McElrath met many celebrities with heart and some without a heart. He knew and liked movie and country-music stars. He idolized the late Casey Tibbs, world champion bronc rider from Fort Pierre.

He recalls a facedown with Clint Eastwood, whom he convinced that he liked Eastwood's latest movie.

McElrath added announcing to his rodeo skills. He noted in one aside: "It's hard to have a good rodeo without a good announcer and it's a waste to have a good announcer without a good sound system."

Miraculously, McElrath escaped serious injury and counted only a few broken bones from mishaps. He was injured fewer than a dozen times during his 50-year career.

When McElrath was on the road, he often slept in his pickup and ate food from a store.

He wrote that costs were low including rodeo fees. "I usually spent $10 or $15 per event and could win up to $160."

There were still plenty of summers when he barely made enough money to buy a cup of coffee and enough gas to get home. "When I saw the $3.2 million prize money at the National Finals Rodeo in Las Vegas this year (1996), I about fell off my recliner.

"Who would ever have dreamed of that kind of money? Not me. I can remember being thrilled to win $300 in a weekend."

McElrath still likes South Dakota the best. His three favorite residences have been Sioux Falls, Canistota and Las Vegas.

He has worked as a security guard in Sioux Falls and Las Vegas. He looks back on life with the maturity of 63 years and excellent health.

His book offers the reader samplings from press clippings and photo albums. There are Argus Leader clippings and a reprint of a Ford Truck Times magazine article featuring him.

His last chapter is unusual. He lists 16 pages of names of individuals, including his ex-wives, who have touched his life.

It's also a roll call of national celebrities and Sioux Falls and other South Dakota individuals. Names include the Suttons, rodeo family at Onida; fair secretary Myles Johnson, and Denny Oviatt, radio and horse-show announcer.

Also included on the list: former Arena manager Bob Kunkel, and Dean Kjelden and Bob Bennis, whom McElrath termed great bosses at Ben Hur Ford, and the late Mayor Mike Schrimer.

THIS CUSTER BIO ALSO LOVE STORY

Argus Leader, Sunday, Dec. 21, 1997

Widow spent 57 years standing up for him
"Touched by Fire—The Life, Death and Mythic Afterlife of George Armstrong Custer"
Author: Louise Barnett
Henry Holt and Company. 540 pages

This is an engrossing account of the many images of Lt. Col George A. Custer and his beloved wife, Elizabeth, who devoted 57 years of widowhood to standing up for her man and his reputation.

Author Louise Barnett. a Rutgers University professor, has painstakingly examined Custer's misfortune in losing his own life and his entire immediate command of the 7th Cavalry: 210 men killed at the Last Stand and 53 elsewhere on the battlefield at the Little Big Horn in Montana Territory on June 25, 1876.

The biography is also a love story about Custer and Libby.

The United States of 1876 and its white leaders and citizens could not believe that the Union Army's youngest Civil War general and outstanding cavalry leader had been wiped out by a much larger force of Indians.

That started the myth.

Custer was the brave, invincible field commander whose cavalry tactics greatly helped the Union at Gettysburg and other battles.

How could the Sioux and their allies possibly defeat him?

Writers, historians and others have sought the answer—unsuccessfully for the most part—in the 121 years since the battle.

Barnett's book considers viewpoints of both Custerphiles and Custerphobes.

Her narrative of Libby Custer following Custer is well done and sympathetic to him and his wife.

During the Civil War Custer's commander allowed Libby to visit her husband in camp near battlefields close to Washington.

She followed him to the Plains where he pursued Indians after the Civil War and also to Fort Lincoln, Dakota Territory.

From there, opposite Bismarck on the Missouri River, Custer rode to Yellowstone, the Black Hills, and finally to his fatal rendezvous in what is now Montana.

Sitting Bull, the great Hunkpapa medicine man, spiritual leader and nemesis of Custer, receives sympathetic attention.

Sitting Bull's death and the execution-type slaying of his 14-year-old son by Indian police on the Standing Rock Reservation in 1890 are related.

South Dakotans will find the book very interesting.

Sioux descendants of the tribes which fought Custer and the U.S. Army live on and off reservations in the state.

South Dakota has a city and county named for Custer and dozens of locales from Yankton to the Black Hills that have a Custer connection.

The Indians of 1876 faced relentless pressure from gold prospectors and white settlers seeking their land and sacred Black Hills. The Indians were in a war they could not win.

Even so, they overwhelmed Custer, a favorite of the Army's top commanders because of his Civil War record.

This had helped him return to duty in Indian country—after a court-martial for disobeying orders.

Libby spent the rest of her life defending her husband's record. She was successful in publishing several books of her life with Custer and lecturing.

The author answers many questions about Custer, including his gambling, possible dalliances with attractive women and his poor business judgment.

His feelings for Libby are depicted as loyal and constant. They were married only 12 years when he died. She died on April 6, 1933. Barnett's sensitivity and feminine viewpoint enhance her biography of Custer.

RIGGS STORY IS TREASURE OF EARLY S.D.

Argus Leader, Sunday, April 26, 1998

"Sunset to Sunset: A Lifetime with My Brothers, the Dakotas"
Author: Thomas Lawrence Riggs as told to Margaret Kellogg Howard, South Dakota State Historical Society Press

This is an old treasure first chronicled in 1958 by the South Dakota State Historical Society in its collections and reissued recently with a new introduction.

The Rev. Thomas Riggs was a Congregationalist minister and missionary to the Sioux from the 1870s to the 1920s, working from his base at Oahe Mission north of Pierre.

Riggs established small churches and mission outposts, mainly on the Cheyenne River Indian Reservation. He had an extraordinary understanding of Indian people, their language and their plight.

Besides his missionary spirit and intellectual skills, he was, as his oldest son, Dr. Theodore Foster Riggs, a Pierre surgeon, described him: a skilled carpenter and stone mason, an excellent oarsman, a strong swimmer and a master horseman.

He used all these skills in traveling by horseback or wagon team in Dakota Territory and nearby Minnesota and Nebraska. He bonded with his horses and sometimes swam the Missouri River with his teams.

He knew hundreds of Indians and some chiefs, including Sitting Bull, the Hunkpapa medicine man. No one wanted to bury the seven Indians killed with Sitting Bull when he resisted arrest by Indian police on the Standing Rock Reservation during the Ghost Dance crisis in 1890. Riggs persuaded relatives and acquaintances of the dead men to help him bury them.

Indian friends invited him to accompany them on the last winter buffalo hunt of the Dakotas during 1880-1881. The hunting party brought back about 500 robes from the hunt south of Slim Buttes.

Riggs' account is fascinating. He was the only white man on the three-month expedition. He sat in on councils which planned the hunt.

His perspective was unique. He was a son of the Rev. and Mrs. Steven Return Riggs, Congregationalist couple who ministered to the Sioux in Minnesota.

The family narrowly escaped death during the 1862 Sioux uprising in Minnesota. Thomas Riggs had only one career choice: to continue his father's work.

He writes poignantly of the death in 1878 of his first wife, Nina Foster, in childbirth in the sixth year of their marriage, and how his second wife, Louisa Irvine, helped him raise his first family and their second one.

As a boy, Riggs and a brother accidentally set fire to their log cabin in Minnesota. Fire destroyed his wooden mission home at Oahe in 1898. He built a stone house to avoid another fire.

He died in 1940 at age 93. Louisa died in 1951. Riggs, his two wives and two daughters are buried in the family cemetery at Oahe. The graveyard and stone home are under 200 feet of water in the Oahe Reservoir.

Riggs recorded his memories through talks with his niece, Margaret Kellogg Howard. The reissue is enhanced by a new introduction by Paula M. Nelson, professor of history at the University of Plattesville in Wisconsin. New photographs and an index also enhance the work.

Nancy Tystad Koupal, director of the society's research and publishing program, said: "A generous gift from Rev. Riggs' granddaughter, Elizabeth Riggs Gutch of Sioux Falls, has enabled us to bring this remarkable story to a new generation of readers."

Gutch, who was born when her grandfather was 72, has great memories of Thomas and Louisa. Gutch's father was Robert, oldest son of the second marriage, who helped work the mission farm. Gutch lived at Oahe Mission until her family moved to Pierre when she started eighth grade.

Gutch recalls Grandfather Riggs reading from the Bible before meals. When the grandparents didn't want the children to know what they were discussing, they quickly switched to Lakota.

SOUTH DAKOTA TRAILS AND TRACKS

TRACING THE WAGON TRAIL

Argus Leader, Sunday, April 1, 1979

There are still traces of the wagon trail in northwestern South Dakota over which freight from Bismarck was sent to the mining towns of Deadwood and Lead.

The Bismarck Trail generally followed the route that Brig. Gen. George Custer took back to North Dakota, following his exploratory expedition to the Black Hills in the summer of 1874.

Custer, who was to lose his scalp two years later at the Battle of Little Big Horn in Montana, had 1,000 men, six mule teams drawing 10 wagons and 300 head of beef on the hoof on his Black Hills expedition.

Besides his troopers, the expedition included engineers, geologists, naturalists, practical miners, Indian scouts, a newspaperman and a photographer.

Custer entered the Black Hills from the northwest, and headed south to near Custer where Horatio N. Ross, one of his miners, found gold along French creek. From there the expedition traveled north up the east side of the Black Hills and left them near Bear Butte.

The legacy of the Custer expedition in data, maps, discovery of gold and photography was a bounty for a nation less than 100 years old. What Custer and his companions put on paper was more meaningful to posterity than his military defeat in Montana at the hands of Dakota Chief Sitting Bull and other Sioux warriors. His trip, the lure of gold and the subsequent opening of the Black Hills led to the tribe's last big battle at the Little Big Horn.

For the history buff with a liking for photography, the pictures from the Custer expedition are among the best "then" shots extant for comparison with the same terrain "now." In most cases, the Black Hills tree cover and vegetation show improvement today over what they were nearly 105 years ago.

Custer and his troopers left the written record of the white man's first organized and scientific trip into the Black Hills. The wagon ruts of the Bismarck trail are visible evidence of a freight route that long ago supplied Deadwood and Lead before the local railroads in the Black Hills linked up with the Burlington from the south in 1890.

When the first explorers reached the Black Hills and the rich, gold-bearing placer veins near what became the Homestake Mine at Lead is lost in obscurity and time, with only a hint as to when they were there.

Captain Seth Bullock, a frontiersman and the first sheriff of Deadwood, wrote in his diary:

"Shortly after the close of the Civil War, Father DeSmet, the heroic missionary, stated at a dinner party in the home of General Ewing at Columbus, Ohio, that he had repeatedly seen gold dust in the possession of the Sioux Indians. They told him that they got it in the Black Hills and that there was 'heap plenty of it.' Where and how the Sioux got the gold which they had from time to time, is a controversial matter, If it was from the Black Hills, it is an almost assured fact that it came from the section now embraced in the county of Lawrence, as their trail through the Hills skirted Deadwood Gulch, crossed the Homestake Belt and the rich placer deposits in the gravels near Central City."

Father DeSmet's trips to the area of the Black Hills are documented in church records. He was there in 1848 and again in 1851, 1864 and 1870.

There's another written record, scratched on a sandstone tablet found in 1887 by Louis Thoen near Spearfish that puts white men in the Black Hills in 1833. The sandstone bears an inscription, apparently made with a knife, that says:

"Came to these hills in 1833 seven of us DeLacompt, Ezra Kind, G.W. Wood, T. Brown, R. Kent, Wm. King, Indian Crow, all died but me Ezra Kind Killed by Ind. behind high hill Got our gold dust June 1834."

The reverse side carried this legend:

"Got all the gold we could carry Our ponies all got by the Indians I have lost my gun and nothing to eat The Indians hunting me."

The stone tablet may or may not be authentic. But if no one can prove it valid, no one can say it's not. When the stone was found it had the appearance of having been in the same spot for many years.

Its discovery on a trail which connected a fur trading post near modern Belle Fourche to the main Indian trail up Deadwood Gulch gives it considerable credence.

The tablet is in the Adams Museum in Deadwood, which has memorabilia of the Black Hills and its history. A history buff can spend a day or more in the museum for an exciting look back at South Dakota's gold boom days of 1876 and what followed.

The miners who flocked to Deadwood in late 1875 and 1876 didn't find any "Kilroy was here" signs. But they found other traces of prospectors before them, including skulls, hatchets, mining picks and abandoned shafts.

If dead men could tell tales and Black Hills pine could whisper a hint of what went before the big gold rush of 1876 along Deadwood creek, South Dakotans would have an even stranger chronicle to tell.

Perhaps a hiker will turn up another stone tablet. Perhaps someone will find another diary like Captain Bullock's.

It makes an American of today's times wish that the adventurous men of long ago had taken more time to write home, or relate more of their finds in Deadwood Gulch, to pioneer Black Hills journalists.

CUSTER AN ARDENT BLACK HILLS BOOSTER
His official reports to Congress were filled with praise for the area

Argus Leader, April 11, 1982

When Gen. George A. Custer kissed Mrs. Custer goodbye at Fort Abraham Lincoln, Dakota Territory, on July 2, 1874, there were rumors that Sitting Bull and his warriors were lying in wait about 70 miles south.

Sitting Bull's plan, according to scuttlebutt, was to intercept Custer's Black Hills Expedition and to contest every foot of their journey. As it turned out, the thousand-man contingent encountered only a few Indians on the two-month trek.

Custer and his men headed southwest from Fort Lincoln, which was on the west side of the Missouri River near Bismarck. The expedition's mission was to explore the Black Hills.

Custer had 10 companies of the 7th Cavalry, one each of the 20th and 17th Infantry, a detachment of 100 Indian scouts—Rees, Santees and a few Sioux—and guides, interpreters and teamsters.

His wagon train had 110 wagons, each drawn by six mules, and some ambulances. There were 1,000 cavalry horses and 300 cattle, to be slaughtered as needed.

Custer's staff included Capt. William Ludlow, his chief engineer; a couple geologists, two naturalists, a chief medical officer who was also the botanist, and newspaper correspondents. There were two practical miners, Horatio Nelson Ross and William T. McKay.

W. H. Illingworth was the photographer. His remarkable pictures of the Black Hills in 1874 have drawn new interest in recent years. The comparison of his pictures with some taken in the last decade at identical sites generally is favorable for the white man's stewardship of the Black Hills National Forest.

✦ ✦ ✦

There probably has never been a more eloquent and ardent booster of the Black Hills than Custer. His descriptions of the terrain, wild flowers, grass, game and other natural features of the Hills are detailed in his official reports to the War Department and Congress.

The expedition traveled south along what is today the Wyoming side of the Black Hills, turning eastward into what is now western Pennington County, S.D.

Here's part of Custer's description of the line of march in what he named "Floral Valley": "Every step of our march that day (July 24, 1874) was amid flowers of the most exquisite colors and perfume. So luxuriant in growth were they that men plucked them without dismounting from the saddle....It was a strange sight to glance back at the advancing columns of cavalry and behold the men with beautiful bouquets in their hands, while the headgear of the horses was decorated with wreaths of flowers fit to crown a queen of May.

"General Forsyth, at one of our halting places, plucked 17 beautiful flowers, belonging to different varieties....Professor Donaldson estimated the number of flowers (species) in bloom in Floral Valley at 50...."

Custer compared another vista "with the loveliest portions of Central Park" (in New York).

After camping on French Creek near modern Custer, where miner Ross found gold, Custer summarized his impressions of the Black Hills:

They consist "of beautiful parks and valleys, through which flows a stream of clear cold water, while bounding these parks or valleys is invariably found unlimited supplies of timber, much of it capable of being made into good lumber.

"In no portion of the United States, not excepting the famous blue-grass region of Kentucky, have I ever seen grazing superior to that found growing wild....On Harney's Peak I could contrast the bright green verdure of these lovely parks with the sunburned and dried yellow herbage to be seen on the outer plains.

"Everything indicates an abundance of moisture....The soil is that of a rich garden....We have found the country in many places covered with wild raspberries, both the black and red varieties....Cattle could winter in these valleys without other food or shelter other than that to be obtained from running at large...."

All good things come to an end—and Custer sensed it in writing about the expedition's last bivouac in the Black Hills. The site was northwest of today's Rapid City. Custer wrote:

"A march of an hour....through a pine forest brought us to a beautiful park, containing thousands of acres and from which we obtained a fine view in the distance of our old acquaintance—the plains. Here we pitched out tents for the last time in the Black Hills; nearly everyone being loath to leave a region which had been found so delightful in almost every respect.

"Behind us the grass and foliage were clothed in green of the freshness of May, in front of us, as we cast our eyes over the plains below, we saw nothing but a comparatively parched, dried surface, the sun-burnt pasture of which offered a most uninviting prospect both to horse and rider....A march of 26 miles, gradually bearing northward, brought us to the base of Bear Butte."

The expedition camped near Bear Butte Aug. 14-15, east of what would become Fort Meade and Sturgis, S.D.

They headed north into North Dakota and then east to Fort Lincoln, arriving there Aug. 30, 1874.

Less than two years later—on June 25, 1876—Custer and 264 soldiers of the 7th Cavalry were killed in the Battle of the Little Big Horn in Montana. The toll includes 224 men who were with Custer in his "last stand" on the hillside and 40 others in units that failed to reach him.

Sitting Bull was credited with masterminding Custer's defeat.

❖ ❖ ❖

Strangely enough, the town of Custer, S.D., originally was called Stonewall for the Confederate general, Stonewall Jackson, according to "South Dakota Place Names." That book, published in 1941, was compiled as a joint project of the Works Progress Administration and the University of South Dakota.

There must have been a "Johnny Reb" among prospectors who wanted to strike it rich after Custer's expedition discovered gold. The name of the town was later changed to Custer. Custer County was created in 1875 and organized in 1877.

It's a footnote of history that the expedition's cattle got fat on Black Hills grass.

ARMY AVENGED CUSTER'S DEFEAT WITH ATTACK IN NORTHWEST S.D.

Argus Leader, March 21, 1982

Look at the upper left hand corner of a South Dakota road map and spot the legend—Battle of Slim Buttes—near Reva on Highway 20.

That was a major battle won Sept. 9, 1876, by the U.S. Army and its first success in the aftermath of General Custer's defeat.

Sitting Bull and other hostiles escaped from the Army after Custer's disaster in June. Custer and 264 soldiers of the 7th Cavalry were killed June 25, 1876, in his "last stand," the Battle of the Little Big Horn in Montana during the Sioux Indian War.

Among other Army commanders, General George C. Crook spent the rest of the summer chasing the hostiles. Crook pursued the Indians with several units of cavalry and infantry. They eluded his grasp.

By September Crook's column was at the headwaters of the Heart River in North Dakota.

His troopers and horses were tired; their gear was practically worn out and their provisions were exhausted. Crook decided to head for Deadwood, Dakota Territory gold mining town and the nearest place he could get supplies.

The story of the march and the battle is told by Gen. Charles King in his book, "Campaigning with Crook."

Other western authors have recounted the Battle of Slim Buttes. They include Doane Robinson, early state historian and author of his "Encyclopedia of South Dakota," and Cyrus Townsend Brady, author of "Indian Fights and Fighters."

By Sept. 7, Crook's command halted near the headwaters of the Grand River in South Dakota. Maj. Anson Mills was sent ahead with 150 men of the 3rd Cavalry to find the Black Hills, purchase supplies and quickly return to Crook's main body.

Mills, however, had to change his own orders. As his scouts rode south, they discovered a large village of 40 or 50 Indian lodges in the Slim Buttes. The buttes, a prominent landmark, rise several hundred feet from the rolling rangeland of northwestern South Dakota. Today, they're a part of Custer National Forest, named for the general.

❖ ❖ ❖

Mills decided to attack the village at dawn and sent a messenger back to Crook for assistance.

Mills' attack was successful, although he and his troopers were heavily engaged. They held off a larger Indian force until Crook arrived about noon with some 2,000 men.

The sight of the enemy was an boost for the soldiers. They saw Custer's guidons and Army uniforms, what King called "trophies and evidence at once of the part our foe had taken in the bloody battle of the Little Big Horn."

Late in the day Crazy Horse arrived on the scene with approximately 600 warriors, believing he had to contend only with Mills' small group. After several clashes with the reinforced troopers, Crazy Horse broke off the engagement.

Following very sharp fighting the cavalry convinced some of the Sioux, who were hidden in ravines and gullies, that their lives would be spared if they would come in and surrender.

One of the captives was the warrior American Horse, dying with a massive hole in his side. He lay in an Indian lodge that the Army converted into a field hospital.

Dr. Clements, one of the Army surgeons, did everything he could to help him although he knew he couldn't save him.

American Horse spurned chloroform and ordered a squaw to bring him a stick which he thrust between his teeth while the surgeon attempted to ease his pain. American Horse died before dawn.

Although there were large numbers of combatants in the Battle of Slim Buttes, casualties were comparatively small on both sides in fighting that lasted from dawn to dusk.

The soldiers captured 400 ponies with the Indian village. This immediately changed their diet to some fat, grass-fed pony roasts.

The troopers had been eating tough and stringy horse meat from their own mounts they had slaughtered. They had been riding or marching constantly for more than a month, equipped mainly with what they could carry on their saddles or on their backs.

❖ ❖ ❖

After the battle, Crook and his men still had several days of marching in rain through unfriendly territory—about 70 miles—to reach the Belle Fourche River.

There were no further clashes, although one scout, who rode ahead of his party in pursuit of an antelope, was killed by Indians on the last day of the march.

The soldiers carried their wounded in Indian travois they had fashioned from lodge poles after the battle.

Constant rain gave them many problems as they headed south for the Black Hills. King's account mentions "badlands"—a reference to rough terrain and gumbo flats northeast of today's Newell. Their landmarks included Deer's Ears and Bear Butte.

They forded the Belle Fourche River, swollen by rains, on Sept. 12 and 13, 1876.

The soldiers' problems of lack of food, blankets and basic comfort were soon ended. They were met by soldiers and civilians bringing wagons from Deadwood and Crook City. They carried supplies purchased by the quartermaster and also furnished by the grateful people of those Black Hills towns.

The soldiers bivouacked several days in Whitewood Valley, visiting the mining camps at Deadwood and being entertained by the local residents.

Their next mission took them south through the Hills and on to Red Cloud Agency in Nebraska to disarm and unhorse reservation Indians. That, however, is another story.

Crook, like many Army men, had a sympathetic view of his foe. He wrote in 1878 that the white man had "come and occupied about all the lands the Indians derived their living from.... The disappearance of the game, which means starvation, may seem a small thing to us, but to them it is their all, and he must be a very contemptible being who would not fight for his Life."

IMAGINATION TAKES A JOURNEY TO GHOST TOWNS
Argus Leader, Sunday, April 15, 1984

Riders of range and mountain trails in South Dakota this summer might ponder the way things were in ghost towns in Dakota Territory and early statehood days.

Today's riders—except for an adventuresome few who might load a saddle horse in a pickup or resort to motorcycles—generally are bound by circumstance to highways or local roads or trails.

They might find nothing at the site except a lone building or footings to mark Main Streets of yesteryear.

Visitors with vivid imaginations could recreate—from Gunsmoke and other television and movie tales of the Old West—what it must have been like in Two Bit, Dakota Territory, in 1877.

The Lawrence County town started up after a promising lead in a gold claim owned by A. M. Hardin. Two Bit had a post office, daily stage line from Deadwood and flourished briefly with saloons, stores, boarding houses and all the establishments that make up a boom town.

The town was so named, according to South Dakota Place Names, because prospectors along Twobit Creek picked up nuggets worth 25 cents, or a mine on the creek yielded only 25 cents' worth of gold a day. The town faded when its gold strike played out.

Custer County, where Gen. George Armstrong Custer's miners found gold in 1874, had an early mining camp named Bugtown. It was named after log cabins which were heavily infested with bugs. Bugtown was deserted in the 1880s after a boom of a few years.

Carwye in Lawrence County was a railroad and lumbering town which sprang up at the end of one of the Homestake Mining Company's narrow-gauge railroad lines. To save backing the trains many miles, a Y was installed at the end of the line and the station was called "Car Y" which soon became Carwye. The town had several stores, saloons and boarding houses and homes of railroad workers and lumbermen employed by Homestake. The railroad was torn up after a few years and Carwye practically vanished overnight.

Today's Belle Fourche might have been Minnesela, 3½ miles southeast of the present Butte County seat. Minnesela citizens hoped to convince the railroad, being built north from Whitewood in 1890, that their town should be the terminus instead of Belle Fourche. They succeeded with sales literature and oratory in stymieing the sale of lots at the Belle Fourche site for one day, but the railroad won and most Minnesela businesses moved to the new site.

Only one man remained loyal to Minnesela to the last. He took over the abandoned hotel building, cut it to one-third its size and successfully farmed and ranched for the rest of his life. He lived with a beautiful yard and flower garden at the old townsite until he died in 1936.

Minnesala, the Indian word for red water, was named because of its location on Redwater Creek.

❖ ❖ ❖

There was a cattle trail—a six-mile right-of-way granted by Indians through the Cheyenne River Indian Reservation—that led from northwestern South Dakota to two new railroad towns on the east bank of the Missouri River.

Evarts, built by the Milwaukee Railroad, flourished from 1900 until 1907. The town's population of approximately 500 was swelled during the spring and fall shipping seasons by several hundred cowboys, buyers and drifters who had some boisterous times at trail's end. Thousands of cattle were herded from ranches west of the Missouri River across a pontoon bridge at Evarts and shipped to eastern markets.

Evarts lost its reason for existence when the railroad decided to cross the Missouri River at a point 12 miles north which had a better foundation for a bridge. That site became Mobridge; practically the entire town of Evarts moved to the new location by 1909.

LeBeau, a few miles south along the Missouri River, was Evarts' competitor for cattle shipments. LeBeau was the end of the line for the Minneapolis & St. Louis Railroad. It was one of the nation's largest cattle-shipping points between 1907 and 1910. A ferryboat was used to carry cattle across the Missouri to the railhead.

LeBeau was crowded with cowboys and Indians during the fall when cattle where shipped east. A fire in 1910 swept away part of the town and most of the damaged district was never rebuilt. LeBeau faced new competition from the Milwaukee Railroad, which had extended branch lines southwest from Mobridge. Trains kept coming for a few years, but in 1923 the rails were torn up and LeBeau faded away.

Two other river towns—Pierre and Chamberlain—were important rail shipment points for West River livestock before the railroads crossed the Missouri and headed west. Today, there are tracks but no trains west from Chamberlain to the Black Hills and only a few trains west from Fort Pierre.

Pierre and Chamberlain still retain their links with the range country to the West. Both river cities are proud of their historical roles as cowtowns when South Dakota was younger.

❖ ❖ ❖

Many South Dakotans have personal recollections of small towns that are no more—or post offices that were discontinued long ago. Few individuals will take the time or trouble to put their own memories on paper.

Fortunately, the South Dakota Writers' Project during the 1930s developed a priceless compendium on how the state's cities, towns and geographical features got their names. The writers talked to many persons who had direct knowledge of homesteading, settlement and mining. They were there when history was made.

South Dakota Place Names, from which most of today's column is derived, was published by the University of South Dakota in 1941 as a project of the Writers' Program of the Works Progress Administration. Edward C. Ehrensberger, head of the Department of English at the University of South Dakota, directed the project. Many English students, graduate students and others contributed to the wealth of material in the book.

Virginia Driving Hawk Sneve, the South Dakota author, edited a revision of the original book. Her compilation was published as *South Dakota Geographic Names* in 1973 by Brevet Press and is available in some local and state bookstores.

Relatives who have to dispose of the personal papers, photographs and memorabilia of older South Dakotans should take some care to determine if they have historical significance.

There may be a part of the state's history in letters and papers left behind in an elderly parent's or aunt's attic.

Wayne Petersen, promotion director of the Center for Western Studies at Augustana College, says the center will be glad to determine upon request whether such papers have historical significance.

Your relatives' personal treasures could yield worthwhile additions to local or regional South Dakota history.

ASH BLAZED TRAIL INTO SOUTH DAKOTA HISTORY
Argus Leader, Sunday, July 7, 1985

Ben Ash was a trailblazer in Dakota Territory.

When he was 11 years old in 1862, he drove a team and buggy for the U.S. marshal in Yankton, territorial capital.

At age 17, he was appointed U.S. deputy marshal and served for seven years.

When he was 20, he took a crew of men from Yankton 450 miles up the river to the townsite that would become Bismarck.

In December 1875 when he was 24, Ash and several other men left Bismarck in December bound for the Black Hills. Their route became the Bismarck-Deadwood trail.

On Christmas night 1875 the contingent camped on the Moreau River in what became Perkins County in northwestern South Dakota.

The next day Ash, S.C. Dodge, Russ Marsh, Ed Donahue and Stimmy Stimson saw the Black Hills from the divide 10 miles south of the Moreau.

When he was in his 90s, Ash said that if he ever got his eyesight back, he'd return to the spot where they first saw the Black Hills and erect a monument to Dodge's memory.

Ash didn't make that last trip before he died at 94 in 1946. But his wish was realized when South Dakota dedicated a monument to Ash and his companions in 1949.

The monument is high on a windy hill on the south side of Highway 212, one mile west of the former post office of Cedar Canyon and 36 miles west of Faith.

It's 50 miles from the monument to Bear Butte—maybe an hour by car via Newell. It took Ash and his friends four days to reach Bear Butte Valley. There they found the track of Gen. George Custer's 1874 expedition to the Black Hills.

Ash was a friend of Custer and had been the 7th Cavalry's wagonmaster on the 1873 expedition to the Yellowstone Country.

But Ash's December 1875 trip to the Black Hills was a surreptitious one, commissioned by Bismarck businessmen. Bismarck had fallen on hard times when the railroad was completed. Its leaders wanted a share of the gold boom in the Black Hills. The U.S. Army was still trying to keep white men out of the region.

Ash and his party followed part of Custer's trail in the Black Hills. They talked to miners and took some gold back to Bismarck. They were gone 20 days and didn't see an Indian. The weather was pleasant.

Custer learned of their trip before they returned, but he didn't send any troopers to arrest them. Instead he dispatched a lone messenger to confirm the report that they were safe at home.

Ash was intrigued by the Black Hills and western range country. He and Dodge resolved to start ranching along Rapid Creek the next spring.

But it was not to be. Custer asked Ash to remain in office as deputy marshal temporarily. Dodge returned to the Black Hills to start their ranching enterprise, and during a cattle drive was ambushed by Indians.

Before Custer left Fort Lincoln with the 7th Cavalry, he asked Ash to estimate how many Indians were with Sitting Bull. Ash said they would number in the thousands. Custer said he expected to find six or seven hundred and not more than a thousand—that the 7th Cavalry could handle them.

On July 4, 1876, Bismarck and the nation celebrated 100 years of independence. Two days later Custer's supply steamer, the "Far West," reached Bismarck with the wounded from the Battle of the Little Big Horn and news of the death of Custer and 264 soldiers of the 7th Cavalry. A few days later Ash drove a heartbroken Mrs. Custer to the railway station.

Ash left Bismarck in 1880 and moved down river where he helped found Pierre. He was Hughes County sheriff for two terms and agent of the Lower Brule Reservation for five years.

He bought the Quarter Circle W horse ranch on the Moreau River during the 1880s. The ranch was near where he had camped on Christmas night 1875. He built it into a large cattle ranch and later switched to sheep following the coming of homesteaders (1909-1910). He and a friend also started a bank in the new town of Faith. In 1917 he had a livestock sale and moved to Sioux Falls, and later to Florida.

Ash's career is well told by Don Patton in "South Dakota Historical Collections, Volume XXIII, 1947," from which most of this material was obtained.

Ash is featured as "the patriarch of South Dakota's pioneers" in "Faith Country Heritage," published last winter for Faith's 75th jubilee. The observance will be celebrated at Faith's annual stock show Aug. 7-11.

PAPER POINTS OUT ATTRACTIVENESS OF HIGHWAY 212

Argus Leader, Sunday, Nov. 24, 1996

Two years ago the State Department of Tourism left U.S. Highway 212 out of its list of corridor highways with the most marketing potential for rural tourism development in eastern and central South Dakota.

The omission piqued Walter Mundstock, the energetic and promotion-minded publisher of the Redfield Press which is located on Highway 212.

His response was a newspaper insert, "Prairie Highway," extolling tourist attractions along 212. The 1996 edition carries stories and photographs taking the traveler from Watertown to Faith.

The cover says: "Travel South Dakota's "Prairie Highway" 212 Experience rural life!! The fantastic things to see/The wonderful things to do/The beautiful people to meet/Where to eat—Where to shop."

It's a shame that the Washington, D.C., and Colorado consultants who compiled the Rural Tourism Assessment couldn't have seen Mundstock's work before they completed their master plan for tourist development in eastern South Dakota.

Mundstock said that he had planned to publish such a tourist guide before the Rural Tourism Assessment report was made. The omission prompted him to bring out the guide in 1995. It was revised this year and will be revised again for 1997.

The Rural Tourism Assessment report acknowledges that the Highway 212 "corridor has some strengths, primarily the resources of Watertown and Gettysburg, and the fact that it is one of the shortest routes between Minneapolis and the Black Hills. However, the road geometry, width and conditions are detractions."

While the report lists attractions at key towns along U.S. 212 in its county summaries, it doesn't see potential development for corridor treatment.

The report recommended development along these five key corridors: Sioux Falls/Rapid City (I-90), Oyate Trail (SD 50/US 18), Black & Yellow Trail (US 14), Yellowstone Trail (US 12) and Interstate 29 (North Sioux City to North Dakota border).

Mundstock's travel guide crew included a writer, ad salesman and himself as photographer. They developed interesting stories, like Memorial Day services near Clark for the "Little Fellow." He was a young boy who in the 1880s greeted Chicago, Northwestern train crews with a friendly wave. A conductor missed him one day and discovered he had died of smallpox. Train crews stopped for years to decorate his grave, a custom now carried on by the Clark Rotary Club.

Doland's tribute on its Heritage Wall to three of its high school graduates—Vice President Hubert Humphrey and Olympic wrestlers Dennis and Duane Koslowski—is chronicled.

There are articles on Redfield's local history, Fisher Grove State Park and Faulkton's Pickler Mansion and carousel.

Gettysburg's fishing on the Missouri River and the Whitlock Bay Spawning Station with its fish ladder for salmon and trout are described.

The Cheyenne River Sioux Tribe's H. V. Johnston Lakota Cultural Center at Eagle Butte is pictured. Faith's Durkee Lake, municipal swimming pool and availability of working ranch tours are included.

Historically, U.S. 212 has not enjoyed a high priority on government construction and other plans.

This writer as a ranch boy lived alongside 212 during the 1930s. It was a dirt grade for about 45 miles west of Faith until it was blacktopped after World War II. When it rained, gumbo made this federal highway impassable.

Then as now, Highway 212 gives you countless panoramas equal to scenery in Kevin Costner's "Dances with Wolves."

From Faith west Highway 212 takes you through Newell and Belle Fourche into Wyoming and Montana. The scenery from Watertown east to Minneapolis is also excellent.

Write for a free copy of "Prairie Highway" to Redfield Press, Box 440, Redfield, SD 57469-0440.

SCENIC SOUTH DAKOTA

S.D. TRAVEL OFFERS BEAUTY WITHOUT CROWDS

Argus Leader, Dec. 8, 1991

When the weather outside is frightful, it's a good time to think about next year's travels.

For some of the nation's most spectacular scenery, explore western South Dakota.

Kevin Costner's *Dances With Wolves* has won rave reviews for the remarkable outdoor scenes filmed northwest of Pierre on former Lt. Gov. Roy Houck's buffalo ranch.

The movie cameras didn't lie. They captured the appeal of the "big sky," the open range and what life on the frontier must have been like in territorial days.

That scenery can be duplicated many times in western South Dakota as you drive great distances: from Pierre to Sturgis via Highway 34, from Gettysburg to Belle Fourche via Faith and Newell, from Mobridge to Buffalo and on Highway 85 from the North Dakota line through Buffalo to Sturgis.

There are also South Dakota big sky vistas from Platte through Winner to Martin, Pine Ridge and Hot Springs and from Pickstown through Gregory, Winner, White River, Cedar Pass and Scenic to Rapid City.

The variety of scenery is compelling: hills, buttes, long low-lying ridges, river and creek bottoms, grasslands that meet the sky and hilltops that reveal another valley and another range of hills to climb.

Costner saw South Dakota's big sky from afoot and horseback. You can see it from your favorite vehicle.

Part of the appeal of western South Dakota is the scarcity of people. It's easy to commune with nature when you and your companion are driving roads with few other vehicles. That's a plus of living in a state with a large area (South Dakota ranks 15th) and a small population (No. 45).

South Dakota has about 700,000 people who live within 77,116 square miles. That figures out to a population density of about 9.1 persons per square mile. Of course, there are many square miles in the countryside that have no residents.

South Dakota tourism not many years ago used the slogan "Roam free," a message that has not been lost. It is one reason the Black Hills Motor Classic at Sturgis is so popular. Motorcyclists come to South Dakota because they can enjoy their bikes on our uncrowded highways. It's no fun riding busy interstates and other highways in urban areas.

South Dakota has many other outdoor attractions that can enhance your life during the four seasons. The Great Lakes of the Missouri, the northeast lake region and the vast expanse of prairie from Minnesota and Iowa to the Missouri River all have appeal. The state's parks, hunting and fishing are among the least crowded in the nation.

The Black Hills offer great mountain scenery with variety. Mount Rushmore National Memorial, born-again Deadwood and lowstakes gambling, Crazy Horse Memorial, Custer State Park, Wind and Jewel Caves and skiing and snowmobile trails are among top attractions.

If your family is planning a reunion next summer, now or January is the time to make arrangements. Choice campgrounds, motels or other accommodations require reservations many months in advance.

SOUTH DAKOTA'S INFINITE MIX OF SIGHTS LEAVES A LASTING IMPRESSION
Argus Leader, Jan. 19, 1985

Here are several vignettes of the author's favorite South Dakota scenes—compiled from countless trips across the Land of Infinite Variety.

Hay bales and stacks that never end—like the year during the 1960s when ranchers along Highway 34 in Hughes, Hyde, Buffalo and Jerauld counties had a crop that grew and grew. There was so much hay after the first cutting that there was jubilation for ranchers and frustration for motorists in trying to count the stacks. Surplus from that crop lasted a couple of years. The greening of South Dakota over the last several years and accompanying excellent hay crops have given Coyote State livestock producers something to cheer about. There's another bonus in the expanse of wide open green spaces: tourists want to return to South Dakota.

The sight of irrigation water being sprayed on South Dakota fields that once were dependent entirely on rainfall is a welcome change of the last decade or two. Whether you're driving from Sioux Falls to Brookings, Vermillion, Pierre or Aberdeen, you can see fields where the operator has resorted to irrigation to reduce his gamble with the weather. There are other areas in South Dakota where irrigators have tapped wells to ensure a crop. The total acreage isn't large—but it shows what South Dakota could do. Mist from an irrigation rig isn't as colorful as a rainbow arched over growing fields, but it's a lot more certain.

Harvest gold, whether grain flowing from combine to truck or maturing corn in row upon row, is a sight to please farm and city dwellers alike. Cornfields last fall had a classic look that triggered recollection of golden pheasant years when hunting was much better. There was also the happy comparison, for 1984's crops, with years when early snowfall prevented a complete harvest of the fields.

Somewhere west of Pierre and north of Kadoka, Philip and Rapid City are those countless South Dakota hills where cattle become grass fat in good years. To see Herefords or Black Angus heifers with calves tagging along at their side on a nice day is a treat for this highway-bound traveler. Opportunities for cattle watching are much better along highways 63, 34, 14, 212 and 73 than beside Interstate 90. Almost anywhere in Stanley, Haakon and Meade Counties there are western range scenes in spring or summer that would gladden the heart of any urban cowboy from Sioux Falls or Rapid City. Climb a hill on Highway 63 between Hayes and Eagle Butte, and there's another panorama of grass-covered valleys, buttes and hills ahead. Or leave the interstate at Wasta and drive north to Enning for more cattle country vistas. But do it on a summer day. It's not a winter diversion.

One vivid winter recollection centers on newly completed Interstate 29 between Sisseton and New Effington. The roadway, ditch and horizon blended together in a whiteout as complete as any in Alaska one day in bitterly cold December 1983. A young student couple from Fargo had just spun into the ditch. Within minutes a South Dakota trooper had a wrecker on the way to pull their car out so they could resume their journey. In summer or fall, the trip from Watertown north to North Dakota offers pleasing views of the Prairie Hills and the pretty countryside in the Minnesota Valley. Not that time, in 40 below zero windchill and big trucks whipping ground snow into a frenzy when they passed. A motel in Fargo, N.D., was the best sight of the day—at about 6 p.m.

Other views that thrill this South Dakotan: Tall tails of B-52s lined up at Ellsworth Air Force Base. Mount Rushmore framed in the tunnels of alternate Highway 16, between Custer State Park and Keystone. Trout jumping at Deerfield Reservoir on a sunny June day. Northwestern South Dakota from atop Bear Butte. Lake Oahe and the other bluewater Great Lakes, whereever one happens to cross the Missouri. Jet contrails in South Dakota skies and trains back on track that once seemed lost. Seeing the lights of Sioux Falls and home again after another trip.

PIERRE, BUFFALO, STURGIS, FAITH ARE A JOY TO VISIT
Argus Leader, June 6, 1987

Here are some of my favorite South Dakota destinations.

• Pierre and Fort Pierre: South Dakota's capital city, the capitol and Fort Pierre across the Missouri River have never looked better.

See the Verendrye plate at the Robinson Museum in Pierre. The lead plate was buried by the Verendrye brothers of Canada in 1743 to claim the area for France. The plate was discovered by Fort Pierre school children in 1913.

A monument in Fort Pierre marks the discovery site. There is a magnificent view from the monument of Pierre and the wide Missouri. Joseph LaFramboise started a fur post at Fort Pierre in 1817; it is the oldest continuous white settlement in South Dakota. The Verendrye Museum and Cowboy Hall of Fame in Fort Pierre have excellent exhibits.

Oahe Dam, fishing on the Missouri, and Farm Island State Recreation area three miles east of Pierre are other attractions.

• Faith: Population 575 and my hometown, is the little town that could. It built a 2,500-seat grandstand in 1976, spurning federal aid. During the same year Faith entrepreneurs opened the one-block Prairie Oasis Mall, replacing pioneer Main Street buildings that were erected soon after the town was founded in 1910.

Faith's annual Stock Show and Rodeo, held in August, routinely presents such celebrities as Loretta Lynn, Charlie Pride, Merle Haggard, Ronnie Milsap, Louise Mandrell, Tom T. Hall, Mel Tillis and Jeannie C. Riley.

Faith is in the heart of livestock country. Faith Livestock Commission Co. is a major livestock auction for cattle and sheep. Faith is also a rodeo center. The town is 110 miles northeast of Sturgis, the county seat, and is in the middle of South Dakota's version of the "Big Sky Country" which Montana calls its own wide-open spaces.

• Buffalo: County Seat of Harding County, is in the northwestern corner of South Dakota and offers additional "Big Sky" vistas. Montana and North Dakota are next door. Here is where deer and antelope roam and Williston Basin oil wells dot the landscape.

Harding County is the home of the Slim Buttes and the South Dakota part of Custer National Forest, which extends into Montana. General George A. Custer traversed the area in 1874 on both legs of his scientific expedition's journey from Fort Lincoln near Bismarck to the Black Hills and return.

Buffalo, population 453 and one of South Dakota's smallest county-seat towns, is neat and trim. It has a monument to Tipperary, the famous bucking horse.

The ramparts of the Slim Buttes rise east of Buffalo. A monument 2 miles south of Reva on Highway 79 marks the battle of the Slim Buttes between U.S. cavalry and Sioux Indians on Sept. 9, 1876.

The cavalry surprised and defeated a small band of Sioux and held off an attack by Crazy Horse. The Sioux were returning to reservations from the Battle of the Little Big Horn in Montana. There Custer and 225 soldiers of the 7th Cavalry under his immediate command had died June 25, 1876, in his last stand against the Sioux.

• Sturgis: Has two outstanding attractions in Bear Butte State Park and the Old Fort Meade Museum. Bear Butte, an ancient volcanic bubble, is a sacred mountain to the Cheyenne and Sioux Indians.

Climb Bear Butte, elevation 4,422 feet, for a dramatic view of western South Dakota's rangeland to the north and east. Turn around and enjoy the panoramic sweep of the nearby Black Hills and Fort Meade, constructed in 1878 as the "peace keeper frontier post." Its mission was to contain the Sioux on their reservations in what is now western South Dakota.

The museum is on the grounds of the Fort Meade Veterans Administration Center, a mile east of Sturgis on Highway 34.

It was at Fort Meade in 1892 that the 8th Cavalry started playing The Star Spangled Banner at retreat formations on the parade ground. This eventually resulted in Congress designating the song in 1931 as the national anthem.

Fort Meade outlived all other frontier posts of the Upper Missouri region. It became a Veterans Administration Hospital in 1944.

CATTLE COUNTRY OFFERS COLOR TREAT

Argus Leader, Oct. 24, 1987

October's changing leaves have been spectacular in South Dakota.

The switch from green to yellow and many shades of red has delighted viewers who enjoy a change of season.

Fall's vivid colors are fading fast, but there are other landscape treats in prospect.

There's a fine mix of blue sky and brown grass in cattle country in western South Dakota. Bare fields, stubble fields and harvested corn rows offer a pleasing patchwork of country scenes in eastern South Dakota. Various breeds of cattle, horses and sheep offer variety in colors as they dot the countryside.

Bright days have flashed glints of sunlight from soft yellowed stalks. Wind and colder temperatures have wafted snowflakes earthward in varying amounts across the state. Higher elevations in the Black Hills have already had measurable snowfall.

Given the best of weather worlds snow would come at ideal times for kids' play and ski journeys to the Black Hills. There would be no Armistice Day blizzard on Nov. 11 and South Dakota would enjoy a white Christmas. Then there would be a repeat of last year's mild winter, with ample precipitation for crops.

We're probably fortunate that man is helpless when it comes to dictating the weather.

One way to heighten viewing pleasure is to drive different routes.

Recently, my wife and I took Highway 79 north from Newell to Reva for the first time. Butte County's wide open spaces are as spectacular on the east side of the county as along Highway 85 north from Belle Fourche. On 79 you get a great view of the Castle Rock Buttes, elevation 3,741 feet, 17 miles north of Newell.

Route 79 takes you past Hoover and across the home range, between the forks of the Moreau River, that the Flying V ranch had nearly 100 years ago. The road offers a nice drive in

Harding County between escarpments of the southeastern leg of the Slim Buttes, a part of Custer National Forest.

There's a historical marker 2½ miles west of Reva on Highway 20 which commemorates the battle of the Slim Buttes between the U.S. Army and Sioux Indians on Sept. 9, 1876. Go farther west to see Buffalo or Camp Crook.

Highway 20 from Reva east to Bison and Highway 73 south to Faith offer a glimpse of wheat fields between buttes and hills in Perkins County. Forget the road signs for a moment and you could be almost anywhere in South Dakota's northwest or North Dakota's southwest corner.

Meade County, South Dakota's largest, has an excellent network of graveled roads in ranching country, thanks to Minuteman missile sites.

Driving from Faith, you can leave Highway 212 or 34 and reach Rapid City without going through Newell or Sturgis.

Many country stores and post offices that once served ranchers in western South Dakota are locked up or have disappeared. It's part of the statewide trend toward larger farms and ranches.

Fifty years ago there was a thriving village—with a store, handset weekly newspaper and a school—at Chalk Butte in the center of Meade County. Chalk Butte has vanished with its buildings that were hauled away.

A few miles north, the Stoneville store has closed. A few miles west, Fairpoint's store is closed. Opal has a post office at a ranch home, but the former store a couple of miles away is closed. Maurine has a filling station/garage, but no store. And so it goes.

One country gasoline dealer told me he was worried about strict new requirements for gasoline tanks that could put him out of business, because of the cost. He believes, and I agree with him, that environmental standards for a country filling station where there is no threat to underground water need not be as stringent as those in Sioux Falls or rural Minnehaha County.

So many country gas stops have disappeared that you risk running out if you drive on half a tank. Be sure to fill up before leaving the interstate or small towns to savor western scenery.

STOPOVERS ACROSS STATE PROVIDE GOOD PLACES TO VISIT
Argus Leader, Sunday, April 16, 1989

Here are a dozen scenarios for places to see and things to do during South Dakota's centennial year.

1. Stop over in Sioux Falls on your way to or from the faces at Mount Rushmore National Memorial.

Visit the Great Plains Zoo and Delbridge Museum of Natural History. The zoo's more than 300 birds, reptiles and mammals are well displayed. The museum features 175 mounted animals bagged by Henry Brockhouse, a Sioux Falls businessman, on many safaris around the world. A mounted panda is a gift from the People's Republic of China.

Drive by Oscar Howe School, named for South Dakota's great Indian painter, and Laura Wilder School, named for the author of Little House on the Prairie. Tour historic districts, the Old Courthouse Museum and Pettigrew Home and Museum. Bike on city trails.

2. Visit the South Dakota Art Museum in Brookings. See art of the Sioux, including Howe paintings, and Harvey Dunn paintings depicting life on the prairie and other exhibits. Tour South Dakota State University's campus.

3. Visit DeSmet. See the childhood home of Laura Ingalls Wilder and many other places she mentioned in her books. See the statue honoring Father DeSmet, Jesuit missionary who spent his life among the Indians. Drive west to Huron, State Fair city, and one of former Vice President Hubert Humphrey's South Dakota hometowns.

4. See glacial lakes in northeastern South Dakota. Tour Fort Sisseton State Historic Park, a well-preserved frontier army post built in 1864. Visit Watertown and Aberdeen. See the Sitting Bull monument west of Mobridge.

5. See musical instruments from around the world at the Shrine to Music Museum on the University of South Dakota campus at Vermillion. The museum has a gallery of Oscar Howe originals. Howe was university artist in residence during the later years of his life. See the DakotaDome. Drive west to Yankton, capital of Dakota Territory from 1861 to 1883.

6. See the World's only Corn Palace, Oscar Howe Art Center and Enchanted World Museum at Mitchell.

7. See one or more of the four dams and four Great Lakes of the Missouri, depending on where you cross the river.

8. See the Oahe Dam at Pierre. Tour the new Cultural Heritage Museum that opens to the public May 5. See South Dakota's Capitol, restored in recent years to its original beauty. Watch the ducks and geese on Capitol Lake.

9. Walk the streets of Fort Pierre. Drive to the Verendrye Monument that marks the spot where school children in 1913 found a lead plate buried in 1743 by the Verendrye brothers.

10. Drive through Badlands National Park for great views and pictures.

11. Tour the Black Hills. Pick up the trail of Lt. Col. George Custer's 1874 scientific expedition to the Black Hills. See Gutzon Borglum's carvings of four presidents at Mount Rushmore National Memorial. Observe work continuing on Korczak Ziolkowski's monument to Crazy Horse. Visit Lead and its new mining museum. See the Homestake Mine. Walk the streets of historic Deadwood.

Climb Bear Butte near Sturgis. Visit the Cavalry Post Museum at Fort Meade and see Custer's last camp site in the Black Hills. See the Passion Play at Spearfish.

12. Head north from the Black Hills. Stop in Belle Fourche. Picture you and yours at the geographical center of the United States, about 25 miles north of Belle Fourche on Highway 85.

Visit Buffalo, oil center of South Dakota. See Custer National Forest, the Slim Buttes and the monument west of Reva that commemorates the Battle of the Slim Buttes in 1876.

S.D. BECKONS FOR TRAVELERS
Soak up history on back roads

Argus Leader, June 6, 1993

Travelers in South Dakota will find a scenic smorgasbord everywhere this summer season.

It's a good time (weather permitting) to turn off your air conditioning, roll down the front windows and explore country roads.

Southeastern South Dakota's farmsteads, planted fields and trees surrounding houses or buildings offer pleasant vistas. They may trigger your memory's tape recorder: That looks like Grandpa's house. Or, that barn is just like the one Uncle had.

If you're driving on Sunday morning, you can guess the size of a church turnout by the number of cars in the parking lot. White, frame country churches with their steeples, groves of trees and neatly trimmed grounds may also trip memory's skein of childhood days.

Churchyard cemeteries and those that stand by themselves along a country road are part of South Dakota's outdoor pageantry. Every headstone represents memory of a loved one and heartbreak. Time eases grief and mends hearts of the living. Cemeteries in green summer raiment reflect sylvan repose.

Senior citizens who remember gravel roads and dirt grades of the 1930s are thankful that today they're traveling on all-weather roads. Electric lights seen at every farm home today were not there 60 years ago. Rural electrification, most of it accomplished after World War II, lit up the countryside.

Today's infrastructure in most cities and towns is much improved. Homes are better everywhere. Some small towns have senior centers, parks and swimming pools.

Sadly, much of the countryside has become depopulated and many small towns have withered. Deserted farm houses and gas stations mark lost dreams of somebody's friends who had to move because of changing circumstance.

Happily, most county seats and towns with good trading areas have kept pace with the times. There are small industries in the countryside that weren't there 10 or 15 years ago. Tourism and historic preservation have provided new jobs with prospect of more to come.

State or national parks and recreation areas are within easy reach.

It's enjoyable to scout areas away from home: the lake region in the northeast, Missouri River breaks from North Dakota to Nebraska and the hills, buttes and draws that unfold in cowboy country west of Pierre.

Kevin Costner's "Dances With Wolves" dramatized South Dakota's remarkable western scenery. There's a lot more of it—virtually all of South Dakota west of the Missouri River.

Drive west from Mobridge on Highway 20 through Timber Lake, Isabel, Bison and Reva to the ramparts of the Slim Buttes. Enjoy picnic areas in Custer National Forest and visit Buffalo, the state's oil capital and Harding County seat. That is the land where antelope roam.

Take your RV, 4x4 or family station wagon and explore the western side of the Black Hills of South Dakota. Buy some topographical maps and explore back roads to your heart's content.

Fish for rainbow trout at Deerfield Reservoir or other Black Hills lakes. Pet the burros in Custer State Park. See the four faces on Mount Rushmore and the emerging face and head of Crazy Horse on Crazy Horse Mountain. Thread your way through the Needles Highway. Stop in Hot Springs for the best swim in South Dakota at Evans Plunge. See ancient bones of Columbian mammoths at the Mammoth Site.

Other Black Hills attractions you should see: Deadwood and its gambling revival; the Fort Meade Museum and Bear Butte State Park at Sturgis and the Rushmore-Borglum Story at Keystone.

South Dakota's restored State Capitol is one of the nation's most beautiful statehouses. When in Pierre also visit the South Dakota Cultural Heritage Center. Its museum and view from its hilltop setting are inspiring.

NICOLLET'S TOWERING S.D. FEATS HONORED

Argus Leader, Sunday, Aug. 3, 1993

There's a scenic and historic treat for visitors at the Nicollet Tower and Interpretive Center 3.5 miles west of Sisseton.

The 75-foot tower and center memorialize Joseph Nicolas Nicollet, French mapmaker and scientist. He was fascinated by the spectacular view at the site, atop the Coteau des Prairies (Hills of the Prairies). There the prairie rises 800 feet above the valley floor to the east.

On a clear day climbers can see three states and the Continental Divide from the tower. Highway 10 which runs alongside the tower practically defines the divide: the area north of the highway drains into Hudson Bay; the area south of the road, into the Gulf of Mexico.

Nicollet wrote about "the magical influence of the prairies....Their sight never wearies...to ascend one of its undulations, moving from wave to wave over alternate swells and depressions, and finally to reach the vast interminable low prairie, that extends itself in front, be it for hours, days, or weeks...pleasurable and exhilarating sensations are all the time felt....I pity the man whose soul could remain unmoved under such a scene of excitement...."

Nicollet visited the Sisseton region in 1838 and 1839.

Nicollet's journeys resulted in the nation's first accurate map of the Upper Mississippi and Missouri River Valleys. He located the headwaters of the Mississippi, trekked from Fort Pierre to Devils Lake, visited the Pipestone Quarry and traveled along or near the Big Sioux and Minnesota Rivers, among others.

Nicollet tower near Sisseton.
—Anson Yeager photo

He used steamboats, canoes and saddle horses. He carried his gear in a wagon. He made thousands of topographical readings and many sketches. He used a telescope, chronometer and barometer to determine locations and altitudes.

Nicollet's name is on the U.S. War Department map published in 1843, the year he died. The map is displayed in the Interpretive Center. His calculations proved to be very accurate.

A 12-minute tape gives visitors highlights of Nicollet's work. Ten murals by John S. Wilson, South Dakota artist, depict the region and Nicollet's role. He made friends with many Indians along the way.

Nicollet traveled without a military escort but accepted Lt. John Charles Fremont, 23 years old, as his assistant. Fremont named Lakes Poinsett, Preston, Benton and Albert for friends or benefactors. Fremont later won fame for his explorations in the West.

Nicollet was born in 1786 in the French Alps. He was appointed professor and astronomer in the Royal Observatory in Paris during the Napoleonic era. His career was cut short by turbulent French politics. He sailed alone to the United States in 1832. After some exploratory work, he was appointed to lead the U.S. Army's newly formed Corps of Topographical Engineers.

The Redlin Art Center at Watertown exhibits paintings of wildlife and early American life by Terry Redlin, a native South Dakotan and one of the nation's foremost artists. The Center, which also includes a theater, is Redlin's gift to the people of his home community and state.

Although Nicollet's work was well known to South Dakota historians, research work since the 1960s in Minnesota has contributed additional information.

Martha C. Bray and Edmund C. Bray of St. Paul translated and edited Nicollet's detailed journals from French in the 1960s and 1970s. The Minnesota Historical Society published their book, "Joseph N. Nicollet on the Plains and Prairies," in 1976.

Harold L. Torness, president of Roberts County National Bank in Sisseton, was so fascinated by the book that he spearheaded a fund drive to build a monument to Nicollet. Some longtime residents contributed $25,000 each. Some services were donated. Cost of the tower and center was approximately $385,000, all of it privately donated and none of it from tax money.

The tower was dedicated Oct. 5, 1991. More than 10,000 visitors saw the tower during a short summer season last year.

SOUTH DAKOTA SPECTACLE

SIOUX TIES TO LAND ENDURING, REVERENT

Argus Leader, Sunday, Aug. 23, 1981

Tim Giago, the editor and publisher of The Lakota Times, a weekly newspaper at Pine Ridge, S.D., questions the Indians' occupation of Wind Cave National Park this summer. His editorial is reprinted below.

Giago makes a point about the religious significance of the Black Hills to Indians.

Perhaps Indians who have taken part in the encampment at Wind Cave and also the media have put too much emphasis on the political struggle.

That should not minimize the depth of feeling that Sioux Indians have for the Black Hills. It is akin to the reverence in which they hold their windswept reservation lands in South Dakota.

◆ ◆ ◆

Perhaps no other Americans feel so deeply about the land upon which they live as the Sioux Indians of South Dakota.

They relate to the land—whether they are among the older generation, some of whose grandparents knew Sitting Bull, or younger Indians. Many of the latter have dismissed pleas to find schooling or jobs elsewhere and have stayed on the reservation.

Life on the reservation is difficult at best. There are few jobs and few opportunities. But there is the land—and ties to home and village.

The land is where parents, grandparents and other kin lived—after their ancestors were put on the Great Sioux Reservation in western South Dakota.

It is the sky, the sweep of hills in western South Dakota, the pine and brush in the ravines, the sun and the wind.

Home on the reservation has always been modest, and often a shack. Sometimes home has been a tent.

Years ago I talked to an Indian mother and her two school-age children—happy and making do in late April on the Pine Ridge reservation. They had no sad tale to relate because they were still in the white-wall tent in which they spent the winter.

An Indian youngster, like his white counterpart, knows that land is limited.

The sons of a white rancher in South Dakota realize that there isn't enough land for all of them to stay home.

"The Ways of the People" exhibit depicts the Sioux Indians of South Dakota

An early Indian woman at work.

The Indian boy, whose chances of making it on a ranch are considerably less, more often views it as a matter of hope and faith—and is disappointed.

Family land holdings on reservations have been handed down from generation to generation, despite their small size and fractionalization. It is the tie that binds many Indians to a part of South Dakota.

❖ ❖ ❖

Trying to persuade Indians to leave their land for relocation and jobs in cities like Minneapolis, Chicago and Los Angeles was a plan that failed during the 1950s.

Some transplants stayed, of course, but the land pulled many Sioux back to the wooded hills around Sisseton and to the rangeland on the reservations in western South Dakota.

A friend of mine once asked a successful young Indian woman why she wanted to go back home to the reservation where the amenities of daily life did not compare with her working-day role.

"Why does anyone want to go home?" she replied.

Some of the homesteaders who settled on West River land in 1908-1910 found themselves attracted to the wide open spaces in a way comparable to the feeling Indians have for South Dakota's "big sky" country.

Most of the homesteaders didn't make it when drought came. They left South Dakota over a period of several decades through the 1930s to find a living on the West Coast or Southwest. Something about the land has pulled them or their children back to South Dakota time and again.

It isn't a religion with the settlers or their descendants, but it is a yearning for roots, a desire to see a spot of soil on the plains that once was hearth and home.

For the Sioux, it's communion with the outdoors.

❖ ❖ ❖

The Buffalo was a key part of the Indians' sustenance on the plains.

It's 105 years since Sitting Bull and his warriors vanquished General Custer and his contingent at the Battle of the Little Big Horn. It is almost 91 years since Sitting Bull was killed by Indian police on the Standing Rock Reservation.

In more than four generations on South Dakota reservations, the Indians' regard for the compressed area in which the United States put them is as strong as ever.

A hundred years from now, some of the descendants of today's Indians will still be on the land to which their forefathers became so attached.

The Black Hills, which are lost forever to the tribes except in their symbolism, will still have a religious appeal to the Indians.

Some South Dakotans can remember Indian families driving teams and wagons to camp out at reservation towns during fairs and celebrations. The Indians were at home in the outdoors, like their ancestors and like today's Indians at Wind Cave.

A few can remember full-blooded Indian braves with long braided hair and big felt hats who sat on the steps of village stores or post offices on the reservation—and reminisced among themselves about another era.

No one can bring it back.

No one should minimize the Indians' feelings for either the Black Hills or the land on the reservations.

Hopefully, someone during the next 100 years will find a bridge of understanding between the two races. Of all the social change that cries for departure from the past, this is both South Dakota's biggest problem and opportunity.

For Indians, it will mean playing a much bigger part in the outside world than is the case today.

Like the settlers, they can do it—without losing their link to the land. The mystique will remain—but the jobs Indians need will be off the reservation.

Pope John Paul II examines a bronze cast of sculptor Korczak Ziolkowski's smallest scale model for his Crazy Horse mountain carving in the Black Hills. Bishop Harold J. Dimmerling, left, of Rapid City, presented the scale model to the pope at the Vatican.

POPE PLEASED BY CRAZY HORSE SCALE MODEL, INVITED TO VISIT

Argus Leader, Sunday, Jan. 22, 1984

Here's a potpourri of recent developments affecting South Dakota's Polish-connection.

✦ ✦ ✦

Pope John Paul II, Poland's most famous native son, has a bronze cast of sculptor Korczak Ziolkowski's smallest scale model of his Crazy Horse mountain carving.

Ziolkowski was born in Boston of Polish descent and devoted most of his adult lifetime to carving a mountain near Custer, S.D., to honor Crazy Horse, famed Indian chief.

The Most Rev. Harold J. Dimmerling, bishop of the Rapid City Catholic diocese, presented the scale model of the mountain carving to the pope on a recent trip to the Vatican. Dimmerling said, "The pope was extremely pleased with the Crazy Horse bronze. He examined and scrutinized it very carefully."

The cast of the 1/1,200ths scale model mounted on a piece of polished Crazy Horse granite was a gift to the pope from Mrs. Korczak Ziolkowski and family. The sculptor died at age 74 on Oct. 20, 1982. His wife and large family are dedicated to carrying on his work according to the detailed plans he left.

Mrs. Ziolkowski said: "Korczak would have been greatly honored and humbled by the pope's acceptance of his work. Korczak had the greatest admiration for Pope John Paul's faith, courage and wisdom. He followed very closely the pope's religious and political struggles in Poland before he was elected pontiff. Although he always said he was an American, Korzcak was very proud of his Polish ancestry."

Dimmerling said, "The Holy Father and I talked about the Indian people in our diocese. He was somewhat surprised to learn that there are five reservations in our diocese. I shared with him that the Jesuits, Benedictines, Sacred Heart fathers and a Dominican were ministering to the Indian people. He was pleased to hear this, but cautioned that we must always respect the culture of our Indian brothers and sisters. I assured him that we always tried to do this, and I informed him that some of our priests were taking time to learn the Lakota (Sioux) language."

Mrs. Ziolkowski expressed the hope that Pope John Paul II can visit Crazy Horse on a future visit to North America. That would excite many people, especially Americans of Polish descent. It would be a tremendous publicity boost for the Black Hills and South Dakota.

The pope was well received in Iowa on Oct. 4 1979, when he visited the Living History Farms on the outskirts of Des Moines.

In the year since Ziolkowski died, his family—working under Mrs. Ziolkowski's supervision—has blasted another 200,000 tons off the mountain carving.

Approximately 7.6 million tons has been removed in blocking out the sculpture of Chief Crazy Horse in the round. When completed, Crazy Horse will be 563 feet high and 641 feet long.

♦ ♦ ♦

Robert Karolevitz, the Mission Hill, S.D., author and part-time farmer, is the other part of today's Polish equation. His paternal grandparents came to the United States from Poland.

Bob has been known to tell many Polish jokes on the banquet circuit in South Dakota—plus Norwegian and other nationalities. He plays the field—and does it in good humor.

Now he's poked some fun at himself in his 21st book, "Tears in My Horseradish", a collection of humorous weekly columns he's written during the last year for Bernie Hunhoff Jr.'s Observer, at Gayville, S.D. The book was published by The Observer.

One column is entitled "How to OVER-DO It Yourself." It includes eight steps to fun and fractures. Rule No. I is "always pick jobs you know nothing about." Another: "Never ask for help." The last: "When everything else fails, read the instructions."

Karolevitz says he hopes his eight rules might help some other Handy Andy out there, Polish or otherwise. A picture showing him at work, safety visor pushed up, is captioned: "I almost burned the barn down when I tried to weld a couple of 2x4s together."

Although Karolevitz is not in favor of regimentation, he wrote that he could support a National Nametag Law that would impose a $5,000 fine and 10 years of hard labor for anyone who starts a conversation at a class reunion with the question: "You don't remember me, do you?"

Robert F. Karolevitz

The 130-page paperback is on sale at some regional bookstores; the suggested price is $7.95, plus tax. It was the third book Karolevitz did last year. The other two were a history of Douglas County and Public Relations, a how-to-do-it book for the health care industry.

Karolevitz says that three books in one year were almost more than he bargained for.

This year he'll be working on a biography for a Seattle area banker/developer and a history of community newspapers in the United States for the National Newspaper Association's centennial convention in the fall of 1985.

The centennial newspaper volume was inspired by a similar book he did for the South Dakota Press Association. His With a Shirttail Full of Type—The Story of Newspapering in South Dakota helped the state press association celebrate its centennial in 1982.

Karolevitz knows that he's going to be very busy in the months ahead. What happens when he finishes books No. 22 and 23?

"I'd like to take a little rest."

STATE HONORS THE LIVING
Argus Leader, July 16, 1989

South Dakotans and their state and local governments have a neat way of honoring outstanding citizens—naming buildings, schools or airports for them while they are still alive.

Webster, population 2,417, on July 1 renamed its airport in honor of its most famous resident, former Gov. Sigurd Anderson.

His daughter, Kristin, wrote a bylined article about the dedication for the Watertown Public Opinion. She quoted her dad: "I thought it was a great day, and I am most appreciative of the community's efforts. Sometimes it's hard to put such personal feelings into words."

The town of Webster and many of Anderson's friends from around the state turned out to wish him well. He's 85.

Anderson's name is also on a state office building at Pierre, an honor that came to him in June 1975. Gov. Richard Kneip dedicated two buildings that day—the other one to former Gov. Joe Foss.

There was controversy at the time about naming the buildings for living persons, and particularly for naming a third building for Kneip, the incumbent.

Foss in his inimitable way said that he was darned pleased by the honor and that it was great to be able to enjoy it while he was still alive. Anderson expressed similar sentiments. He had left the governor's office in 1955; Foss, in 1959.

Gerald Andrews, Kneip's administration commissioner, said in 1975 that Kneip knew nothing of the plan until after the commission made the decision.

Kneip resigned as governor July 24, 1978, to become President Jimmy Carter's ambassador to Singapore. He resigned in 1980 and returned to Sioux Falls to enter business. Kneip died in Sioux Falls March 9, 1987.

Sioux Falls did some trail blazing in 1955 when the city and the Chamber of Commerce named the municipal airport Joe Foss Field. Foss was in the third month of his first term as governor. He was a hometown boy who won fame in World War II by shooting down 26 Japanese planes over Guadalcanal. President Franklin D. Roosevelt awarded him the Congressional Medal of Honor. Foss is now 74.

Another famous South Dakotan, Sioux Indian artist Oscar Howe, was present Sept. 21, 1980, when the Sioux Falls School District dedicated the elementary school in his honor.

Howe's response was in calligraphy. His scroll said in part: "I am glad to be here in person for this most memorable occasion....It's an honor I shall always remember."

Howe died Oct. 7, 1983.

South Dakota's major precedent for honoring the living probably was set in 1911 when a statue of Gen. William Henry Harrison Beadle was placed in the Capitol at Pierre. The man who saved the state's school lands and funds was 73 and present for the dedication. He died in 1915. His statue is still on display in the Capitol at Pierre.

CENTER FOR WESTERN STUDIES PRESERVES, INTERPRETS HEARTLAND
Argus Leader, Sunday, Jan. 23, 1994

Think tank exponents of writing off this region of the United States as a buffalo commons haven't researched Augustana College's Center for Western Studies.

The center's mission is to preserve and interpret the historical record of the northern heartland of South Dakota and adjoining states.

To Arthur R. Huseboe, onetime college instructor of 18th century English literature who guides the center as executive director, there is no more interesting region in the world.

"This is a marvelous microcosm of the world. We have here some of the most diverse people in the world. Geographically, this territory is one of infinite variety: mountains, desert, forest, but no ocean. There are no great cities in Buffalo Commons. The rest of the world...doesn't know how adaptable we have become: We don't plow ranchland. We have learned how to use this land."

He said that half the people who settled the West were foreign born. He has a passion for preserving their histories and translating and publishing them from Scandinavian and German frontier documents. He is also passionate about preserving Indian history and art. He is elated that one can hear Lakota spoken in the countryside.

The Center this year and next is observing its Silver Anniversary Year. Augustana College in 1970 expanded the center as an integral part of the college directly under its president, who was then Charles Balcer.

Professor Herbert Krause, noted author, became its first director. The Center had been founded under his leadership in 1964 as

Arthur Huseboe's *An Illustrated History of the Arts in South Dakota* interprets the arts of the state from Territorial days to the present. Here Huseboe (left) and Harry Thompson, the Center's managing editor (right), accept the first copy at Christmas time 1989 from Keith Severson of Sioux Printing.
—Center for Western Studies photo

part of the Augustana College English department. Huseboe became the center's fifth director in 1989.

The Center occupies part of the ground floor of Mikkelsen Library. Many scholars, authors and history buffs beat a path to its archives and library. The center is also a museum and art gallery and is the largest academic publisher in South Dakota. The Center has published 40 books and plans new titles.

"Yanktonai Sioux Water Colors" by authors Martin Brokenleg and Herbert T. Hoover published last year has 23 stunning color plates of paintings by John Saul, Crow Creek artist. Saul painted them for the Works Progress Administration in the 1930s. He was artist Oscar Howe's mentor and helped him paint the Indian murals at the Mobridge Auditorium. Saul's paintings are at the center.

An Oklahoma author recently found interesting material about the death of Sitting Bull in letters of Episcopal and Congregational missionaries that are filed in archives at the Center.

The Center has published the first paperback books in its new Prairie Plains group. One is "Duke's Mixture," a collection of essays by Frederick Manfred, regional author.

Another paperback is Sig Mickelson's "The Northern Pacific Railroad and the Selling of the West." This was Mickelson's master's thesis at the University of Minnesota in 1940 and was left unpublished for 50 years. Mickelson was a 1935 graduate of Augustana who became president of CBS News in 1959.

The center's 14th annual Plains Art Show and Sale is scheduled Feb. 18-20. Fourteen American artists will show paintings in 14 booths rented for $100 each. Sales are expected to total about $10,000, Huseboe said. Dean A. Schueler, the center's development director, handles the art show.

Harry F. Thompson, curator and managing editor, shepherds the annual Dakota History Conference sponsored by the Center and the South Dakota Humanities Council. The conference will be held at Augustana College June 2-4.

Current exhibits include memorabilia of Sheldon F. Reese, South Dakota grain dealer and philanthropist, and original paintings by Roger Preuss, waterfowl and wildlife artist.

There is much more at the center including 30,000 volumes on the American West. Center hours are 8 a.m. to 5 p.m., Monday through Friday.

EX-WASHINGTON HIGH COACH SETTLES IN THE HILLS

Argus Leader, Sunday, Oct. 1, 1989

Happiness is being a campground manager in the Black Hills, especially if you're the third generation in tourism.

Meet Al Johnson, 36, 6-foot-11, who is winding up his 13th year as manager of Mount Rushmore KOA (Kampgrounds of America) and Palmer-Gulch Lodge near Hill City.

His boss, Sioux Falls lawyer Richard A. Cutler, who hired him, said: "We've never had anyone challenge Al Johnson."

The former Western Illinois University center towers over everyone at the campground, but not in a formidable way. He's at ease in his job, whether talking to guests, one of his 40 summer staff members or responding to problems:

• Like switching water valves to a reserve supply at 6 p.m. when a guest tells him there is no water in the showers.

The Mount Rushmore KOA near Hill City is nestled in Palmer Gulch, below Harney Peak. —Anson Yeager photo

• Or retrieving his pride and joy, the red Bristol British double-decker bus, stalled in Rapid City.

The campground acquired the bus about five years ago to run free shuttles to the night lighting ceremony at Mount Rushmore, five miles east on Highway 244.

The bus is one of many features that helps Palmer Gulch Resort pack in guests at 325 sites and 18 full-service cabins with daily maid service. The campground also has 17 KOA Kamping Kabins for guests who carry sleeping bags and kitchen gear.

The campground is on a 132-acre gulch that was an early gold mining claim.

"Our location (at the foot of Harney Peak) is unbeatable," Johnson says. "But the real secret of our success is people having a choice of what they want to do. We have trail rides and a water slide. We have put in volleyball. We have two playgrounds areas, free movies and activities—Indian dances, hay rides, watermelon feeds.

The campground's restaurant and lounge, trail rides and Old West Town are concessions. Rental cars and bus tours are available so campers don't have to drive their RVs through the hills.

Johnson is active in tourism organizations. He was president of the South Dakota Campground Association in 1987.

He thinks tourists would like to see more of Sioux Indians and their culture. He said Indian dancers, who drew evening crowds of several hundred last summer, were the most popular free attraction of recent years.

The campground closes today until next May 1.

SOUTH DAKOTA SPECTACLE

Camping vehicles are shoe-horned into slots lining campground access roads. —Anson Yeager photo

The lodge at Palmer Gulch, on the grounds of the Mount Rushmore KOA, offers luxurious accommodations in a spectacular setting. —Anson Yeager photo

Johnson finished college with an English major at the University of South Dakota in 1975. He taught a year and a half at Washington High School in Sioux Falls and was its first girls basketball coach since the 1930s.

Elton Byre, then boys basketball coach, knew Cutler was looking for a manager and told him about Al, who wanted to return to his Black Hills roots.

Johnson also directs the Rapid City KOA of 270 sites, but says it requires very little of his time because it has an excellent manager.

Both campgrounds enjoyed record sales this year, Cutler said. He's president of Satellite Cable Services, which owns the campgrounds. Sales of Palmer Gulch exceeded $900,000 and at Rapid City, $300,000. "We have a lot of family reunions at Palmer Gulch," Cutler said.

Satellite Cable Services offers cable TV in 40 eastern South Dakota towns. Stockholders are Cutler, some of his colleagues in the Sioux Falls legal firm of Davenport, Evans, Hurwitz & Smith, and various managers, including Johnson.

Cutler's interest in the Black Hills stems from boyhood trips from Wessington Springs, his hometown. Cutler and three other Sioux Falls men bought Palmer Gulch in 1972 and built a Holiday Inn Travel Park. The cable company bought it in 1976 and switched to KOA about two years later.

A grizzly sculpted in wood is an attraction in the Palmer Gulch Lodge. —Anson Yeager photo

Cutler said that the two campgrounds make the firm one of the 50 largest KOA franchises.

Palmer Gulch Resort is the largest privately owned campground in South Dakota open to the public.

NEW LODGE HAS RUSTIC APPEAL IN HILLS

Argus Leader, Sunday, Sept. 15, 1996

HILL CITY, S.D.—Gather around, Happy Campers.

There's a new side to camping at Palmer Gulch Resort, a scenic mountain campground nestled in pines 5 miles west of Mount Rushmore.

The Lodge, a $2 million motel with 62 deluxe rooms, is the new attraction. It joins Palmer Gulch's 30 full service cabins with kitchen and fireplaces and the Mount Rushmore-Hill City KOA with its 500 campground sites and 51 KOA Kamping Kabins.

The Lodge, which opened in June 1995, helped Palmer Gulch reach sales expected to top $2 million this year during a season when camping was down.

The two-story motel is nestled among Ponderosa pines in one of the Black Hills' most spectacular settings. Look south 2-1/2 miles and up nearly two thousand feet to Harney Peak, elevation 7,242 feet, highest point in South Dakota and in the United States east of the Rocky Mountains.

Palmer Gulch Resort has pitched the Lodge's appeal to business and other groups to hold retreats at the motel. Family reunions have long constituted much of the resort's business.

The Lodge has log accents, outdoor balconies in most of the rooms and natural wood decor and furnishings. There are four suites with fireplaces and kitchenettes. Other facilities include a spa and sauna, free cable TV with HBO and a meeting room with an impressive log balcony.

The most spectacular furnishing is Beauford Woodrow, a 3,000-pound bear carved from California redwood. The nine-foot high bear had to be placed in the lobby before the building was enclosed.

Al Johnson, Palmer Gulch manager, credited local companies for excellent workmanship in everything from the construction to locally made furnishings. Paul Waldum, a local artist, created the in-room and lobby art. Silhouette lighting featuring Black Hills scenes adorns the vestibule, lobby and meeting room.

Johnson said, "We are especially grateful to Ruth Ziolkowski for providing blast fragments from the Crazy Horse Memorial for our massive fireplace and lobby rock work."

Johnson, in his 20th year with Palmer Gulch, said that during the summer season the resort falls in the top 30 South Dakota cities, about the size of Custer (population 1,741) or Deadwood (population 1,830) in population.

"We are the grocery store, gas station, restaurant, laundry, arcade and shopping center for quite a city in the summertime," Johnson said.

There's a strip mall of half a dozen stores across from the KOA store and office. Swimming pools, a water slide, outdoor stage which features Indian dancers, miniature golf and trail rides and the Ponderosa Inn are among attractions.

Richard A. Cutler, a Sioux Falls lawyer, is president of Satellite Cable Services which owns Palmer Gulch and six other campgrounds. He said the company hopes to acquire three more large franchises to reach a goal of 10 KOA campgrounds.

The firm this year purchased campgrounds in Seattle, Wash., and Harper's Ferry, W. Va. Other franchises are at Rapid City, Fort Myers-Pine Island, Fla., Cody, Wyo., and Astoria, Ore.

Cutler said he expects the firm's national campground sales to reach $7 million this year.

Cutler, at 55 the senior active member of a prestigious Sioux Falls law firm, said, "I would never have guessed that I would get into the campground business."

Cutler said ownership in Satellite Services has broadened somewhat from earlier years when his law partners were the principal shareholders. Satellite Services, based in DeSmet, S.D., also provides cable service to 57 small towns in eastern South Dakota and owns a half-interest in cable operations at Brookings.

Last year Cutler and his wife, Sharon, were presented KOA's national franchisee of the year award, the first time it had gone to individuals not actively managing a campground.

Palmer Gulch services include rental cars, shuttles to Mount Rushmore and Crazy Horse (Memorial Day to Labor Day) and other features which appeal to a wide variety of campers.

BLIZZARD BAFFLES TODAY'S TRAVEL ADVANTAGES

Argus Leader, Jan. 19, 1997

Today's jet-age travelers have many advantages that earlier Americans couldn't have imagined.

But when all is said and done, even modern Americans can't do anything about the weather.

That has been demonstrated countless times in recent weeks by frigid whiteouts in South Dakota, floods in California and the Pacific Northwest, and stormy weather in most of North America.

It's easy to reserve flights that will whisk you from Sioux Falls to Honolulu by midafternoon, but it is something else when you're snow-bound in Yankton 85 miles from Joe Foss Field. Interstate 29 was shut down and so was virtually all of South Dakota.

So Ada May and I canceled our Jan. 10, 7:05 a.m., United flight out of Sioux Falls on the preceding morning. A few hours later the airport was closed because of the winter storm, so the flight for which we were booked didn't occur anyway. Commercial air service was shut down along with virtually everything else that South Dakotans do on normal winter days.

If you're going to be snowbound, you'll be lucky if you're staying at Days Inn in Yankton, a comfortable motel on the city's north side.

Shirley Stoebner, manager since the motel opened in May 1992, delights patrons by decorating for Valentine's Day, Easter, Halloween, Thanksgiving and Christmas. It's fun to see her extensive decorations.

Our snowbound stay was between decorations. Swirling snow in big scenic gulps and whiteouts through motel windows had to do.

A port in a storm

Inside senior citizens, young families, business travelers and truckers found her motel a welcome port in a storm. There were card games in the lobby during snowbound nights and snacks.

Travelers who reached the motel Jan. 9 described conditions close to Yankton. One couple said both had to watch from open windows in their car to make the five-mile drive, and they couldn't see anything. Another couple related how their problems began quickly after leaving Sioux Falls that morning on Interstate 29 and worsened between Irene and Yankton on Highways 46 and 81.

Truckers parked their big rigs in front and settled down. Pizza vendors delivered to the motel, which doesn't have a restaurant. Sunshine Foods kept their deli open during two white-out days to help snowbound travelers.

Stoebner, a 1955 graduate of Menno High School, has been in the hotel business for 42 years. She started in her hometown during high school and has worked for six South Dakota hotels during her career. She went from Menno to the former Sheraton-Cataract in Sioux Falls and helped open a Holiday Inn in Sioux Falls. She also has worked in Aberdeen and Pierre.

She celebrated her birthday on the job at Yankton's Days Inn on Jan. 11—the day South Dakota partially reopened the interstates after the whiteout subsided.

We had arrived in Yankton on Jan. 8, the day before the storm. We stayed at Yankton until Sunday morning.

We used the Yankton visit—to help our oldest daughter, Karen, celebrate her birthday—as a test of our packing for the Honolulu flight. We packed our carry-ons about the way we wanted them for the Hawaiian trip. I also brought along my new laptop computer to be sure I had everything I would need in Honolulu.

Packing for Honolulu

Our other packing for the Honolulu trip involved laying out a minimum list for a two-week stay, in which we would have access at son Terry's home in Honolulu to a washer and dryer.

It's convoluting to think about T-shirts, shorts and socks for 85-degree days in Hawaii when the weather outside is so frigid.

Here's what I took to Honolulu in my carry-on: electric razor, toiletry kit, medicine, camera, flashlight, small radio, change of clothes, two books and Time magazine. My laptop was the second carry-on.

United made new reservations. We took a cab to the airport with a minimum of heavy clothing.

Another expedient was to mail a package of winter gear to Denver for a weekend visit with our daughter, Ellen, on the way back.

We managed to board the plane with less stuff than usual.

Even today's jets have to defer to the weather at times, but comfort and convenience factors are greatly improved.

Our last trip to Europe (in 1994) took about seven hours from the East Coast. The writer's first flight to Britain via military propeller aircraft in 1944 during World War II took almost 24 hours of flying time via Newfoundland, the Azores, Casablanca and Scotland. Today's seats are much more comfortable than bucket seats alongside the walls of transport planes.

Given two weeks in Australia, the only way you can see Sydney, Melbourne, Perth, Alice Springs and the Great Barrier Reef is to do much of your traveling by plane. That was our 1992 overseas trip. It also allowed us to take the train to Perth. We had a third week to see New Zealand.

One lesson from this is to consider how large your destination is. Australia is almost the size of the 48 mainland states of the United States. During two recent trips to Alaska we used air transportation to see Kotzebue, Nome and Juneau from our base in Fairbanks.

One thing we've never endured is a 14-hour nonstop flight from Los Angeles to Australia. Instead, we broke up our flights with stopovers in Hawaii. When you book a tour, insist on a stopover.

Planning a trip and then doing it is a lot of fun. But don't forget that Northern Plains winter weather can stymie the best of plans. Trying to prevail over life-threatening conditions is stupid.

Be thankful for state, law enforcement and other individuals who help South Dakotans survive the storm.

Also, say a thanksgiving prayer for all state, highway and other workers who helped South Dakota survive the blizzard's fury.

STATE-CITY-GOVERNMENT; S.D. POLITICS

S.D. PUBLIC FIGURES AS CLOSE TO CONSTITUENTS AS NEAREST PHONE

Argus Leader, Sunday, Nov. 22, 1981

Jottings from an editor's notebook—telephone and other trivia about public figures that may or may not boggle your mind.

South Dakota's First Family—is in the phone book in Pierre. There's a listing for William Janklow—no title—and a separate phone for the children.

Gov. and Mrs. Janklow and the youngsters have kept the same phone numbers for several years, from before the move into that large, white frame home by the lake in 1979.

South Dakota mansion expense, according to a survey by the Minneapolis Star, is the least expensive in the region, or $51,316 for fiscal 1981. Wisconsin topped the list with $338,564; other states were Minnesota, $163,969; Iowa, $129,893, and North Dakota, $77,911.

Mayor Rick Knobe and some other Sioux Falls citizens with top public jobs are like Janklow—they're in the phone book.

Commissioners Harold Wingler and Richard Peterson are listed. So is Senior U.S. District Judge Fred J. Nichol.

M. E. (Mike) Schirmer, chairman of the Minnehaha County Commission and a former mayor, is in the phone book.

So are Richard Bohy, chairman of the Board of Education and John W. Harris, superintendent of schools. There are three John Harrises in the book and two John W's. The superintendent lives at 1620 S. 5th Ave.

School board members, superintendents—and principals—probably get more phone calls than anyone else in South Dakota. State legislators would be a close second, counting telephone calls to the capitol—called "heat from home"—when they're in session.

People who want unlisted numbers shouldn't run for office—or have a public job.

And here's a commercial for Ma Bell and all the independent phone companies in South Dakota. Your public servant is as close as your telephone.

The state's heritage as an open society—with easy access to public officers—makes it that way. Any officeholder who gets lofty ideas about being above the crowd soon finds himself looking for new employment in the Coyote State.

SOLONS' ORDEAL

Argus Leader, Sunday, Feb. 12, 1978

PIERRE, S.D.—How do the legislators do it?

That's the question Capitol observers ask about the strenuous demands a session of the Legislature places on the 105 members in dealing with the people's business.

In this 30-day session, legislators have considered more than 700 bills. In doing so, they've worked from morning to late at night, in committee sessions, hearings and floor work that involve questions important to South Dakota citizens and also to the bureaucracy. Some legislators complain they're jumping for both the Pierre and Washington bureaucracies.

Weekends for many legislators find them flying or driving home to talk to constituents at public meetings on a Saturday. For many of them, the phone rings off the hook from the time they reach home until they leave. The phone also rings in Pierre—and legislators try to answer the calls. They're helped or badgered by lobbyists, depending on the individual legislator's viewpoint.

In 30 days in even-numbered years and 45 days in odd-numbered years the members are charged with coming up with the answers to simple questions that involve only a few, and complicated matters of taxation or consumerism that can affect virtually all the state's citizens.

In committee hearings and in floor debates, the participants are expected to have the answers. The members have the benefit of a sophisticated and experienced Legislative Research Council to help them with the answers. They've used interim studies, special hearings between sessions and their own personal inspection trips to state institutions on their own time to try to come up with information to help them in their decisions.

The Legislature has tightened its rules to expedite filing of bills and their passage through the Legislature. The Legislative Research Council uses the benefit of computer technology to keep track of bills and to print them—tasks that once were performed manually or keyboarded by stenographers and printers. Time saved by the computer amounts to several precious days each session. These steps have all helped legislators cope with the mass of bills and the people's business thrown at them during a session.

There has also been a bit of backsliding in expediting the Legislature's work. That is the tendency in recent years for more bills, killed in committee, to surface on the floor of the House or Senate. The process is democracy in action: if a legislator can get a bill out of the committee and onto the floor, he or she has an opportunity to change some minds.

What, then, can be done to lighten some of the rigors of an annual session of the South Dakota Legislature? One possibility, which is remote, would be to lengthen the session by adding legislative days. Voters have turned down several such proposals in recent years involving constitutional changes.

They'll have a chance this November to decide on annual 40-day sessions, instead of the present 30- and 45-day sessions each two years.

There have been suggestions in the Capitol that legislators conduct sessions on Monday, Wednesday and Friday, and use Tuesday and Thursday for hearings.

Under this concept, the length of the legislature could be stretched out somewhat, counting only session days as legislative days.

This could effectively reduce the demanding pace during a session and eliminate some 14-hour days. Legislators would have more time to consider involved questions. It has an advantage in giving the public more time to make a better showing before a committee. But it has a drawback: elements of subterfuge in not counting hearing days as part of the session. The legal question would have to be resolved.

There is no logical way to curtail any legislator's right—or citizen's recourse—by limiting the filings of bills. Many observers think that the only way to reduce the problem of 700 bills during a 30-day session is the use of a hardboiled steering committee which would determine which measures are serious and which are of limited interest or frivolous. The marginal measures would not reach a standing committee for legislative action, under this concept. Rules would make it more difficult to get bills out of the steering committee for action by the body.

This Legislature, like its predecessors, has referred some knotty questions, like the proposed Department of Energy and appointment of public utilities commissioners, to an interim study. There is a limit to such referrals, too—a limit which legislators recognize. When the buck stops, it's up to them to vote "yes" or "no."

The Legislature has reached the point where most of the efficiency steps have been taken. There's a limit to what can be done in 30 or 45 days at Pierre. Only a stringent steering committee concept could lighten the present load. Beyond that, more time in Pierre is the only way to reduce the demands on legislators in conducting the state's business. That's a decision for both legislators and the electorate. Citizens should not expect their elected representatives to be supermen or superwomen.

VEEP'S TRIP A GROUNDBREAKER

Argus Leader, July 22, 1979

What's in a Sioux Falls visit for a vice president?

A chance to see and be seen. To help the president. To come to the aid of his political party. And, perhaps, make contacts or lay groundwork that would be useful in his own campaign for president in circumstances not foreseen in the present.

Vice President Walter Mondale, protege of the late Hubert Humphrey, South Dakota's most famous native son, did all of that in the state's largest city last week.

He gave some youngsters and their mothers a thrill when he shook hands with greeters. He was at ease before a friendly luncheon crowd at the Downtown Holiday Inn.

At a briefing for editors on the SALT-II treaty, Mondale walked around the table in a hotel conference room and shook hands. He said, "Glad to see you again" to some regional acquaintances and "Nice to meet you" to others:

At 51, he's trim, vigorous and looks a bit older than a few brief years ago when he was U.S. senator from Minnesota. Unlike Humphrey, who looked eternally young with his hair tinted to match ebullient spirits, Mondale has allowed the grey to show through. His outlook, though, is positive and upbeat.

The man who's two heartbeats away from the highest elective office in the world helped his president with the selling of the SALT-II Treaty, one of a number of vexing problems for President Jimmy Carter.

If circumstances should put Mondale into the presidency some day, his Sioux Falls visit will take on more significance for residents who saw him Wednesday or shook his hand.

As vice president, Richard Nixon was in South Dakota several times during the 1953-1961 period. He helped his president, Dwight Eisenhower. Nixon lost a close race to John F. Kennedy in 1960. During the next eight years Nixon returned to Sioux Falls as a private citizen to help Republicans and himself with political appearances.

Humphrey was in South Dakota often as vice president under President Lyndon B. Johnson. Humphrey's South Dakota connection helped Johnson carry this then normally Republican state against Sen. Barry Goldwater in 1964.

As vice president, Humphrey enjoyed his return trips to see his mother at Huron to renew acquaintances with friends and the family drug store. He flew into Sioux Falls occasionally. In his own campaign for president in 1968, he met some of the civic leadership at Joe Foss Field in a brief stop in which he handed out Humphrey pens. He followed up by mailing autographed photographs to his greeters. Humphrey lost that election to Nixon and with it his last real hope of becoming president.

Vice President Spiro T. Agnew was still riding high as Nixon's No. 2 man and critic of administration opponents when he flew into Sioux Falls in the 1970 fall campaign. But Agnew's appearance didn't make the difference that year. Democrats won the governorship with Richard Kneip and the two congressional seats with Frank Denholm and James Abourezk. Agnew was forced to resign in 1973, a path Nixon would take 10 months later in 1974.

Neither former President Gerald Ford nor Johnson was in South Dakota as vice president. Ford came as president. He had campaigned in South Dakota when he was a Michigan congressman and party leader.

Johnson was in South Dakota twice in 1960. In May he set off a dynamite blast at groundbreaking ceremonies at the Big Bend Dam. He was majority leader of the Senate. He was in Sioux Falls that September as Kennedy's No. 2 man on the ticket.

The band at Joe Foss Field that bright September day played the "Yellow Rose of Texas" for Lady Bird Johnson, who was presented a corsage of roses in that hue. Slightly more than three years later, Johnson succeeded Kennedy following his assassination in Dallas.

The late Nelson Rockefeller, whom Ford appointed vice president in 1974 following Nixon's departure from government, was in Sioux Falls in June 1968 in quest of the Republican presidential nomination which Nixon won.

If history repeats itself, Mondale will be back in Sioux Falls and South Dakota. If Carter's present political fortunes change for the better with no battle among Democrats for the 1980 presidential nomination, Mondale's role on a return trip likely will be as vice president campaigning for reelection of his boss.

MILWAUKEE'S HISTORY WON'T DIE

Argus Leader, April 29, 1979

There's a feeling of sadness in seeing the Milwaukee Road go belly up.

The railroad reached Sioux Falls 100 years ago. The Milwaukee and its historic competitor, the Chicago and North Western Railway, opened up South Dakota to settlement before statehood.

Their tracks extended westward to the Missouri River and crisscrossed eastern South Dakota in patterns that provided roadways for immigrants and shipment east for grain.

The westward march of their steel ribbons that bound hamlets and countryside to the Midwest sparked the Great Dakota Boom of the 1880s.

By 1880 the Milwaukee had reached Chamberlain. Along the way its surveyors laid out the town site of Mitchell, destined to become a key railroad center on the prairie.

Meantime, the North Western had reached Pierre. Chamberlain and Pierre became jumping off places for wagon freight lines to the Black Hills. This business was lost several years later to a direct rail link to the Hills from Nebraska.

Milwaukee agents during the 1890s constructed water dams at 25-mile intervals along a trail in Lyman County so early cattle companies could move their herds to Chamberlain.

In northeastern South Dakota the Milwaukee devastated Big Stone City's dreams of glory by platting the town site of Milbank in 1880. Aberdeen was platted in 1881. By 1883 the Milwaukee was in Ipswich.

By 1900 the new Milwaukee railroad town of Evarts on the Missouri River was a load-em up, ship-em out point for cattle trailed across the Cheyenne River Indian Reservation.

The excursion train at Wylie Park on the northwest side of Aberdeen carries passengers under the Milwaukee Road insignia. The train circles Storybook Land, with its settings and characters from The Wizard of Oz. Wylie Park, one mile north on U.S. 281, has a wildlife area exhibit and a recreational vehicle campground.

Cattlemen on the Moreau and Grand Rivers in northwestern South Dakota used a right-of-way across the reservation that the railroad negotiated with the tribe. The Indians got a toll of 25 cents a head for all cattle and horses. The railroad had a pontoon bridge across the Missouri at Evarts for a year and provided ferry service.

Those were the days when four big cattle companies, including the Matador and the Diamond A, leased a million and a half acres of reservation land.

The Milwaukee was bound for the northwest. The road's decision to cross the Missouri eight miles to the north at what became Mobridge meant the end of Evarts in 1906.

By 1910 the Milwaukee road had sent branch lines south and west from Mobridge to Isabel and Faith, serving some of the last homesteaders in South Dakota. The Isabel and Faith lines were approved for abandonment within the last several months.

The news out of Chicago, headquarters of the Milwaukee, is that the bankrupt railroad may survive if it's shrunk from its present 9,800 mile system to about 2,400 miles. South Dakota, unfortunately, is not in those plans.

Hopefully, Interstate Commerce Commission and court proceedings will see another railroad—probably the Burlington Northern—taking over the Milwaukee's main line through Milbank, Aberdeen and Mobridge to the Pacific Northwest. Some other Milwaukee trackage would also be useful to South Dakota's rail plan for the future, but what it might be is not certain.

The businessmen, surveyors, rail gangs and train crews who built the Milwaukee Road in South Dakota's pioneer days had dreams and matched them with building savvy and action.

Proceedings in federal bankruptcy court and before the ICC would be foreign to them.

They were part of South Dakota's history and comparatively recent past. Some old cowboys alive today rode Milwaukee cattle trains out of the West River country.

Other railroad buffs tell the story about the Faith to Mobridge train crew stopping along the way to hunt during an era that wasn't so hurried. Faith, at the end of the line, used to claim it was the largest initial shipper of grain on the entire Milwaukee system.

In today's times shippers can't get boxcars. Trains, when they run, often go very slowly because the track can't take it. Deferred maintenance would be an unknown term to the crews who laid the rails.

In World War II the Milwaukee Road, with other railroads, did its part to help a nation at war. Servicemen and servicewomen, bound for Chicago and their individual destinies in wartime, said their goodbyes to family and friends at the old depot in Sioux Falls. Crowded troop trains headed for Pacific Northwest ports whistled along the main line through Aberdeen: at war's end, they helped Johnny come marching home.

The Milwaukee's Arrow made its last passenger run into Sioux Falls in September 1965. Nearly 14 years later, Sioux Falls faces the prospect of seeing the last Milwaukee freight train. What lines will survive in South Dakota is not clear.

The Milwaukee Road is 116 years old. But it was a Johnny-come-lately as a transcontinental railroad. The Union Pacific and Central Pacific linked up at a golden spike at Promontory, Utah, in 1869 to establish the first cross-country route to the Pacific coast. Other railroads beat the Milwaukee to the Pacific Northwest.

That was probably part of the Milwaukee's trouble. Its westward expansion came late. The expectations of heavy settlement and volume of traffic didn't follow the pattern of the Midwest closer to Chicago.

The Milwaukee's old rival, the North Western, which has had troubles of its own, may wind up with some of its competitor's track in South Dakota.

This state for years had no stronger booster than the Milwaukee Road. It helped build South Dakota.

A railroad dream is dying in bankruptcy court in Chicago. But these modern-day proceedings can't dim the Milwaukee's historic role in opening up South Dakota, nor the derring-do of an earlier breed of railroaders

SAVING STATE TRACK A WISE MOVE

Argus Leader, Sunday, March 16, 1980

It takes a compelling circumstance for a governor of South Dakota to call a special session of the Legislature.

There hasn't been one for 30 years. There may be a brief session later this year, but don't count on it.

Legislators specified that their approval would be necessary before Gov. William Janklow—through the Division of Railroads—could hire an operator for a state railroad, pay for or subsidize service or purchase or control any rolling stock. Such arrangements take time.

Their consideration likely will come at the next regular session in January, barring a sudden realization by South Dakotans before harvest time that there won't be trains in much of the state.

And although the governor didn't get everything he wanted in the rail package passed in the closing hours of the 1980 session, South Dakota's step toward acquiring up to $25 million worth of track is a significant one.

It could guarantee that South Dakota, both the end and the start of the line in transportation, will have the rail routes and tracks for a basic system in a future when energy prices will rise dramatically. Like $3 a gallon or higher gasoline by 1990. South Dakotans should be glad, then, that Janklow and the legislators saved the rails.

Most of the track the Division of Railroads expects to purchase includes some of the lines idled by the Milwaukee Road's shutdown. However, the authority for purchase includes some lines abandoned or to be abandoned by other railroads in eastern South Dakota.

❖ ❖ ❖

The 1950 special session, called by Gov. George T. Mickelson, passed a consumer power district law after 11 days of deliberation.

The session was preceded by intensive preparation and necessitated by the fact that a measure had failed to gain final passage by one vote in the 1949 regular session.

Public power proponents had hoped for legislation that would permit formation of districts by petition, similar to Nebraska, a public power state. But what was enacted carried a provision requiring an election in both rural and urban areas.

Former Gov. Joe Foss, then a member of the House, was successful in his push to require a majority vote in both cities and the countryside.

That was one major alteration of a bill which a bipartisan fact-finding committee of legislators wrote for Mickelson. The measure had provided for a 51 percent petition in rural areas and a majority vote in cities and towns.

The only other major alteration in the measure was a provision permitting a power district to negotiate the sale of bonds, instead of putting them up at public auction.

The 1950 special session also acted on 20 other measures, most of them comparatively minor. However, the special session did boost the gasoline tax by two cents a gallon and also appropriated $1.2 million for matching federal highway funds. Roads were a problem then, as now.

Legislators also passed a law to permit cities to cooperate in housing and redevelopment projects to create low-rent units.

❖ ❖ ❖

The 1950 special session was the ninth in the state's history. Gov. Peter Norbeck called three special sessions. One was in 1918 to help prosecution of World War I. Another was to ratify the woman suffrage amendment in 1919. Norbeck's third session was in 1920. The Legislature enacted 92 laws to adjust state affairs to condition resulting from the war.

Gov. Frank M. Byrne called the first special session in 1916 to amend the Richards primary law, eliminating one of the primaries in presidential election years.

Gov. W. J. Bulow, the state's first Democratic governor, had to call a special session in 1927 to enact the general appropriation bill which the Republicans had failed to act upon in the regular session.

Gov. Tom Berry, the state's second Democratic governor, called two special sessions. One in 1933 provided revenue for care of indigent persons. The other, in 1936, enacted an unemployment compensation law.

Gov. M. Q. Sharpe called a special session in 1944 to enact laws permitting members of the armed forces to vote in absence.

There has been less urgency for calling a special session since the Legislature went to annual instead of biennial sessions in 1964.

Republicans in recent years introduced the idea of delaying the final legislative day so they could act on the vetoes of Gov. Richard Kneip, a Democrat. The majority party has retained the practice during Janklow's administration.

Last week, the 30th day, plus Janklow's request to legislators to return a day earlier to facilitate the decision-making process, eliminated the need for a special session.

Legislators were able to enact compromise rail legislation, tie up other loose ends, including tax boosts for gasoline and Homestake's gold, and invite Citibank of New York to South Dakota. That invitation may mean 2,500 new jobs if Citibank moves its credit card operation to Sioux Falls, or 300 jobs for another division of the nation's second largest bank.

ONLY FIVE OF 23 S.D. SENATORS FROM WEST RIVER, PRESSLER BOOK REVEALS

Argus Leader, Sunday, Nov. 21, 1982

Sen. Larry Pressler's book, "U.S. Senators from the Prairie," is a fascinating look at the 23 individuals who have served as South Dakota's U.S. senators since statehood in 1889.

There's an interesting biography of each senator and a selection of important speeches on key legislation or issues.

Pressler captures key nuances of South Dakota politics: the heritage of self-reliance and independence from frontier and Territorial days, the emphasis on the individual instead of party which occasionally has broken the state's generally Republican pattern and the tendency to elect senators for only a term or two.

Only three senators have been elected to a third term: Peter Norbeck, who served from 1921 until his death in 1936; Karl Mundt, who completed a fourth term before he retired in 1972, and George McGovern, who won his third term in 1974 and served until Jan. 4, 1981.

Pressler has included a wealth of detail, most of it significant, some of it minute.

For instance, most of the state's senators have come from the southeastern corner of the state and only five from the Black Hills and West River areas.

The first westerner was Gideon Moody, a Deadwood judge and a lawyer in Rapid City. It was his misfortune to draw the two-year term in 1889 when South Dakota sent him and Richard Pettigrew to the U.S. Senate. Moody failed to win re-election from the South Dakota Legislature.

It wasn't until Francis Case was elected senator some 60 years later that South Dakota had another senator from the western half of the state.

Subsequently, Joe Bottum, James Abourezk and James Abdnor were elected from the West River.

Only three senators have come from the northern section of South Dakota: James Kyle of Aberdeen and Harlan and Vera Bushfield of Miller.

Only 10 of South Dakota's senators were born in the state and only seven of these were elected to full terms. Since 1948, the only non-native senator has been Case, who was born in Iowa.

Five senators served South Dakota as governor: Coe Crawford, Norbeck, William McMaster, William J. Bulow and Harlan Bushfield.

Pressler became the state's youngest senator when he was sworn in at age 36; the oldest senator to begin service was Herbert Hitchcock, who was appointed at 69. The oldest South Dakotan to serve was Mundt, who retired at 72, after serving 24 years in the upper house.

The only senator ever indicted was Pettigrew, who was arrested on a charge of sedition during World War I for speaking against American military involvement. The fiery Pettigrew fought the charges, which were dropped after he hired Clarence Darrow, a famous defense attorney, and other lawyers. Pettigrew, a Sioux Falls lawyer and businessman, served two terms, leaving the Senate in 1901.

In religious affiliation, all but two of South Dakota's senators have belonged to the Protestant faith. The exceptions are Abourezk, a Syrian Orthodox Christian, and Pressler, a Catholic.

Larry Pressler.

Eight South Dakotans have held Senate committee chairmanships. Among them Alfred Kittredge of Sioux Falls was chairman of the Committee on Interoceanic Canals in 1903 during the hearings on the proposed Panama Canal. Norbeck directed investigations of the influential committee on Banking and Currency. Chan Gurney chaired the Armed Services Committee immediately after World War II.

Neither Mundt nor McGovern was chairman of a regular standing committee, although Mundt presided over the Government Operations Committee during the Army McCarthy hearings and McGovern chaired the Agriculture Subcommittee on Food and Nutrition.

Mundt as a House member won national fame as the acting chairman of the House Un-American Activities Committee during its hearings in 1948 on spy charges against Alger Hiss, a State Department official. Mundt's close friend, Richard Nixon, was on the committee. In 1954, Mundt presided over Senate hearings on Sen. Joe McCarthy's charges that the Army was harboring subversives.

◆ ◆ ◆

You'd never guess Pressler's partisan ties by reading this book. He has taken an objective and scholarly approach in analyzing the careers of the state's senators. He has known them all since Mundt and Case.

To retain that objectivity, Pressler asked Douglas L. Miller and Gwen Gibson to write the chapter on himself. Miller is a former professor of political science and chairman of the Department of Social Services at Northern State College. Gibson is a Washington, D.C., free lance writer and journalist.

McGovern in a foreword says, "My colleague, Larry Pressler, has provided a valuable historical perspective on South Dakota's U.S. senators." William O. Farber, professor emeritus of political science at the University of South Dakota, in foreword remarks says Pressler "has demonstrated a sense of history and an awareness that progress must be based on the past."

Sen. Howard Baker Jr., majority leader of the U.S. Senate, calls "U.S. Senators from the Prairie" "a valuable addition to the body of literature devoted to the Senate.

Pressler in his acknowledgements said he is especially indebted to Dr. Alan Clem of the University of South Dakota Political Science Department.

The volume has been several years in the making. Pressler did much of the writing while riding an airplane. It could be called a spare time venture and a labor of love.

In April 1981 Pressler said, "I haven't spent a lot of time on it." He also said the idea for the book came from C. J. Dalthorp's book on South Dakota governors, published in 1953.

All proceeds from Pressler's book will go to the University of South Dakota Foundation. It will be available soon in retail outlets, or from Dakota Press, Vermillion, S.D. 57609, for $8.95 softback and $11.95 hard cover. Add $1.50 for handling by mail from Dakota Press.

PANDA DIPLOMACY REFLECTS CHANGING WORLD TIMES
Argus Leader, June 22, 1985

What a difference 13 years makes in relations between the United States and the People's Republic of China.

It was very evident on a sun-splashed Saturday afternoon when two Chinese officials presented a stuffed giant panda to the Great Plains Zoo and Museum in Sioux Falls.

Leland Lillehaug's Municipal Band played the Chinese National Anthem, followed by the Star Spangled banner.

China's flag was displayed with the Stars and Stripes in front of the bandstand.

Lin Zhiying, first secretary to the Chinese ambassador in Washington, called the day a notable one in relations between the two countries. He expressed confidence that both nations would continue to improve friendly contacts and cooperation.

Chang Jun Fu of the Chinese Forestry Ministry said he hoped that Americans would help his country improve the survival chances of the panda, an endangered species.

Zhiying spoke excellent English. Fu spoke through an interpreter.

South Dakota's two U.S. senators, Larry Pressler and James Abdnor, and Lt. Gov. Lowell Hansen participated in the ceremony.

The day's event would not have been possible if it hadn't been for President Richard Nixon's historic trip to China in 1972.

For nearly 23 years relations between the United States and the Communist government of mainland China had been hostile.

China entered the Korean War in November 1950, after Gen. Douglas MacArthur's forces reached the Yalu River bordering Manchuria. The Chinese pushed the Americans and their U.N. allies below the 38th parallel.

President Harry S Truman removed MacArthur, who had threatened China with air and naval attack, and replaced him with Gen. Matthew B. Ridgway.

An armistice, negotiated by Gen. Mark Clark, was signed in July 1953. Even today, no peace treaty has been signed between the combatants in Korea.

During the 1950s John Foster Dulles, Eisenhower's secretary of state, emphasized support of the Nationalist Chinese government on Taiwan. Dulles on one occasion at an international meeting snubbed Chinese Premier Chou En-lai who had attempted to talk to him.

In 1971 the United Nations General Assembly expelled the Taiwan government from the U.N., and seated the People's Republic in its place.

The deep freeze between China and the United States was warmed only by ping pong diplomacy involving exchange matches by teams from both countries.

Chou En-lai invited President Nixon to visit China. His visit of eight days there in February 1972 ended years of enmity between the two countries. Nixon called his trip a journey for peace.

President Jimmy Carter formally recognized the People's Republic of China in 1978 as the sole legal government of China. Premier Zhao Ziyang in January 1984 visited the United States and signed agreements with President Ronald Reagan on industrial cooperation, science and technology.

Reagan, who for many years was a blunt critic of Chinese policies, visited China in April 1984 and was well received.

Panda diplomacy had its start with C.J. Delbridge, Sioux Falls lawyer and benefactor of the Great Plains Zoo, who wanted to obtain a panda for the zoo and museum.

He asked Pressler to help contact the Chinese embassy in Washington. Initially, the Chinese were reluctant but a promise to raise donations to help save the pandas in their diminishing habitat in China helped materially in the negotiations.

The saga of the Sioux Falls panda has many other interesting sidelights, including midnight telephone calls to China extending over the last year and Delbridge's sending Ernest G. Carlson, a friend, to Peking last winter to see government officials.

Delbridge and his wife bought the renowned Henry Brockhouse stuffed animal collection for Sioux Falls with the understanding the city would provide a suitable building. The Delbridge Museum of Natural Science at the Great Plains Zoo is the city's and taxpayers' part of that bargain.

Pressler called China's gift of the panda an historic one for Sioux Falls and South Dakota. It is believed to be the first gift that the People's Republic of China has made to the United States.

Presentation of the panda came on a weekend when bad news—the TWA hijacking in the Middle East—dominated the international scene.

Person-to-person diplomacy in Sioux Falls gave both the visiting Chinese and South Dakotans a lift.

Now's the time for zoo visitors to purchase a miniature stuffed panda or donate directly to China's Save the Panda fund.

One international good turn deserves another.

VOTERS' WATCHFUL EYES HAVE ALWAYS FOCUSED ON CITY HALL

Argus Leader, Sunday, July 28, 1985

City Hall watchers are nothing new to Sioux Falls.

They've been circulating around city government since the days your favorite town and mine was a village in the 1870s.

City Hall watching became more intense when Sioux Falls obtained a city charter from the Territorial Legislature in Yankton in 1883.

One of the most earnest observers of the local government scene 99 years ago was one Ralph Jaybush.

His mission was to prod the council into adopting a uniform street numbering ordinance.

Jaybush showed up at almost every session of the city council during April, May and June of 1886. He wanted authority to affix numbers to residences and business buildings in the city.

H. W. Ross was the mayor. Each of the four wards in the city was represented by two aldermen.

The city council responded by passing a motion to prepare an ordinance that would include territory on the east side of the Big Sioux River.

The matter was referred to the city attorney, Dana Reed Bailey, a native of Vermont and resident of Sioux Falls for three years.

Bailey thought the motion was made as more of joke than in earnest and neglected to prepare the ordinance.

Jaybush at the next council meeting succeeded in getting the mayor to reprimand Bailey. Some aldermen mildly informed Bailey that he had better prepare the ordinance if he expected to hold his position.

Bailey quickly discovered the difficulties of uniform street numbering because of the haphazard manner in which they were named.

Phillips Avenue, for instance, became Third Avenue at its south end. What is now Main Avenue was then Main Street and Second Avenue. What is now 13th Street was then Frank and River Streets.

Bailey decided he would give the council something to think about in earnest. He fixed upon the corner of 9th Street and Phillips Avenue as the center from which to commence numbering. Names of 17 streets and avenues were changed. All streets would run east and west and all avenues north and south; each street would have only one name.

Bailey's proposed ordinance came up for passage at the August council meeting at which Jaybush was present. The committee on streets and alleys reported it had not examined the report very much, but favored its passage.

The ordinance was read and Bailey was asked why the names of so many streets and avenues had been changed.

With respect to changing Frank and River Streets to 13th Street, the city attorney said that presumably Frank Street was named for Frank Pettigrew.

Pettigrew broke in and said: "No, that street was named after W.S. Bloom's dog Frank."

As Bailey wrote some years later, "This remark seemed to settle the question that it was more desirable to have the streets named with some degree of system, than to retain the original names given in honor of some pet canine or the fancy of the persons making the original plats."

The ordinance was passed Aug. 6, 1886, and a happy Ralph Jaybush got the contract for numbering the buildings.

Bailey served three more years as city attorney. His "History of Minnehaha County, South Dakota" from which this anecdote was taken was published in 1899.

Another excerpt from Bailey's book will interest today's City Hall observers.

Sioux Falls in the spring of 1888 urgently needed to pave Phillips Avenue between 5th and 12th Streets to get the downtown out of the mud.

There was a question whether the city had authority under its charter to assess adjacent property for the improvement. Despite some doubts, the city council decided to go ahead. The city awarded its first paving contract in June 1888; property owners were assessed $2.13 per square yard for Sioux quartzite paving and 70 cents per lineal foot for curbing with Drake's jasperite.

Bailey wrote, "Some of the adjacent property owners refused to pay the assessments and litigation followed. Since then considerable paving has been done in the city and the same material has been used." A civic booster, Bailey praised quartzite paving for its durability.

Today's street renewal projects undertaken by Commissioner Loila Hunking dwarf in size and cost the city's improvement projects of the last century.

So does the $30 million downtown renewal package on the ballot Aug. 13. It is much more complex in its financial makeup than street assessments for paving.

What hasn't changed in 100 years is the voter's watchful eye on City Hall.

JANKLOW OFFERS SOUND IDEAS FOR HELPING WITH LOCAL GOVERNMENTS

Argus Leader, Nov. 9, 1985

"I'm not saying that most communities are terminally ill....What scares me most is that the cost of services is going up and property values are going down."

That's part of what Gov. William Janklow last week (Oct. 31) told a conference at Mitchell which delved into "Adapting Local Government to a Changing Rural South Dakota."

The changes find the countryside being depopulated as farms and ranches become larger. A smaller population supports local government in rural areas. Per capita costs rise for tax payers who remain.

Farmland values have dropped an average of 34 percent statewide and as much as 46 percent in southeastern South Dakota from their peak in 1981. Janklow said that when property values drop sharply, the average South Dakota citizen believes taxes should also decrease.

Some county officials before the conference opened were ready to do battle. They told the Legislature's Local Government Study Commission that consolidation of local governments would weaken services and take away local control.

A day and a half later, after listening to some of South Dakota's most knowledgeable political scientists, legislators and local officials, there was a different perception.

The approach to solving the problems was perceived as cooperation between local governments, not change mandated by the Legislature. Cooperation would be fostered by changes making it easier for counties and cities to adapt to today's demographics and economy.

As Janklow said, no governor nor Legislature can determine what individual cities, towns and counties should do about their future. "Only local people have the ability to make that kind of decision," he said.

Janklow thinks those choices will revolve around how to fund services adequately in the future, rather than adding new programs. He sees a need to spend better and for smaller counties and cities to help each other.

Janklow has some assistance in mind. He would use $10 million of a substantial state cash balance as a one-time boost in the $40 million annual payment to local government for personal property tax repeal.

He will also propose to the 1986 Legislature a new Cabinet agency—a Department of Local Government Affairs—to work with local government.

Janklow said the new agency would try to provide the maximum amount of non-economic aid to local government. The agency would provide technical assistance. The department wouldn't tell local government what to do, but would lay out options it could follow.

For years, Janklow has preached partnership between local governments and joint use of city, school and county facilities as a way to contain costs. He says the same taxpayer picks up the tab.

He has urged cities and counties which have duplicate motor vehicle shops or radio dispatch centers to pool resources. He acknowledges that achieving such cooperation is difficult. But he says the taxpayer who dials 911 for help couldn't care less whether the lawman who arrives at the scene of an emergency is a sheriff's deputy or a city policeman.

Janklow termed Main Street very important to South Dakota's future well-being. He said that for every 10 farms or ranches that close, one small town business is lost.

He believes that in most communities, school buses and local government cars could be repaired more cheaply in a local garage than in local government facilities. He said such a contract might make the difference in keeping a Main Street business.

The conference viewed consolidation of counties with each other as an unlikely scenario for changes. Cooperation, transfer of functions between cities and counties and more efficiency were seen as the likely progression.

Individuals and their organizations, like Russell Smith, director of the Governmental Research Bureau of the University of South Dakota, and Bob Burns, professor of history and political science at South Dakota State University, will help the process.

Smith organized the Mitchell conference. Burns compiled data on the way municipalities and counties cooperate. Janklow said he sees USD and SDSU adding their resources to the Department of Local Government Affairs.

Jack Lintz, of Custer, president of the South Dakota Association of County Commissioners, considers Janklow's proposals worthwhile and said he would recommend cooperation.

Rep. Royal J. Wood, R-Warner, chairman of the Local Government Study Commission, believes technical assistance from the new state department will be helpful to counties. His commission expects to offer permissive legislation that would allow counties to seek change without going into home rule.

Janklow's analysis of the crises rural South Dakota faces is well based. The Legislature should follow his recommendations.

PUT SOME WARMTH IN YOUR WINTER: TAKE A TRIP TO THE LEGISLATURE

Argus Leader, Jan. 19, 1986

If you want to make this long, long winter more interesting, visit the Legislature.

It's the best show in South Dakota.

Besides, the state Capitol and Pierre are among the friendliest places around.

Legislators, despite their long hours and demanding schedule, like to see constituents in Pierre.

One hundred five men and women, among them some of South Dakota's finest citizens, do their best to represent their districts.

In doing so, most legislators also represent the state's best interests.

The lawmakers are a remarkable cross section of the state.

Collectively, they reflect the hopes and fears of South Dakotans in every walk of life.

You'll hear from legislators about the farm crisis and how small towns are fading away.

And about education, the low-level nuclear waste question, highways, railroads or anything else you might be interested in.

You'll get capsule solutions for a wide range of state problems in quick visits over coffee or brief exchanges in legislative halls.

You'll enjoy some sharp and pointed debates in the House and Senate on some big issues and less serious ones as the session progresses.

You'll see Appropriations Committee members scrutinizing the state's spending, sometimes line by line, in hearings on department budgets.

You'll watch from the galleries as lawmakers introduce school children or constituents—possibly you among them—as visitors of the day.

You'll see visiting farmers, businessmen and women, beef growers, hog growers, cowboys and cowbelles roaming Capitol halls.

You'll see (and be seen by) some lobbyists whose business it is to know who's in town and for what reason. If your business or farm group has a lobbyist in Pierre, he or she will be glad to see you.

If you're unhappy with local government back home, the Legislature is the place where you can change the rules.

If you think you're taxed unfairly, your legislators are the individuals who can change that, too.

If you believe South Dakota is OK the way it is, Pierre is a good place to proclaim it.

There's no pretense in South Dakota's seat of government. People call legislators, the governor and other top officials by their first names.

Pierre is also a good place to develop a statewide acquaintance. It's easy to do, given a state of only 700,000-plus residents.

You'll meet somebody from almost anywhere in South Dakota who knows someone you know.

Your capital city does a fine job year in and year out of hosting visitors.

Pierre's citizens since statehood have paid attention to the capital's main business: state government.

Pierre people make a point of providing a friendly setting for state government.

There's also a strong tie to the Old West in Pierre and Fort Pierre, the capital city's smaller and much older neighbor across the wide Missouri.

Blizzards may tie up South Dakota and prompt Gov. William Janklow to shut down Interstate 90.

But the state's business goes on despite South Dakota's deep winter chills. It would take a once-in-a-century storm to seriously affect a legislative session's routine in the Capitol.

Nearly everyone who's seen state government in action likes to go back for another look.

If you're headed southwest for warmer climes, you'll find many South Dakota snowbirds in Mesa, Ariz., and elsewhere in the Phoenix metro area.

This year's Arizona committee is headed up by the following Sioux Falls winter sojourners: Art and Ione White, chairmen; Ernie and Freda Carlson, vice chairmen; Maxine Seeman, secretary and Jean Haber, treasurer.

Three dinner meetings have been scheduled at the Mesa Elks Club: this Wednesday (Jan. 22); Feb. 12 and March 12. Cocktail hour starts at 5 p.m., meals are served at 6:15 p.m. and programs start at 7:30 p.m.

Reservations should be made with one of the committee officers listed above. You may also write The Arizona Committee, c/o Maxine Seeman, 2929 E. Main #476, Mesa, AZ. 85203.

The Sioux Falls and vicinity meetings in Mesa have become one of the most popular winter events for South Dakota visitors. You see so many friends that it's as if you never left home.

TWO OF STATE'S OLD POLITICAL NAMES FACE NEW AND EXCITING CHALLENGES

Argus Leader, Saturday, June 21, 1986

There's a sense of maturity for South Dakota in the 1986 governor's race: sons of former governors are opposing each other for the office.

Republican George S. Mickelson's father, George T. Mickelson, was governor from 1947 to 1951. Democrat Lars Herseth's father, Ralph Herseth, was governor from 1959 to 1961.

One governor's son will take office in January for a four-year term. The new governor will return to the rambling white house by the lake in Pierre in which he lived as a boy.

The governor's office in the Capitol where his father served will be his. He'll address the Legislature in which both he and his father served.

There will be strong memories from boyhood days in Pierre pulling at the new governor. He went to school in the capital city, enjoyed meeting his father's friends and liked the excitement of living in Pierre.

There'll be reminiscing, too, of countless roll call votes in the House, of committee work and all the friendships that spring from service in the Legislature.

Even so, the administration of Gov. Lars Herseth or Gov. George S. Mickelson will be a new adventure, both for the individual and South Dakota.

It will not be a reprise—something both South Dakota Republicans and Democrats have avoided even for well liked leaders of the past. Republican voters in 1964 said no to a return to the office by former Gov. Sigurd Anderson. Democrats this year told ex-Gov. Richard Kneip the same thing.

Whether the new governor is Herseth or Mickelson, he will be expected to provide his own scenario and influence to fit South Dakota's circumstances from 1987 to 1991.

The governor's term will come during the second century of settlement in South Dakota. The state in 1989 will observe the centennial of its admittance to the union.

South Dakota is vastly different from pioneer days of the last century and the eras in which the fathers of this year's gubernatorial candidates served.

The computer age finds the state's business, from making laws and budgets to conducting government, facilitated by electronics. The governor and state officials

R. Lars Herseth.

have mountains of data readily available on a video screen by merely touching a button. How to act on that information is the challenge.

Television—commercial and public—has given South Dakotans new interest in what is happening across the state. Local and civic problems that concerned only one community 20 years or more ago have become statewide topics.

When the elder Mickelson was governor, state legislators often argued about the facts. They had to rely mainly on themselves or a friendly lobbyist for essential data and research. That situation changed with establishment of the Legislative Research Council in 1951 during Anderson's first term.

Today, debate is still an essential part of government. But the arguments usually are not about the facts but what they mean. Thanks to interim studies and the year-round functioning of Legislative Research Council staffers, there is more continuity in state government. It has become more sophisticated, as have the voters.

Both Mickelson and Herseth demonstrated an understanding of practical politics by winning their party's nomination in the primary without a runoff.

The new governor will benefit from Gov. William Janklow's initiatives of the last eight years and the cooperative work of the Legislature.

Such major hurdles as saving the rails, reorienting water policy and adopting a new state water plan have been met. The state now seeks to develop 10 or more smaller water projects on a priority basis instead of betting on one big one, like the defunct Oahe Irrigation Project. South Dakota has attracted many new businesses, including Citibank and other credit card firms and their high-tech ways.

Serious problems remain for South Dakota, including agriculture, the continuing decline of the smaller towns and depopulation of rural areas. School financing and the last place national ranking of teachers' salaries are among other major issues that need resolution. Gaining new jobs is a continuing need.

Mickelson and Herseth will have to address these problems in the campaign. How well they do it will determine the outcome of the November election and the course of events in South Dakota for the next four years.

Both difficult and interesting days are the prospect for November's winner. His most nostalgic time will be observance of the centennial in 1989. It will be exciting for the next governor to lead South Dakota into its second century.

Like father, like son, the new governor will be a popular one.

GAMBLING WOULD HELP DEADWOOD

Argus Leader, Jan. 31, 1987

More perils than one can imagine will confront Deadwood proponents in their quest of limited gambling for their historic city.

The 1987 Legislature will be asked to refer a constitutional amendment to voters authorizing limited gambling in Deadwood only.

If South Dakota voters approve the measure in 1988, Deadwood voters would have to decide in a city election whether they want gambling.

If Deadwood voters approve, legal gambling could be started in 1989, the state's centennial year.

Proposed licensing fees and part of a city sales tax on gambling would be earmarked for restoration and preservation of Deadwood's history. Deadwood is the only city in South Dakota designated a historic landmark.

A preliminary draft of the proposed legislation provides that gambling in Deadwood would include blackjack, poker and slot machines. Wagers would be limited to five dollars a bet. The city of Deadwood would issue licenses for $2,000 a year for each gaming device, such as a slot machine or table.

Rep. Harvey Krautschun, R-Spearfish, and Sen. Jim Dunn, R-Lead, are sponsors of the legislation. Deadwood city officials have praised the proposal as a way to keep tourists coming to Deadwood and to celebrate the state's centennial.

Proponents acknowledge that an amendment giving only Deadwood the right to license gambling would raise objections from other communities that want gambling. But they say exclusivity would eliminate fears about gambling spreading to other towns.

Some backers say that the Deadwood experiment could show how limited gambling could affect small town South Dakota in the future. Proponents expect objections on moral grounds.

It will take all the persuasion the Lawrence County legislative delegation can muster to limit the proposed amendment to Deadwood.

Other tourist towns may want to offer gambling. Charitable, veterans, religious and civic organizations likely will see a threat to their present monopoly on bingo and lotteries.

Legal gambling could aid Deadwood greatly in attracting tourists. It could help ensure that Deadwood's historic fixtures would still be around for the start of the city's third century in 2076.

Gambling was an intrinsic part of gold mining history in Deadwood Gulch starting in 1876. Tourists today enjoy the re-enactment of Jack McCall's trial for the murder of Wild Bill Hickok while he was playing poker in saloon number 10.

It's interesting for tourists to think about the pairs of black aces and eights—the "dead-man's hand"—that Hickok held. But it would be more fun to play. The prospect could give Deadwood a modest year-round tourist draw.

Illegal gambling has also been a part of Deadwood's history. Attorney General George T. Mickelson, father of the present governor, closed down Deadwood's gambling casinos in 1946.

As governor from 1947 to 1951, Mickelson and Attorney General Sigurd Anderson were tough enforcers. They cracked down statewide on gambling and slot machines which flourished briefly in South Dakota and neighboring states following World War II.

South Dakotans in 1970 amended the Constitution to allow the Legislature to authorize games of chance provided they are conducted by public service organizations. The 1973 Legislature authorized bingo and lotteries.

In 1982, South Dakota voters by a margin of nearly 58 percent turned down a constitutional amendment to permit individuals or businesses to conduct gambling. In 1986, voters approved a state lottery, which will require enabling legislation from the 1987 session.

No one expects a bonanza from a South Dakota lottery. Neither should anyone expect Deadwood, with limited gambling, to become another Reno or Las Vegas with topflight entertainment to complement gambling.

South Dakota is a flyover state and cannot, like Nevada, draw on millions of neighbors in adjoining states.

Deadwood could, if voters permit, gain new jobs and underwrite perpetuation of its historic setting. There would be a modest tourism gain for the state.

South Dakotans should help Deadwood help itself.

MUNDT ARCHIVES OFFER NOSTALGIC VIEW OF STATE'S LONGEST-SERVING LAWMAKER

Argus Leader, Wednesday, Feb. 3, 1988

MADISON—There's a treasure trove of recent South Dakota and U.S. history in the Karl E. Mundt Historical and Educational Foundation in Madison.

A tour of the foundation offers a fascinating glimpse of the man who served in Congress 34 years, longer than any other South Dakotan. Mundt's five House and four Senate terms spanned 1939 to 1973. He died in 1974.

Students and adult study groups will find much that is interesting. Older South Dakotans who remember Mundt's service will encounter political nostalgia.

Exhibits accurately portray Mundt as a friendly, outgoing man, an influential senator and a great speaker, and, one of South Dakota's most winning politicians.

Scholars from nearly every state and some foreign countries have visited the foundation to examine Mundt's files, documents and other papers.

Karl E. Mundt library on the Dakota State College campus is the repository for Mundt's archives. They include 1.9 million documents that have been catalogued and microfilmed.

There are more than 15,000 pieces of memorabilia from Mundt's personal and political life, including 107 scrapbooks and 2,500 photographs.

The foundation area and the archives are located on the lower level of the library building, which was dedicated June 3, 1969, by President Richard Nixon. The foundation area was constructed and furnished by private donations.

Exhibits and displays give highlights of Mundt's career as one of the nation's most visible Republican legislators.

He changed from a pre-Pearl Harbor isolationist to an internationalist. He served with senators who became president and he knew some of the world's most famous figures.

He was acting chairman of two of the nation's most controversial congressional hearings: the House Un-American Activities Committee inquiry in 1948 into spy charges against Alger Hiss, a State Department official, and the Senate Investigating subcommittee's Army-McCarthy probe in 1954.

He helped form the United Nations Economic, Scientific and Cultural Organization and cosponsored the bill that established Voice of America broadcasts.

The foundation, appropriately, is on the campus where Mundt and his wife, Mary, taught from 1928 to 1936. He was chairman of the speech department; she taught English and drama classes.

Mundt's Senate office is recreated and preserved behind glass as it was in Washington—with one major difference. The portrait on the wall behind Mundt's desk is that of President Ronald Reagan, the incumbent.

Karl E. Mundt

On another wall is a large painting of Gen. Douglas MacArthur, presented to the Mundts by their friend, Jean MacArthur, wife of the general.

The foundation now is featuring an exhibit marking the bicentennial of the U.S. Constitution.

Margaret Phillips, executive director of the foundation, said that a 28-minute film of Mundt's life and career will be completed as a gift to the South Dakota centennial. The film will be distributed statewide to service clubs and schools. A seven-minute excerpt will be put on a monitor as an introduction to tours.

Other projects involve transferring 480 reels of Mundt's weekly TV reports from film to tape, similar preservation of movie film of the Army-McCarthy hearings and transferring 100 phonograph records to video audio cassettes.

The foundation provides student scholarships, awards prizes for essays and oratorical contests and gives grants to many major projects such as the Dakota State College History Conference and the Prairie Repertory Theatre.

Phillips said school or group tours may be arranged by phoning the foundation or writing to her at the Mundt Foundation, Dakota State College, Madison, S.D. 57042. Hours are 8:30 a.m. to 4 p.m. Monday through Friday. The public is welcome.

You'll enjoy visiting the foundation.

"FAIR CHANCE" OFFERS INSIGHT TO FAMOUS POLITICIAN
Argus Leader, Feb. 12, 1989

Scott Heidepriem's biography of Karl Mundt, a South Dakotan who won fame in Congress, is fascinating.

The book, *A Fair Chance for a Free People*, provides a scholarly and detailed look at the forthright Republican orator who was one of South Dakota's greatest boosters.

Mundt knew U.S. presidents and world leaders. He helped both Dwight Eisenhower and Richard Nixon become president.

He served longer in Congress—34 years—than any other South Dakotan. His five House and four Senate terms spanned 1939 to 1973.

When Democrats controlled Congress, as they did for most of his career, Mundt was often a national spokesman for the Republicans. He enjoyed campaigning.

Mundt was an educator, a champion of international understanding and an opponent of communism. He believed in equality for Congress with the executive branch, and particularly in the legislative right to investigate.

Heidepriem has skillfully traced Mundt's rise from his roots to become one of South Dakota's winningest politicians.

Mundt was born June 3, 1900, in Humboldt, the only child of Ferdinand and Rose Mundt. He excelled in high school and college debate. His speech students at Eastern Normal (now Dakota State College) ranked high in state and national competition.

As a new congressman, Mundt in 1939 started a weekly column, Your Washington and You, which appeared in many South Dakota weekly papers. Heidepriem has drawn extensively on the columns, the senator's files at the Mundt Library in Madison and other sources.

United States entrance into World War II changed Mundt from an isolationist to an internationalist almost overnight.

The author devotes a chapter to Mundt's service on the House Indian Affairs Committee and his role in helping to investigate conditions on reservations. The inquiry was prompted by a resolution of the South Dakota Legislature.

Most of today's political fans will be astounded to read that Mundt spent less than $8,000 for his first Senate campaign in 1948.

Heidepriem describes Mundt's role as co-chairman of the Republican Speakers' Bureau in 1952, when Eisenhower won his first term. A controversy over Nixon's secret Senate expense fund threatened his place on the ticket with Eisenhower. Mundt acted as an intermediary to keep Nixon as the vice presidential nominee.

There's much more in Heidepriem's book: about Mundt as an investigator, as a proponent of a generous farm policy and his opposition to and dislike of Ezra Taft Benson, Eisenhower's secretary of agriculture. Mundt's interest in international student exchanges, the United Nations Educational, Scientific and Cultural Organization and his legislative counter-measures against the Soviet Union during the Cold War are also detailed.

The book's foreword, by Robert L. McCaughey, Mundt's former administrative assistant, is highly interesting, too. McCaughey describes the stroke that incapacitated Mundt on Nov. 22, 1969, and his wife Mary's refusal to let the senator resign. Mundt never returned to his office, which his staff handled until his term expired in January 1973. Mundt died in 1974; his wife, in 1985.

Heidepriem is a Miller attorney and a state representative. His book on Mundt started out in 1982 as a master's thesis. He became so interested that he wrote the book, sponsored by the Mundt Historical and Educational Foundation.

The result is excellent reading for South Dakota's centennial year and a fine addition to state biography.

A Fair Chance for a Free People, a Biography of Karl E. Mundt, has 258 pages and costs $30 plus tax. It's available from Cover to Cover in Sioux Falls and Brookings, Books 'n' More in Yankton, and the Mundt Foundation, Dakota State College, Madison, S.D. 57042, or by calling 605-256-5212. By mail, it costs $35, which includes $5 for postage, handling and tax.

ABOUT MAYORAL LONGEVITY—

Argus Leader, Sunday, August 7, 1983

You'll like it.

About mayoral longevity—

Mayor Rick Knobe of Sioux Falls has a good roll going. He has less than a year to serve in his second five-year term, and has already been in office longer than any other mayor except George W. Burnside and his 26 years.

So, what would Knobe have to do if, perchance, he wanted to top Burnside's record? He would have to win four more five-year terms.

That would mean winning re-election bids in 1984, 1989, 1994 and 1999.

Knobe would pass Burnside's record sometime in the year 2000 when Knobe would be 54 on his birthday. He is now 36 years old.

I doubt that the mayor has even considered such a scenario. He's taking his political decisions one at a time these days, and they don't extend beyond next year.

First, Knobe will decide by September whether to challenge U.S. Rep. Tom Daschle for Congress in 1994. If that answer is no, Knobe will make up his mind by about the first of the year whether to go for a third term as mayor,

Every mayor elected since 1942 has served more than five years, with one exception: Henry B. Saure, elected to one term (1949-1954) which he completed. Other mayors and their time in office were C.M. Whitfield (1942-1949), Fay Wheeldon (1954-1961), V.L. Crusinberry (1961-67) and M.E. Schirmer (1968-74).

Crusinberry defeated Wheeldon in a recall election. Crusinberry died in office on Dec. 12, 1967, before completing the full five-year term to which he was re-elected.

Earl McCart was acting mayor of Sioux Falls, in addition to his duties as water commissioner, for five months following Crusinberry's death.

Schirmer, now Minnehaha County Commission chairman, was elected mayor in April 1968 to fill Crusinberry's unexpired term. Schirmer was unopposed for re-election in April 1969, but lost to Knobe in a run-off in 1974.

Rick Knobe returned to radio as a commentator and talk show host after serving as mayor of Sioux Falls.

PROFILES

"TIRED AMERICAN" AREA PRIZE

Argus Leader, Sunday, July 29, 1979

Alan C. McIntosh, the country editor at Luverne whose way with words brought him international renown, served his community and his readers very well during 28 years as a publisher.

From 1940 when he bought the Rock County Star until he sold the Star-Herald in 1968 and retired, he did the things he liked the best: publishing his paper, expressing his views, selling ads, playing his community role in Luverne. He also found time to serve on special state and federal commissions.

His death at 73 Monday and services Thursday at Luverne brought recollections of his colorful and pertinent writing, his business acumen and recognition that came to him in his profession.

His best known editorial, "I am a tired American," summarized the frustrations of a citizen in the nation's heartland with the trends of the times in the early 1960s.

McIntosh began his 1964 editorial, "I am a tired American.

"I am tired of being called the ugly American.

"I'm tired of having the world panhandlers use my country as a whipping boy 365 days a year...."

He related his weariness over the stoning and burning of American embassies and information centers abroad, and over beatniks "who say they should have the right to determine what laws of the land they are willing to obey...."

"I am a tired American—who is getting madder by the minute at the filth peddlers who have launched Americans in an obscenity race, who try to foist on us the belief that filth is an integral part of culture....

"I am a tired American—sickened by the slack-jawed bigots who wrap themselves in bedsheets in the dead of night and roam the countryside looking for innocent victims...."

When he wound up it with the following summation, he had touched America's nerve and heart:

"I am a tired American—real tired of those who are trying to sell me the belief that America is not the greatest nation in all the world—a generous-hearted nation—a nation dedicated to the policy of trying to help the 'have nots' achieve some of the good things that our system of free enterprise brought about....

"I am an American who gets a lump in his throat when he hears the 'Star Spangled Banner'....

"I am a tired American—who thanks a merciful Lord that he was lucky to be born an American citizen—a nation under God, with mercy and justice for all."

McIntosh's editorial was reprinted by countless newspapers and magazines. It appeared on David Lawrence's editorial page in U.S. News and World Report magazine in 1966. It won for him the George Washington Gold Medal award from Freedoms Foundation and other honors.

McIntosh told Bob Renshaw, Argus-Leader reporter and photographer at the time, that the editorial came close to being thrown into the hell box without being used. The editorial was set into type and lay around the Star-Herald shop for several weeks before extra type was needed on the editorial page one week.

The reprints in this country and abroad brought a deluge of mail to McIntosh. At first he answered with personal replies, but later had to resort to form letters. McIntosh said that for an editor who was accustomed to being damned for what he writes, it was a pleasant change of pace to have seven out of 10 letters say, "God bless you."

In other writings he reflected the concerns and the feelings of his town and community. He traveled frequently and used his observations as the basis of many columns and editorials in the Luverne Star-Herald.

He was equally at home commenting on the Luverne, Minnesota, national and world scenes. The world was his oyster. His wife and daughter accompanied him on a trip around the world in 1963. This was not a pleasure trip for McIntosh. As he described it the trip was "a family study mission—to better inform ourselves, as newspaper people, about this changing world." His Star-Herald articles on the trip were compiled in book form.

Among other offices, McIntosh had served as president of the Interstate Press Association, Minnesota Newspaper Association and the National Newspaper Association. He received the University of Nebraska's Distinguished Service Award as an alumnus in 1968, the year he sold his newspaper.

He came to Luverne from Lincoln, Neb., in 1940 and enjoyed the transition from daily newspaper work to weekly publication. In the years that followed, his role in community journalism in Luverne made him a national expert in the field. He was sought out for his views and expertise and lived his role as a country editor to the hilt. In the process he made a lasting and worthwhile contribution to his community, state, nation and profession.

His longtime friend and former employee, Irid Bjerk, had a short, snappy lead on Al McIntosh's obituary story in the Star-Herald last week: "The 'Tired American' is dead at 73." I think McIntosh would have approved of that.

He was a fine citizen, a dedicated newspaperman and an American who never tired of emphasizing the pluses of the "land of the free and the home of the brave." This area was fortunate to have him in its midst.

CARNEGIE'S ZEST BORN IN S.D.

Argus Leader, Sept. 16, 1979

Dale Carnegie, who parlayed his speaking skills into one of the greatest adult education programs in the modern world, had his first successful career in South Dakota.

The author of "How to Win Friends and Influence People" and other renowned books on speaking and personalities was a meat salesman in South Dakota for Armour & Co. of Omaha. Carnegie took a territory for Armour that had been a loser and in two years boosted it to first place among 29 routes out of Omaha.

Six months later when he was 22, his bosses wanted to promote him to manager of the Des Moines branch. He declined because he had already decided to go to New York to study at the American Academy of Dramatic Arts. He tried the stage for one year and in 1912 started to teach public speaking at the 125th Street YMCA in New York.

Why did Carnegie succeed in selling meat in South Dakota on a salary of $17.31 a week plus traveling expenses when others before him had failed? Enthusiasm. It was the trait that brought him success after his first selling job ended in failure. It was the mark of his lifetime's work.

Carnegie was a Missouri farm boy who decided that public speaking was the best way for him to win fame at the State Teachers' College in Warrensburg. He was too small to be an athlete. He practiced speaking by the hour, haranguing pigeons in his father's barn about the necessity of halting Japanese immigration.

He met with defeat after defeat in speaking contests and then started winning. That led to his first job as a salesman for International Correspondence Schools. His prospects were ranchers in the hills of western Nebraska and eastern Wyoming.

Enthusiasm didn't work on this job and he wound up making only one sale. A friendly cracker salesman in Scottsbluff, Neb., heard his tale of woe and told him, "Son, you haven't got a real job at all. You don't have any repeat sales." That decided it for Carnegie. He resolved to sell ham and bacon and lard for Armour or Swift.

Jerry Simmons.

The job with Armour found him crisscrossing South Dakota. "I was determined to make good no matter what the cost, because I knew that if I failed, I would have to go home and admit failure....Besides, my work was far more interesting and far more lucrative than milking cows, shucking corn and cleaning out the henhouse on the farm."

Carnegie said he probably worked harder than other salesmen in South Dakota. He rode the caboose of freight trains. He ran uptown while the train was switching cars and called on butcher shops and grocery stores. His coattail flew in the wind when he ran back to catch the moving train. On a 40-below day he froze both his ears in running from depot to Main Street.

Carnegie rode stagecoach and horseback in covering western South Dakota. He slept in pioneer hotels where the only partition between rooms was a sheet of muslin.

His friend, Lowell Thomas, whom he helped with his speaking, wrote that Carnegie "studied books on salesmanship, rode bucking broncos, played poker with squaw men and learned how to collect money."

Sometimes when a storekeeper couldn't pay cash for the bacon and hams he had ordered, Carnegie would take a dozen pairs of shoes off his shelf, sell the shoes to the railroad men and forward the receipts to Armour & Co.

Carnegie liked South Dakota and particularly the Black Hills. He always wanted a Black Hills home. He didn't realize that ambition before he died at 67 in 1955. But his widow, Dorothy Carnegie, did. She has a ranch near Sundance, on the Wyoming side of the Black Hills, where she spends her summers.

Mrs. Carnegie directs the worldwide Dale Carnegie organization from New York. It operates in the United States, Canada and 56 other countries. Enrollment last year was approximately 104,000.

The firm licensed Nettleton Commercial College in Sioux Falls in 1947 to offer its courses in South Dakota. Since then there have been 386 classes with an average of about 35 students per class, or a total of 12,000.

Jerry Simmons, owner of the Dale Carnegie license for this region since 1968, said that 1,000 of those enrollments have come in the last 12 months. He estimates that he has worked with more than 7,000 men and women in Dale Carnegie courses since 1955 when he joined Nettleton (which he and Gene Reinholt have owned since 1973).

Simmons wound up in Dale Carnegie work because of a speech he gave at the Old Normandy restaurant in Sioux Falls. He was in law school at the time. The speech didn't impress the late J. D. Coon, Sioux Falls lawyer who was a Dale Carnegie instructor.

"I can see there's room for improvement in you as a public speaker," Coon told Simmons. "What can I do?" Simmons asked. "Take my course," was J. D.'s advice. It worked. Although Simmons finished law school, his career 24 years ago took the public speaking turn that Dale Carnegie embarked upon long ago.

Simmons has commuted all over South Dakota giving Dale Carnegie courses in about 40 towns including such diverse places as Buffalo, Bison and Lodgepole, a post office town of six in Perkins County.

I ran into Jerry once at a restaurant in Gettysburg. He had stopped for a sandwich on a wintry day while hurtling on snowpacked roads between Bison or Lodgepole and Sioux Falls in his Volkswagen Beetle. With enthusiasm.

Classes run once a week for 12 or 14 weeks and include speaking, sales and management courses. There are 11 instructors, all graduates of an 18-month training program. Simmons directs Dale Carnegie courses, offered in North Dakota and parts of Iowa and Nebraska as well as South Dakota, from offices at 208 W. 9th St. in Sioux Falls.

A photograph of a confident Dale Carnegie, which Simmons received for serving as president of the national firm's Sponsors Association in 1977-78, is on the wall by the receptionist. Simmons likes that—and also, a certificate from the Accrediting Commission of the Council for Noncollegiate Continuing Education.

That's what Dale Carnegie started out to do in New York in 1912—helping adults learn speaking skills they needed in a hurry. The courses since then have taken a broader scope, as Carnegie went into the human relations part of telling the world "How to Win Friends and Influence People."

With enthusiasm.

A TALE OF TWO AREA CONTRIBUTORS

Argus Leader, Jan. 13, 1980

Samuel W. Masten of Sioux Falls, who practiced in Canton for many years and died Jan. 4 of cancer at Iowa City, was regarded as a giant among lawyers.

Memorial services were held for him in Sioux Falls last Sunday. He lived here at 908 E. 35th St. with his wife, the former Kathryn Kaltsulas of Vermillion and their twins, Alison and Monte, now almost 18. There are three older children.

The people of Lincoln County who took their legal problems to Sam Masten since 1946 and elected him state's attorney regarded him as their friend and champion. He also had served as city attorney of Canton.

V. A. Lowry.

Masten and V. A. Lowry of Madison, for whom services were held Friday, both played unique roles in their chosen South Dakota home towns. As the long-time president (1933-1962) of General Beadle State Teachers College (now Dakota State), Lowry was a mover and a shaker both in the state and in Madison.

Lowry helped save the college several times from politicians who thought South Dakota had too many schools. And thousands of students knew him: as Madison High School coach (his basketball team won the state championship in 1921), as coach at Eastern Normal (an earlier name for Dakota State) and as president. He served longer as president at the Madison campus than any other individual in that job.

Masten, who was 64, was born in Nemo in the Black Hills and went east to Canton, S.D., to pursue his legal career. Lowry died Tuesday at 83. He was born in Hubbard, Ind., and went west to teach. The lives of both men included some fine contributions to their professions, community and state.

As Federal Judge Fred J. Nichol said of Masten: "He was a giant in the legal profession and an outstanding example of what effect one man can have on a whole state, coming from a small community. His death represents a great loss.

"He tried many cases in my court, both when I was a circuit (state) judge and a federal judge. His ability was outstanding." Nichol said Masten was a "scrapper" and a "lawyer's lawyer."

Masten practiced alone for much of his career. He was highly regarded as a member of the Sioux Falls firm of Davenport, Evans, Hurwitz and Smith during his three years (1966 through 1968) there.

Deming Smith of the firm said, "Sam was certainly an effective and outstanding lawyer of his time in South Dakota. Any lawyer of the state would say that. He was great to work with and he was a formidable opponent on the other side."

Masten's work in the South Dakota Bar Association was significant and extended over many years. This included chairmanships of the association's judicial reorganization committee from 1952 to 1958 and in 1960 and of the judicial qualifications commission from 1975 to 1977. Masten was president of the State Bar Association in 1964-65.

His recognition included the Dean Marshall McKusick Award from the University of South Dakota law school, the highest award given any South Dakota lawyer. He had graduated magna cum laude from the law school in 1946.

Masten also received the Herbert Lincoln Harley Award, the highest honor of the American Judicature society, for his efforts in court on behalf of consumers.

Masten's memberships included fellow of the American College of Trial Lawyers, a distinction granted to only one percent of the trial lawyers in America.

Two of his children became lawyers: Jeff an attorney at Canton, and Mary, who is public defender in Rapid City.

Ed Dirksen, a retired banker in Madison, lived next door to Lowry all the years that he was president of the college. Dirksen called him by his first name, Vayne, but to most of Madison Lowry was "V. A." The middle name was Arnold.

Said Dirksen, "He was a wonderful man, a good friend of mine, a good Christian man. He was a good leader and always interested in our community." Dirksen recalled how effective Lowry had been in championing the college. "He stood pat and kept it going."

One of the first major threats to the future of the college came in the 1930s, when South Dakota was hard hit by the Depression. Lowry had assumed office as president in 1933; he soon found himself in the middle of a battle for survival of the college.

Madison business leaders, alumni and friends of the college united to win the fight in the Legislature to keep the college going.

Dirksen said of his presidency: "He did a good job. Our school is is still serving well today. He helped many young men and women during their school courses to obtain good jobs and successful careers."

Dirksen recalled that Lowry had served for many years on the board of the Madison Community Hospital and was its president during some particularly difficult years.

His neighbor mentioned a bit of heartache that has come to many American families in this century. The Lowry's second son, Robert Charles, was killed in action in World War II.

Said Dirksen: "It was kind of hard on him when he lost his son in France. He never got over it."

Another good turn of Lowry's was serving as state chairman of the USO (United Service Organization, which looked after servicemen) and the National War Fund during World War II years. He was also a scouter and held the Silver Beaver Award from the Boy Scouts.

The community of Madison paid its respects to Dr. and Mrs. Lowry April 24, 1961, at a banquet tribute attended by more than 250 friends and associates. He retired June 30, 1962. He was in charge of the Smith-Zimmerman State Historical Museum in Madison from 1962-72.

The long-time college president and his First Lady, Daisy, whom he married in Indiana and who survives him, made hundreds of friends on and off the campus during his 60 years in Madison.

South Dakota lost a part of itself in the deaths of Lowry and Masten. Each contributed to a better South Dakota.

And each will be going home. Some day when she can find the time and bring herself to do it, Mrs. Masten will scatter Sam's ashes from a plane over Nemo. He wanted that. Dr. Lowry will be buried in Culver, Ind.

BALCER'S ROLES

Argus Leader, Sunday, May 25, 1980

Dr. Charles L. Balcer has provided farsighted leadership for Augustana College during the last 15 years. He relinquishes the presidency July 15. After a year at the University of Arizona as a visiting scholar, he will return to Augustana as a distinguished service professor.

Balcer delivered a remarkable speech to Augustana's 1980 graduates last Sunday. It was his last as president. He gave the class of 1980 some words to live by—advice pertinent to these and other times, too.

Charles Balcer.

The regents of Augustana properly recognized Balcer with their medal for his service. His tenure came at a difficult time in American campus history—with turmoil from the Vietnam War and unrest in the nation affecting students everywhere. But this did not deter Balcer from his goal of helping young people acquire quality education.

In his first speech on the campus, he said: "Ours is the business of educating Christian young men and women to assume positions of responsibility in a rapidly changing world."

Midpoint in his presidency, on Founders Day in 1973, Balcer reminded his audience that the American system of higher education had originally been founded on a religious base. "A society like ours needs colleges like Augustana, because we have an obligation to concern ourselves with moral learning. Knowledge is....power, and any power unrestrained by moral sensibilities is a dangerous and capricious instrument."

Balcer has expressed pride in Augustana's ability to merge the liberal arts with professional studies programs in ways which recognized the importance of each. As he said, "We have tried to help people prepare how to live as well as how to work."

Balcer also said, "We have made a very concerted effort to improve our communications with Sioux Falls and the surrounding region." He has also worked for increased cooperation with Sioux Falls College and North American Baptist Seminary.

Balcer's contributions to education in the community and in civic pursuits have been noteworthy and extensive.

The capital improvements at Augustana College during his tenure have been impressive. As the regents said in their citation: "Eight new buildings have been added to the campus, an all-weather track installed, two buildings remodeled and an energy-saving tunnel project completed during Dr. Balcer's 15 years as president. Sixty percent of the college's graduates enrolled in the past 15 years and the endowment fund has grown from $763,000 to $2,126,000."

There are few individuals in today's times who have the inclination or the daring to start anew or to leave a position of power. That is what Balcer is doing, at age 59, in willingly turning over Augustana College to Dr. William C. Nelsen, president-elect, on July 15. Nelsen is academic dean and vice president at St. Olaf.

As Balcer said in a farewell comment for a campus publication, "Many people have asked why I chose to leave at this time. I think it's time for Augustana to have new leadership and it's time to shift gears and do something else. I'm convinced the board chose wisely in electing Dr. Bill Nelsen. He has the same eagerness and excitement about coming to Augustana that I had 15 years ago."

It is characteristic of Balcer that he will return to the classroom in his major discipline: speech and communication which he used so effectively as president. We are confident that he will make a fine contribution in his new teaching role, too.

CALIFORNIA WINE PRODUCER MAKES A NOSTALGIC RETURN TO S.D.

Argus Leader, April 27, 1980

Last Monday, Jerry Lohr, a California wine producer, spent 12 hours on an International tractor plowing some of his wheat land near Raymond, S.D.

That was a prelude to a nostalgic week in which Lohr, born and raised near Clark, extolled the joys of wine sampling to audiences in several South Dakota cities.

He starts this week in Boston, introducing his firm's Monterey Gamay wine to Massachusetts Bay wine writers.

His current trip schedule broke his usual Saturday afternoon routine—inspecting the Turgeon and Lohr vineyards near Carmel, Calif., astride an International tractor.

He thinks this is the way for a "farm boy" from South Dakota to look after his labor of love. At 43, he's enjoying wine making as an avocation to which he devotes about half his time. The other half goes to his home building business in Saratoga, a city of 31,000 in the San Jose area on the south side of San Francisco Bay.

Lohr's partner in the building business is Bernard Turgeon, also his wine partner. Turgeon, who served in General George Patton's 3rd Army in France during World War II, married a French girl. He and his wife look after the Turgeon and Lohr Winery in San Jose while Lohr supervises the vineyard.

Lohr, who has painstakingly walked vineyards in France, believes the gravelly soil and cool, windy weather in Monterey County, Calif., where their 280-acre vineyard is located, lends itself to producing grapes that are comparable to those grown in France.

His interest in wine began about 15 years ago when he and his wife began visiting California wineries. Such sampling tours are a way of life in the Golden Gate state.

His South Dakota background, plus his civil engineering degree from South Dakota State University at Brookings, heightened his interest in approaching wine production both as a farmer and engineer.

Lohr and Turgeon started their winery in 1972, and bottled their first wines in 1975.

Their wines are now available in 31 states. They will sell from 70,000 to 75,000 cases or approximately 900,000 bottles of wine this year.

How "J. Lohr" wines, as they are labeled, wound up in South Dakota started with a trip Ted Muenster and two of his colleagues at Sodak Distributing Co. in Sioux Falls made to California about a year ago in search of new wines for this market.

Jerry Lohr shows Ada May Yeager details of grape care in a 1998 visit to one of his vineyards in Monterey County, California.
—Anson Yeager photo

They heard about Lohr's wines in the process of visiting California vineyards. Someone told them the new winery had gained prestige and recognition in the California market and "that fellow, Lohr, is from the Dakotas."

The Dakota connection resulted in Muenster's signing Lohr and Turgeon. J. Lohr wine was served at the annual legislative dinner of the South Dakota Chamber of Commerce in Pierre during the 1980 session. That's the dinner where public officials are "roasted."

Lohr enjoyed introducing about 100 individuals to a wine tasting session at the Ramada Inn Wednesday night. He emphasized the importance of sniffing the wine to enjoy its aroma (fragrance from the fruit) and twirling the glass before drinking to enhance the bouquet or taste. That also requires savoring your drink in the mouth instead of gulping it down.

He took his audience through eight samples, and enjoyed the nostalgia of being back home in South Dakota. He also saw some old friends, including Lois Mehrbach Axlund of Sioux Falls, who grew up a mile from Lohr's home place in Clark County.

Wine tasting, Lohr was careful to explain, does not require anyone to empty a partially filled glass by consuming it. Tasters dumped the excess in a plastic container set in the middle of Ramada Inn tables. Each taster had two glasses, one for the red wines and rosés, the other for white wines.

And wine, Lohr said, should be used in the company of friends or to heighten enjoyment of food. Never drink wine alone, he cautioned.

His South Dakota itinerary last week included similar wine tasting sessions in Yankton, Pierre and Rapid City. And a visit with his parents, Mr. and Mrs. Walter Lohr, now retired from farming, who live in Clark. A brother, Alan, lives in Huron.

The South Dakota connection is a strong one for Clark. He was back four times last year.

South Dakota ties in the San Francisco Bay Area are also strong. The South Dakota State alumni chapter met in San Jose March 1—and 115 members toured the winery.

After Lohr graduated from State in 1958, he took graduate work at Stanford University, where he met his future wife, Carol, a native of New York. They have three children.

From 1965 through 1978, Lohr and his partner designed and built some 700 custom homes. At present, they are concentrating on town houses in their construction business.

From a volume standpoint, the two partners have the same goal for their winery now as when they started: 125,000 cases a year. This year, they will bottle 100,000 cases. Last year, sales totaled about $1.4 million on 45,000 cases. This year, sales will be about $2.1 million on 70,000 to 75,000 cases.

Lohr thinks the technical approach to winegrowing—developed from a blend of his farm and engineering background—is important. But so is that Saturday afternoon inspection tour on his tractor—and the opportunity to talk with his workers in the vineyard about what needs to be done.

The grape, of course, is the key to winemaking. It determines the taste and quality of the product. How their grapes are treated—both in the vineyard and the winery—gives two construction partners and their families another pursuit that is exciting and thrilling in today's California.

FULLER, A LAWYER'S LAWYER, DEVOTED TO CHURCH

Argus Leader, Sunday, March 8, 1981

Howell Fuller, who died at 71 on Feb. 27 and for whom services were held last Monday, was a lawyer's lawyer.

He was also much more—lawyer and chancellor for his church and lawyer for his university fraternity. Through the years he rescued many much younger fraternity brothers from the clutches of the law.

He was a devoted family man, proud of his wife, children and grandchildren.

Fuller had quiet, unassuming ways and gentle humor. He was something like the late Vice President Alben Barkley, who said he liked to serve the Lord by being a parishioner in the back pew.

Fuller's colleagues—lawyers and secretaries at the prestigious firms of Wood, Fuller, Shultz and Smith in Sioux Falls—miss him. And so do many others.

Bishop Walter Jones of the Episcopal Diocese of South Dakota praised Fuller's work for the church. As chancellor of the diocese for more than 25 years, Fuller was on the executive committee and faithfully attended more than 100 quarterly meetings, plus innumerable special ones.

Howell Fuller.

"For me, he had been a tremendous help," Jones said. Fuller advised Jones and his predecessors on legal and other matters. Jones said he would quietly suggest a change in wording in a difficult letter that would solve the problem. He also saw the humor in a vexing situation.

When a change in the diocesan Constitution or Canons was necessary, Fuller had the wording. When a new tax law several years ago affected the church's ownership of some 200 pieces of property in South Dakota, Fuller did the necessary paper work to keep the diocese in compliance.

Fuller and his wife, Ruth, faithfully attended Calvary Cathedral. Two Supreme Court justices and many members of the bar were among mourners who consoled Mrs. Fuller and family members at Fuller's service at Calvary Cathedral

♦ ♦ ♦

As Francis M. Smith, a senior partner of the law firm, recalled his association with Fuller: "I don't think that I have ever encountered a finer legal mind than Howell.

"He was a man absolutely without pretense. I have had more than one judge tell me it was a joy to have Howell try a case in his court. He knew exactly where he was going, he didn't get sidetracked.

"It is certainly a fact that all of us, when we started to practice, would beat a path to Howell's door. He had a tremendous facility for recalling cases by name and even by citation. Everyone in this office would go to him with a problem and he would remember a case where he would pull out the file and say, 'There's your answer.'

"He was truly a lawyer's lawyer." That was a characterization with which his brother, the late "Had" Fuller, a Mitchell lawyer, agreed. "Had" called Howell "his lawyer."

Law ran in the family. Howell's grandfather was a justice of the South Dakota Supreme Court. Smith recalled that at one time during his legal career Fuller was invited to apply for appointment to the court.

Fuller's father was a lawyer in Milbank, and two of his three brothers were lawyers.

Fuller's son, Bill, is a junior partner in Woods, Fuller, Shultz and Smith—and will carry on as the fourth generation in the profession.

A daughter, Mrs. Aune West lives in Sioux Falls; another daughter, Mrs. Mary Madden, lives in Fargo, N.D. There are 10 grandchildren.

❖ ❖ ❖

There was a conservative side to Howell Fuller that showed in his reaction to the move to the law firm from the Bailey-Glidden Building on North Main Avenue in the late 1950s.

Fuller bought along his old desk and used it until his death. Other offices have fancy new ones.

He also snorted a bit about the extensive recent interior remodeling of the law firm's colonial-style office at 310 S. 1st. Ave.

The firm has comfortable lawyers' offices, conference rooms in tasteful decor, carpeting, bookcases down the middle and a colonial staircase leading to an unused second floor.

"It was sort of a game with Howell," Smith said. He used to shake his head and mumble that "if we got any more fancy equipment there wouldn't be enough room for the books."

Fuller, who was admitted to the bar in 1931, had used dictating equipment for years. He also saw the switch to word processing machines (typewriter keyboards with a video screen, printer and computer hookup) in his lifetime.

Smith said, "He could write and say something in 500 words that would take some of us 2,500 words or more to say it as well."

Fuller, Smith said, "was the only one who could read his own writing."

William G. Taylor Jr., a junior member of the firm, recalled Fuller's role as an officer of the Beta Theta Pi fraternity for many years. Fuller was instrumental in putting together the financing in 1966 for a new chapter house at the University of South Dakota campus in Vermillion.

"He was always considered chapter counsel and bailed many of the boys and the chapter out of trouble on numerous occasions," Taylor said. "I first met Howell in 1964 when he was at the chapter house unwinding one of our complicated problems."

Although Fuller never sought top leadership posts in civic and other groups, some of them came to him. He had been president of the Second Judicial Circuit Bar Association and of the Downtown Rotary Club. He was exalted ruler of the Sioux Falls Elks in 1940-41.

❖ ❖ ❖

Fuller used to enjoy golf, but like the firm's head and senior partner, M. T. Woods, enjoyed his work the most.

Said Woods, "What I think about Howell is that he was just a damned good lawyer. He had some good results in his handling of titles and mortgages and foreclosures. Probably, there was nobody in the state that could match him (in that field)."

Woods recalled another good lawyer, Bob Jones of Milbank, who knew Fuller when he was growing up. "Jones said Howell as a kid and child would ask more questions than any youngster in town."

That inquiring mind led Fuller to a legal career that spanned more than half a century, counting law school days in Vermillion.

As Smith told the ministers at Calvary Cathedral, "We've lost a good one."

PROFILES

40 YEARS' WORTH OF CHANGES

Argus Leader, Sunday, April 5, 1981

What a difference 40 years, plus or minus, makes in the affairs of men and governments!

Consider Tony Javurek, who retired in 1974 with 45 years service at John Morrell & Co. For 35 years Tony was the plant tour guide and photographer.

He was an extraordinary plant guide, a smiling individual with a distinctive whistle. When he needed to get someone's attention, Tony whistled. And they listened.

He pleased groups of school children and adults alike on their tours of the meat packing plant.

One of Tony's most eventful days as photographer was when Maj. Joe Foss, Marine Corps ace and hero of air battles in the Pacific, returned to his hometown for a war bond appearance in 1943.

Foss was in a parade that wound up at the Morrell plant that day. He talked to employees from a stage outside the building. Needless to say, Foss sold a lot of bonds.

Sioux Falls' and South Dakota's hero, who had received his Congressional Medal of Honor from President Franklin D. Roosevelt, had the undivided attention of plant workers, as shown in Tony's photograph.

Foss, of course, went on to organize the South Dakota Air National Guard, become governor of his state and organizer and commissioner of the American Football League. He's retired now, living in Arizona.

Tony at the time he pictured Foss wasn't long for civilian life. He served three years in the Army and wound up in Czechoslovakia where his folks were born.

Tony could speak and write the language and acted as an interpreter when his outfit—the 16th Armored Division—liberated Pilsen, Czechoslovakia. His distant cousins were glad to see him and other GI liberators.

Tony came home to resume his work at Morrell. He took great delight in looking at a name on a visitor's card and calling out a greeting in German, Dutch, Latvian or Bohemian.

Possibly half a million persons encountered Tony in Morrell tours. He mixed whistles with his philosophy—"all people are wonderful if approached in the right manner." His audiences included Sen. Hubert Humphrey and Adlai Stevenson.

Away from work, Tony began entertaining groups in the early 1930s as a result of winning contests in the old Orpheum Theatre's amateur nights. He continued entertaining through the years, appearing in most Sioux Falls churches and on various programs to give his whistling routine. He also took pictures of weddings and other events.

Tony conducted his last tour in May 1974 and was the last tour guide employed by the firm. Federal safety regulations forced a halt of public tours.

He lives at 1509 S. Wayland Ave., his home since 1950. Tony's wife, Audrey, died in 1959. He's proud of his two sons and a grandson, Benjamin, age 10. Ben lives with his mother in Deadwood. Tony's sons are Dr. Anthony (also called Tony) of Vermillion, Ben's dad, and Martin, Deadwood.

Tony, who'll be 69 May 25, has retained his interest in photography since retirement, taking occasional pictures of family reunions and birthday parties. A younger Tony in his tour cap may be compared with John Danicic's picture of him taken recently in the Argus Leader newsroom.

Yes, Tony still smiles. And he can still whistle! Most of us can't return the whistle, but who wouldn't smile back at Tony Javurek?

KOPLOW NEVER FIRST IN LINE—SALUTE TO REMARKABLE VET
Argus Leader, Sunday, May 24, 1981

Memorial Day weekend is a time when members of the American Legion, Veterans of Foreign Wars and other patriotic groups help this country remember its war dead and veterans.

And it's a good time to remember a quiet Sioux Falls Legionnaire—Nathan Koplow.

He spent much of his lifetime remembering his fellowmen, serving mainly in the rear ranks of two veterans organizations and doing his part in his chosen country.

Few Legionnaires or members of other veterans' groups serve their organizations for so long or take such an active role as he did.

Nathan, who died in Sioux Falls at 89 on May 7, was born in Poland.

He came to the United States in 1910 and eventually to Sioux Falls to be near two of his three brothers. He homesteaded near Timber Lake, S.D., in 1914.

He volunteered for the U.S. Navy in World War I, but was drafted into the Army before acceptance. He served in France in 1918.

After the war, he became a Legionnaire and was a member for 62 years. He was also a member of the 40 et 8 Voiture for 41 years.

And he remembered his childhood sweetheart, Goldie. He returned to Poland and married her in 1921. They settled in Sioux Falls.

During his lifetime, he was a plumber, homesteader and businessman. He particularly liked his Legion and 40 et 8 affiliations.

He enjoyed enrolling Legionnaires. For years he led Post No. 15's "go-getters" group, signing up 100 or more new memberships or renewals.

He was friendly and quick to offer assistance. He didn't seek the limelight but contributed year in and year out to the good of the organization.

When there were patriotic observances, he was there. When there were post meetings involving financial and other problems, he was there. He seldom missed a meeting.

Sioux Falls Post No. 15 recognized him as the Legionnaire of the year in 1972.

Gene Pruitt, Sioux Falls lawyer and a Legion friend of Nathan Koplow for years, said of him in a eulogy during services at the Miller Funeral Home on May 10:

"Nathan was always last—he was never first in line. He first assured himself that everyone else had been taken care of before he would get in line. This was typical behavior for Nathan. He was appreciative—never did a kind act or a thoughtful deed or a gift go unacknowledged. Almost immediately, he would respond, returning the gift, deed or act with something of kind...."

"Nathan loved America. I am sure this accounts, in part, for his great love of the American Legion and 40 et 8."

Koplow through the years also participated in B'nai B'rith and the Sons of Israel Congregation serving in numerous capacities in each organization.

His wife died in 1962. Survivors include two sons, Ira of Kansas City, Mo., and George of Rock Island, Ill.; two daughters, Mrs. Henry (Pauline) Hausdorff, Baltimore, Md., and Mrs. Al

(Sylvia) Polen, Wickliffe, Ohio; five grandchildren, four great grandchildren and a brother, Isadore, Cleveland, Ohio.

He lived modestly and usually traveled by bus when he went out of town. He liked to visit his children and would often recount the experiences he encountered while traveling. He had a good sense of humor.

Throughout the United States, there are counterparts of Nathan Koplow in local veterans' organizations.

They're the members who unselfishly set aside time today or tomorrow to mark graves and salute the memory of men and women who served their country.

They also serve throughout the year in various post and community activities. And they're on call to act as pallbearers or members of an honor guard, firing squad or some other detail expected of a veterans organization.

Like Nathan Koplow, they quietly serve their veterans' post with concern for comrades, their widows and their children—and not for themselves.

It's part of the spirit of the United States. Koplow found that spirit in Sioux Falls, in homestead days in South Dakota's West River and during his service with the Army in France.

It became an inseparable part of Nathan Koplow. And it showed throughout his lifetime in Sioux Falls.

KROEGER HELPED BUILD BOYS AND STRUCTURES

Argus Leader, Tuesday, Feb. 16, 1982

Jean R. Kroeger, a talented architect who devoted countless hours to the Boy Scouts of America and Sioux Falls civic endeavors, leaves many good works and a fine record of service in a busy 32 years in Sioux Falls.

Kroeger, a senior partner of Fritzel, Kroeger, Griffin and Berg, died Saturday at age 58. Services will be at Calvary Cathedral today at 11 a. m.

Among many building projects in which he played a key role as an architect are Costello Terminal at Joe Foss Field, the main office of the First National Bank in Sioux Falls, the Northwestern Bell Telephone Company's office building, and the DakotaDome at the University of South Dakota, Vermilion.

Kroeger was president of the Sioux Council of the Boy Scouts of America for eight years, first from 1964 to 1969 and again from 1972 through 1974.

He served on the National Cub Scout Committee, was chairman of its regional organization and helped organize its Wood Badge Program for leaders. Kroeger was presented the Sioux Council's Silver Beaver award in 1966 and the region's Silver Antelope Award in 1969.

Kroeger was chairman of the Sioux Falls Planning Commission at the time of his death. As chairman he played key roles in developing the city's Year 2000 plan and the river greenway. He had served as president of the State Chapter of the American Institute of Architects and of the Downtown Kiwanis Club.

He was also a past president of the Sioux Falls Junior Chamber of Commerce and received its Distinguished Service Award in 1956. He had been a national director of the Jaycees.

Kroeger, a native of Mankato, Minn., and a graduate of Watertown High School, was a World War II Air Force pilot. He held the Air Medal and a presidential citation from service in Europe. He returned to Iowa State University after the war to complete his college work. Like many other veterans, he liked what he saw in Sioux Falls.

Kroeger had many interests. He was a lay reader in his church, helped found the Sioux Empire Kennel Club and was its third president. He conceived, developed and became the first editor of the Canine Currier, which won national honors in 1964.

He will probably be remembered best for his volunteer work as a scout leader and as chairman of the Planning Commission. Both endeavors demonstrated his good purpose and concern for the future. His contributions to scouting and his effective work in planning and other civic endeavors long will be remembered.

Sioux Falls was fortunate to have him—as a designer of brick and steel who was also interested in building boys.

◆ ◆ ◆

Jean Kroeger

Jean R. Kroeger, 59, of rural Sioux Falls died Saturday at Sioux Valley Hospital.

He was born Oct. 19, 1923, in Rapidan, Minn. He grew up in Watertown, S.D., and graduated from Iowa State University in 1948. He married Jackie Horney June 12, 1947, in Kansas City, Mo.

They moved to Sioux Falls in 1950. He was a partner in the architectural firm of Fritzel, Kroeger, Griffen and Berg for 32 years.

Survivors include his wife; two sons, Jean R. Kroeger, Jr., and Kevin J. Kroeger, both of Sioux Falls; his mother, Mrs. Louise Kroeger, Watertown; and a sister, Mrs. Rex (Elizabeth) Gereau, Watertown.

Services will be 11 a.m. Tuesday at Calvary Cathedral. A private burial will be after the services. Expressions of sympathy can be sent to the Sioux Council of Boy Scouts of America.

DEATH ENDS BRILLIANT CAREER OF CANTON NATIVE WHO HELPED U.S. WIN WWII

Argus Leader, Sunday, May 30, 1982

Merle Antony Tuve, physicist and one of a trio of Canton, S.D., natives who won worldwide renown as scientists, died May 20 in a Bethesda, Md., hospital. He was 80.

His recollections of his boyhood in Canton appeared in the Argus Leader's May 2 "People" edition.

Tuve's experiments with short-pulse radio waves have been accepted as the basis for development of radar.

A research group he organized in World War II led to the development of the proximity fuze, a radio device for antiaircraft or artillery shells that sets off the explosive as it nears the target.

The fuze was used effectively against Hitler's V-1 rocket bombs aimed at Britain and by U.S. field artillery against ground forces in Europe and the Pacific.

Tuve responded promptly from his Chevy Chase, Md., home about two months ago when I wrote him asking for his recollections of South Dakota.

They offered a unique glimpse of how two scientific careers were stimulated or inspired by a friend's offer in 1915 or 1916.

Verne Kennedy was back in Canton for the summer after completing his sophomore year at Boston Tech (which became the Massachusetts Institute of Technology).

Kennedy told Tuve: "If you two (Tuve and "Ernie" Lawrence) will drop by after supper, say around 7:30, I'll show you my 'slip stick' or slide rule...."

Lawrence of course, became the nuclear physicist who invented the cyclotron and won a Nobel prize. He was director of the Lawrence Radiation Laboratory, named for him, at the University of California in Berkley. Lawrence died in 1958.

The other member of the famous Canton scientific trio is Dr. John Lawrence, younger brother of Ernest. John pioneered in nuclear medicine and directed the Donner Laboratory at Berkley. He is active in retirement. His recollections of South Dakota appeared May 16.

Tuve's death was chronicled in Newsweek's Transition and Time's Milestones. The New York Times on May 22 carried an obituary under a two-column headline.

Tuve was born at Canton on June 27, 1901, the son of Anthony G. Tuve and Ida Marie (Larsen) Tuve. He attended Augustana Academy from 1915 to 1918 and was graduated in electrical engineering from the University of Minnesota in 1922.

He taught at Princeton University for two years and at John Hopkins University, where he received his doctorate degree in physics in 1926. He joined the staff of the Carnegie Institution where his research brought him international recognition.

During the 1930s his studies included the first measurements of nuclear forces which bind neutrons and protons together. He helped develop high-voltage accelerators to examine the structure of the atom.

During World War II Tuve volunteered to do research for the war effort. Among his awards was being made a Commander of the Order of the British Empire for his work on the proximity fuze.

After the war, he developed techniques for seismic studies of the earth's crust, using explosions. Another research project, which extended from 1953 to 1966, was in radio astronomy. During 1967-1969 he did a monograph on atomic hydrogen clouds of "our galaxy." He retired in 1970.

Tuve is survived by his wife, Winifred Whitman, Chevy Chase, Md., and a daughter, Lucy Tuve, Schenectady, N.Y.

There must have been something more than coincidence that saw three Canton boys do so much to further mankind's knowledge of the atom, radio waves and nuclear medicine.

And there must have been some thing keen about Tuve's outlook on life. His Argus Leader recollections started out: "Of a hundred vivid memories of my youth in Canton I shall remark on only one which resulted in a permanent stimulus for Ernest Lawrence and for me, both of us as high school freshman."

Tuve concluded his article about being initiated into the mysteries of a slide rule: "This little capsule of experience was one of the item's leading Ernie and me to study mathematics and physics a few years later. In two hours of that evening the generous demonstration that simple means could give us immediate numerical answers to a whole galaxy of problems opened our eyes and excited our ambition to learn more about science and mathematics. Ernest Lawrence and I several years later went on in college to do just that."

South Dakota can count Tuve as one of its greatest native sons. His research helped the United States and Great Britain win World War II and helped unlock secrets of the nuclear age and the galaxy.

FLOYD LEBLANC DIDN'T TAKE PHARMACY FOR GRANTED

Argus Leader, Sunday, July 18, 1982

Most of us take the pharmacy part of modern drug stores—whether they're on a neighborhood corner or part of a large retail store—more or less for granted.

One man who didn't—Floyd J. LeBlanc, dean emeritus of South Dakota State University—died at age 85 in the Brookings Hospital Monday.

He had a lot to do over a 43-year period in training pharmacists. As an instructor at SDSU from 1924, the year he graduated with a B.S. degree, and as dean of the college of pharmacy for 25 years, he touched the lives of hundreds of students.

He inspired many youth in the region to attempt and complete the rigorous academic and laboratory requirements leading to licensing as a pharmacist. And he was as cognizant of the other merchandising aspects of drug stores as proprietors.

LeBlanc's big opportunity for service in his academic career came in 1941, when he was named dean of pharmacy. He was dean until 1965 and continued on the faculty as professor of pharmaceutical chemistry until 1967.

Floyd LeBlanc.

Harold S. Bailey Jr., vice president for academic affairs at SDSU who had served on the faculty with LeBlanc for a number of years, recalls:

"Floyd was a quiet man. Although he received a number of honors in his career, his greatest enjoyment came from his instructional responsibilities and contact with the college students. He knew every one of the graduates of the College of Pharmacy by name and much of their background."

"He was not only interested in them as students but also intensely interested in their goals and their dreams and on many occasions gave good advice to those who were in need of advice. Dr. LeBlanc was proud of his college, his faculty and the graduates. He followed the careers of his graduates and was pleased to renew these acquaintances at meetings of the South Dakota Pharmaceutical Association and other occasions."

"Although he was the dean of pharmacy, his faculty always thought of him as a colleague and a friend to whom they could turn in cases of professional as well as personal advice. He was proud of his Upper Midwest heritage and let it be known to newcomers to his faculty from outside of South Dakota that there was no better place in which to work, to play or to pursue your lifetime goals."

LeBlanc was born in Minnesota and spent nearly all of his adult lifetime in South Dakota. There were several interruptions in his longtime residence in Brookings during the 1930s to gain his doctorate degree at Purdue University.

When he applied for a job as instructor at SDSU, his resume listed several years of clerking in drug stores. His annual salary in 1916-1917 was $900; he got a raise to $1,080 by switching drug stores the next year. He was manager of a drug store for three summers, 1924-25-26, between college terms at a salary of $160 per month.

Phil Von Fischer, a 1952 pharmacy graduate and manager of Lewis Drug Southgate, recalls that LeBlanc's favorite expression was "Say"—like, "Say, Phil..." or "Let's say we'll do it this way."

His way was exacting, Von Fischer said. LeBlanc stressed accuracy and excellence in compounding prescriptions to exact and professional standards, the performance that the public expects so routinely.

"Those of us who graduated under him had the highest respect for him," Von Fischer said.

Jack Halbkat, Webster druggist and a 1962 graduate of the College of Pharmacy, recalls, "The dean's door was always open. If we had a problem he listened and was sympathetic."

One of those problems was a yearlong course in physics, required for Halbkat's class. The course was taught by the College of Engineering. Student classroom performance reflected something less than enthusiasm for being transplanted to another discipline.

The instructor, Halbkat said, threatened to flunk the whole class if they didn't shape up. LeBlanc solved that problem by getting on the telephone to the dean of engineering. There were no more threats.

"He was a dedicated educator and a professional," Halbkat said. The Webster druggist is president of the South Dakota Pharmaceutical Association.

Harold Schuler, Pierre, secretary of the association and of the South Dakota Board of Pharmacy, says: "He was always a very fine, gracious person. He had a good working relationship with the board and South Dakota pharmacists."

LeBlanc is survived by his wife, Eleanor. Private services were held in Brookings. Memorials may be directed to the Floyd LeBlanc Scholarship Fund, established by the association in 1980.

A measure of LeBlanc's dedication to his students was his decision over a $500 check which the Osco Drug Co. gave him as a personal retirement gift in 1964.

Instead, he decided to deposit the money at 4 percent interest and use it as a discretionary loan or scholarship fund for worthy and financially hard pressed students.

It is a footnote of campus history that LeBlanc's striving for excellence included inspiring his pharmacy students to win the outstanding or most beautiful float category in countless Hobo Day parades.

A FREE SPIRIT WHO LIVED FOR EACH DAY

Argus Leader, Sunday, Sept. 5, 1982

John Wooley was a free and blithe spirit.

He was a newspaperman with an extra quotient of inquisitiveness.

He liked people—very much.

He was a good husband, proud of his wife, their three daughters and their husbands.

He was a doer who made every day count: the day at hand.

And he was a fighter.

"He was terribly strong," his wife, Karen, told me in a telephone chat Friday.

She described her husband's reaction seven years ago to a diagnosis of lymphoma, cancer of the lymph system.

John came home to Pierre and wrote a column. The doctors tell me, John wrote, that I have five years to live. His column's message was that he was going to make the best of it—a day at a time.

As it turned out, John got two extra years.

Most of his friends realized that he was working on borrowed time. But you forgot about that when you saw John occasionally. He was always up beat. He gave every day his best shot—a characteristic of his even before that ominous diagnosis.

◆ ◆ ◆

John was an aggressive and well-liked young reporter on the news staff of the Argus Leader for four years from 1958-62.

Assigned to cover the Navy's Blue Angels acrobatic team which performed at Joe Foss Field in 1960, he got a 40-minute demonstration flight. That made him an honorary Blue angel and for a short time a fledgling astronaut.

"The trip was wonderful," Wooley told Herb Bechtold, city editor and "Round Robin" columnist. "But the hot beef sandwich I ate just before takeoff wasn't actually conducive to some of the maneuvers. I didn't actually get sick, but a few more rolls of the jet would have fixed me up good."

The best part of the flight was reaching a point on a parabolic curve that resulted in weightlessness, the same as astronauts experience. There were more thrills on descent, Wooley said.

While vacationing in a suburb northwest of Chicago in September 1961, Wooley did a column for Bechtold about the crash of a commercial airliner 2 1/2 miles away and the tragedy's impact on the neighborhood.

Wooley wrote about the curious jamming roads in the vicinity of the crash and suburbanites living in the shadow of O'Hare Field who were unafraid that rapidly increasing use of the airport would bring additional air disasters.

He had talent for relating events to the people equation: aptitude that he used effectively later as staff writer and Pierre correspondent for The Associated Press for six years and in a number of other media and public information roles.

Wooley became a partner in Thompson Publications in Pierre in 1973—and was the driving force behind creation of the Pierre Times. It won acclaim for editorial content, makeup and photography.

Wooley published the Pierre and Fort Pierre Times until 1981, when the corporation was sold to Hipple Printing Co. Most recently he had been Hipple's advertising manager and a columnist for the Daily Capital Journal and the Times.

◆ ◆ ◆

Karen, whose training as a registered nurse helped her husband greatly, praised the help that the University of Minnesota research center had given John.

She said nearly all the last seven years were very good—that chemotherapy mitigated John's condition. Treatment, however, didn't seem to handle the illness in the last few months.

Even so, the last trip to Minneapolis on July 15 was not unlike the others. Karen drove John all over Pierre, so he could do some errands. He applied for his antelope license. He made some notes about future columns he had in mind.

They flew home to Pierre Aug. 24. John died the next night at St. Mary's hospital.

One thing that Karen didn't tell him was that he didn't get his antelope license this year.

◆ ◆ ◆

Terry Wooster, editor of the Capital Journal, wrote a column about Wooley, who had hired Wooster for the Times. "With John, I learned about caring for people. I never learned as much about it as he obviously knew, but I learned a little."

"More than anyone else I've known, John cared about people. Young, old, famous, obscure. It didn't matter. Each of them was a story. Not because he was in the business of stories, but because he just liked people. He wanted to know who they were, what they liked, how they lived....He was someone special."

That column meant a great deal to Karen, as did a column by John Hipple, business manager of Hipple Printing Co., and a radio editorial by Dean Sorenson of KCCR in Pierre.

The capital city, of course, is people-oriented. Pierre folks and many others liked John Wooley. He packed a lot into 47 years—especially since July 1975 when he resolved to welcome each day as it came.

MADISON WOMAN CHRONICLES PRAIRIE MEMORIES
Argus Leader, Sunday, Jan. 23, 1983

Mrs. Esther M. Gross of Madison, who is 85, took her grandchildren's advice seriously.

When she used to relate incidents of the past, they would tell her: "Grandma, you should be writing these things down."

She started chronicling her memories during the winter of 1980—and finished them on her 85th birthday last March.

With some help from her son, John C. Gross of Madison, other family members and friends who helped her put her book together, she has told her life story and that of her family in "My Garden of Memories."

It's an account of life on the prairie: in South Dakota, Montana, North Dakota and near Madison since 1929 when she and her late husband, Ellwood Gross, moved to his family's farm, Ash Grove.

He was a teacher at her family's school in Montana. He gave her a nice quarter-carat diamond ring that came from Sears Roebuck and cost $48.

On their wedding day they got up at 3 a.m., taking horses and a wagon 20 miles to catch the train—but it didn't stop. So they hired a car for the 40-mile ride to Roundup, Mont., where they were married Jan. 11, 1919.

"It was a cool ride, though it was a thawing day. We got to the county seat just in time to get the license," Mrs. Gross wrote.

She relates the ups and downs of homesteading in Montana, the move to a farm in North Dakota and how she and her husband settled down at Ash Grove.

Her perspective is many-faceted, as a wife and mother, as a daughter and daughter-in-law, as a grandmother and great-grandmother.

She tells the joys and the pains of raising six boys and one girl and the loss, through plane crashes, of two sons in military service: one during World War II and the other in 1956.

Esther M. Gross.

Her account preserves for her family the feelings she and her husband had in June 1942 when a War Department telegram informed them their son, Emerson, had been killed in a plane crash. He could have bailed out—but he stayed with his plane to keep it from crashing on a schoolyard full of children.

The book has a picture of the Air Corps escort officer who brought Emerson's body home. He was the first casualty from Lake County in World War II.

Fourteen years later, in June 1956, their son Wallace, who had survived World War II and made his career in the Air Force, was killed in a plane crash. A flight engineer on a tanker, he and his crew had been on an evening mission to get in their flying time. The family drove to Roswell, N.M., in one day to attend his funeral service.

Most of the book, however, tells a happy story: of children being married, the first grandchildren, their weddings, how the family spread out and summer reunions.

What Mrs. Gross calls "a big surprise" was her award in 1959 as an Eminent Homemaker of South Dakota, conferred by Hilton Briggs, then president of South Dakota State University.

The citation mentioned her activities in church, 4-H and Extension—and her advice to young farm couples: "Do things together. When children get old enough get them into a 4-H Club, work with them and guide them into useful activities. If this is done, the future of South Dakota farm living will be bright and young folks will be more content on the farm."

That November day was a happy one, but reaching Brookings on icy roads took some doing.

As the Gross family met the 1960s she wrote: "We were really having good times. I think we went to Montana most every year (to see a son and his family and other relatives). Ellwood would buy a new Rambler every other year and we did enjoy rambling."

The couple's first flight to California and her husband's illness and death in 1966 are other milestones.

There are historical references, too, like Mrs. Gross' recollections of President Richard Nixon's visit to Madison in 1969 to dedicate the Mundt library. Madison's centennial observance in 1980 was a happy time; the family had a picnic at Ash Grove on July 4.

Mrs. Gross splits her time between the home place five miles north of Madison and Modesto, Calif., where she spends winters to be near her daughter, Viola.

Sometime in the next century, great grandchildren of Mrs. Gross will have a family history that tells them how life was on the prairie in this century.

She writes in a foreword: "No doubt your great grandchildren will someday say, 'You know grandma was 85 years old when she wrote this and she may have imagined some of it.'"

Perhaps. As she says, "This is the way I remember it."

Her chronicle—with its anecdotes about farm life and snapshots of smiling youngsters, grooms and brides—represents a treasure for her family.

Her efforts should inspire more mothers and grandmothers to tell their family story.

THIS FELLOW RENTS MOST EVERYTHING, AND HAS BOXES OF IDEAS

Argus Leader, Sunday, Sept. 25, 1983

Talking to Robert C. Elmen, whom we'll henceforth call Bob in this column, is like getting so many ideas that a writer doesn't know where to start.

Robert C. Elmen.

So we'll begin by saying that Bob enjoys directing business operations that includes 25 Rent All stores and seven Mini Stor All operations in five states and real estate holdings in Sioux Falls and elsewhere.

His comfortable second story office on West 12th Street overlooks the Elmen Rent All store across the street. Nearby is the latest evident Elmen enterprise, a rent-to-own appliance store.

Another new business, Elmen Rent All by catalog, with service from present rent all stores via United Parcel Service, is ready to do business. So far, the phones haven't rung, but Bob isn't worried.

He reasons that sooner or later someone in Buffalo, S.D., or some other town in the five-state region will use his new service to rent tools to repair his own car.

Six hundred thousand catalogs, detailing what's available at Elmen Rent All locations, have been mailed. Bob has an initial stock of 1,000 cardboard boxes of maximum size to send whatever tool that customer in northwestern South Dakota might want. When the home fixer finishes his repairs, all he has to do is return the tool in the same package.

Bob believes that going mail order was a logical extension of his rental stores. He based part of the decision on changing demographics so he could tap the upscale side of the market.

He said 10 years ago 65 percent of the people were middle income; today, the figure is 46 percent, with more rich and poor people on either side of the middle.

The new appliance store is an an approach toward the lower income part of the market.

❖ ❖ ❖

Bob during 1984 and 1985 plans to spend $800,000 building new or expanded Mini Stor All facilities in Sioux Falls; South Sioux City and Lincoln, Neb.; Rochester, Minn.; and Grand Forks and Fargo, N.D.

That expansion is based on on some highly desirable occupancy rates for the firm's existing storage facilities: Sioux Falls is 95 percent full; Rapid City, 88; Sioux City, 95; Grand Forks, 93 and Fargo, 97.5.

Again, a study of population characteristics convinced him that this was a service that would be used. Americans are mobile, there are more apartment dwellers than ever before and many are divorced.

Storing household goods or a car becomes a real problem, whether you're an airman at Rapid City with orders for the Far East or a retail employee who's being transferred.

"People store things they really don't need," he said. "People can't throw something away." He said they'll keep an old adding machine that cost $500 and weighs 60 pounds when today they can buy an inexpensive hand-held calculator.

The solution, according to Bob, is to rent a space for your own personal warehouse. The 10x10-foot size is the most popular.

Several weeks ago he sent me two clippings.

One was an Ann Landers column from November 1981 in which "Cramped in Michigan" wrote that she was sick of running a warehouse for her grown children to store their junk. Elmen whipped off a letter at the time to Landers, suggesting that for as little as $10 a month "Cramped in Michigan" could put the children's treasures in a self-storage unit and get back her garage, basement and spare bedroom.

Another clipping was this writer's column of Aug. 21 wondering how parents of college students could persuade their children to store their stuff in the college town instead of having to haul it home next spring for the summer.

Bob's solution, of course, is for the collegians to use his facilities. He said many of them do, in the college towns served by his self-storage units.

◆ ◆ ◆

One prominent American who read newspapers thoroughly and regularly related the news to national economic problems was financier Bernard Baruch, who was an unpaid adviser to every president from Woodrow Wilson to Dwight D. Eisenhower.

Like Baruch, Bob tries to relate his reading to economics and, specifically, his business enterprises.

He does a lot of reading—starting at 4 a.m. Bob gets by on 5 hours of sleep a night, which allows him time for all the things he wants to do, including studying, planning and addressing trade conventions.

He regularly reads the Argus Leader, USA TODAY, Wall Street Journal, Corporate Report, Forbes, Fortune, Business Week, U.S. News, Consumer Reports and some special tax and other digests.

In the last month he has read eight books on the mail order business. He keeps up with such contemporary authors as John Naisbitt (Megatrends) and Alvin Toffler (Previews and Premises) who portray changes in the American economic scene.

Bob's interest in statistics and economics is longstanding.

He took postgraduate work in economics at Augustana College, his alma mater, and earned an M.S degree at South Dakota State University in 1966. He wrote his master's thesis on "Some Operational Aspects of the General Rental Industry" and sold it as a book, now out of print. It is considered a model financial study of the trade.

Week before last Bob was featured speaker at a rental association convention in Clearwater, Fla. At noon Tuesday he'll address a Small Business Clinic at the Town House Motel on business changes ahead in South Dakota over the next five years.

He's happy in his hometown and he has truly made it big.

◆ ◆ ◆

Bob is author of more than 80 articles on the rental business. During the last five years he wrote an article each month for Rent All, a national magazine based in Duluth, Minn., which suspended publication earlier this year.

He enjoyed doing the articles—at $175 a piece—but is glad that he doesn't have to face a monthly deadline any more.

That association led to Ron Brochu, the former editor of Rent All, writing a three-page article profiling Elmen and his family business operation for a rival publication, Rental Equipment Register. The article was carried in its July issue.

Bob is pictured on the cover of Rental Equipment Register, with one little gliche, repeated inside: the magazine put him in Sioux City, S.D.

National publications have a hard time keeping Sioux Falls and Sioux City, North and South Dakota, the Black Hills and other geographical fixtures of this region straight.

Like the futurist authors he reads, Bob is thinking five years ahead about more business changes. Meantime, he likes what he and his brother, Jim, vice president of Elmen Rent All Inc., are doing with their various enterprises.

The Elmen businesses are deep into computers, as anyone who's been in one of their stores lately knows. A customer gets his itemized bill on a power sander or section of scaffolding in a flash.

But Bob, who optimistically sees a potential market of 9,000 rental stores in the United States for the computer system programs his stores use, has no plans to start running a computer himself.

He's too busy.

MR. BOOKSTORE
He's turned life's pages forward for many a SDSU student

Argus Leader, Oct. 30, 1983

There are many vignettes from the past crowding through Mel Henrichsen's mind this weekend in Brookings.

He's thinking about his retirement coffee party Monday afternoon to note his 38 years working for his alma mater, South Dakota State University. He's 69.

Memories have come crowding in about a variety of jobs he's handled for SDSU in addition to his main job of directing the Student Association Bookstore.

There was the time right after World War II when Henrichsen was managing housing for returning GIs, fitting them into house trailers and converted barracks according to the size of their families.

"I'll never forget one morning when a student came to me and said his wife had just delivered twins—and they needed a bigger apartment.

"We worked it out," Henrichsen said. He arranged a quick move from their one-bedroom apartment to larger quarters.

During the years he was resident manager of Eastmen's and Brown Hall dormitories, telephone calls sometimes awoke him and wife Al Vina in the middle of the night.

Henrichsen became the messenger of bad news, telling students that a family member had died in an automobile accident, from a heart attack or, occasionally, suicide.

The messenger's job didn't end there. Henrichsen sometimes accompanied a student home, helping him meet family members or attending the funeral. Such tasks weren't difficult for Henrichsen, partly because of his lay work in his church.

It has been said many times on State's campus that Mel and Al Vina Henrichsen have probably touched the lives of more students than any other couple. No matter what his job, both have tried through the years to give students a helping hand.

❖ ❖ ❖

One former student at SDSU told me that he would never have made it through four years at Brookings if it hadn't been for Henrichsen and the credit he extended at the bookstore for books and supplies.

Henrichsen is one retailer who hasn't had any trouble with credit, nor with bad checks.

Mel Henrichsen.

"We still issue credit to needy students," he said. "We carry about $30,000 to $35,000 on credit each semester." There is no carrying charge.

"We close out very few accounts for non-payment. It's the same with checks. It's unbelievable how many checks we cash. We will end up a year sometimes with only $100 or $120 in bad checks."

Henrichsen said the lack of credit and check problems is a reflection of the good people heritage of the students.

One of Henrichsen's biggest surprises since arriving on the State campus as a student in 1933 is the increase in the cost of text books: "Unbelievable. Just like breakfast food."

He recalled paying $3, $5 or $6 for books when he was a freshman. Today, the average book costs $25 and many go up to $35 or $40.

That accounts for part of today's annual bookstore sales topping $1.5 million, a volume that is another surprise to Henrichsen. It may be compared with yearly grosses of $30,000 to $50,000 in an earlier era.

Another factor is a 10-fold increase in enrollment in 50 years to more than 7,000 students.

A campus bookstore, of course, has some things going for it. Henrichsen said that college students like to buy T-shirts for younger brothers and sisters, as well as themselves. This accounts for up to $150,000 of the yearly volume.

Books make up 60 percent of sales, and supplies, sweat shirts, T-shirts, etc., 40 percent.

Today's bookstore in the Student Union has 10,000 square feet of retail space, compared with 3,500 square feet in the former Pugsley Union.

Henrichsen has relied on 30 to 35 part-time employees to supplement five full-time people in the bookstore.

The National Association of College Stores in 1970 named Henrichsen College Store Manager of the Year, a distinction that meant a great deal to him.

Another activity he enjoyed was being state chairman for about 12 years of the Lutheran Layman's League This is the Life program. He and his wife traveled throughout the state.

The Henrichsens have lived in South Dakota all their lives. He was born at Altamont, S.D.; she was born in Sioux Falls. He taught at Elkton and later worked in Watertown. He joined State in 1945 as director of the Student Union. She has taught at Altamont, Clear Lake and Arlington. They have two sons, Melvin, Terre Haute, Ind., and Dean, Rapid City, and three grandchildren.

❖ ❖ ❖

There were other honors for Henrichson and his wife this weekend.

During halftime at the State-U game yesterday, the band dedicated its performance to Henrichsen.

Friends are setting up a Mel and Al Vina Henrichsen Scholarship Fund through the Greater State Fund. Several scholarships will be awarded, as earnings permit.

Priority will go to a Student Association Bookstore Honors Scholarship, for a student employee of the bookstore. Other scholarships will include an athletic one, a Mt. Calvary Lutheran Church Scholarship recognizing the Henrichsens' service to their church and an achievement scholarship.

Walt Conahan, SDSU director of development, said: "We have established the scholarship to recognize the faithful service and friendship by the Henrichsens to thousands of students and alumni of SDSU to whom they have given so much of themselves over the years."

That's a fine tribute for two South Dakotans who've spent their lifetimes in their home state.

RETIRING REA HEAD'S HAPPIEST JOB MOMENT: WHEN RATES CUT 25%

Argus Leader, Sunday, Jan. 15, 1984

Virgil Herriott, who retires Wednesday as general manager of Sioux Valley Empire Electric Association, can't remember whose idea it was to use a circus tent for the REA's annual membership meetings at Colman.

But he clearly remembers the reason: a very hot day in the park east of Flandreau in June 1953 when sunburn was one of the by-products of the meeting.

The tent has been a staple of Sioux Valley's annual membership meetings ever since. Herriott said the idea must have resulted from the REA staff's group think sessions.

Oddly enough, there has been only one time in the last 30 years that it rained all day and all evening for an annual meeting. That was last June.

Another time in the early or mid-1960s, a 9-inch afternoon deluge on a Sunday afternoon in June left water standing in the northeast corner of the tent—but the rest of it was dry for the Monday meeting. Herriott recalled that one REA colleague brought his motor boat for rides on the REA grounds.

✦ ✦ ✦

Staff and employee participation has been characteristic of Herriott's management style since he started the job Jan. 19, 1953. Managing Sioux Valley Electric has never been a one-man show, an associate of his said. The REA is South Dakota's largest, with 10,000 members. It is considered one of the nation's best managed cooperatives.

Herriott said he's had a lot of happy moments on the job. One of the happiest was in 1958, when the REA reduced rates by 25 percent. "It didn't seem like it at the time, because a reduction of that size didn't mean as much then as now. During the last 10 years we have had to raise rates almost annually, although we've gone 22 months without a rate increase.

"There have been many other joys, too: especially the idea that we could bring something as important as electricity to people to help them in their daily lives."

Herriott said that financing problems will always be a part of the future for rural electrics. "Consumers' reaction to higher costs ultimately will work its way out as people realize that other forms of energy increase in cost as much as electricity."

Storms bring crises to any rural electric, but Herriott said there's an important difference from yesteryear in the dependence of people on electricity.

"Thirty years ago a four-, five- or 10-hour loss of service was inconvenient. Today, it's a catastrophe." Herriott said the goal must be to provide better continuity of service despite problems from the weather.

❖ ❖ ❖

Throughout his career at Sioux Valley, Herriott has taken a wide and continuing interest in community and area development. Sioux Valley under his guidance provided office space and other assistance for area rural water groups when they began their development.

A co-worker said that Herriott had encouraged innovation, including testing of new laminated poles manufactured from wood chips and had shown a keen interest in alternate forms of energy.

Herriott has participated in various rural electric and related regional associations and served on many boards and commissions. He kept in close touch with state and national legislators, and helped foster programs bringing urban legislators, such as House Speaker Tip O'Neill, to the South Dakota countryside.

A transport pilot during World War II, Herriott saved his time and that of associates by piloting Sioux Valley's plane from an airstrip east of Colman. He racked up more than 4,000 hours as a pilot but hasn't flown for about a year since the REA sold the plane.

"I miss flying," he said. "It takes more time to travel."

❖ ❖ ❖

Next Thursday, his longtime friend and associate, assistant manager James Kiley, whom he hired in 1953, will succeed Herriott.

Virgil and his wife, Ruth, will head their Cadillac for Tempe, Ariz. He wants to time their travel to avoid any more snow shoveling at this end, but return before South Dakota becomes green.

Three granddaughters, daughter Teresa and husband James Morse, who live in White Bear Lake, Minn., are another reason the Herriotts will be heading northward before springtime.

Herriott is looking forward to retirement because it will free him from the bounds of the clock and a workaday schedule. He has friends and family to visit, including his parents in Iowa.

There are some community responsibilities he wants to take care of, too, at Lake Poinsett where the Herriotts live.

He's chairman of the board of the Lake Poinsett Sanitary District. He hopes that engineering studies of the lake and its problems this year will lead to a wastewater collection system in 1985 or 1986. The project needs some volunteers and local support.

Another project that he's looking forward to is the Herriott Tricentennial Family Reunion: an event that he and several other individuals are trying to put together.

Virgil Herriott.

The first Herriott arrived from Scotland in what is now New Jersey in December 1685: Herriott said descendants want to hold either a national reunion or a series of regional family reunions in 1985.

Herriott said much depends on one of the descendants at Stanford University, who's working on his Ph.D. and has access to a computer.

Herriott started his REA career as a cashier-receptionist with the Guthrie County Rural Electric Cooperative at Guthrie Center, Iowa, in May 1946 when he returned from the service. He was manager of Codington-Clark Electric Cooperative in Watertown for 4½ years before joining Sioux Valley.

His association with REAs spans more than 37 years. That is the difference between doing line work by hand or using large bucket trucks—and office machines of long ago and today's computers.

"This has been a very satisfying career," Herriott reflected. There are thousands of REA members in South Dakota who would term it superlative.

GORDON OLSON VIEWS RETIREMENT LIKE LIFE'S WORK: POSITIVELY

Argus Leader, Sunday, March 18, 1984

Gordon Olson, who retires April 1 as secretary-manager of the Sioux Empire Fair, could give Norman Vincent Peale some tips on positive thinking.

Olson is also a booster, an expert in his own fields—particularly Chamber of Commerce and fair promotion—and a blithe spirit.

Sioux Falls knew it had a remarkable person in Olson when he served as executive secretary of the Junior Chamber of Commerce and then as assistant secretary of the chamber.

There was something about him—his forward look, his optimism and can-do spirit. That combination stayed with him from the first telephone call or public contact in the morning until the last one at night.

Spencer, Iowa, lured him away for four years as secretary of its Chamber of Commerce. He came back home in 1953 to manage the Sioux Falls Chamber and stayed 15 years. The chamber named him executive vice president.

He saw his favorite town expand mightily during the boom following World War II. He helped that growth in countless ways.

The big guy—he's 6-foot 2 and hope's he's holding at 230 pounds—delighted wheeling his tiny White TR3—a British sports car—around the city on his way to chamber meetings. Several years later he graduated to a silver Corvette Sting Ray.

"I wish I had both of them now," he said. "They'd be worth three or four times what I paid for them."

Olson later progressed to antique cars—a hobby that he might take up again.

He's as enthusiastic about retirement pursuits as he is about his job.

He's looking forward to doing some traveling, hunting and fishing and work in his yard. He's interested in photography, reading and a host of outside interests, including his church, the Nordland Fest and Augustana Fellows.

He and his wife, Phyllis, to whom he's been married 37 years, plan to do some traveling and make a trip to Florida.

But they won't be snowbirds. Olson figures that two weeks of the Sunbelt will be enough—and they'll be back home.

♦ ♦ ♦

"Gordie" Olson was a fine practitioner of Chamber of Commerce work. He liked both the inside and outside aspects of his job. Olson worked hard in mastering chamber procedure—and used his inborn enthusiasm to get things done.

He was one of the first 34 managers in the country to be named a Certified Chamber Executive, the highest recognition of the American Chamber of Commerce Executives. He was a member of the organization's board of directors for three years and served a year as secretary-treasurer.

He also served on the Board of Regents of the National Chamber Institute Program and on the faculties of chamber management institutes at the University of Montana and the University of Colorado.

Gordon Olson.

In 1968, the Chamber of Commerce of the United States persuaded him to become district manager for Ohio. In 1970, Olson became the chamber's manager of the Western Division, consisting of nine states including Hawaii and Alaska.

The job was interesting and vital—but there were some drawbacks to spending a lifetime on airplanes and in hotel lobbies while on the road to San Jose, Calif., where they lived.

"I was so lucky to be able to come back to my roots," he said. "I was in love with this city."

He became manager of the Sioux Empire Fair Jan. 15, 1978. The job fit Olson's knowledge of the community and area.

His new work was soon interrupted—when doctors in 1980 found a massive abdominal cancer. "It was a shock," Olson said.

One of his surgeons asked if he wanted a second opinion, from Rochester. Olson declined. He told me last week he had every confidence in Sioux Falls medical care.

He was away from work for 13 months, spent 127 days in the hospital and thought it probably was a good thing he didn't realize how sick he was. He never lost his optimistic outlook.

He credits Phyllis' encouragement—he called her a tower of strength—and the care and concern of doctors, nurses and many others with helping him to pull through. His last checkup—week before last—came out fine.

♦ ♦ ♦

Olson will be 62 Tuesday—and he's pleased by the many pursuits he can follow in retirement.

His working career has spanned 50 years—and he's never been unemployed.

"I started selling Argus Leaders when I was 12 years old. I sold papers at the corner of 12th and Phillips."

During World War II, Sgt. Olson of the Signal Corps routed messages in Gen. Douglas MacArthur's headquarters signal center in the Southwest Pacific. Olson was on MacArthur's journey back to the Philippines, starting in New Guinea.

Olson saw the general several times and remembers his corncob pipe. "He was tall, impressive, looked like a leader. I had a lot of respect for him." As it happened, Olson went to Okinawa from the Philippines. He missed seeing Tokyo.

◆ ◆ ◆

Why could Olson give Dr. Peale tips about positive thinking? For one thing, he's followed Peale's advice, gleaned from several of his books. Olson liked the message.

For another, Olson was greatly impressed by Dale Carnegie and his books, including How to Win Friends and Influence People.

Peale and Carnegie were the inspiration—but Olson has mixed that with his own brand of enthusiasm, nurtured in his hometown of Sioux Falls.

LAWYER HAS RECORD OF ACCOMPLISHMENTS
Argus Leader, May 14, 1986

When lawyers hold the annual meeting of the State Bar of South Dakota in Sioux Falls next month, some of them will probably talk about Mead Bailey.

Likely, they'll run down the list of contributions the retired Sioux Falls lawyer has made to the legal profession.

They'll tick off some of the following:

• Bailey's chairmanship of the bar's Public Information Committee between 1955-1961. He begged, borrowed or wrote pamphlets for public consumption on general legal matters and figured out a rack for their display in a law office.

• Originated the bar's Newsletter in 1956 and was its editor until 1961. His editorializing on controversial subjects resulted in some disagreements.

• Among other things, he backed having the Supreme Court hold sessions outside of Pierre, permitting its justices to live at their homes instead of requiring them to live in Pierre, having a full-time secretary-treasurer of the bar and revising the code of laws of South Dakota. All these ideas became fact.

• Served 22 years on the Statute Compilation Commission and its successor, the South Dakota Code Commission, from 1964 to 1986. He was the first chairman of the Compilation Commission and was vice chairman of the Code Commission.

Thanks to the two commissions, the state's law was revised to reflect accumulated changes between 1939 and 1966 and provide for updating the code on a continuing basis by publishing supplements and replacement volumes. It became much easier for lawyers and laymen alike to check current law.

Bailey is pleased by the continuity provided by Thomas R. Vickerman and his chairmanship of the Code Commission. Vickerman is code counsel of the Legislative Research Council.

• Originated South Dakota Barrister, publication of the South Dakota Trial Lawyers Association, in 1966 and was its editor through June 1985. He is now editor emeritus and contributes a column.

• Developed in 1973 an academic course for clinical training of senior law students of the University of South Dakota. He taught the course for 11 years as a professor on the School of Law faculty. During that period he looked after more than 325 students who interned for a semester or summer term in private or public law offices.

"The university law school hired me on a contract basis to just think it up," Bailey said of the clinical or intern course. "It was fascinating." He'd go out to lunch to discuss the intern plan

Mead Bailey.

with lawyers, asking them what they could and would do. The program started in Sioux Falls and after about a year spread westward to Rapid City.

"I went to Francis Dunn (then state Supreme Court chief justice) and asked him if we could please redraw the rule of student practice. I contacted Chief Judge Fred Nichol in Federal Court....so the intern could in effect practice in state or federal courts: intern versus intern....This was not moot."

As Dunn relates it, "Bailey put the course together and made it meaningful. The change (permitting an intern to try a case with the consent of the client) was a step ahead. It provided more interest for the intern."

Nichol, now U.S. senior district judge, said: "I thought it was probably the best clinical law program in the country. I wrote a letter about it to Chief Justice Burger. It is a very fine program and a practical one."

Cathy Piersol, a Sioux Falls lawyer, said of her internship under Bailey: "It was an excellent experience. He was very good about providing a good framework of knowledge about what is expected of you as a lawyer." Her assignment was to the Minnehaha state's attorney's office. She said the trial experience was a real good way to get to know the profession.

Bailey said getting a new group of interns three times a year and watching them develop was heartwarming. "It kind of kept me young, I think." He's 67.

The 1986 Legislature by joint resolution recognized Bailey's work on the commissions and his contributions to the legal system, law school, Legislature and the people.

Bailey's office these days is on the basement level of his home along Beaver Creek south of Brandon. His wife, Jean, who is an artist, works in her living room studio just above his office. He uses his computer to write his column for the Barrister and other articles on law office management.

His articles on office management have been widely reprinted in legal journals. One of them, Have You Called Yourself Up Lately? has appeared in more than 20 publications. The article deals with phone and office situations that irritate clients. Bailey developed an office management course for the law school.

He contends that the two deadly sins of the lawyering process are lack of communication and procrastination. He started the Newsletter and South Dakota Barrister out of a desire to improve communication.

As Dunn said of Bailey's practice in Municipal and Circuit Courts in Sioux Falls, he was always ahead of the pack in his challenges of the status quo.

The question for South Dakota lawyers is who's going to champion the kind of change Bailey has spurred along for so many years?

Profile

Name: Mead Bailey (Theodore Meade Bailey Jr.). Fourth-generation lawyer. Grandson of pioneer Sioux Falls lawyer C.O. Bailey, co-founder of Bailey and Voorhees law firm which is now Woods, Fuller, Shultz and Smith.

Date of birth: Jan. 15, 1919. Hometown: Sioux Falls.

Occupation: Retired since June 30. He was in private practice in Sioux Falls for 26 years starting in 1947. Was with Bailey, Voorhees, Woods and Fuller for about seven years, then entered practice for himself. Professor, University of South Dakota School of Law, 1974-1985.

Education: Graduate of North Hollywood, Calif., High School, 1937. B.A., Carleton College, 1941. J.D., University of South Dakota School of Law, 1947.

Family: Wife, Jean; son, Theodore Mead Bailey III, Boston; two daughters, Sallie Schott, Kansas City, Mo., and Alice Nervig, Nine Miles Falls, Wash.; four grandchildren.

Interests: Writing, reading, photography, "busted knuckle" home mechanics.

MINISTER'S FRIENDS, COLLEAGUES PAY THEIR LAST, LOVING RESPECTS

Argus Leader, Feb. 7, 1987

How do you say goodbye to a South Dakota Methodist minister who loved his work for the Lord, fought the good fight—and died all too soon on Jan. 31 at age 62?

With joy, great feeling and very few tears. At least, you didn't see many tears among 500 who turned out to pay their last respects to the Rev. Lloyd K. Grinager at his funeral service last Tuesday.

There were 35 ministers in the choir at First Methodist Church. The Rev. Glenn Hammerlee of Watertown directed his colleagues in hymns of hope and feeling: "It Is Well with My Soul" and "Blessed Assurance."

The Rev. John Jacoway read Grinager's obituary because the deceased a few days before his death said there is an important difference between something voiced during a funeral service or merely seen on the printed page.

Jacoway knew his subject well. He had succeeded Grinager as pastor of Wesley United Methodist Church in Sioux Falls last summer after Grinager's health failed. Grinager retired but continued as Wesley's associate pastor until his death.

The obituary related his birth at Canton April 2, 1924, graduation from Canton High School, his three years of World War II Army service, marriage to Dorothy Rasmussen of Parker, graduation from Augustana, theological training, love of family, and his lifetime of service in the Methodist Church.

There were many church assignments: in Harrisburg, S.D., and New York City and area as a student pastor, pastor of Asbury in Sioux Falls from 1952 to 1957 and of churches at Milbank, Pierre and Yankton. He was district superintendent in Rapid City from 1965 to 1971 and was executive director of the Methodist Foundation in Mitchell from 1974 to 1982. He returned to Sioux Falls in 1982 to be pastor at Wesley.

The Rev. Edwin C. Boulton, bishop of the United Methodist Church Dakotas Area, flew down from Fargo to give his tribute to Grinager. Said Boulton:

"There is something more excellent than extolling famous persons. The better thing is to recognize a truly good person, good as judged by excellence of character, charity in judgment,

Rev. Lloyd Grinager.

gentleness in demeanor, and inner strength which grows up out of one's faith in God, oneself and others."

"Such a person was Lloyd Grinager. He was an outstanding influence in the life of the South Dakota Annual Conference, the United Methodist Church here and beyond, and in the community at large."

The Rev. Richard O. Moberly, Huron, superintendent of the Northern District, said: "Lloyd was my dearest friend. We met while we were still in college, and we decided to attend seminary together. We lived with our spouses in the same run-down duplex near Drew Seminary, killed cockroaches together, washed clothes at the village laundromat while our wives struggled with first borns back at the house...."

"Lloyd was a leader. He led the churches he served with sound doctrine, a warm and caring concern for people, a strong stewardship emphasis, and a belief that God would win victories. He was a leader on behalf of pastors in devoting almost his entire ministry on the conference level to upgrading ministerial pensions and providing a better retirement for 'worn out' preachers, their wives and widows."

"Lloyd became director of stewardship in our conference. This gave him rich opportunities for sharing his principles of Christian stewardship in every United Methodist Church across the state. Many wills were written by people which have benefited our conference's institutions greatly under his influence and guidance...."

"He was above all a man of faith. He was a man of hope. He believed in victory beyond defeat, in triumph beyond tragedy....The world is richer because he lived, worked, and died in the faith of the Lord Jesus Christ."

Moberly noted that two of Grinager's sons are Methodist pastors in South Dakota, another is in seminary and a fourth son and his daughter are active lay persons in their churches. He praised Dorothy Grinager's roles as wife and mother and her contributions to the church.

She shook hands with hundreds at the lunch following the service. Many ministers, their wives and parishioners past and present recalled something special about her husband.

ANDERSON KNEW STATE INSIDE OUT

Argus Leader, Dec. 30, 1990

What was it about former Gov. Sigurd Anderson that made him so popular?

He put himself in the other person's place. He could relate to people from his own experiences in growing up in South Dakota following immigration from Norway with his parents when he was two years old.

He could speak only Norwegian when an older neighbor girl in 1910 walked him to start country school near Canton. He became a fine extemporaneous speaker and debater, a country school teacher and a teacher in Rapid City and Webster, which he made his legal home in 1932. He learned basic politics in Day County in successful campaigns for state's attorney. He was elected attorney general twice and governor twice.

Anderson lived in half a dozen places in South Dakota. He never forgot a friend, nor a new acquaintance's name. My first contact with him was along the campaign trail in 1948 when he was running for re-election as attorney general. I was a reporter for the Argus Leader. He asked me where I was from. I told him Maurine, a general store and post office between Faith and Newell. He knew a Maurine family I knew who had moved there years ago from Kingsbury County where he taught a rural school.

I recall his appearance in the early 1950s at the Republican tent at the Sioux Empire Fair. A woman in her 40s challenged him with, "I bet you don't know my name." She stumped him initially, but in a moment he told her her family name on the basis of facial resemblance. She had been a neighbor years before in Lincoln County.

Sigurd Anderson.

Anderson confounded political experts during the 1950 Republican primary when he won the governor's nomination with slightly more than the required 35 percent of the vote in a field of five. He talked philosophically in an interview with this writer in July 1953, during his second term as governor.

Anderson said: "We in South Dakota don't conduct government on a striped pants basis at all. The governor of South Dakota has to be able to talk to the cowboy, the miner, farmer and rancher, businessman and housewife. And sometimes you have to say it in Norwegian."

"South Dakota is a small population state and the people are still the good neighbor type. When I was elected governor, I told the people to come and see me. They surely have."

There was no pretense in Anderson or his wife, Vivian. What you saw was what you got. They were friendly, direct and gracious. The most exciting personal news of the Andersons' life in the governor's mansion was the birth of their only child, Kristin Karen, in 1954 after 17 years of marriage. His wife died in 1981.

Anderson had two major political disappointments. In 1962 Republicans selected Joe Bottum over Anderson and others to fill the vacancy caused by the death of U.S. Sen Francis Case. In 1964 Anderson resigned as Federal Trade commissioner to try again for the governor's office. He lost the nomination to Nils Boe, who as governor appointed Anderson a circuit judge.

My last visit with Anderson was a year ago last summer in his hotel room at Webster. He had almost total recall—and pertinent comments on current events. Over coffee and cake Anderson quipped that Democrat Joe Robbie, whom he defeated for governor in 1950, owed him one. Otherwise, Robbie probably wouldn't have gone on to fame and fortune as owner of the Miami Dolphins.

Anderson enjoyed many honors in his retirement years. A state office building in Pierre was named for him in 1975. Webster renamed its city airport for him in 1989. A state historical marker on Highway 12 at Webster has long hailed Anderson as the city's and Day County's most distinguished citizen. The one-room country schoolhouse in which Anderson taught in 1927-28 is on the grounds of the Laura Ingalls Wilder Memorial Society at De Smet.

Anderson died in Webster at age 86 on Dec. 21; his service was held there Friday.

HISTORY BUFF PUSHES IDEA OF LIVING-HISTORY FARM FOR S.D.

Argus Leader, Sunday, Oct. 9, 1994

Mel Thorne, Brookings oxen team owner and history buff, dreams of the day when tourists and school children will visit a Dakota Living History Museum at Fort Pierre.

At age 77, he wants to give something back for the life he's enjoyed in South Dakota. That something is a better understanding of the heritage of his home state. He believes that young people would be inspired by seeing actors portray Native Americans and pioneers of Dakota Territory in natural settings along the Missouri River.

He has no land to sell for the museum. He has no organization, but said one is needed.

He's not looking for federal or state help. He's looking for interest, not money. "I don't worry about where the money is coming from. If people get excited about it, it will happen," Thorne said.

He said Fort Pierre, only 32 miles from Interstate 90 at Vivian, could tap a constant stream of tourists bound for Yellowstone National Park. The museum would prompt most of those who stopped to stay an extra day in South Dakota, thus adding to tourist revenue.

Fort Pierre has historic advantages. It's in an area that was inhabited by Arikara (or Ree) Indians. They tilled crops between 1600 and 1792. Fort Pierre started as a fur trading center in the last century. It was a shipping point for wagon trains for the Black Hills.

Thorne's plan envisions Indian tribes joining with other groups to present exhibits. He said, "I have talked to all the tribes in the state. They can do their own thing, sell their wares."

Tourists could see how Indians lived in villages along the Missouri and on the Plains. They could view fur traders bargaining for pelts and homesteaders plowing the plains.

Mel Thorne in garb of a Dakota Territory Pioneer.
—Anson Yeager photo

They could visit a school and church, a homestead and the home of a newly arrived immigrant family. There would be a log cabin, a store and blacksmith shop.

Tourists could join narrators in performing frontier or farm tasks. Children could observe farm animals and attend a class in a frontier school. A visit would take about four hours.

Thorne has studied virtually every facet of frontier life from the food people ate to care of livestock. Oxen, for instance, were superior to horses for pulling wagons because, unlike horses, they needed no feed supplement for heavy work. He and his wife, Arlyce, drive their team of four oxen at various events. The team was in South Dakota's Centennial wagon train.

Thorne in talking to South Dakota groups these days dresses like a pioneer: big hat, boots, loose fitting cloth shirt, neckerchief, suspenders and work trousers.

He has a wealth of South Dakota lore gained from his own career.

He was born at Stickney and lived on his grandparents' farm at Mount Vernon. He played football at Philip and Lead High Schools. He also caught the attention of the J.C. Penney Co. manager at Lead who put him to work after school, starting him at 20 cents an hour. That led to a 10-year management career with Penney's in South Dakota and region after his graduation from Lead High School in 1935.

He opened Thorne Clothing Co. in Gettysburg in 1945 and soon started selling mobile feed mills. He saw the mills as a way for farmers to increase their income and his clothing store sales by feeding livestock. He operated the store into the 1950s. He became the nation's first franchiser of campgrounds in 1961 when he started Camp Dakota. A camp near Salem was the first; Camp Dakota near Hartford, the second of about 35 campgrounds. He got out of that business in 1974.

Thorne donated two years of his talent, time and labor to building the South Dakota Centennial Pioneer Cabin in Brookings' Pioneer Park. The project was financed by donations.

ENOCH L. SCHETNAN

A previously unpublished essay by the author

Enoch L. Schetnan, Editor and Publisher of the West River Progress at Dupree and the Eagle Butte News, was one of South Dakota's most remarkable country editors. He was deaf and had never heard the English language spoken, but through perseverance and sheer guts, he found ways to report the news by writing notes to people he interviewed. He took strong editorial stands. Some of his readers said that he did a better job of reporting than many editors who had their hearing. Schetnan was born at Fevaag, near Trondheim, Norway, on May 9, 1884. He lost his hearing when he became sick aboard ship en route to the United States. He attended the School for the Deaf at Vancouver, Washington, and later St. Olaf College at Northfield, Minnesota. Enoch married Cora Reed on June 18, 1909, and moved to South Dakota the next year to homestead near Dupree. In 1921 they moved to Red Elm, where he published the Red Elm Record, which later became the West River Progress.

This writer met Mr. Schetnan in Faith about 1936, when Schetnan was setting type on the Faith Gazette as a trade for setting type for his Dupree paper. Later, Mr. Schetnan purchased his own linotype. The author worked for Mr. Schetnan in the summer of 1939 and put out his paper while he took a vacation. By this time, Schetnan had acquired the Eagle Butte News. Its office, in Eagle Butte, had room for a two page press and some other equipment. This writer recalls that after putting out the West River Progress, Mr. Schetnan and I would take the morning Milwaukee train from Dupree to Eagle Butte. We carried galleys of type to the railroad station and took them aboard the caboose for the ride to Eagle Butte. At Eagle Butte we made up the front and back page of the Eagle Butte News and printed the paper on a two page press. We put the paper in the post office before returning to Dupree on the evening train. (The train was the Mobridge-Faith branch line, which at the time ran a train each way.)

Schetnan had a newsy paper with many personal items about his subscribers and news of Dupree and area. He was a strong Republican and it showed in his writings.

The following is excerpted from the Dec. 26, 1957, West River Progress.

Mr. Schetnan published the West River Progress in Dupree for 23 years and the Progress, which reported his death on Dec. 19, 1957, had this sidelight:

Mr. Schetnan, not being able to converse with anyone except by those knowing the deafs' finger language, worked alone. In spite of the tremendous amount of work involved in not only publishing his paper, but also supplying local business people with stationery, etc., he never missed publishing an issue, with the exception of the time when he was injured in a car accident a few months ago.

Mr. Schetnan was keenly interested in South Dakota's education for the deaf and followed the state's handling of deaf education matters closely.

E.L. Schetnan.

NATIONAL GUARD, MILITARY

"JUSTY" STARTS NEW CHAPTER AFTER 37 YEARS IN COCKPIT

Argus Leader, Sunday, June 22, 1980

What do you do when you're a brigadier general, retired, with 11,000 hours of flying to your credit?

You think about the fabulous men and women in the 114th Tactical Fighter Group which you've commanded since 1966, those overseas Air Guard trips and the readiness role of the outfit in U.S. defense planning.

And with your 58th birthday coming up July 22, you think about your home, 30 acres and a dozen horses south of Sioux Falls, where you can do some riding and other things and enjoy retirement with your wife, Pat.

Gen. Justin Berger is comfortable and happy about recent milestones in his life. One was his confirmation as a general officer by the U.S. Senate on May 29 (he had been a bird colonel since 1968). Another was his retirement from the South Dakota Air National Guard on June 12.

That was the day he took his last military flight, leading four A7D fighters to Volk Field, Wis., and its gunnery range. They rendezvoused later over Hartford, S.D., with three South Dakota fighters which had flown to Salina, Kan. They lined up over Hartford for the flyby over Joe Foss Field.

The reception ceremony on the field with personnel waiting for a fond farewell, saw him doused with a fire extinguisher loaded with champagne. And at 4:30 that afternoon there was a small change of command ceremony in the office, in which Lt. Col. John Olson took over the group.

There was another event Wednesday night—an informal retirement party at the Air Guard Base at Joe Foss Field—which heightened his good feeling about starting a new chapter in life.

Daughter Becky, married to a Coast Guard officer who is stationed in Ponce, P.R., was home for that and a 10-year class reunion.

Maj. Gen. and Mrs. Duane L. Corning ("Duke" and Cathy) were among the guests. "Duke," of course, helped Joe Foss, now in retirement in Arizona, organize the Air Guard in Sioux Falls after World War II. Corning is adjutant general of the South Dakota National Guard.

Looking back, "Justy," as nearly everyone in and out of the Air Guard calls him, never thought he'd get his general's star. Back when he joined the Air Guard in 1947 as a second lieutenant, "Everybody was on top," he said.

As a lieutenant, he was one of the original members of General Foss' acrobatic team, the "Red Devils."

And now, after 37 years in the cockpit, it seems hard to give up flying.

Berger enlisted in the Army Air Corps in September 1942, entered pilot training the next year and was commissioned in 1944. He served as an instructor in P40 and P38 fighters.

He has qualified in perhaps 18 or more airplanes. He praises the A7D in which he made his last military flight and which he flew to Norway in 1977. "That is the most capable airplane I have ever flown," Berger says.

The fighter, used for air to ground support, carries computer and other equipment which lets a pilot set the map coordinates and leave the heading and other calculations to black box wizardry.

GIs of South Dakota's 196th Regimental Combat Team display their unit designation at Seattle before embarking for voyage to Haines, Alaska, in July and August 1951. —U.S. Army photo

That technical expertise was within three or four miles of pinpointing the location of Rygge, Norwegian Air Force base south of Oslo, which was a 4,000-mile nonstop destination from Joe Foss Field.

"We left Sioux Falls (in the fighter planes) at 1:30 a.m. in the morning and got to Norway at 4:30 their time, that afternoon," Berger said.

He recounted the thrill pilots never cease to have in sighting landfall: Newfoundland south of Gander, northern England and the continent. Greenland, Iceland and Norway were socked in.

The fighters were refueled four times en route. They landed in an overcast and below minimum field conditions at Rygge. That feat amazed the Norwegians, who had some doubts about utilizing reserve units in their Air Force.

Most of the 350 South Dakota Air Guard personnel made the flight to Norway in Starlifter transport planes. Part of the military freight was 600 pounds of sirloin tips, which the Air Guard barbecued for Norwegian guests. They enjoyed that South Dakota treat.

One hundred Norwegian relatives of the Air Guard contingent showed up at the barbecue. Over half of the South Dakota Air Guard personnel had relatives in the country. Many family ties were renewed during the 17-day encampment.

Both Berger and his wife have relatives in Norway, whom they hope to meet next spring. Part of the joy of retiring is planning for that trip to Norway, which they'll make with Harry and Faith Tunge, Air Guard friends of many years. Mrs. Tunge has relatives in Norway, too.

Berger hopes to renew acquaintances with the Rygge base commander, Brig. Gen. Thurmann Nielsen, now retired and whom he's seen a couple of times since the Air Guard's tour in Norway.

Berger's last international duty was at Cold Lake, Canada, northeast of Edmonton, in May. "Maple Flag" was an exercise to train air crews in the techniques of surviving their first five or 10 combat sorties.

Air Guard defense assignments in Panama (three in the last year or so), two tours in Alaska and active duty training in Italy were part of Berger's routine during the 1970s. In Panama the Air Guard was the backup for the United States in the Nicaraguan crisis.

Berger sees continued reliance on the Air Guard during the future. He says the cost effectiveness and lower cost of maintaining units of citizen airmen and women, in contrast to the higher cost for regular Air Force outfits, will guarantee the Air Guard's defense role for years to come.

Brig. Gen. Justin Berger.
—S.D. Air National Guard photo

He also believes that Defense Department plans for increased reliance on the National Guard and reserves will call for greater understanding by private employers of the sacrifices reservists make. These include using their own vacation time for annual Guard duty and being at their country's call ahead of family plans or a company's requirements.

Berger's praise and feeling for the dedication and expertise of his Air Guard personnel are deep and well-founded. He's proud of their spirit, their performance and their loyalty. And he also worries about the problems of the regular military in today's times.

The Air Guard, for instance, has consistently been just below full strength, somewhere in the range of about 90 to 95 per cent. Guard equipment is older than that in the Air Force, but personnel are experienced and turnover is slight.

That situation has required considerable work and recruiting effort by the Air Guard through the years. The retention rate of the 114th is one of the highest in the nation.

Regular Air Force units, on the other hand, have later planes and other equipment, but officer and noncommissioned ranks often lack experience or the right numbers because turnover is higher. Many pilots and technicians have left the regular military forces in recent months because pay and benefits don't match what they can earn in civilian life.

Berger will be thinking about things like that in the months to come. There'll be no more rising early to be on the base at Joe Foss Field shortly after 7 a.m. to check maintenance, operations and supply.

There'll be time to ride his favorite horses and enjoy retirement just outside his home town—a way of life that General and Mrs. Berger have already found enjoyable.

And likely, "Justy" will also have an eye and an ear tuned skyward. That comes from years of flying everything from World War II's propeller planes to today's jets.

It also comes from thinking about the 800 men and women who make the 114th Tactical Fighter Group such a proficient military team.

If the need had occurred, they would have followed "Justy" anywhere. And as it happened, many of them saw a lot of the world with General Berger.

FOSS HAPPY SPREADING "THE WORD"
Argus Leader, Tuesday, Jan. 6, 1981

If any flier ever had God or Jesus as his co-pilot, it would have to be Joe Foss whose interest in Christianity turned from largely ceremonial to intense about 10 years ago.

Bob Lee, editor of the Sturgis Tribune and Black Hills Press for the last 20 years, has written a fascinating update about Foss's continuing interest in Christianity. Lee was executive secretary for Foss when he was governor of South Dakota from 1955 to 1959.

Lee chronicled the appearance of Foss before the Christian Businessmen's Committee in Sturgis in his editor's notebook column in the Tribune. Foss spoke there in early December.

The column also happens to be one of Lee's last efforts for the Tribune. That paper and the Press were sold effective Jan. 1 by publisher Morris Hallock to Vernon Allison of the Allison Publishing Co. in Sturgis. The Tribune has been merged into Allison's Meade County Times published at midweek; the Press continues publication on Saturday.

Lee's journalistic efforts will continue, however, in The Tri-State Livestock News of which he is editor. The weekly livestock paper is published by Black Hills Publishers, Inc., which owned the Tribune and Press and which Hallock heads.

Here are some extracts, condensed in places, from Lee's column:

Ex-Gov. Joe Foss feels that he's a changed man since he "got religion." But he sounded like the Joe we've always known when he began telling stories on himself. Foss has never claimed to be a polished speaker, but he has a charisma that sets him apart as an outstanding story teller.

You get to know a fellow pretty well when you work for him so closely in such a pressure position (as executive secretary while he was governor), and we saw him function under all kinds of circumstances. He made enemies, as all those in politics somehow manage to do, but he has always been widely admired and respected even by those who don't share his political views. He still is, simply because he's such a likable guy.

Joe told his Sturgis audience that he always considered himself a Christian. (We recall that he taught Sunday School in the Methodist Church at Pierre while he was governor.) But he confided that he really didn't accept Christ as his Saviour until recent years when he faced death (for the umpteenth time) and eluded it. Since then, he's figured God must have had a purpose for his life and he guessed it to be "spreading the word." That's what Joe's been doing, in his own inimical style, in recent years.

Joe faced death many times in World War II when he became the first ace to equal Eddie Rickenbacker's World War I record of 26 enemy planes shot down, and won himself the Congressional Medal of honor as a Marine Corps pilot in the Pacific.

Joe's own account of how he was shot down during the war and forced to ditch his plane in the wide Pacific is so graphic that listeners almost feel they're in the plane next to him. But there was no co-pilot in his Grumman fighter. It was an especially traumatic experience for Joe

Joe Foss, right, and Yeager reminisce in editor's office. —© John Danicic, Jr., The Argus Leader

because he couldn't swim and was kept afloat by the Mae West (life jacket) that was standard gear for all pilots.

(A native saw Foss' plane crash near an island. The native notified a Belgian priest. They pulled him out of the water at night and hid him from the Japanese until an American seaplane picked him up.)

Foss opines that he wouldn't have survived if that lone pair of eyes on the island hadn't seen his plane going into the sea. But he now believes somebody else was watching, too.

The former Marine hero had some narrow escapes after the war, too, when he and Duke Corning, now adjutant general of the South Dakota National Guard, ran a charter airplane service out of Sioux Falls. He told about the time he crash landed at night on a newly-sodded lawn on the outskirts of Minneapolis during a storm, and it was an exciting story, too.

It was a few years ago (while he was filming an episode for his national television show— Joe Foss, Outdoorsman—) that Joe became deathly sick and a whole corps of specialists couldn't diagnose his illness. Joe was near death when it was discovered that he had been accidentally poisoned. He recovered and got back into shape by quitting smoking (he was an inveterate cigar smoker during his war service and while governor) and adopting the Canadian Air Force's regimen of physical exercise.

Now, at 64, Foss is as trim as a halfback in the American Football League of which he was commissioner after his stint as governor. He's still a good looking guy with curly black hair, softened a mile by streaks of gray, who looks more like a movie star than a rugged ex-war hero and grass roots politician.

Joe was stricken some time later with what he feared was a heart attack and was rushed to a military hospital (in Texas). He was somewhat apprehensive when the doctor attending him there turned out to be Japanese. He figured the doctor may have known about Joe knocking 26 of his former countrymen out of the skies during World War 11.

But as it turned out, the doctor, now an American citizen, was a man of integrity as well as competence and Joe fully recovered. His illness was traced to a serious virus rather than to a faulty heart.

After so many brushes with death, and at the urging of his wife, Joe began going to church more regularly and listening to the sermons with more intensity and thought than ever before. It was during this time that he realized God had a mission for him, and he began spreading "the Word" in talks all over the country.

Joe's speeches, while not polished, are colorful and he has a knack for graphic description. For instance, he described his mother (now dead) as having a face that looked like it had been carved out of a redwood stump. We knew his mother and it was a perfect description of her classic pioneer countenance.

Joe doesn't sermonize as most ministers do, and he doesn't try to force his religious beliefs on anybody. He just tells what's happened to him throughout his life and how he's convinced there is a God in heaven looking out for all of us—if we just turn to Him.

We've heard Joe give talks before Black Hills audiences at least three times during the past year. Each time he told how happy he was to be here, and how grateful he was (and is) for every day God gives him. He exudes joy and faith, and he isn't bashful about sharing it.

If Joe had campaigned as effectively for himself while in politics as he now does for the Lord, he'd still be governor today. But he wouldn't be anywhere near as happy. Praise the Lord!

◆ ◆ ◆

And thank you, Bob Lee, for that glimpse of Joe Foss. He's one of those rare individuals who is a legend in his own lifetime and absolutely unspoiled by fame.

Foss's credits are too numerous to mention here. But he was the co-founder (with Corning) of the South Dakota Air National Guard. Joe Foss Field is named for him. And so is a state office building in Pierre.

Foss was feted in Sioux Falls May 16, 1975, at a dinner recognizing his retirement as brigadier general from the National Guard. That was a nostalgic evening of anecdotes and toasts.

Foss still flies his own plane when he's in a hurry, which is most of the time. He is public affairs director for KLM Royal Dutch Airlines. His office is in New York; his home is in Scottsdale, Ariz.

Foss also has a summer home on Sand Creek west of Spearfish which he frequently visits. He's in and out of Sioux Falls occasionally—and always on the run to another destination.

S.F. NATIVE GOVERNOR OF WAKE ISLAND

Argus Leader, Sunday, March 7, 1982

When collect phone calls from amateur civilian or military radio operators reach the Rapid City home of Sandy Rayl and daughters Wendy, 10, Heather, 8, and Becky, 6, they're quickly accepted.

They know that the military governor of Wake Island is on the line. He's Capt. Thomas J. Rayl, calling home on a radiotelephone patch to talk to his family.

Rayl, a native of Sioux Falls and a 1966 graduate of Worthing, Minn., High School, has one of the U.S. Air Force's more unusual one-year assignments.

As governor of Wake Island—which is important for its airstrip—he manages the affairs of the installation and governs its population, usually 200 to 225 residents.

The telephone calls to Rapid City, however, are not official business. They supplement U.S. mail which provides a constant exchange of information and souvenirs between the captain on Wake Island and his family in Rapid City.

The postman about two weeks ago delivered four boxes of colored slides and a tape in which Rayl narrates the island's scenic attractions.

The island has an area of 2½ square miles in the shape of a horseshoe, 12 miles of coast line, some palm trees and nice homes. The land is the coral outcropping of an extinct volcano.

You can look in any direction and see water. The scenery is both lovely and desolate.

There are no sandy beaches—but the scuba diving is excellent. There are remnants of the Japanese occupation during World War II, including bomb shelters, bunkers and tunnels.

Mail from Rapid City, Mrs. Rayl said, has included tapes of what the girls are doing at home, such as Becky's reading lesson and other activities. One of the souvenirs from Wake Island was a T-shirt for Mrs. Rayl, showing the outline of the island.

Rayl has orders to return to Ellsworth Air Force Base at the end of the year. Mrs. Rayl said the family hopes he will win assignment to the U.S. Air Force Academy from which he and his twin brother George were graduated in 1970.

Meantime, they're looking forward to Rayl becoming a major, possibly by May 1, and returning home on leave in late June for a couple weeks. His parents, Mr. and Mrs. J. R. "Bob" Rayl of Worthington, will be celebrating their 40th wedding anniversary.

Capt. Rayl was assigned as a B-52 pilot to Ellsworth Air Force Base in 1975. Since then the Rayls have been "civilians" for a year and a half at Purdue University where he obtained a master's degree in management. He left for Wake Island Jan. 2.

His assignment on Wake Island is on non-flying status with the Air Force's civil engineering branch.

❖ ❖ ❖

Rayl and his twin were born in Sioux Falls June 18, 1948, when their father, Maj. Rayl at the time, was with the 147th Field Artillery at summer camp in Rapid City. Papa arrived by plane on a weekend pass about 10 hours after their arrival.

The family was with Maj. Rayl in Alaska in 1951-52 when the South Dakota National Guard was on duty there during the Korean War. After their return, they moved to Worthington.

George Rayl left the Air Force in 1980 and is now flying a 737 for a commuter airline based in Newark, N.J.

Thomas Rayl's wife is the former Sandra Berger of Worthington. Her husband follows many military governors who've supervised Wake Island. It has been administered by the U.S. Air Force since 1972.

The U.S. flag was hoisted over Wake Island July 4, 1898, by Gen. F. V. Greene, commanding, the 2nd Detachment, Philippine Expedition. Formal possession was taken Jan. 17, 1899.

Wake, of course, is on the direct route from Hawaii to Hong Kong. It lies about 2,300 miles west of Hawaii.

During the 1930s, Wake Island assumed new importance as a landing strip for trans-Pacific flights. Following the attack on Pearl Harbor Dec. 7,1941, a gallant U.S. Marine garrison held off the Japanese for 14 days until Dec. 24, 1941. The Japanese surrendered the island to the United States Sept. 4, 1945.

President Harry S. Truman met Gen. Douglas MacArthur on Wake Island Oct. 15, 1950, for conferences, after MacArthur's forces had repelled the North Koreans from South Korea.

Many other American leaders have stopped at Wake Island for refueling on their way to and from Asia. Meeting or taking care of them is one of the duties that falls to the governor of Wake Island. Capt. Rayl is taking that chore in stride this year along with other duties and scuba diving.

MANN LEAVES GUARD AFTER LONG, DISTINGUISHED CAREER

Argus Leader, Sunday, Nov. 14, 1982

> *"Over hill, over dale, we have hit the dusty trail*
> *And those caissons go rolling along."*
> —From Edmund L. Gruber's "The Caisson Song," 1908

"The Caisson Song," with its "hi-hi-yee for the field artilleree," could well be Brig. Gen. Dean D. Mann's theme song.

He enlisted in Headquarters Battery of the 147th Field Artillery Battalion in Sioux Falls in 1949 while he was a junior at Washington High.

He was in the artillery until two years ago when he became assistant adjutant general for the South Dakota Army National Guard.

His two-year term as assistant AG ended Oct. 1. For the next two years Mann will be a general officer in the federal inactive reserve.

His comrades—active army and air guardsmen and retired ones, their wives and others totaling 367 guests—turned out a week ago Saturday night for a dress blue dinner at the armory in Mitchell to note Mann's retirement from the National Guard.

They praised his service. He said it was a team effort—and anything worthwhile that was accomplished resulted from the efforts of a lot of people.

Mann has been a consummate team player. There's no other way he could have done so much and worn so many hats through the years.

His praise at the Mitchell banquet for the support he had from wife Lorraine and daughter ReNae during his military career struck a familiar note with National Guard couples. "You need their support ... Lorraine and ReNae supported me," the general said.

The demands on a guardsman's time, aside from his regular vocation, are heavy.

❖ ❖ ❖

There was Fort Carson, Colo., and Alaska duty for Mann in 1950-52 during the Korean War. He was a fire direction sergeant and later operations sergeant. By the time the Berlin Crisis of 1961 rolled around with its year of active duty at Ft. Sill, Okla., he was a captain. He was promoted to major in 1963.

He served variously on the 147th Artillery Group staff as S-3 (plans officer) and later as executive officer (lieutenant colonel). He became commander of his old outfit, the 1st Battalion, 147th, in 1970.

Mann in 1976 received the Army Commendation Award for his work in guiding the battalion through nuclear weapons proficiency. The 1st Battalion was the first reserve component battalion in the United States to successfully complete this test. It is now standard for all artillery battalions.

He became commander of the 147th Field Artillery Brigade (and a bird colonel) in October 1977, a post he held until becoming assistant adjutant general.

He managed to find time to graduate from the Army's Command and General Staff School at Ft. Leavenworth, Kan. This included attending the U.S. Army Reserve School in Sioux Falls once a week, attending two weeks of classes each summer at Ft. Leavenworth for three years and eight weeks in 1973 when he graduated with honor. The Leavenworth classes were in addition to two weeks of summer camp.

Meantime, following graduation from Augustana College in 1957 he was successively a business education teacher at Washington High School, assistant track coach, and head track and cross country coach for nine years. He was cross country coach of the year in 1977 when his Orange and Black team won the state Class AA cross country title, ending Lincoln's seven-year reign.

He resigned from his coaching duties in 1979 when he became chairman of Washington High's Business Education Department. "There are seven of us in the department," Mann says. It's a team operation, too. He teaches shorthand, typing and senior office procedures.

❖ ❖ ❖

There aren't many perquisites in the South Dakota National Guard. Mann borrowed a staff car from the 1st Battalion at the Sioux Falls Armory when one was available. Otherwise, he headed his LTD across the state on inspection trips.

Mann said, "I tried on weekends or during annual summer training to visit every company and battery sized unit." Soldiers want to see their leaders, and vice versa.

Looking back, he says the good things from National Guard duty "were the people I have met and worked with. There's lots of patriotism and team work." He said the 1st Battalion's becoming the first nuclear qualified reserve outfit was team work.

Was he disappointed that Gov. William Janklow didn't reappoint him?

A bit, but it doesn't show.

"I have never regretted being in the National Guard," Mann said, acknowledging that it's difficult when part of a career ends. "I understand the system." He says his successor, Col. John Powell of Pierre, is a very excellent choice for assistant adjutant general for the Army National Guard.

"I appreciate Gov. Janklow's confidence in appointing me two years ago and I thank him for putting me into that position," Mann said.

Brig. Gen. Dean Mann.
—S.D. Air National Guard photo

♦ ♦ ♦

And what did Gen. Mann do last week?

For one thing, he flew to Colorado Springs to attend a seminar at the Air Force Academy on how committees can do a better job of screening applicants for appointment to the academy. Mann is chairman of Sen. Larry Pressler's committee which recommends selections for all the academies.

For another, Mann delivered the Veterans Day address at Mitchell on Thursday.

Friday, it was back to the high school classroom for this citizen soldier, age 50. He's done a great deal for state and country over the last 33 years—and inspired hundreds of students, military and otherwise, in the process.

This writer has to admit a certain prejudice in writing about Dean Mann, having been one of his battery commanders long ago and on the same dusty trail at many summer camps.

Well done, General!

EULOGY
CITIZEN-SOLDIER SCURR GAVE MUCH TO STATE AND COUNTRY

Argus Leader, Saturday, July 5, 1986

This is an appropriate weekend, following Independence Day, to remember a remarkable South Dakota citizen-soldier and engineer.

He was Col. Kenneth R. Scurr of Pierre, who died June 19 at age 90. His life spanned approximately the last 43 percent of the 210 years the United States has been a free country.

Scurr had a distinguished career as a bridge engineer. As a young engineer in the 1920s he helped South Dakota bridge the Missouri at Mobridge, Forest City, Pierre, Chamberlain and Wheeler. As state bridge engineer 30 years later, he directed construction of replacement bridges required by the dams across the Missouri.

His career was interrupted three times by military service during, World Wars I and II and the Korean War.

He left his engineering studies at Iowa State College in 1917, was commissioned from ROTC and served as a lieutenant in France with the 10th Field Artillery, 3rd Division.

He was called up as executive officer with South Dakota's 147th Field Artillery Regiment in 1940. He was with the unit and its successor from Fort Ord, Calif., to Australia, the East Indies and the Philippines. He was the regiment's acting commander when it was deactivated overseas in 1944; he then assumed command of the 147th Field Artillery Battalion. He served five years.

Scurr was inducted again in September 1950, as commander of South Dakota's 196th Regimental Combat Team. He led the unit during two years of active duty at Fort Carson, Colo., and Fort Richardson, Alaska. The 196th was part of the Alaskan defense force during the Korean War.

After World War I, Scurr returned to Iowa State to get his B.S. degree in civil engineering. He was excused from June 1920 graduation ceremonies so he could start work in March in Pierre for J. E. Kirkham, his former structures professor. Kirkham had been hired by South Dakota as a consultant to develop a bridge program to span the Missouri.

Scurr's recollections many years later for an oral history project were vivid. Scurr said, "The dominant personality throughout the program was Gov. Peter Norbeck. He pushed the necessary legislation through the Legislature to create the Highway Commission, retained Mr. Kirkham as bridge engineer and supported him at all times, both as to the location and financing arrangements to enable the bridges to be finished expeditiously." Controversy arose over the sequence in which the bridges would be built. Scurr recalled, "The basic legislation provided for a one-tenth mill levy, and the bridges were to be constructed only as funds became available. This would have stretched the construction period over eight or nine years."

Doane Robinson, state historian, proposed a plan for simultaneous construction of all five bridges which was accepted. The Legislature authorized communities along the roads leading to the bridges to advance funds to the State Bridge Fund; later they were reimbursed. All five bridges were opened by 1926 at a total cost of about $2.1 million. The bridge at Mobridge cost the least $339,123; the Pierre bridge, the most $461,124.

The federal government underwrote much greater costs for replacement bridges in the 1950s and 1960s as the Missouri River reservoirs began to fill. New bridges at Mobridge and Forest City (the Highway 212 crossing west of Gettysburg) cost approximately $4,500,000 each. The bridges were higher and longer—about 5,000 feet.

Col. Kenneth Scurr, commander of 196th Regimental Combat Team, embarks at Seattle on July 26, 1951, for voyage to Haines, Alaska, aboard the "Pvt. Sadao Manemorix. —U.S. Army photo

The Wheeler bridge spans were barged upstream to Chamberlain and twinned with its bridge spans on higher piers for local traffic to Oacoma. The Platte-Winner bridge and a 4,500-foot bridge over the Grand River for Highway 12 were added because of the dam program.

Scurr was civil and structural engineer with the state Highway Commission from 1921 to 1931. He became state bridge engineer in 1931. He returned to that position after World War II and Korean War duty. He retired in 1963 and was a consultant until 1968.

Scurr joined the South Dakota National Guard in 1921. He commanded Battery C of the 147th at Pierre from 1922 to 1938. Later he was a battalion commander before induction in 1940.

Back home in South Dakota after World War II, Scurr switched to infantry and became commander of the 196th when it was activated in 1946. The combat team was called to active duty in 1950 because of its excellent training record.

Scurr looked after his officers and men—whether guardsmen, draftees or reservists—and they responded in kind. He was at ease in escorting such top brass as Gen. Mark Clark or Gen. J. Lawton Collins, U.S. Army chief of staff, on inspections of the 196th.

Scurr was born Jan. 15, 1896, at Creston, Iowa. He married Lucille Pettyjohn Oct. 12, 1921, in Pierre. She survives him. He was preceded in death by their son, Kenneth R. "Bud" Scurr Jr., who died while serving in the U.S. Army.

Few South Dakotans have served their country and state so long and well as Col. Scurr. His devotion to duty and competence as a citizen soldier and state bridge engineer became legendary long before he left either role in retirement.

S.D. LOSES ANOTHER GOOD ONE

Argus Leader, Aug. 23, 1986

"We lost another good one."

South Dakotans who've served Uncle Sam and the state in the National Guard often use the expression when a comrade-in-arms dies.

Many friends are saying that about Robert D. Chalberg, who died at age 65 Aug. 16 at his home in Rapid City. Services were held there Wednesday at South Canyon Lutheran Church; burial with military honors was at Black Hills National Cemetery, Sturgis.

Chalberg is remembered in Sioux Falls and the area for his long service with the 147th Field Artillery Battalion and its successor, the 1st Howitzer Battalion of the 147th Artillery Group.

Chalberg joined the 147th Field Artillery Battalion in 1947, following its reorganization as a National Guard unit after World War II. He served as adjutant and became the unit's first full-time administrative assistant. He also served as a battery commander.

Those were the days when the 147th's Sioux Falls armory was in the Coliseum Annex on North Dakota Avenue. The annex, which later was destroyed in a fire, adjoined the Coliseum on its west side.

When the 147th was mobilized after the Korean War broke out in 1950, Capt. Chalberg commanded Canton's C battery on active duty at Camp Carson, Colo., and Fort Richardson, Alaska. He resumed his job as administrative officer in Sioux Falls in 1952 upon returning from active duty.

It was Chalberg's job as administrative officer to assist his battalion commander: first, Lt. Col. Orvel B. Swenson and later Lt. Col. Thomas R. Iverson.

Chalberg's duties included administration, supervision of caretakers in each battery, handling recruiting and working with the army advisor.

When howitzers rolled out of local armories for summer camp at Ripley in Minnesota, McCoy in Wisconsin, or Guernsey in Wyoming, Chalberg had a lot to do with planning and execution of the training exercise.

When the phone rang with directions from higher headquarters, Chalberg usually was the intermediary. He got the word to the troops. He lent many a helping hand to citizen-soldiers who had to juggle their military duties with their civilian occupations. He encouraged guard personnel who wanted to improve their military capabilities.

He was a cheerful individual who carried over Army engineers' can-do spirit from World War II to the day-by-day routine of administering an artillery battalion.

Chalberg transferred from Sioux Falls to South Dakota National Guard headquarters in Rapid City in 1963. He held various key state staff positions, including officer candidate school commandant at Camp Rapid, until 1976 when he retired from the National Guard. He attained the rank of colonel. He was Pennington County Civil Defense director from 1976 to 1980, when he retired.

After retirement he underwent multiple bypass heart surgery, a necessity and a challenge that he met confidently. The operation was successful and he subsequently enjoyed several good years with his wife, Helen, and family and friends. He was a good husband and father and a happy grandparent.

Chalberg belonged to that comparatively small group of South Dakota National Guardsmen who have been called up three times. His first was in 1941 when he was mobilized with

Madison's 109th Engineers. He was commissioned as a second lieutenant in 1942 and served in Europe during World War II.

His second active duty tour was during the Korean War. The third came in 1961 when the 1st Battalion was mobilized during the Berlin Crisis: The 1st served one year as school troops at the artillery school in Fort Sill, Okla.

Chalberg had many friends and was a good friend himself. He attended Sioux Falls College and was graduated from General Beadle State Teachers College (now Dakota State) in Madison. He taught and coached at Humboldt High School, his alma mater, before becoming the 147th's administrator in 1948. He enjoyed the camaraderie of a statewide acquaintanceship developed during his guard service.

He contributed much to the National Guard and its concept of reliance on citizen-soldiers to bolster the nation's preparedness. He helped make the system work.

Col. Robert Chalberg.

IVERSON WAS ALWAYS ON GUARD TO PROTECT STATE, COUNTRY

Argus Leader, Sunday, Sept. 26, 1993

Relatives and friends said goodbye Tuesday to Colonel Thomas R. Iverson, U.S. Army Retired, at East Side Lutheran Church and Hills of Rest Memorial Park.

He was buried within a few miles of his Route 2 farm, to which he returned three times after being called to service in World War II, the Korean War and the Berlin Crisis.

Our nation's military has been built upon the response of citizen-soldiers in time of national emergency. Iverson's service was remarkable, for which his fellow Americans owe him.

Friends remember him as an unflappable, thoughtful officer whose service in the South Dakota National Guard and the U.S. Army spanned 33 years. Officers and GIs alike could talk to the tall, lean commander who understood their problems and their Army jobs because he had done many of them himself.

Relatives remember him as a fine husband and kind father. He and his wife, the former Janet Brokaw of Sioux Falls, and family endured a great deal of living apart because of military service.

One of the family's crowning moments came two years ago this fall when Col. and Mrs. Iverson celebrated their 50th wedding anniversary at the Legion Hall in Valley Springs. Iverson proudly introduced their four children and their children to Guard and other friends.

He began his service with the Guard in 1931 as an enlisted man in Company B of the 109th Engineers at Brookings while attending State College. Two years later he enlisted in

Colonel Thomas R. Iverson, 1955 picture at Camp Ripley. —Gordon Guy photo

Headquarters Battery, 1st Battalion, 147th Field Artillery Regiment in Sioux Falls. He served in communication, the scout and instrument section, as mess sergeant and as first sergeant.

He was commissioned a second lieutenant Nov. 25, 1940, when the regiment was inducted into federal service. He transferred to the 31st Reconnaissance Squadron of the Air Corps in September 1941.

Iverson was promoted to major in February 1944. During service in Europe he was awarded, among other decorations, the Air Medal and Bronze Star and the French Croix DeGuerre with palm.

Iverson took a reduction in rank to captain to become Headquarters Battery commander in February 1947 in the reorganized 147th Field Artillery Battalion in Sioux Falls. He became battalion executive officer several months later. The unit was called up with the 196th Regimental Combat Team in 1950-52 for service in Ft. Carson, Colo., and Fort Richardson, Alaska during the Korean War.

Iverson became commander of the 147th Field Artillery Battalion in South Dakota in December 1952. The unit later became the 1st Howitzer Battalion in the 147th Artillery Group. He was the battalion's commander at Ft. Sill, Okla, in 1961 during the Berlin Crisis. It had batteries from Sioux Falls, Howard, Flandreau and Canton. He relinquished command in July 1964 when he accepted a promotion to colonel in the U.S. Army Reserve.

At the time Iverson retired from the National Guard, Brig. Gen. Duane L. Corning, adjutant general, in a letter of commendation praised his service as outstanding. Corning said Iverson had "demonstrated superb initiative, reliability and soundness of judgment" and that his "selfless devotion to duty has won the admiration and respect of all."

Corning noted that because of Iverson's supervision of training, administration and supply matters prior to entry into federal service during the Berlin crisis, the unit was able to complete all Army training tests in record time.

Iverson was born March 10, 1912, on the farm on which he died Sept. 18. He was graduated from Washington High School in Sioux Falls in 1930 and with a B.A. degree in economics from Augustana College in 1937. He and his wife were married Nov. 8, 1941, in Sioux Falls. He retired from farming in 1976.

COMMENTARY

BOOK CHRONICLES DIVERSIFIED ROLE OF "PEACE KEEPER FRONTIER POST"

Argus Leader, Sunday, Nov. 30, 1980

The officers and men of the U.S. Army, many of them Civil War veterans, who founded Fort Meade in 1878 could not have foreseen some of the missions their successors at the Black Hills military post would undertake.

Their immediate mission, of course, was to be Washington's deterrent against the Sioux Indians, held on the reservations in western South Dakota after Sitting Bull and his allies vanquished Gen. George Custer and part of his command in Montana in 1876.

The cavalrymen and infantrymen who were stationed at Fort Meade performed their mission very well. Their role earned for Fort Meade the title of "peace keeper frontier post. "

The 8th Cavalry rode out of Fort Meade in 1890 to intercept Big Foot's band of runaway Sioux near the Cheyenne River east of the post.

The Indians slipped away during the night for a tragic rendezvous at Wounded Knee with troopers of Custer's old command, the 7th Cavalry. They were sent to South Dakota from Fort Riley.

The last mission involving Indians for the Fort Meade garrison spanned 1906-1908. Not a shot was fired. The troopers caught up with a band of 400 Ute Indians in Montana who were on their way to the Cheyenne Indian Reservation in South Dakota.

Army officers persuaded the Utes to winter at Fort Meade. A year's lease arrangement on the Cheyenne Reservation didn't work. Again, Fort Mead officers persuaded the Utes, who also showed restraint, to quit the Cheyenne Reservation peacefully. The soldiers escorted the Utes back to Utah in 1908.

These roles and others are well told in articles written by Army personnel, Sturgis residents and South Dakota historians, including Bob Lee and the late Richard B. Williams of Sturgis.

The articles appear in a centennial commemorative book entitled "Fort Meade, Dakota Territory/South Dakota, 1878-1978." The book relates the history of the U.S Army and Veterans Administration at Fort Meade.

Chaplain Herbert B. Cleveland, chief of chaplains at Fort Meade, compiled the book as a VA project for the 1978 centennial year for Fort Meade and Sturgis. Copies are still available.

❖ ❖ ❖

In 1927, Troop C of the 4th Cavalry, plus some other men from the post, went to the State Game Lodge in Custer State Park for three months for guard and support duty while President Calvin Coolidge was in the Black Hills for the summer.

The troopers saw Coolidge close-up in the vacation that he probably enjoyed the most. He learned to wear a 10-gallon hat. He drove to Rapid City to conduct presidential business at offices in the high school. After hours and back at the Game Lodge he fished for trout, conveniently planted for his enjoyment.

It was in Rapid City on Aug. 2, 1927, that Coolidge issued a terse typewritten statement: "I do not choose to run for president in nineteen twenty-eight."

About a week later, Coolidge spoke at Mount Rushmore, praising the work of sculptor Gutzon Borglum. It was Coolidge's first prepared address of his summer vacation.

❖ ❖ ❖

Another historic role, this one related by Cleveland, found the cavalrymen helping the U.S. Army Air Corps and the National Geographic Society unlock secrets of the stratosphere.

The troopers handled the ground work and other support for flights from the Stratosphere Bowl near Rapid City in 1934 and 1935. The flights were Fort Meade's and South Dakota's introduction to the space age.

Capt. Albert W. Stevens and Capt. Orville Anderson took their balloon, Explorer II, to a record altitude of 72,395 feet on Nov. 11, 1935.

Their headquarters was at Fort Meade. Troopers helped launch the balloon, and also drove across South Dakota to near White Lake, where it landed, to pick up the balloonists and the gear. Some intrepid civilians also chased the balloon from the Black Hills to White Lake.

Later, the two Air Corps captains received congratulations from President Franklin D. Roosevelt in the White House. What they learned on their flight contributed greatly to the success of high altitude flying during World War II and space projects that followed.

As Cleveland wrote about the Armistice Day 1935 flight, "After months of preparations, trials and planning at Fort Meade, S.D., the space age began on Nov. 11, 1935."

◆ ◆ ◆

Another role for Fort Meade during the 1930s was part of President Franklin D. Roosevelt's New Deal.

Fort Meade was the headquarters for all Civilian Conservation Corps camps in South Dakota. Fourth Cavalry officers headed the camps. Hundreds of young men worked in the camps on forest projects, construction of picnic areas, buildings, etc.

There were horses at Fort Meade until the summer of 1942. The 4th Cavalry was mechanized during maneuvers in Louisiana and returned that fall without the horses. The regiment left Fort Meade for overseas duty in January 1943.

In February 1943 the 88th Glider Infantry moved to Fort Meade. Its officers and men had an exciting mission: to be prepared to enter Bavaria and rescue German scientists before the Russians got them.

The Army chose the Black Hills because of their similarity to the Black Forest and sections of Bavaria in Germany.

The infantrymen maneuvered on the back paths of the Black Hills, usually from Fort Meade to Pactola.

The rescue mission never materialized for the glider troops. Their exploits in the closing months of World War II in Europe are chronicled in the epic movie, "A Bridge Too Far."

The last Army role for Fort Meade was as a prisoner of war camp.

Approximately 600 Germans, most of them captured in the North African campaign, were shipped into Fort Meade in 1944. They worked in beet fields in the nearby Belle Fourche Irrigation Project. Some of them were used to help convert barracks buildings into hospital wards. Fort Meade became a Veterans Administration Hospital in 1945.

Summer tourists will find the history of the "peace keeper frontier post" well told in the Old Fort Meade Museum. It's open daily from Memorial Day through Labor Day. The museum is in the former Army administration building.

If you can't wait to see the museum until next summer, you may arrange tours for either individuals or groups by contacting the chaplain's office at Fort Meade.

COMMENTARY

THE NATIONAL ANTHEM AND S.D.
Argus Leader, Sunday, Dec. 27, 1981

How the custom of playing "The Star Spangled Banner" at retreat formations had its start at an Army post in South Dakota, resulting in its becoming the national anthem, is a fascinating story.

Many South Dakotans know the general history of Fort Meade, the "peace keeper frontier post" established during the winter of 1878-79 near Bear Butte to protect gold miners and settlers in the Black Hills from the Sioux Indians.

Perhaps only a few South Dakotans know the details about how and why the 8th Cavalry started playing "The Star Spangled Banner" on the Fort Meade parade ground in 1892.

Col. Caleb Carlton, 8th Cavalry and post commander, and his wife discussed the need for a national air. At her suggestion, Carlton concluded that it should be "The Star Spangled Banner." He then required that it be played at retreat and at the close of parades and concerts at Fort Meade.

As General Carlton wrote in 1914: "When Governor Sheldon of South Dakota visited Fort Meade, our custom was explained to him. Later I attended a reception given by Governor Hastings of Pennsylvania at the governor's mansion in Harrisburg and he promised me that he would try to have the custom established among the state militia.

"Not long afterward I had an interview on the subject with the Secretary of War, Daniel E. Lamont, and my impression is that it was but a few months later that he issued an order requiring 'The Star Spangled Banner' to be played at every Army post every evening at retreat.

"In addition to this I tried to enforce respect for our national flag by having every one rise and remove their hats when the colors passed them."

The Adjutant General of the U.S. Army designated "The Star Spangled Banner" as "The National Air." President Woodrow Wilson ordered it played by military and naval services in 1916. It was designated the National Anthem by Act of Congress, March 3, 1931.

Most of us get a shiver or tingling in the spine when "The Star Spangled Banner" is played. It must have been that way, too, for the colonel and his troopers at Fort Meade nearly 90 years ago.

Fort Meade outlived all other frontier posts in this part of the nation, surviving as a military installation until 1944 when it became a Veterans Administration Hospital.

Fort Meade is a mile east of Sturgis on Highway 34. There's an excellent museum, open daily Memorial Day through Labor Day. The museum faces the parade ground where a historical marker recounts Fort Meade's part in making "The Star Spangled Banner" our national anthem.

ANNIVERSARY OF V-E DAY STIRS MEMORIES FOR AMERICAN VETERANS
Argus Leader, May 12, 1985

Victory in Europe 40 years ago this month was remembered and chronicled well by newspapers and the TV networks.

Coverage of the anniversary brought back a flood of memories for veterans about where they were when Germany surrendered.

It also prompted World War II veterans to subtract 40 from their age today and exclaim: I was young then.

This writer was in the woods of South Carolina on V-E Day.

I was the company commander of 220 fine young Americans—mostly 18 or 19—who were being trained as infantry replacements.

Their instructors were a cadre of non-commissioned officers who had served overseas in the European or Pacific theaters.

Their platoon leaders were second lieutenants—either newly commissioned from 90-day officer candidate school or retreads from anti-aircraft artillery who were transferred to infantry.

The company was in its final weeks of training—climaxed by a field exercise and bivouac in the woods.

Our first knowledge of the German surrender came from the mess sergeant who was returning to the bivouac area from a trip to camp for provisions.

"It's over, the Germans surrendered," he yelled as he ran down a trail in bright morning sunshine.

What he meant was that the war was over in Europe.

The Japanese were fighting fiercely—practically to the last man—on Okinawa. Their Kamikaze (suicide) pilots were divebombing their planes into our Navy ships on the picket line off Okinawa.

The United States was starting to shift its men, planes, ships and tanks to the Pacific for the forthcoming invasion of Japan.

The rest of the field training period was anti-climactic.

Back in camp a few days later, the company and everyone else at Camp Croft marched into theatres to see a War Department orientation film on the Army's new mission in the Pacific.

In a nutshell, the film said Victory in Europe made it one down and one to go.

Trainees who shipped out of Camp Croft henceforth knew that they would be needed in the battle to defeat Japan.

What they and the public didn't know was that the atomic bomb—top secret to all but a few Americans—would end the war in August and render an invasion of Japan unnecessary.

But on V-E Day the bomb hadn't even been tested. The first atomic bomb was exploded at Alamagordo, N.M., on July 16, 1945. The second bomb was dropped at Hiroshima, Japan, on Aug. 6, the third at Nagasaki on Aug. 9. Japan surrendered Aug. 15, 1945.

Victory in Europe was a tonic for everyone at Camp Croft, including German prisoners of war. Many of them worked in the peach orchards for nearby farmers.

Some POWs were cooks in the officers' mess, where they couldn't help but see many German names on our helmet liners. I often wondered what they thought of frying breakfast eggs and fixing meals for the likes of Americans named Schultz, Schmidt, Yeager, etc.

There were several things about those young trainees, their lieutenants and cadremen in Company B, 36th Infantry Training Battalion, that I'll never forget.

They trained hard and willingly. They put up with long days, six days a week, for 17 weeks, with a minimum of griping.

They made the most of strenuous marches, hot days on the firing range and crawling under machinegun fire and barbed wire.

Their sergeants and corporals did their best to impart combat savvy to them in field exercises and appreciation of the need for spit and polish in the barracks.

COMMENTARY

Those teen-age trainees were superb, and so was their physical condition as the training cycle neared completion.

There was no bigger thrill for a company commander, age 25, than leading a column of young GIs through the woods or on the parade ground at Camp Croft.

But that was 40 years ago.

The anniversary of Victory in Europe is a good time to wonder what happened to yesterday's comrades in arms.

No veteran can possibly know what happened to all of them. But it's interesting to think

-About the tall young Regular Army corporal from Appalachia who had a plan in the summer of 1942 for getting rid of Adolf Hitler. The corporal believed the U.S. Army should sacrifice a few men on a suicide mission to kill Hitler and end the war sooner.

-About all the friends who didn't come back and what America owes to those who gave their lives for freedom.

-About war and luck. War is mostly luck. Except for circumstance, those of us who remember V-E Day in Europe during this merry May of 1985 would be among the remembered instead.

MEMORIAL IS A TOUCHING TRIBUTE TO VICTIMS OF AN UNPOPULAR WAR

Argus Leader, April 19, 1986

There is an intangible quality about the Vietnam Veterans Memorial in Washington, D.C., that makes a tourist stop and think.

Two 250-foot walls of black marble are set against the earth near the west end of the Washington Mall. To the east is the Washington Monument; to the southwest, the Lincoln Memorial. Constitution Avenue is nearby. Unless you look closely, you might miss the Vietnam Memorial.

As you approach it, your eyes are drawn to three golden-bronze figures, slightly larger than life-size, which depict the Vietnam War's fighting men.

Army nurses who served in Vietnam think there should be a fourth figure—one of them to represent women veterans. That would enhance a memorial that is already superlative. The nurses' role in caring for the wounded and sick soldiers in Vietnam is a story of extraordinary devotion to duty.

Near the statue of the three GIs are several waist-high stands covered with glass, which protects what looks like big city phone books. Instead, they carry the names, in alphabetical order, of some 58,027 American servicemen and women killed or missing in action in Vietnam between 1959 and 1975.

The first name on the list is that of a Sisseton, S.D., man, Gerald L. Aadland, a specialist 4 in the Army. The one-line listing says he was born March 29, 1945, and died May 30, 1968. The list tells you his name is on line 14 of panel 63 west.

The directory, which has 763 pages, prepares the viewer for the walk alongside the memorial's walls. You step down a slight slope. Green grass of the Washington Mall caps the top of the walls. Each wall has 70 separate granite panels: Aadland's name was easy to find.

On Memorial Day next month, 96 more names will be added. They include casualties that were overlooked or not counted initially for one reason or another during the progression of this country's longest war.

There were flowers placed by relatives or friends below some of the panels. Some tourists had their pictures taken as they pointed to the name of a loved one or acquaintance.

A viewer has to think about several things when observing the Vietnam Memorial. These were men and women who gave their lives in an unpopular war while the nation enjoyed great prosperity.

Each name represents heartache for the deceased's family and friends. It is grief borne for many years in American homes for those who did not come back from the conflict.

This was a war in which the first U.S. casualties were military advisers or pilots assigned to help South Vietnam resist the incursion of North Vietnam. As U.S. involvement grew, losses included the young man—draftee or career serviceman—from your town or mine.

The memorial was dedicated Nov. 13, 1982. It was recognition long overdue for the sacrifices of a generation of Americans whose service was not appreciated by much of the public at the time. Although this country and its ally, South Vietnam, lost the war to North Vietnam, the U.S. stand nevertheless contributed to stability along the Pacific Rim. Friends and allies, like Australia, Japan and South Korea, were sustained by the United States in its role in Asia. Malaysia and Indonesia remained oriented to the West.

The power of the Vietnam Veterans Memorial lies in its chronicling the names of all those like Aadland who gave their lives. The thousands of names chiseled on the memorial's black surface are more compelling than the most carefully drafted prose hailing the sacrifices of those who died.

The roll call is a message, too, for President Ronald Reagan and other presidents who will follow him to avoid courses of action that could result in another Vietnam. The American public could not bear, nor would it tolerate, being engulfed halfway around the world in another war in which this nation's own most vital interests are not at stake.

◆ ◆ ◆

Here are other observations gained in Washington while attending the annual convention of the American Society of Newspaper Editors.

• Reagan, at 75 our oldest president, looks fit and trim. He easily handled an appearance before the editors at a noon luncheon. He was the biggest draw of the convention.

• Lee Iacocca, chairman of Chrysler Corporation, was a close second. Editors and their spouses enjoyed his candid comments. He spoke with good humor about many of the country's problems. Calling himself a non-politician, he said neither his company nor the country can afford giant swings in oil prices or interest rates. He also said he's not running for president, but some of his listeners thought he'd make an excellent candidate.

• Washington in the week before the U.S. attack on Libya was more preoccupied with Moammar Khadafy and terrorism and Nicaragua and the Contras than the 1988 presidential aspirations of its politicians.

45 YEARS AGO—U.S. GOES TO WAR

Argus Leader, Saturday, Dec. 6, 1986

What was probably the biggest news story of this century happened 45 years ago this weekend.

Japanese planes bombed the U.S. Pacific fleet at Pearl Harbor, Hawaii, while Japan's diplomats were delivering a formal message carrying no hint of war to Secretary of State Cordell Hull in Washington.

COMMENTARY

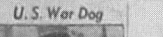

THE DAILY ARGUS-LEADER
South Dakota's Leading Newspaper

EXTRA — EXTRA

SIOUX FALLS, SOUTH DAKOTA, SUNDAY, DECEMBER 7, 1941 — PRICE FIVE CENTS

350 KILLED AT HAWAIIAN BASE
Japs At War With U. S.; FDR Summons Cabinet

The surprise dawn attack came on Sunday morning, Dec. 7, 1941. President Franklin D. Roosevelt called it "a date which will live in infamy."

This year's December calendar coincides to the day with 1941.

There were hints of a worsening crisis in the Far East on page one of the Saturday afternoon, Dec. 6, 1941, Daily Argus-Leader. The big, bold headline across the top said: SINGAPORE PREPARED FOR CRISIS.

The news story said Great Britain suddenly recalled all fighting men to their posts at Singapore. Australia arranged to send tank troops to help defend the Dutch East Indies in case of war.

The same story said that the Japanese press sharpened its attacks against the United States. One Tokyo newspaper declared that in the event of "American aggression a billion people of East Asia would become bombs" against Britain and the United States.

At the top of page one another headline heralded: NAZIS HURL HUGE ARMY AT MOSCOW. Another story reported that the British had repelled three German and Italian attacks southeast of Tobruk in North Africa.

Britain was in its third year of war against Adolf Hitler's Nazi Germany. Germany was in its first year of war against the Soviet Union. The Japanese, having invaded French Indo-China in 1940, seemed ready to move again.

Sunday morning's paper on Dec. 7 carried a large two-line headline across the top of the page: Roosevelt Sends Note to Emperor of Japan as Clouds of War Darken.

Japanese planes struck Pearl Harbor on Sunday morning at 7:55 a.m. Hawaiian time, or 12:25 p.m. CST. The first radio bulletins of the attack came early Sunday afternoon.

The Argus published an extra late in the day. The headline across the top of page one read: 350 Killed at Hawaiian Base. Below it, in larger type, was a two-line headline: Japs at War with U.S.; FDR Summons Cabinet.

The Pearl Harbor casualties were much higher than reported initially. The U.S. Navy had 2,117 killed, 960 missing and 876 wounded; the Army, 226 killed, 396 wounded.

The battleship Arizona was lost; four battleships and three destroyers were severely damaged. A number of other battleships and cruisers were damaged and repaired. The U.S. lost 80 Navy and 97 Army planes. The Japanese lost 48 planes and three submarines.

The main story on Monday, Dec. 8, 1941, reported Congress' declaration of war against Japan. The Senate vote was 82-0; the House, 388 to 1. The state's congressional delegation—Senators Chan Gurney and W. J. Bulow and Representatives Karl Mundt and Francis Case—voted for the declaration.

The big story on Thursday, Dec. 11, was the declaration of war on the United States by Germany and Italy. Later in the day, the Argus published an extra to report that Congress declared war on Germany and Italy.

Most of the news that first week was grim as Japan's Pacific island conquests unfolded. There were false air raid alarms in San Francisco and New York.

South Dakotans didn't know where their 147th Field Artillery was—and the War Department wouldn't tell. The National Guardsmen were on a troop transport southwest of Hawaii on Dec. 7 with secret orders for the Philippines.

On Friday, Dec. 12, 1941, a page one story said no news about South Dakota men in service was good news. On the day before Christmas the Argus quoted Mundt with a report that all men in the 147th were safe and well, but their location could not be told. It was learned much later that the convoy was diverted to Australia and the 147th landed at Brisbane Dec. 22, 1941.

COMMENTARY

They later became part of Gen. Douglas MacArthur's troops in the long island-hopping campaign to regain the Philippines.

There was only one thing on the mind of Americans from Pearl Harbor day forward: to win the war. They were unified as never before or since, when the United States would endure the Korean and Vietnam wars.

TOUR OF EAST OFFERS LOOK AT OLD BATTLEFIELDS
Argus Leader, Sunday, May 7, 1989

One advantage footloose senior citizens have is that they can add attractions to their travel schedule.

A recent trip to Washington, D.C., and North Carolina and a return home by way of Tennessee offered several bonuses.

First was the opportunity to see Gettysburg, Penn., and the National Military Park which memorializes the Civil War battlefield.

Gettysburg, 1,200 miles from Sioux Falls via Interstate except the last 30 miles, is an easy three-day drive. You can arrive in time to visit the National Cemetery before dark and stand where President Lincoln gave his famous Gettysburg address. You can also sign up at the motel for a two-hour bus tour of the battlefield the next morning.

No matter how well you remember your Civil War history lessons, seeing where 51,000 Americans were killed, wounded or captured in three days in July 1863 is a moving experience. Gen. George G. Meade, commander of the Union Army, turned back the Confederate forces of Gen. Robert E. Lee, changing the course of the war.

The bus ride follows the action. Statues of generals, state memorials to Union and Confederate units, and artillery pieces are sited throughout the park.

The electric map at the Visitor Center enhances understanding of positions and tactics. The Cyclorama Center features a remarkable painting of the battlefield by French artist Paul Philippoteaux.

Downtown Washington is only 80 miles from Gettysburg. It's a pleasant drive through Pennsylvania and Maryland countryside, but not much fun after you reach city traffic. The good news is that the Interstate to Virginia is readily accessible from downtown Washington.

April in Washington, Virginia, North Carolina and Tennessee offers many visual charms. Dogwood in white and occasionally in pink, azaleas and red blossoms on many trees provide a festive air.

North Carolina's marvelous pine trees stretch endlessly from the Atlantic Ocean to the Great Smoky Mountains in the West.

There's something inspiring about spending a night on the coast, walking the beach and watching waves roll into shore. One ritual is to put your hand in the ocean. It was too cold to wade.

By coincidence we toured the U.S.S. North Carolina Battleship Memorial in Wilmington the day after the turret explosion killed 47 sailors on the U.S.S. Iowa.

Climbing into a gun turret on the North Carolina and looking down four stories at the maze of ammunition hoists and hatches was a somber experience.

The North Carolina was the first big battleship constructed by the United States just before World War II. The ship entered action against the Japanese in the Pacific in July 1942. The

North Carolina earned 15 battle stars during 40 months of combat duty. These engagements took the lives of only 10 of the North Carolina's men; 40 others were wounded.

North Carolina school children and citizens with their donations saved the battleship from the scrap heap in 1960. The 728-foot battleship was berthed at Wilmington in 1961 and became a state memorial to all World War II service personnel. A roll of honor carries the names of 10,000 North Carolinians who lost their lives in the conflict.

If traveling through Chattanooga, Tenn., take time to see the Chickamagua and Chattanooga National Military Park. It straddles the Georgia and Tennessee border.

The three-day battle of Chickamagua in September 1863 was a defeat for the Union Army, which withdrew to Chattanooga. Two months later, Union forces under Gen. Ulysses S. Grant defeated the Confederates at Chattanooga and Lookout Mountain.

Like Gettysburg, there are many statues, memorials and cannons in the military park. Chickamagua was one of the bloodiest battles of the Civil War. Lookout Mountain offers a grand view of Chattanooga, the Tennessee River and the battlefields.

PARK MEMORIALIZES MONUMENTAL BATTLE
Vicksburg is an education on Civil War

Argus Leader, Sunday, March 18, 1990

VICKSBURG, Miss.—There's no better place than the Vicksburg National Military Park to take an easy course in Civil War history.

You can do it from your car or van, using tapes or a guide book. Or you can hire a licensed guide.

You'll leave your vehicle often during the 12-mile drive through the park to read markers and walk historic ground in pleasant Mississippi spring weather.

Vicksburg's bluffs sat on a hairpin curve of the Mississippi River. Confederate guns on the heights and at the river's edge controlled navigation and access to the city. Vicksburg was the only river and rail junction between Memphis and New Orleans.

Blue and red markers delineate positions of Union and Confederate troops, respectively, around Vicksburg during the 47-day siege from May 18 to July 4, 1863. The Confederates didn't run out of courage, but they exhausted their ammunition and food supplies.

More than 100,000 men—some 31,000 Confederates and up to 75,000 Union forces—fought each other, sometimes from lines only yards apart.

Monuments and markers recount valor and devotion to duty on both sides. The battle became an artillery duel and waiting game in trenches.

States have erected elaborate monuments. Some families have paid for statues or markers of officers. But don't try to stop at each monument—you'd be in the park all summer. There are approximately 1,600 plaques or statues.

Artillery pieces are placed along the many ridges facing hilltops held by the enemy. Fields of fire, fortifications and positions where sharpshooters guarded gun crews and picked off the enemy are described.

A bigger than life statue of Gen. Ulysses S. Grant astride his horse is near his field headquarters on the park's Grant Avenue.

A statue of Gen. John C. Pemberton, the Confederate commander at Vicksburg, is on Pemberton Circle along Confederate Avenue. He was a Pennsylvanian and like Grant a graduate of the U.S. Military Academy. There's also a statue of Jefferson Davis, another West point graduate, in the park.

Grant's victory on July 4, 1863, when Pemberton surrendered Vicksburg, split the South in half. The Union gained control of the Mississippi River from Cairo, Ill., to the Gulf of Mexico. The Confederates lost their railroad link to Louisiana, Arkansas and Texas.

The Union on July 1-4, 1863, defeated Gen. Robert E. Lee's forces at Gettysburg, Pa. Until July 4, 1863, the Confederacy had hoped to win.

Most important from the Union standpoint was Grant's emergence from Vicksburg as a master military strategist. In less than a year President Lincoln would name him commander of all the Union armies.

Grant's campaign to capture Vicksburg involved Navy forces, amphibious operations to ferry his troops across the Mississippi and feints to confuse Confederate commanders. Grant's decision to cross the Mississippi below Vicksburg and attack overland from the east was a brilliant stroke that ran counter to his orders from Washington.

The salvaged remains of the Union ironclad gunboat Cairo are in the park. Confederates sank the Cairo in the Yazoo River north of Vicksburg on Dec. 12, 1862. The Cairo was the first vessel in history to be sunk by an electrically detonated mine. The entire crew escaped.

DON'T PASS UP MILITARY MUSEUMS

Argus Leader, Sunday, July 1, 1990

The next time you visit a son, daughter or other relative in the military service, tour the museum on the base.

You'll gain a new perception of World War II, the Korean War and the Vietnam War—conflicts that are fast receding into history.

You'll also come away with a better understanding of the valor and sacrifices of the nation's servicemen and women. For veterans and spouses, such visits will be a trip down memory's lane.

Battlefields and national military parks in the East and South reflect images of battles fought with colonial muskets and the more lethal weapons of the Civil War. Revolutionary and Civil War heroes invariably are generals or other officers on horseback portrayed in marble or bronze.

Visitors at national military museums quickly sense the changes in warfare. The horse is missing from World War II and later exhibits, replaced by military hardware. GIs are depicted with Jeeps and tanks. Fliers are shown with their planes and sailors with their ships.

The difference is dramatic at the Patton Museum of Cavalry and Armor at Fort Knox, Ky. The museum is dedicated to General George S. Patton Jr. and to the evolution of cavalry and armor.

Patton, called "Old Blood and Guts" because of his tough manner, started his U.S. Army career in the cavalry. But he made his mark developing tank tactics between the world wars and as a field commander in North Africa, Sicily and Europe in World War II.

A special section of the Patton museum is devoted to his life. Among exhibits are his Jeep and staff car from the European campaign. The general, riding crop in hand and an ivory-plated revolver in his belt, is depicted in a wood carving. Museum exhibits trace the use of armor by all nations from World War I to the 1978 prototype of the M1 Abrams tank.

Patton raised storms of controversy during World War II. In one incident he slapped a soldier in a hospital because he thought he was malingering. In another, he told reporters that Nazis were like losers in a U.S. political contest. On the battlefield, his leadership and tactics were superb.

Patton died from injuries in an accident in his staff car in December 1945, some seven months after victory in Europe. But he refused to blame his driver or the other military driver, saying on his hospital bed it was simply an accident. His peers and Army friends remembered him fondly. The son of a wealthy California family, he was a West Point graduate and won fifth place in the 1912 Olympic pentathlon.

The National Infantry Museum at Fort Benning, Ga., follows the footsteps of the American foot soldier across two centuries of courage and determination.

A weapons exhibit depicts the evolution of the infantryman's rifle. Another display honors General of the Army Omar Bradley, Patton's commander in Europe during World War II. (Bradley was professor of military science and tactics in 1919-1920 at what was then South Dakota State College in Brookings.) An outstanding diorama shows airborne troops. Fort Benning's parachute school has trained thousands of airborne troops since World War II.

Two other national military museums will make any veteran's vacation day. They are the U.S. Air Force Museum at Dayton, Ohio, and the U.S. Naval Aviation Museum at Pensacola, Fla. Plane displays, aviation art and historical summaries are outstanding.

Closer to home, the South Dakota Air and Space Museum at Ellsworth Air Force Base near Rapid City displays planes and chronicles base history. At Pierre, the South Dakota National Guard Museum emphasizes the role of citizen soldiers in the Coyote State.

A MILITARY ON THE MARCH
Current reservists follow state's proud tradition
Argus Leader, Dec. 9, 1990

Call-up of reserve units and individuals for service in the Persian Gulf is like a TV rerun for many older South Dakotans.

They remember well when their units were called for World War II, Korean War and Berlin Crisis service. Theirs was another time, another place but the scenario is much the same.

Trading civilian jobs for a uniform breaks the familiar cycle of job, home and daily routine. One day you're eagerly pursuing a career and enjoying home life. The next day, you're packing. Uncle Sam becomes your drum major and you march to his tune.

Today's National Guardsmen and women and reservists in the Navy, Air Force and Army cannot know how long their service will last. They cannot read the future and know what will happen by Jan. 15, the United Nations' deadline for Saddam Hussein to have Iraq's troops out of Kuwait.

Fifty years ago on Nov. 25, 1940, South Dakota's 147th Field Artillery Regiment was inducted into federal service in eight South Dakota cities. The guardsmen belonged to units in Sioux Falls, Mitchell, Aberdeen, Pierre, Flandreau, Yankton, Vermillion and Parker. The regiment left 10 days later for Fort Ord, Calif.

South Dakota units that were part of the 34th Division waited until Feb. 10, 1941, for their call-up. These units included the 34th Signal Company from Watertown, 109th Engineers from

Rapid City, Madison, Brookings, Huron, Hot Springs, Lead and Sturgis, and the 109th Quartermaster Regiment from Aberdeen, Mitchell, Edgemont, Brookings and Pierre.

The November 1940 and February 1941 call-ups furnished 2,263 officers and men to the Army of the United States. The late Lt. Col. Richard Cropp in his book The Coyotes—A History of the South Dakota National Guard noted: "This sizeable contingent exempted South Dakota from the first Selective Service drafts, a matter of small satisfaction to the guardsmen."

Wartime journeys for both groups were long and difficult.

The 147th on Dec. 7, 1941, was on a troop transport 1,500 miles southwest of Pearl Harbor when the Japanese attacked that U.S. naval base. The South Dakotans were among the first Yanks assigned to Gen. Douglas MacArthur in Australia. They fought in the long island-hopping drive to the Philippines. The last guardsmen were rotated home by June 1945.

The 34th Division was the first American combat unit to go overseas to Europe. Cropp wrote, "Legend says that the first Yank ashore in North Ireland (in January 1942) was a South Dakotan." The Coyotes (South Dakota National Guardsmen) fought in North Africa and Italy. They sailed for home on Oct. 25, 1945.

South Dakota's 196th Regimental Combat Team and 147th Field Artillery Battalion served two years following call-up on Sept. 1, 1950. The unit trained at Fort Carson, Colo., and garrisoned in Alaska for a year during the Korean War.

The Air Guard's 175th Fighter Squadron was mobilized in Sioux Falls on March 1, 1951, served at Joe Foss Field until August and at Ellsworth Air Force Base near Rapid City until released from federal service on Dec. 1. 1952.

The 1st Battalion 147th Field Artillery from southeastern South Dakota and separate Guard companies at Lemmon, Yankton and Winner and a reserve company from Aberdeen were called up in the Berlin Crisis in 1961, serving a year. The 1st Battalion served at Fort Sill, Okla.

Military duty produces countless legends for future reunions. That's probably the last thing today's reservists are thinking about. Even so, World War II 147th veterans had a super time at their 50th reunion in Sioux Falls last September.

VETERANS CONSTITUTE 11 PERCENT OF STATE

Argus Leader, Sunday, Nov. 10, 1991

While you're thinking about observing Veterans Day Monday, here's a profile of South Dakota veterans.

There are about 76,500 veterans in South Dakota, according to Don Tiede, public affairs officer for the Veterans Administration in Sioux Falls. Thus, veterans make up nearly 11 percent of the state's population of about 700,000.

The largest veterans group—some 24,300—served during World War II, according to Gale Reiners, chief of the Veterans Services Division in the Veterans Administration regional office in Sioux Falls. The figure is for March 31, 1989, when the last compilation was made.

The average age of World War II veterans hovers between 69 and 70, Reiners said.

There were 600 World War I veterans in South Dakota nearly two years ago. Their average age is between 95 and 96.

South Dakota has some 22,000 veterans of the Vietnam era whose largest segments average between 43 and 44 years of age.

South Dakota counted 15,200 Korean War veterans as of March 31, 1989. Those veterans now average between 57 and 58 years of age.

The March 31, 1989, compilation lists 8,400 veterans who served after the Vietnam era, 8,600 who served between the Korean and Vietnam Wars and 400 other peacetime veterans. No figures are available for Persian Gulf veterans.

One of South Dakota's most visible tributes to veterans is Black Hills National Cemetery several miles south of Sturgis. The cemetery lies in a scenic mountain valley. Its white headstones, row on row, are visible from Interstate 90. The land originally was part of Fort Meade, frontier U.S. Cavalry post.

A U.S. Flag flies 24 hours a day at the cemetery. Dan Nelson, director, said that as a mark of deep respect and mourning, the flag is lowered to half mast each day one half hour before the first committal service. It remains at half mast until one half hour after the last service. It is then raised to full mast.

Visitors will find fathers, sons, mothers, daughters, uncles and aunts, other relatives and friends buried at the cemetery. They will also find famous South Dakotans:

• Sgt. Charles Windolph, who won the Medal of Honor for holding a position that secured water for the 7th Cavalry at the Battle of the Little Big Horn in 1876. The position was about five miles from where Lt. Col. George A. Custer and his immediate command were killed by Indians. Windolph died at age 98 on March 11, 1950.

• Brig. Gen. Richard E. Ellsworth, for whom Ellsworth Air Force Base at Rapid City is named. He won two Distinguished Flying Crosses and three Air Medals in World War II. He was killed in an airplane accident over Newfoundland on March 18, 1953, while serving as commanding general of the Rapid City Air Force base.

• U.S. Sen. Francis H. Case Sr., his widow, the former Myrie Graves, and their infant son, Francis H. Case Jr. Sen. Case led efforts that resulted in establishment of the cemetery in 1948.

Reiners said Black Hills National Cemetery had 11,058 interments as of Nov. 4.

Reiners said veterans cannot make prior arrangements with the Veterans Administration for burial in a national cemetery. He said they or family members should ask funeral directors to make the arrangements at the time of death. They should have copies of discharge papers available for the funeral director to prove eligibility.

Veterans may call the Sioux Falls VA office toll-free 1-800-952-3550 for information on services and benefits.

WWII BROUGHT MANY MAJOR CHALLENGES TO S.D.

Argus Leader, Dec. 1, 1991

What was South Dakota like on the eve of Dec. 7, 1941, when the Japanese attacked Pearl Harbor?

The Coyote or Sunshine State had 642,961 people, a drop of approximately 50,000 persons from 1930.

Depression, drought and dust storms had forced many South Dakotans to leave for California and the Pacific Northwest. Despite that, there were still 72,000 farms in South Dakota. Today there are only 35,000 farms, and the state's population is a record 696,004 (1990 Census figure).

Then as now, we were one of the nation's most rural states. Although depopulation of the countryside started in the 1930s, most small towns had survived.

The war in Europe in 1941 was in its third year. War news dominated Argus Leader front pages and radio newscasts. The United States was in an uneasy peace. The nation had its first peacetime draft. It was strengthening the military, boosting defense and agricultural production and supplying arms and food to Britain and Russia in their fight against Adolf Hitler's Nazi Germany.

Some 2,263 South Dakota National Guardsmen were serving on active duty, having been called up in November of 1940 and February of 1941.

Manpower demands for the military and defense plants made it difficult for farmers and businesses to keep help. Some farmers enjoyed rural electrification, but most would have to wait until after the war.

On Nov. 22, 1941, South Dakota's 147th Field Artillery which had trained at Fort Ord, Calif., embarked at San Francisco. Their destination was top secret. On Dec. 7th they were in a convoy somewhere west of Hawaii en route to the Philippines, but no one in South Dakota knew that.

Virtually all war news during autumn 1941 was bad. Nazi armies were outside Moscow and occupied most of western Europe from Norway to Spain. They were fighting the British in North Africa. Nazi submarines preyed on Allied and U.S. ships. Japanese forces were moving ominously toward French Indochina.

The happiest news of fall was excellent pheasant hunting, which attracted Clark Gable and his wife, Carole Lombard, to South Dakota.

Harlan J. Bushfield, a Miller lawyer, was governor. William J. Bulow and Chan Gurney were the state's U.S. senators. Francis Case and Karl Mundt were the two U.S. representatives.

Sioux Falls' population was 40,832 in 1940. John T. McKee was mayor on Dec. 7, 1941.

South Dakotans got their first news of the Japanese attack by radio early Sunday afternoon, Dec. 7. I was a State College student in Brookings and heard the bulletins on KSOO. The Argus Leader published an extra early that evening which quickly sold out.

There was good news on the Argus Leader front page on Christmas Eve. Mundt reported from Washington that South Dakotans in the 147th Field Artillery were safe and had suffered no casualties. Their location was a military secret, later revealed as Australia. They would become part of Gen. Douglas MacArthur's campaign to return to the Philippines.

OBSERVANCE, LIKE PEARL HARBOR, CAN'T BE FORGOTTEN

Argus Leader, Sunday, Dec. 15, 1991

HONOLULU—Three generations of American veterans remembered Pearl Harbor in a reflective way on the 50th anniversary of Japan's sneak attack on Dec. 7, 1941.

Survivors of the attack on the naval base, air fields and other Army and Marine facilities on the island of Oahu represented the first generation.

Their children who fought in Vietnam are the second generation. And their children who served in Operation Desert Storm and Desert Shield—today's volunteer military—saluted America's heroes of Dec. 7, 1941.

The day of remembrance dawned bright and sunny in Hawaii.

It was difficult for spectators who were not on Oahu 50 years ago to visualize the horror of shock, bombs and flames in which 2,403 Americans were killed.

But survivors recalled the events of the day as if it were only yesterday.

Spectators at the visitors' center of the USS Arizona Memorial looked across the channel to the gleaming white bridge which straddles, but doesn't touch, the sunken battleship.

Still entombed below its decks are many of the 1,177 Arizona crewmen who died 50 years ago.

At 7:55 a.m., the time of the Japanese attack, the guided missile cruiser U.S. Chosin sounded its ship's whistle as it glided past the memorial. Sailors in white lined its decks.

There was a moment of silence and then the roar of four Hawaiian National Guard F-15s flying in missing man formation to honor their fallen comrades.

President George Bush, speaking to several hundred guests at the memorial, said Pearl Harbor's victims would live forever in our memories.

Spectators at the center watched the president on TV monitors. They viewed the new memorial circle on the grounds of the visitors center, which contains memorial plaques listing the names of the dead on other ships and at various airfields.

The 54 civilians killed in the attack are also named. The names of the Arizona's dead are engraved on walls of the memorial itself.

There were many floral tributes at the memorial circle. States which had namesake battleships moored at Pearl Harbor on Dec. 7, 1941, remembered.

The largest floral wreath was from students of a Wakayama City school in Japan and their principal, Susuma Fujita. They said their wreath is a symbol of peace from the hearts of 150 students in Japan. The wreath was marked "in memory of those who died at Pearl Harbor and all who perished in the Pacific War."

The children donated $5,000 to the Pearl Harbor commemoration.

The U.S. Navy had another salute to Pearl Harbor Day and its veterans: the presence of the USS Missouri moored half a mile from the Arizona memorial. The Missouri, last battleship built by the United States, fought in World War II and the Persian Gulf. It will be decommissioned after returning to the mainland.

Bush, in various appearances, said he held no rancor against the Japanese for the attack. He said the wartime internment of Americans of Japanese ancestry was a great injustice that must never be repeated. He said Pearl Harbor's fallen would say: "Fifty years have passed. Our country is the undisputed leader of the free world. We are at peace.

"Don't you think each one is saying: 'I did not die in vain.'"

Likely, Pearl Harbor survivors and others who were fortunate enough to see the 50th anniversary observance will remember the little things instead of the big picture.

The National Park Service presented survivors who recalled the day and what happened to them. Survivors marched in downtown Honolulu in the most mixed dress (Hawaiian shirts) possibly ever seen in a military reunion.

Veterans and others also had a glimpse of their own mortality. The 18-year-old soldier and sailor of Dec. 7, 1941, is now 68. Twenty-five and 30-year-old veterans of 1941 are now 75 and 80.

There will never be another reunion like this one, which attracted several thousand survivors and family members.

HISTORY ON DISPLAY AT FORT SILL, OKLA.

Argus Leader, Sunday, June 16, 1996

LAWTON, Okla.—Here's an easy-off, easy-on Interstate 44 tour of Fort Sill while you're on your way to or from Texas or the Southwest.

Historic Fort Sill has been the home of the U.S. Army Field Artillery Center and School since 1911. Stone buildings of the frontier post built in the 1870s are preserved as a museum.

COMMENTARY

Walk tree-lined streets to view old post headquarters, barracks, chapel, homes, stockade-type corral and other structures.

Lawton, population 80,561, and Fort Sill, 12,107, make up Oklahoma's third most populous urban center, after Oklahoma City and Tulsa.

Lawton adjoins the Fort Sill Military Reservation on its southeast side. You may enter Fort Sill from several interstate exits or via Fort Sill Boulevard, a north-south thouroughfare connecting Lawton and the Army post. The Fort Sill Military Reservation sprawls over 94,000 acres and adjoins the Wichita Mountains Wildlife Refuge on the reservation's northwest side.

Fort Sill has played historic roles in both the 19th and 20th centuries. It was founded by Gen. Philip H. Sheridan in 1869 during a winter campaign against the South Plains tribes. It was built by the black troopers of the 9th and 10th U.S. Cavalry, the famed "Buffalo Soldiers."

Geronimo, renowned Apache Indian chief who battled the U.S. Army for more than 10 years in what is now southern Arizona, spent the last years of his life as a prisoner at Fort Sill. He died at age 81 in 1909 and is buried at Fort Sill.

McNair Hall, the post headquarters of Fort Sill, is named for Lt. General Lesley J. McNair, born at Verndale, Minnesota. —Anson Yeager photo

During World War II, the Field Artillery School commissioned thousands of officer candidates as second lieutenants and trained many other soldiers in artillery specialties. This training role has continued.

McNair Hall, post headquarters, is named after Lt. General Leslie J. McNair. He served as assistant commandant of the Artillery School from 1929 to 1933. He was commanding general of Army Ground Forces in the continental United States during World War II. His portrait is displayed in McNair Hall.

McNair was killed in Normandy July 25, 1944, while observing artillery fire. He was the first three-star general in U.S. history to die on the battlefield. His death was a military accident: bombs from U.S. planes fell short of targeted German units.

The Visitor Center is in a building that was used as an infantry barracks.

Historical field artillery weapons of the United States and of some allies and enemies are displayed along Cannon Walk.

The largest weapon is "Atomic Annie", the 280mm gun that fired the world's first atomic artillery round at Frenchman's Flat, Nev., on May 25, 1953. The gun's elevation is set at the mark used to fire the historic round.

A self-propelled gun is one of the many outdoor displays at Fort Sill. —Anson Yeager photo

You'll stroll by the Old Post Guardhouse built in 1873. It's where Geronimo and other Indian leaders were held at Fort Sill. Guardhouse exhibits memorialize hard-riding horse soldiers, slogging foot soldiers and the proud Indian tribes of the South Plains.

Admission to the museum is free and open to the public daily from 8:30 a.m. to 4:30 p.m., except Dec. 25-26 and Jan. 1-2. Allow two to three hours.

Retired military personnel and veterans may want to include a tour of Snow Hall. It is the home of the U.S. Army Field Artillery School. Photographs of school commandants and outstanding artillery officers and historical exhibits are displayed in its corridors.

Many South Dakotans, members of 147th National Guard artillery units, have trained at Fort Sill.

Fort Sill Military Reservation and National Historic Landmark are rated a red star attraction by the American Automobile Association. There are numerous civic attractions in Lawton, including the Museum of the Great Plains and its Red River Trading Post. Lakes Ellsworth and Lawtonka are nearby.

KEY HINTS ON MOTORHOME TRAVEL

TRAVEL VETERANS OFFER HINTS ON LIVING IN MOTORHOME

Argus Leader, Saturday, March 28, 1987

Here are some random observations and motorhome hints from a retired South Dakota couple about travel in the great American Southwest.

A small plastic basket available in any discount store is a great place to store maps and tourist literature. Our map basket sits between the seats in the cab.

The male in this touring family knows the first trip of the year is nearly half gone when his wife cleans out the maps for the states behind us and stores them under the seat in the coach. "What's left now will get us through California and home," she tells me.

Living in a motorhome for a couple of months is made much easier by having a place for everything—and keeping it in its place.

One of the nice things about motorhome travel is that you don't have to live out of a suitcase. You can hang your clothes in closets. Each of us stores clothing changes in baskets that travel in the bunk over the cab.

At least once on every trip the skewer comes out of the refrigerator door, the magnet doesn't hold and some contents land on the floor. No more of that. My wife last week found super safety rails (expandable spring rods) to put across the front of each refrigerator shelf. Now our system should be fail-safe.

My wife and I would find it difficult to carry everything in the family station wagon that we think we need on an extended trip.

My Tandy 200 Portable Computer and a printer are stowed in a drawer under the back bunk of the motorhome. After breakfast dishes are washed and dried, it's a lot easier to type away on a computer than on a portable typewriter.

This particular lesson was learned a couple of years ago when I took along a portable typewriter on our first winter trip to the Southwest. Now, just like at home or when I used a video display terminal at the Argus Leader before retirement, I can utilize a computer's advantages in writing and revising this column. Then all it takes is pressing a button to produce a copy from the printer for mailing home.

This column was written on a sunny morning in a pleasant mountain recreational vehicle camp about 25 miles northeast of San Diego.

My wife, too, has room in the motorhome to carry along family correspondence, household files and her contest entries, including coupons for drawings for a Mercedes Benz and other exotic prizes. She threatens to stop playing postal roulette—unless she gets a major prize (anything more than $100) from her efforts.

Keeping in touch by phone with youngsters in four different time zones while traveling by motorhome is not difficult.

However, we've found that Sioux Falls' mid-nation location does minimize the problem of making connections with either coast.

In California, there's a difference of three hours (half a morning or evening) if we want to talk with a son and daughter-in-law in Boston. It's easier to talk to the son and daughter-in-law in Santa Clara, Calif., and ask about our granddaughter.

Making a phone call without a booth has its challenges if you're on a busy street when an 18-wheeler's going by. Standing up at a pay phone encourages the caller to be brief. The plastic age makes charging phone calls easy.

MOTORHOME TRAVEL NEEDS COMPROMISE
Argus Leader, Feb. 19, 1989

Couples who travel by motorhome should parley once in a while on what the other half would like to see on a trip.

National parks, historic places and a few museums may be great for the husband. But they don't always have that much appeal for the wife.

My wife and I found ourselves in that situation in South Carolina last summer.

We had seen and enjoyed the usual major scenic attractions. But having been on the American road for a month or more, Ada May decided it was time to take a break from the scenic and shop at a mall near Spartanburg.

It was shopping with a difference: in a factory outlet mall of 40 or more stores that offer manufacturers' discounts.

It didn't take long to discover that there were real bargains in clothing and lesser bargains in souvenirs, household knick-knacks and the like.

In many instances, prices were no better than what you'd find in shopping centers or discount stores back home.

Even so, it was fun to see the mall concept employed by an aggregation of factory outlets. Such stores are a common sight along highways in the South.

Motor home travel has pluses for retired couples who like it.

For instance, you can leave Sioux Falls or your Sioux Empire home without packing a suitcase. Hang your clothes in the closets (his and hers). Usually, you can depart in shirt-sleeves, unless the windchill is near or below zero.

There's room overhead, below the bunks and in drawers for nearly everything a couple needs on an extended trip.

It helps if traveling partners observe the old rule of a place for everything and everything in its place.

Daily routine is made much easier if the driver knows where his sunglasses are (mine belong in a pocket on the side of my seat) and if housekeeping chores are performed regularly.

Plastic baskets are invaluable for packing fresh laundry. They're also handy for storing maps and tapes between driver and navigator. Midway in the trip is a good time to sort maps and stow away ones you won't need for the return trip.

My laptop computer is stored in a drawer at the back of the motorhome. When it comes out for production purposes (like writing a column), my wife decides it's a good morning to wash clothes or go swimming.

The computer goes on a removable table, and the printer goes on the floor. The motorhome's big back window and the screen door provide daylight and fresh air, respectively. The morning slips away and both of us manage to get something done.

Here's a list of necessities for motorhome travel:

• Flashlights in the cab, kitchen area and at the back door.

• A tool kit with pliers, hammer, wrenches and screwdrivers. A soldering kit and basic carpenter tools may come in handy during extended stays at a campground.

- A small, portable compressor for inflating flat tires.
- Masking tape for sealing cereal packages, aluminum tape for minor motorhome repairs and a CB radio procedure card.
- A small battery-powered radio if you'll be out in the boondocks with no electricity and no generator aboard your rig. A battery-powered TV set would also be nice.

Enjoying driving requires an optimistic frame of mind.

Acknowledge when you start in the morning that most cars and nearly all 18-wheelers will pass you. Help them do it. On two-lane roads, give cars and trucks an opportunity to pass your motorhome when slow lanes become available. Or turn out and let them by.

Resolve to drive only in daylight except when circumstances require that you complete an hour or two of your journey after dark.

Drive defensively. Try to avoid any problems. And take Texas' advice: Drive friendly!

GOOD TRIP STARTS BEFORE LEAVING

Argus Leader, Sunday, July 15, 1990

Here are some travel tips that may help make your next trip by motorhome or car more enjoyable.

Start planning a major journey well in advance. Events, like a college graduation, dictate making motel reservations months before the happy event occurs. Getting accommodations at the last minute is practically impossible.

Similarly, if you're assembling your tribe of sons, daughters and grandchildren in a Black Hills hideaway or campground, make your reservations early. Six or eight months in advance may be necessary to obtain housekeeping cabins or motel quarters to fit your family's needs.

Campgrounds or motels which have swimming pools, playgrounds and activities offer flexibility to various family members during a stay of several days.

A campground has a further advantage in allowing you to use your motorhome to prepare breakfast and lunches at the picnic table. Run an extension cord from the motorhome to your toaster and coffee maker. Use the barbecue pit for a steak fry. But have a rainy day plan, too. Motorhomes can seat only a limited number of adults and children. Rain may make going to a restaurant the easy way out.

Grandmothers have a knack for advising daughters-in-law about clothing requirements for a summer trip to South Dakota. Jackets and sweaters are a necessity for cool nights in the Black Hills. Family members arriving from diverse locations may not think about that. Grandmothers can help by taking along extra clothing for grandkids and packing a box of toys.

When planning a trip to an unfamiliar region in the United States or Canada, be sure to ask your travel club for maps and routing, literature and other available material. A route map can save you time and trouble and help you to avoid heavy highway construction.

Read the literature and check your maps before departure. If you don't like inner city traffic, take interstate or expressway routes around a big city.

Make it a point to stop at state information centers during workday hours so you can obtain a state highway map. They usually are considerably more detailed than travel club's cross country maps.

Don't hesitate to ask information center personnel for directions to a friend's home or a tourist attraction in a large city. State guides want to help you.

Most border welcome centers along interstate highways have tourist folders on practically every region in the state. If you need hotel or campground reservations at your next stop, try the special offers. You'll get a better rate if you call ahead.

Some states, Texas is a good example, have paperback guidebooks and lavishly illustrated folders. Florida offers new arrivals free orange or grapefruit juice before they start looking at literature.

If your trip is a long one, carry your maps in a plastic basket. Use a manila folder or recycle mailing envelopes to file tourist literature and maps by states. When your return home, save only essentials; toss the rest.

Keep the pertinent map handy for both pilot and navigator. If the routing is complicated, write it on a 3-x-5 card accessible to both. If you have school-age children aboard, give them a duplicate map so they can practice map reading skills. Many Americans grow up unable to use a map.

A magnifying glass is handy for reading fine print on maps, but keep it in a case. If the sun shines on it in a hot car, it may start a fire.

Looking for something in a motorhome or car can be distracting. Follow the sailor's rule—a place for everything and everything in its place—and your trip will be more enjoyable. Gym bags make practical holders for each person's miscellaneous belongings.

MAKE TRAVELING EASIER WITH PLANNING TIPS

Argus Leader, Sunday, Jan. 16, 1994

These tips may help you plan your next motor trip.

Use a road atlas to become acquainted with routes and mileage. Scale your miles per day goal to what you and your traveling companion(s) will find comfortable.

There's no fun in driving 400 or more miles a day and arriving at your destination short on sleep and tired out. Retirees can stretch out their schedule. Take time along the way to see worthwhile local attractions.

Stop in each state at the first highway information or welcome center to pick up the most recent state map available.

South Dakota's map, guides and folders on specific attractions are among the best offered by any state. This material is available to all during the tourist season when interstate information centers are staffed. Elsewhere, Texas, for example, does a fine job. So do Canadian provinces.

When we return home, we file the new maps and toss the old ones.

Use your motor club and other directories to call ahead for motel or campground reservations. This will let you make maximum use of daylight hours for sightseeing and driving.

Save discount coupons and booklets from your motor or other travel clubs and take them along on your trip.

Ask your hotel for the best possible discount. Don't be bashful about requesting a non-smoking room if that is your preference.

Most motel and campground desk personnel go out of their way to help you. Hotels without dining rooms often have discount coupons for meals at nearby restaurants or downtown.

Watch local TV newscasts at night for the latest weather and pick up USA TODAY in the morning for its outstanding weather map. Many large state and metro dailies have copied USA

TODAY's weather, so they're another source, too. Being fully informed about extreme weather conditions is essential to your own safety.

Local radio stations are your best weather source while driving. WNAX's five-state weather forecasts are the region's best. South Dakota's state map lists radio stations and frequencies.

National Weather Service low-frequency 24-hour broadcasts are another excellent source if you're within broadcast range. South Dakota has five stations: Sioux Falls, Rapid City, Pierre, Huron and Aberdeen. Range is approximately 40 miles. There are 380 stations in the nation. You need a special, small weather radio which costs $37 (from Gourley's in Sioux Falls). It operates on house current or battery.

My wife and I keep a destinations folder with clippings about tourist attractions. We also carry American Automobile Association guide books for states through which we'll travel. The guides list main attractions and accommodations. Campground directories are indispensable for recreational vehicle travelers. We've had the best results with Trailer Life Campground Directory.

Packing a car and a motorhome are two different propositions for travelers. Include an overnight bag for your car. It should contain, among other things, a flashlight, small radio and any prescription drugs and other articles you'll need in the hotel room.

It's easier to travel by motorhome because you don't have to pack and unpack. However, limit your clothing to what you'll need between laundry days. Smaller is better for radios, TVs, computers, hair dryers and other gadgets that you can't do without.

A three-step, folding ladder is essential for doing your rig's windshield and windows in an RV park. Knee pads or old rugs are handy for checking underneath your rig.

Finally, carry a couple of suitcases in the motorhome. You may wish to break up your trip with an overnight excursion from a campground. You may also have to fly home during an extended trip.

SOUTH DAKOTANS JOIN THOUSANDS AT TOYLAND FOR MOTORHOMES

Argus Leader, Sunday, March 19, 1995

Las Cruces, N.M.—One rite of winter for motorhome enthusiasts is attending a rally.

It's an opportunity to make friends, brush up on driving skills, motorhome maintenance and quilting or square dancing.

You can also see new models and all the gadgets anyone could desire for their home on wheels.

Nearly 9,000 members of the Family Motor Coach Association met here March 9-11 for their "Fiesta Las Cruces Convention."

There were 5,253 motorhomes including 827 exhibit coaches, many of which were sold. It was an adult toyland.

FMCA volunteers shoe-horned 4,426 motor coaches owned by individuals into parks, streets and open spaces of the sprawling New Mexico State University campus for several days of dry camping. Handicapped who needed electric hookups were accommodated in special lots.

The big draw for most was seeing the 1995 motor coaches. Price tags ranged from about $45,000 to more than $700,000 for luxurious bus-like coaches with high-tech accessories.

Exhibitors included some of the nation's largest recreational vehicle dealers.

Sales people met you, answered questions, pointed out craftsmanship and related the latest technical changes.

There was showmanship. Safari, an Oregon manufacturer, displayed big, stuffed black fabric gorillas. One was driving a motorhome chassis. A couple of gorillas presided amidst palms, over-stuffed lions and other jungle creatures.

Between 300 and 400 firms serving the RV industry had exhibits. Ford, Chevrolet, Caterpillar, Cummings Diesel and other major manufacturers displayed their components.

Two Iowa firms, Winnebago Industries, Inc., of Forest City, and Born Free of Humboldt, were among exhibitors.

Dave Hindt, a retiree from Rock Rapids, Iowa, who used to sell light bulbs to Sioux Falls and other Sioux Empire customers, was with the Born Free exhibit as an owner-agent. Born Free offers cash bonuses to motorhome owners who secure new sales.

Steve Pratt, 45, Born Free factory representative from Humboldt, is confident that the coming surge of baby boomers reaching retirement age will spur RV sales. The 1995 Born Free line is sold out, so Pratt and Hindt are working on 1996 orders. Their next stop is the Coast-to-Coast rally in Phoenix, and after that, an Anaheim, Calif., show.

This was the first FMCA rally for Keith and Doris Lunde of Mitchell, who have spent the winter in Mesa, Ariz. He's a retired loan officer of Commercial Bank in Mitchell.

Tom and Darlene Borzenski of Rapid City made the rally part of their winter travels. He's president of the Black Hills Mavericks chapter of FMCA.

His recommendation for avoiding mountain driving is to take U.S. 385 south from Hot Springs through Chadron and Alliance, Neb. Follow it through Julesburg, Burlington, Lamar and Springfield, Colo., and the Oklahoma Panhandle to Dalhart, Texas. There you can pick up a southwest diagonal route (U.S. 54) into New Mexico.

The FMCA's summer rally will be Aug. 15-17 at Minot, N.D. Merlyn and Doris Dick of Dickinson, N.D., expect to help. Their Rambling Nodaks chapter will serve as greeters.

Dennis Voeller and Jane Bartholomay of the Minot Convention and Visitors Bureau offered attendees a packet on North Dakota attractions. The 1990 Minot rally drew 2,600 coaches.

Robbin Maue, associate editor of Family Motor Coaching and spokesperson, said FMCA rotates its conventions to have summer and winter rallies in each time zone once every four years.

The convention was a pleasant break for Sherman and Lois Visscher of Platte, S.D. He's vice president and manager of First Fidelity Bank in Platte. They're members of Holiday Rambler's Rambling Pheasants chapter.

TIPS CAN HELP PLAN FOR GREAT TRIP IN RV

Argus Leader, April 2, 1995

Here are some travel hints to help you enjoy a gypsy's life while camping out.

Hold a domestic policy session with your partner to plan what you want to do on the next trip.

If both of you like a domestic airline destination, arrange to leave your motorhome or trailer in a campground at a major airline city and fly from there.

We did that two years ago when we flew out of Albuquerque, N.Mex., via Minneapolis to Baltimore to attend a convention.

KEY HINTS ON MOTORHOME TRAVEL

We did the same thing two weeks ago when we flew from Albuquerque to Denver. We landed at the new Denver International Airport (DIA) in a dust storm.

No, United didn't lose our baggage. It was waiting for us after we reached the main building via a keen underground train.

No one checked our baggage stubs to determine if the three pieces belonged to us. The system at John F. Kennedy Airport in New York and at some other airports is better: someone checks your stub before you take away the bags.

DIA, incidentally, looks great. Its big drawback is being 25 miles from downtown Denver. We spent $15 each for a 45-minute van ride to our south Denver destination. Cab fare would be from $38 or $45 to $50 to $60 each.

One could take a city bus (RTD-Regional Transportation District) to downtown Denver for 50 cents, and transfer at the Market Street Station to a DIA bus for $6 or $3 for seniors. Buses run hourly from 5:29 a.m. to 10:29 p.m. Buses also run from the former Stapleton International Airport to DIA.

Denver needs a better solution like light rail from DIA to downtown. That's a goal of DIA, but unfortunately, not of RTD. Such a link seems a long way off.

Other ideas for your next trip

- If someone at home handles your mail, leave them priority mail envelopes addressed to stops along the way. We've received four weekly envelopes on time (two days from Sioux Falls) this trip; one packet to Las Cruces, N.M., arrived on Monday (five days later), instead of Friday.
- Take clothing (wrinkle resistant) for one week. Do laundry at campground stops that are convenient. Pack a small bag of laundry soap and a roll of quarters. If you'll fly to another place, pack some suitcases with a wardrobe to fit the climate.
- Take only what you expect to use. Use specific places in the motorhome or trailer for clothing, medicine, essential correspondence, etc. A small shoulder pack is great for day trips.
- When you read about far-away places that thrill you, clip the item and file it away. Talk about how you can view a new Shangri-la on your next trip.
- Use automatic bank deposit for retirement and other fixed income. Use bank payment plans for utilities and other recurring charges. This will materially reduce correspondence.
- Leave an itinerary with phone numbers where you can be reached with family members or friends.
- Get a cellular phone for your rig. It's a real boost when you need roadside assistance. It also spares you standing or waiting at campground phones.
- If you're driving a class A motorhome (a larger one as opposed to shorter chassis with bunks over the cab) or pulling a long trailer, avoid going through large cities if possible. Take a belt line around a city. For instance, at Amarillo, Tex., you'll save at least half an hour of slow driving and heavy traffic by using Texas 335 around the eastern and southern sides of the city.
- Stop before the 5 p.m. rush. Avoid night travel.
- Obtain big city maps before you leave. Pack a magnifying glass. Get new state maps at welcome centers.
- Let faster traffic (especially big trucks) pass your slower recreational vehicle. Scan ahead and watch your rear. Drive safely and, as they say in Texas, drive friendly.

VAGABONDS LEARN ABOUT LIFE ON ROAD AT RALLY

Argus Leader, Sunday, Aug. 27, 1995

MINOT, N.D.—Some of 4,000 or more vagabonding couples played student by attending classes at the Family Motor Coach Association's annual summer rally in Minot Aug. 15-17, 1995.

The campus was on the grounds of the North Dakota State Fair. Professors were factory representatives of truck, engine and chassis manufacturers and authors on automotive and cooking subjects. Males and a few females attended seminars on motor home maintenance. Some speakers told them to avoid fuel additives and gadgets to enhance performance. Oddly, sales persons pitched such products at nearby exhibits.

Women attended demonstrations on motor coach cooking and how microwave-convection ovens make it easier. Both sexes shopped countless booths. You could buy a portable flag pole or an air mattress with dual controls.

Many motor homes for sale were buslike and luxurious. One was priced at more than $600,000. Some couples drove home in new or different motor homes.

Members of Black Hills Mavericks chapter led by Tom Borzenski of Rapid City were among greeter volunteers. Glenn Addy of Canistota was a captain of greeter volunteers. Among other attendees from South Dakota were Verne and Donna Luke, Sioux Falls.

Many rally goers toured Minot and area attractions. What they saw in Minot:

• Roosevelt Park & Zoo. Built on the banks of the Souris River, the menagerie includes two giraffes, a magnificent Bengal tiger, zebras, llamas, Kodiak bears, a black jaguar, emus and Bactrian camels. There's a splendid North American section with bison, eagles, musk ox and wolf.

• The Railroad Museum's "Magic City Express" is a two-fifth scale miniature Great Northern (GN) train that runs on track on the north end of Roosevelt Park. The train operates from May 1 to Sept. 1.

The GN F8 locomotive weighs 8 tons and has traction on all eight drive wheels. Rolling stock includes open cars and a caboose. Fullsize Burlington Northern and Soo cabooses are on the grounds; also a carousel.

The Railroad Museum of Minot in the Town & Country Shopping Center, 1015 S. Broadway, is open from 10 a.m. to noon on weekdays; it is not open on weekends. Call Betty Berg, office manager and a board member, at (701) 852 7091, or the concession at the park at (701) 838 2205 for possible other arrangements. The Museum has historic photos and memorabilia. A drive seeks funds for a building to be erected at the park.

• The Scandinavian Heritage Center in Shirley Bicentennial Park is across the street from Town & Country Shopping Center. Exhibits include statues of Leif Eriksson, Icelandic explorer; Sondre Norheim, father of modern skiing; and Casper Oimoen, Olympic skier. Norheim and Oimoen, Norwegian immigrants, lived in North Dakota. A Danish windmill and a 220-year-old house and a stabbur (storehouse), both built in Norway, are other park features.

• Minot State University, once a teachers' normal school, now enrolls many students in business. Its Dome seats 12,000 for basketball.

• The Quentin Burdick Job Corps Center of the U.S. Department of Labor teaches approximately 250 students auto mechanics, farm machinery, custodial and other trades. There are dormitories for students and day care for children of single mothers.

- Minot Air Force Base, 14 miles north of Minot, has 12,000 people. The Minot School District runs elementary schools on the base; children are bused to Minot for high school.

DON'T LET THIEVES RUIN GOOD TRIP

Argus Leader, Nov. 19, 1995

HONOLULU—There are so many pleasant things about a trip to Hawaii that it is easy to overlook a few daily perils.

If you don't pay attention to basic precautions, you may wind up losing your rental car or other belongings.

Most rental agencies tell you not to leave anything in your car, not to keep valuables in your trunk and to lock the car when it's parked.

Parked automobiles and personal belongings are easy marks for numerous criminals who support themselves on the tourist economy.

They watch tourists at viewpoints along the highway, on beaches and in parking lots or other places where they think they can steal a car or take belongings while the owners are doing something else.

This writer experienced such an attempt about seven years ago on Oahu. We had stopped at a restaurant in a small town.

Returning to the car, we met a local property manager who had chased would be thieves away before they finished drilling out a lock on our car. His phone call to police resulted in the apprehension of a couple of suspects.

Today in Hawaii, all you need to do is read the newspapers to know that car theft is a big problem.

Rule 1 in Hawaii—Never leave your car unattended when it has property in it. If necessary to keep something in the trunk, put it in before you park so thieves won't see you stow it.

Rule 2—Believe car rental people when they tell you to lock the car.

Rule 3—Believe the rental agent in Molokai, one of the smaller islands, when she says NEVER lock your rental car. Would be thieves will smash the car windows to make sure you didn't leave anything.

The danger from car thieves becomes an annoyance. You find yourself carrying something along on a sightseeing trip that you'd rather not haul into a restaurant or through a museum.

Generally, basic rules for safeguarding property and self will keep you out of harm's way in the Hawaiian islands.

These include care in handling your wallet and currency, carrying necessary valuables in a fanny pack and not showing off jewelry. (My wife says to leave jewelry at home.)

Never let anyone see you with a wad of cash. Wear a money belt and go to a rest room if you have to resort to the bills you carry in the belt.

There's no reason to walk down a dark street at night in Hawaii. Stick to the bright lights of downtown Honolulu or main streets in smaller Hawaiian cities. Or take a cab to the hotel.

When swimming, use a waterproof container for your electronic room key card or key which you can wear in the water.

Most tourist hotels offer a small safe in your room for about $1.50 a day. The safes operate on a combination you choose, or a single key that you take with you. The safes are a good place to keep airline tickets and valuables.

When on vacation, you want to have a good time. You can foil thieves by staying alert.

Author's Notes

Some articles in this book are unabridged and may differ in length or arrangement from the published version in the *Argus Leader*. This applies mainly to articles written after my retirement on June 1, 1984.

The author would like to acknowledge the following individuals who granted permission to reprint from their publications:

Tim Giago for his editorial from the *Lakota Times*, reprinted in the *Argus Leader* August 23, 1981.

Don Ravellette, publisher of the *Faith Independent*.

David Clausen, publisher of the *West River Progress*, Dupree, S.D.

Albert Tims, Director of the School of Journalism and Mass Communications, University of Minnesota, for an article in the *Murphy Reporter*.

I also want to thank Rob DeWall of Crazy Horse for providing photographs of Pope John Paul II and his interest in sculptor Korczak Ziolkowski's mountain carving of the Indian leader.

Finally, I would like to thank my many friends and *Argus Leader* readers who have made many days for me by their volunteered recollection of my stories.

October 5, 2000

Index

A

Aadland, Gerald L. 306
Abdallah, Gene 172
Abdnor, James 172, 180, 235, 237
Abourezk, James 231, 235, 236
Addy, Glenn 326
Adler, Philip D. 90
Afdahl, Anders 23-25
Afdahl, Anders (Mrs.) 24
Afdahl, Calie 133
Afdahl, Elise (see Yeager)
Afdahl, George (half brother) 24, 25, 39, 43, 47
Afdahl, Knud 24, 25
Afdahl Jr., Knud 25
Afdahl, Larry (half brother) 39, 43, 46, 47
Afdahl, Nels (stepfather) 20, 23, 25, 39, 46, 56, 57, 69
Afdahl, Nels Richard (half brother) 39, 43, 47, 50-51
Afdahl, Olav 23, 24
Agnew, Spiro 231
Alba, Alney 97
Allison, Vern 290
American Horse 199
Anderson, Kristin 219, 283
Anderson, Orville 302
Anderson, Sigurd 158, 219, 243, 245, 282-284
Anderson, Vivian 283
Andrews, Gerald 219
Annison, Michael 152
Antonen, Mel 67, 92
Antonen Ray 177, 178, 182
Ash, Ben 202, 203
Ashley, James D. 63, 77, 83
Astor, John Jacob 169
Axlund, Lois Mehrbach 258

B

Bach, Catherine 149, 177
Bailey, C.O. 281
Bailey, Dana Reed 239, 240
Bailey Jr., Harold S. 266
Bailey, Jean 280, 281
Bailey Jr., Theodore Meade 279-281
Bailey III, Theodore Mead 281
Baker Jr., Howard 236
Balcer, Beth 131
Balcer, Brian 131
Balcer, Elizabeth 131
Balcer, Charles 131, 220, 255, 256
Balcer, Mark 131
Balcer, Mary 131
Bannon, John 87
Barkley, Albin 259

Barnes, Sylvester Raymond 188
Barnett, Louise 192, 193
Barnum, Phineus 162
Bartels, Kitty 133
Bartholomay, Jane 324
Baruch, Bernard 272
Bates, Charles H. 127-129, 183
Batz, Heidi 52
Beadle, William Henry Harrison 220
Beardsley, George G. 129
Bechtold, Alta Marie 96
Bechtold, Bridget Anne 96
Bechtold, Charles 96
Bechtold, Daniel 96
Bechtold, F.H. 96
Bechtold, F.H. (Mrs.) 96
Bechtold, Herbert Miles 77, 94-96, 268
Bechtold, Michael 96
Bechtold, Robert 96
Bechtold, Thomas 96
Beck, Louis 167
Bell, C.E. 188, 189
Bennis, Bob 192
Benson, Ezra Taft 248
Berg, Betty 326
Berg, Sherwood 104
Berger, Justin 287-290
Berger, Sandra 293
Berry, Tom 234
Bidwell, Bob 38
Bidwell, Dale L. (brother-in-law) 38, 54, 55
Bidwell, Dwight 38
Bidwell Family Association 36, 37
Bidwell, Ila Mae 54

Bidwell, Joan 37, 38
Bidwell, John 36-38
Bidwell, Lydia (Ada May's mother) 46
Bidwell, Maxine 37
Bidwell, Richard 36-38
Bidwell, Robert 37
Bidwell, Virgil 37, 38
Binger, Bob 131
Bjerk, Irid 251
Blacklidge, Richard L. 90
Bloom, W.S. 239
Boe, Nils 283
Bogert, William 106
Bohnet, Ronald 136
Bohy, Richard 180,
Boone, Pat 105
Borglum, Gutzon 167, 210, 301
Borzenski, Tom 326
Bottum, Joe 235, 283
Boulton, Edwin C. 281
Bradley, Omar 72, 312

Brady, Cyrus Townsend 198
Brady, Jim 106
Bray, Edmund C. 213
Bray, Martha 213
Breum, Ole 128
Briggs, Hilton M. 104, 270
Brinkman, Del 84
Brochu, Ron 272
Brockhouse, Henry 209, 238
Brokaw, Janet 290
Brokaw, Tom 12
Brokenleg, Martin 221
Brown, George L. 104
Brown, T. 196
Brune, Ben 191
Bullen, J.G. 134
Bullock, Seth 195, 196
Bulow, W.J. 234, 236, 308, 315
Burch, Frank 177
Burger, Chief Justice 280
Burns, Bob 240
Burns, Roy D. 132
Burns, Roy D. (Mrs.) 132
Burnside, George W. 248
Burrow, Robert J. 90
Bush, George 316
Bushfield, Harlan 235, 236, 315
Bushfield, Vera 235
Byre, Elton 224
Byrne, Frank M. 234

C

Cannon, John 67
Carlson, Ernest G. 238
Carlson, Ernie 242
Carlson, Freda 242
Carlton, Caleb 303
Carnegie, Dale 251, 252, 279
Carter, Jimmy 219, 230, 231, 238
Case, Francis 100-103, 189, 235, 236, 283, 308, 314, 315
Case Jr., Francis H. 314
Case, Leland 167
Caselli, Bob 52, 54
Casey, Ralph D. 72, 75, 76, 88, 89, 94
Cash, Joseph 181
Chalberg, Helen 298
Cahlberg, Robert D. 298, 299
Chang Jun Fu 237
Chernoff, Howard L. xi, 71
Chief Joseph 169
Chou En-lai 237, 238
Christopherson, Fred C. xi, 66, 71, 76, 83, 99, 101, 102, 107-109, 131, 132
Christopherson, Marie 109, 131
Clark, Mark 106, 297
Clark, William 155, 167

Clem, Alan 236
Clements, Dr. 199
Cleveland, Herbert B. 301, 302
Clinton, Bill 58
Clinton, Hillary Rodham 58
Collins, Lawton 297
Conahan, Walt 275
Conn, Charles G. 162
Coolidge, Calvin 97, 104, 301
Coon, J.D. 253
Coopards, William H. xi
Corning, Duane L. "Duke" 287, 291, 300
Costner, Kevin 5, 171, 205, 211
Crawford, Coe I. 189, 236
Crazy Horse 208, 211, 217, 218
Crook, George C. 198-200
Cropp, Richard 313
Crusinberry, V.L. 249
Cunningham, Lloyd B. 66, 69, 87

Custer, Elizabeth 169, 192, 193, 196, 203
Custer, George Armstrong 49, 169, 176, 192, 193, 195-200, 202, 203, 207, 208, 210, 216, 301, 314
Cutler, Richard 163, 221, 224, 225
Cutler, Sharon 163, 225

D
Dahlin, Sarah 133
Danicic, John 261
Danilco, Roxie 155
Darrow, Clarence 236
Daschle, Tom 12, 180, 249
Davis, Jefferson 311
Day, Charles M. 109
DeLacompt 196
Delbridge, C.J. 238
de Mores, Marquis 170
Denholm, Frank 231
Derscheid, Lyle 190, 191
DeSmet, Pierre Jean 158, 195, 210
Dick, Doris 324
Dick, Merlyn 324
Dille, John F. 90
Dimmerling, Harold J. 217, 218
Dirksen, Ed 255
Dodge, S.C. 202, 203
Donahue, Ed 202
Donaldson, Professor 197
Doyle, Jack 160
Dravland, Tom 172
Drees, Josephine Mary 188
Driver, Julie 133
Dulles, John Foster 237
Duke, Daisy 177
Dunn, Francis 280
Dunn, Harvey 158, 165, 167, 209
Dunn, Jim 245
Dupree, Pete 170

E
Eastridge, Ray 55
Eastwood, Clint 191
Egan, John 65, 68
Ehrensberger, Edward C. 201
Eisenhower, Dwight D. 3, 101, 103, 104, 107, 230, 237, 247, 248, 272,
Ellsworth, Richard E. 314
Ellis, Teri 153
Elmen, Jim 273
Elmen, Robert C. 270-273
Elrod, Samuel H. 188
Emery, Ed 107
Erickson, Dolly 135
Erickson, Grant 135
Eriksson, Leif 326
Erskine, Al 83
Everist, Hubert 163
Everist, Margaret Ann 163
Ewing, General 195

F
Farber, William O. 236
Farrar, Frank 180, 184
Farrar, Pat 184
Fees, Byron 136
Fees, Chris 14
Fees, Darlene 136, 137
Feist, Lynn 141, 143
Finnegan, John 90
Fischer Quintuplets 110
Fishbach, Andrew 144
Fisher, John 141, 143
Flolid, Jodie Egan 72
Floren, Myron 177
Floyd, Joe 105
Floyd Jr., Joe 105
Ford, Gerald 231
Ford, Henry 2, 165
Forsyth, General 197
Foss, Joe 72, 177, 180, 219, 234, 261, 287, 290-292
Foster, Nina 194
Fraser, James Earl 167
Fremont, John Charles 212
Friess, Barb 152
Friess, Richard 152
Fujita, Susuma 316
Fuller, Bill 260
Fuller, Howell 258-260
Fuller, Larry xi, 67, 88-90, 93, 105, 106
Fuller, Ruth 259
Funston, G. Keith 177

G
Gable, Clark 315
Galbraith, Francis 177
Geisler, A.J. (Dick) 166
Geisler, Dave 166

Geisler, David M. 166
Geisler, L.J. (Ms.) 166
Geisler, Vivian 166
Gereau, Elizabeth 264
Geronimo 317, 318
Giago, Tim 214
Gibson, Gwen 236
Gilfillan, Archer 168
Goldwater, Barry 230
Gorgas, William 7
Grant, Lou 65
Grant, Ulysses S. 310, 311
Grauvogl, Ann 110
Graves, Myrie 314
Green, F.V. 293
Grieg, Edvard 22, 31
Griffin, John 101, 102
Grinager, Lloyd K. 281, 282
Gross, Ellwood 270
Gross, Emerson 270
Gross, Esther M. 269, 270
Gross, John C. 269
Gross, Wallace 270
Grube, Frieda 35
Gruber, Edmund L. 294
Gurney, Chan 236, 308, 315
Gustafson, LaVonne 190
Gutch, Elizabeth Riggs 194

H
Haber, Jean 242
Haggard, Merle 207
Halbkat, Jack 267
Hale, Evan 135
Hale, Joseph 156
Hall, Tom T. 207
Hallock, Morris 290
Hamlisch, Marvin 105
Hammerlee, Glenn 281
Hansen, Lowell 237
Harden, A.M. 200
Hargens, Charles 167
Harrington, Frank 72
Harris, John W. 180, 228
Harris, Tommy 54
Harrison, Benjamin 176
Hart, Don 134
Hart, Mary 12
Hart, Mary Ann 134
Harvey, Traci 133
Hastings, Gov. of Penna 303
Hausdorff, Pauline 262
Heidepriem, Scott 247, 248
Henie, Sonja 27
Henrichsen, Al Vina 274, 275
Henrichsen, Dean 274
Henrichsen, Mel 273-275
Henrichsen, Melvin 274
Hepner, H.S. 70
Herriott, Ruth 276
Herriott, Virgil 275-277
Herseth, Lars 243, 244

INDEX

Herseth, Lorna 184
Herseth, Ralph 190, 243
Heyerdahl, Thor 27
Hickock, Wild Bill 245
Hilt, Mrs. 14
Hindt, Dave 324
Hipple, John 269
Hipps, Linda 74, 75
Hiss, Alger 246
Hitchcock, Herbert 236
Hitler, Adolf 19, 34, 133, 264, 305, 315
Hohbach, Sally 125
Holdren, Wauneta 159
Holt, Tom 63
Holter, Joan 163
Holum, Kenneth 177
Hoover, Herbert 3, 221
Horney, Jackie 264
Houck, Roy 5, 205
Howard, H.P. 188
Howard, Margaret Kellog 193
Howe, Oscar 163, 167, 183, 209, 210, 219-221
Hull, Cordell 306
Humphrey, Hubert 12, 72, 104, 204, 210, 230, 261
Hunhoff Jr., Bernie 218
Hunking, Loila 240
Hunter, Alison 133

Huseboe, Arthur R. 220, 221
Hussein, Saddam 312
Hustead, Dorothy 165
Hustead, Rick 165
Hustead, Ted 165
Hustead, William 163-165

I

Iacoca, Lee 306
Illingworth, W.H. 197
Indian Crow 196
Ingalls, Caroline 157
Ingalls, Carry 157
Ingalls, Charles 157
Ingalls, Grace 157
Ingalls, Mary 157
Ingram, Gene 135
Irvine, Louisa 194
Iseminger, Gordon 128, 129
Iverson, Elise 39
Iverson, Hans 39
Iverson, Thomas R. 298-300
Iverson, Thorwald 39, 41, 48

J

Jackson, Stonewall 198
Jacoway, John 281
Janklow, William 12, 89, 91, 150, 177, 178, 180, 181, 228, 233-235, 240-242, 244, 293

Janklow, William (Mrs.) 228
Javurek, Anthony "Tony" 261
Javurek, Audrey 261
Javurek, Benjamin 261
Javurek, Martin 261
Javurek, Tony 261, 262
Jaybush, Ralph 238, 239
Jennewein, Leonard 163
John Paul II, Pope 105, 217, 218
Johnson, All 221, 222, 224, 225
Johnson, Lady Bird 231
Johnson, Lyndon B. 104, 230, 231
Johnson, Myles 192
Johnson, Tim 12
Johnston, H.V. 204
Jones, Bob 260
Jones, Walter 259

K

Kadir, Rashid 168
Kahler, Ernest J. 101-103
Kaltsulas, Kathryn (Mrs. Masten) 253
Karolevitz, Robert F. 218, 219
Kasa, Roger 86
Keavy, Hubbard 98-100
Keavy, Jane 100
Keavy, Jeffrey 100
Keck, Howard B. 102
Kennedy, John A. xi, 101
Kennedy, John F. 230, 231
Kennedy, Verne 264
Kent, R. 196
Kerney Jr., James 90
Ketterling, Bob 159
Khadafy, Moammar 306
Kiley, Mary 153
Kilvey, James 276
Kind, Ezra 196
King, Charles 198, 199
King, George 75
King, George (Mrs.) 75
King, Win 196
Kirk, George 80, 86
Kirkham, J.E. 296
Kittredge, Alfred 236
Kjelden, Dean 192
Klaudt, James 162
Klaudt, Lou 162
Kneip, Richard 84, 85, 111, 180, 219, 231, 235, 243
Knobe, Rick 177, 180, 228, 248, 249
Kolb, Duane 133
Kolb, Kristi 133
Korbin, Jeffrey 100
Korbin, Jerry 99, 100
Koplow, George 262
Koplow, Goldie 262
Koplow, Ira 262
Koplow, Isadore 263
Koplow, Nathan 262
Kopperud, Harmon 177

Koslowski, Dennis 12
Koslowski, Duane 12
Koupal, Nancy Tystad 194
Krause, Herbert 220
Krautschun, Harvey 245
Khrushchev, Nikita 21, 108
Kroeger, Jean R. 263, 264
Kroeger Jr., Jean R. 264
Kroeger, Kevin 264
Kroeger, Louise 264
Kunkel, Bob 192
Kurtenbach, Thomas 10
Kyle, James 235

L

LaDue, Danny 133
LaFramboise, Joseph 207
Lamont, Daniel E. 303
Lamphere, Dale
Landers, Ann 272
Lane, Rose Wilder 158
Larson, Arne B. 162
Larson, John 161
Latza, Greg 59
Lawrence, David 250
Lawrence, Ernest 264, 265
Lawrence, John 265
LeBlanc, Eleanor 267
LeBlanc, Floyd J. 265-267
Ledford, David xi
Lee, Bob 290, 292, 301
Lee, Robert E. 309, 311
Lehman, Marilynn 136.137
Lehman, Mony (aunt) 57
Lehman, Paul 136
Leopard, William H. 80, 83
Levitt, Glenn 131
Lewis, Meriwether 155, 167
Lillehaug, Leland 237
Lin Zhiying 237
Lincoln, Abraham 169, 309, 311
Lindbergh, Charles A. 2, 119
Lintz, Jack 241
Lirus, J. Vangen 23
Little, Karla 135
Little, Laurie 135
Little, Loren 135
Little, Maxine 135
Little, Richard 135
Lohr, Alan 258
Lohr, Carol 258
Lohr, Jerry 257, 258
Lohr, Walter 258
Lohr, Walter (Mrs.) 258
Lombard, Carole 315
Loriks, Emil 131
Lowry, Daisy 255
Lowry, Robert Charles 255
Lowry, Vayne Arnold 254, 255
Lucid, Daniel 125
Ludlow, William 197
Luke, Donna 326

333

Luke, Verne 326
Lunde, Doris 324
Lunde, Keith 324
Lynn, Loretta 207

M
MacArthur, Douglas 72, 237, 247, 278, 294, 309, 313, 315
MacArthur, Jean 247
MacDonald, Peter 90
Madden, Mary 260
Malerich, Jack 97
Mandrell, Louise 207
Manfred, Frederick 221
Mann, Dean 294-296
Mann, Lorraine 294
Mann, ReNae 294
Marsh, Jack xi
Marsh, Russ 202
Masten, Jeff 255
Masten, Mary W. 255
Masten, Samuel 253-255
Masten, Sam (Mrs.) 255
Maue, Robbin 324
McAuliffe, General 25
McCall, Jack 245
McCart, Earl 249
McCarthy, Joe 236
McCaughey, Robert L. 248
McElrath, Jack 191, 192
McElwee, Robert 16
McGovern, George 235, 236
McIntosh, Alan C. 250, 251
McKay, William T. 197
McKee, John T. 315
McKenzie, Edna 167
McKusick, Marshall 254
McMaster, William 236
McNair, Leslie J. 317

Meade, George C. 309
Meaghan, James 177, 178, 182
Meves, Cliff 83
Mews, Ray 110
Mickelson, George S. (son) 185, 186, 243
Mickelson, George T. 234, 243-245
Mickelson, Linda 185
Mickelson, Sig 221
Miller, Carl 160
Miller, Debbie 133
Miller, Douglas L. 236
Mills, Anson 198, 199
Milsap, Ronnie 207
Mitchell, Helen 177
Mix, Tom 165
Moberly, Richard O. 282
Moe, Johan Christian 23
Moe, Mrs. 23
Mohler, Charles W. 58
Mondale, Walter 230, 231
Moody, Charles C. 127, 128

Moody, Gideon 235
Moritz, Jody 158, 159
Morse, James 276
Morse, Teresa 276
Muenster, Ted 257, 258
Muller, Richard 93
Mundstock, Walter 203, 204
Mundt, Karl 72, 235, 236, 246-248, 308, 315
Mundt, Mary 246, 248
Murphy, M.L. 152
Murphy, Benton 58

N
Naisbitt, John 152, 272
Neff, John M. 101-103
Nelsen, William C. 256
Nelson, Baby Face 108
Nelson, Dan 314
Nelson, Mat xi
Nelson, Michael 125
Nelson, Paula M. 194
Nelson, Verlynn (Mr. & Mrs.) 125
Nervig, Alice 281
Nesland, Virgil 144
Neuharth, Al 12, 71, 177
Nichol, Fred 180, 228, 254, 280
Nicolett, Joseph Nicolas 212, 213
Nielsen, Thurmann 289
Nisselius, Arthur 16
Nixon, Richard 230, 231, 236-238, 247, 248, 270
Norbeck, Peter 234, 236, 296
Nord, Evans 105
Norheim, Sondre 326
Norris, Emily 133
Northrup, Joseph 125
Novotny, Joe 105

O
Ochs, Adolph S. 110
Ode, Kim 65
Oimoen, Casper 326
Olsen, O.H. 189
Olson, Alice 161
Olson, Gene 161
Olson, Gordon 277, 278
Olson, Gregg 161
Olson, John 287
Olson, Phyllis 278
O'Neill, Tip 276
Onstad, Niels 27
Oviatt, Denny 192

P
Parker, Jeff 137-140
Parker, John D. 138-140
Parker, Walter 139
Patman, Elmer 102
Patton, Don 203

Patton Jr., George S. 311, 312
Peale, Norman Vincent 277, 279
Pearson, David 104
Pearson, Drew 80
Pemberton, John C. 310, 311
Petersen, Wayne 202
Peterson, Richard 180, 228
Pettigrew, Frank 239
Petigrew, Richard 128, 129, 235, 236
Pettijohn, Lucille 297
Philips, Scotty 170
Phillips, Margaret 247
Piantino, Tammy 133
Pickard, Reginald 127
Piersol, Cathy 280
Pietz, Clyde 162
Polen, Sylvia 263
Pompidou, Georges 32
Powell, John 295
Pratt, Steve 324
Presley, Elvis 22, 165
Pressler, Larry 71, 180, 235-238, 296
Preuss, Roger 221
Price, Bob 14, 15
Price, Kristi 133
Pride, Charlie 207
Pritchard, Shirley 158
Pruitt, Gene 262
Pugsley, Charles W. 104

Q
Qualset, Herb 77, 83
Queal, Dave 11

R
Raasch, Chuck 87
Ragsdale, E.K. 57, 58
Rainey, Anson (great uncle) 39
Rainey, Minnie 48
Rasmussen, Dorothy 281
Rayl, George 293
Rayl, J.R. 293
Rayl, Sandy 292-294
Rayl, Sandy (Mrs.) 293
Reagan, Ronald 103, 104, 106, 107, 238, 246, 306
Redlin, Terry 213
Reed, Clyde 85
Reed, Cora 285
Reese, Sheldon F. 221
Rehfeldt, Sharon xi
Reiners, Gale 313, 314
Reinholt, Gene 253
Renshaw, Bob 250
Rhodes, Dusty 166
Rhodes, Gayl 166
Richter, Charles 55
Richter, William (Mrs.) 54, 55
Rickenbacker, Eddie 290

INDEX

Ridder Jr., B.H. 90
Ridgeway, Matthew B. 237
Riggs, Robert 194
Riggs, Steven Return 194
Riggs, Steven (Mrs.) 194
Riggs, Theodore Foster 194
Riggs, Thomas L. 155, 193, 194
Riley, Jeannie C. 207
Robbie, Joe 160, 177, 283
Robinson, Doane 198, 297
Roche, Catherine A. (Mrs. Herb Bechtold) 96
Rockefeller, Nelson 231
Roosevelt, Franklin D. 3, 15, 107, 108, 120, 187, 190, 219, 261, 302, 308
Roosevelt, Theodore 169, 176
Rose, August Houston 173
Ross, H.W. 239
Ross, Horatio Nelson 195, 197
Ruebel-Alberts, Francie 172
Ruhberg, Gary 106
Ruml, Randall 125
Rumpza, William (Mrs.)
Rush, Rick 180
Ryan, Kathym

S

Salo, Joe 177
Sandven, Olav 23
Sandvig, Spence 77
Saul, John 221
Saure, Henry B. 249
Scheer, Bill 183
Scheer, Jim 183
Schetnan, E.L. 18, 63, 75, 285, 286
Schirmer, Mike 180, 192, 228, 249
Schmitz, Julie 177, 178
Schock, Al 177
Schott, Sallie 281
Schreiner, Tim 87
Schueler, Dean A. 221
Schuler, Harold H. 188, 267
Schultz-Peren, Petter 22
Scurr, Kenneth R. 296, 297
Scurr Jr., Kenneth R. 297
Seacrest, Joe 90
Seeman, Maxine 242, 243
Sellgman, Daniel 103
Shakespeare, William 8, 83
Sharpe, M.Q. 161, 235
Sheldon, Gov. of SD 303
Sheridan, Philip H. 317
Shinneman, Perry 111
Shinneman, Shirley 111
Silha, Otto 90
Simmons, Jerry 252, 253
Simmons, Walter A. 96-98, 177
Sitting Bull 169, 193-196, 198, 216, 221
Skiles, Chad 11
Smith, Dean C. xi, 87

Smith, Deming 254
Smith, Francis M. 259, 260
Smith, Russell 241
Smoker, John J. 57
Sneve, Virginia Driving Hawk 201
Solvie, Lisa 133
Sorensen, Charles M. 35, 36
Sorensen, Delores (Mrs. Charles) 36
Sorensen, Hans Frederick 36
Sorensen, Tom 35, 36
Sousa, John Philip 170
Stevens, Albert W. 302
Stevenson, Adlai 261
Stimson, Stimmy 202
Stoebner, Shirley 226
Streisand, Barbra 110
Strickland, Jack 55
Stroud, Joe 85
Sullivan, Robert A. 177
Suttons 192
Swenson, Orvel B. 298
Swift, Tandi 133
Swift, Tonya 133
Swift, Troy 133

T

Talbot, Lyle 97
Taylor Jr., William G. 260
Tennyson, Alfred Lord 125
Thingelstad, Anders (grandfather) 39, 41, 48
Thingelstad, Hans (uncle) 48-50
Thingelstad, Helen (aunt) 49, 50
Thingelstad, Iver (uncle) 48-50
Thingelstad, Kjersti (Iverson) (grandmother) 39, 48
Thingelstad, Mony (Lehman) 39, 48
Thoen, Louis 196
Thomas, Duane 144
Thomas, Jeff 105
Thomas, Lowell 252
Thompson, Carv 141-143, 148
Thompson, Harry F. 221
Thompson, Jim 112
Thompson, Margaret 148
Thompson, Phatty 170
Thorne, Mel 284, 285
Thune, John 12
Tibbs, Casey 191
Tillis, Mel 207
Toffler, Alvin 272
Torness, Harold L. 13, 213
Townsley, Emeline C. 162
Truman, Harry 72, 77, 107, 237, 294
Tunge, Faith 288
Tunge, Harry 288
Turgeon, Bernard 257, 258
Tuve, Anthony G. 265
Tuve, Ida Marie 265

Tuve, Lucy 265
Tuve, Merle Anthony 264, 265
Twain, Mark 110

U

Ueberroth, Peter 148
Uhrhammer, Ernest 38

V

Vanden Heuvel, Stacey 167, 168
Vedder, Byron C. 90
Verendrye, Louis 154, 207, 210
Vickerman, Thomas R. 279
Virhus, J. Liaton 24
Visscher, Lois 324
Visscher, Sherman 324
Voeller, Dennis 324
Von Fischer, Phil 266, 267
Von Walleghen, Troy 125

W

Wagner, Robert 94
Waldum, Paul 225
Ward, Stephen 132
Warren, Todd 52
Washington, Denzel 110
Watkins, Pierre 97
Welk, Lawrence 16, 170, 171
West, Aune 260
Westfall, Dean 11
Wharon, Clifton 21
Wheeldon, Fay 249
White, Art 242
White, Ione 242
White, William Allen 84, 85, 88, 90
Whitfield, C.M. 249
Whitman, Winfred 265
Wilder, Almanzo 157, 158
Wilder, Laura Ingalls 157, 209, 210
Williams, Richard B. 301
Wilson, Dolores Barnes 187, 188
Wilson, Ival 48
Wilson, John S. 212
Wilson, Woodrow 272, 303
Windolph, Charles 314
Wingler, Harold 180, 228
Wood, G W 196
Wood, Royal J. 241
Woods, M.T. 260
Wooley, John 267-269
Wooley, Karen 267-269
Wooster, Terry 268

Y

Yager, Adam 48
Yager, Ana Marie (Sieber) 48
Yager, Mary 48
Yager, Nicholas 48
Yeager, Abraham 48

Yeager, Ada May (Bidwell) (wife) xi, 36, 37, 44, 46, 49, 52-54, 57-61, 64, 65, 67, 69, 72- 74, 83, 113, 120-122, 128, 208, 226, 257, 319, 320, 327
Yeager, Anson (passim)
Yeager Jr., Anson (son) 59, 64, 69, 74, 121
Yeager, Anson (uncle) 39
Yeager, Charles Franklin (father) 39, 41, 42, 56, 65, 67, 69
Yeager, Elijah Fisk (grandfather) 39, 48
Yeager, Ellen (daughter) 52-54, 59, 69, 74, 121, 227
Yeager, Elise Marie (Thingelstad) (mother) 22, 37, 39, 41, 43, 46-48, 56, 57, 60, 65, 67, 69, 75, 76
Yeager, Fannie Lu (aunt) 39, 69
Yeager, Harry (son) xi, 64, 69, 72, 74, 121
Yeager, Iver (brother) 39, 43, 47
Yeager, Karen Ann (daughter) 46, 64, 69, 74, 226
Yeager, Lillian Lee (Vanover) (aunt) 39
Yeager, Mary (Compere) (aunt) 39
Yeager, Minnie (Rainey) (grandmother) 39, 48
Yeager, Robert Lee (brother) 39, 43, 47, 50
Yeager, Stephanie (Mrs. Harry) 74
Yeager, Terry (son) 64, 69, 121, 227
Yeager, Winnie Davis (aunt) 39

Z
Zhao Ziyang 238
Ziolkowski, Korczak 171, 210, 217, 218
Ziolkowski, Ruth 217, 218, 225